GW00601718

Investment, Risk & Taxation

• • • • • • • • • • • • •

The Official Learning and Reference Manual

2nd Edition, July 2011

This Workbook relates to syllabus version 2.0 and covers examinations from
31 October 2011 to 30 October 2012

PROFESSIONALISM | INTEGRITY | EXCELLENCE

INVESTMENT, RISK & TAXATION

Welcome to the Chartered Institute for Securities & Investment's Investment, Risk & Taxation study material.

This workbook has been written to prepare you for the Chartered Institute for Securities & Investment's Investment, Risk & Taxation examination.

PUBLISHED BY:

Chartered Institute for Securities & Investment
© Chartered Institute for Securities & Investment 2012
8 Eastcheap
London
EC3M IAE
Tel: +44 20 7645 0600
Fax: +44 20 7645 0601

WRITTEN BY:

Dr Harry Thapar and David Smith

REVIEWED BY:

Edward Horgan-Goumas and Jon Beckett

This is an educational manual and the Chartered Institute for Securities & Investment accepts no responsibility for persons undertaking trading or investments in whatever form.

While every effort has been made to ensure its accuracy, no responsibility for loss occasioned to any person acting or refraining from action as a result of any material in this publication can be accepted by the publisher or authors.

A learning map, which contains the full syllabus, appears at the end of this workbook. The syllabus can also be viewed at cisi.org and is also available by contacting Client Services on +44 20 7645 0680. Please note that the examination is based upon the syllabus. Candidates are reminded to check the Candidate Updates area of the website on a regular basis for updates that could affect their exam as a result of industry change.

The questions contained in this manual are designed as an aid to revision of different areas of the syllabus and to help you consolidate your learning chapter by chapter. They should not be seen as a mock examination or necessarily indicative of the level of the questions in the corresponding examination.

Workbook version: 2.3 (February 2012)

FOREWORD

Learning and Professional Development with the CISI

Formerly the Securities & Investment Institute (SII), and originally founded by members of the London Stock Exchange, the Institute is the leading examining, membership and awarding body for the securities and investment industry. We were awarded a royal charter in October 2009, becoming the Chartered Institute for Securities & Investment. We currently have around 40,000 members, who benefit from a programme of professional and social events, with continuing professional development (CPD) and the promotion of integrity very much at the heart of everything we do.

This learning manual (or 'workbook' as it is often known in the industry) not only provides a thorough preparation for the appropriate CISI examination, but is also a valuable desktop reference for practitioners. It can also be used as a learning tool for readers interested in knowing more, but not necessarily entering an examination.

The CISI official learning manuals ensure that candidates gain a comprehensive understanding of examination content. The material is written and updated by industry specialists and reviewed by experienced, senior figures in the financial services industry. Exam and manual quality are assured through a rigorous editorial system of practitioner panels and boards. CISI examinations are used extensively by firms to meet the requirements of government regulators. The CISI works closely with a number of international regulators that recognise our examinations and the manuals supporting them, as well as the UK regulator, the Financial Services Authority (FSA).

CISI learning manuals are normally revised annually. It is important that candidates check they purchase the correct version for the period when they wish to take their examination. Between versions, candidates should keep abreast of the latest industry developments through the Candidate Commonroom area of the CISI website.

The CISI produces a range of elearning revision tools such as Revision Express Interactive and Professional Refresher, which can be used in conjunction with our learning and reference manuals. For further details, please visit cisi.org. The CISI also endorses the workbooks of 7City Learning and BPP.

As a Professional Body, around 40,000 CISI members subscribe to the CISI Code of Conduct and the CISI has a significant voice in the industry, standing for professionalism, excellence and the promotion of trust and integrity. Continuing professional development is at the heart of the Institute's values. Our CPD scheme is available free of charge to members, and this includes an online record-keeping system as well as regular seminars, conferences and professional networks in specialist subject areas, all of which cover a range of current industry topics. Reading this manual and taking a CISI examination is credited as professional development with the CISI CPD scheme. To learn more about CISI membership, visit our website at cisi.org.

We hope that you will find this manual useful and interesting. Once you have completed it, you will find helpful suggestions on qualifications and membership progression with the CISI at the end of this book.

With best wishes for your studies.

Ruth Martin
Managing Director

CONTENTS

It is estimated that this workbook will require approximately 140 hours of study time.

CHAPTER ONE

ASSET CLASSES

This syllabus area will provide approximately 14 of the 80 examination questions

1.   CASH DEPOSITS AND RISK-FREE INVESTMENTS

LEARNING OBJECTIVE

1.1.2   Analyse the main characteristics, risk and returns of cash deposits:
liquidity; rates of interest; past returns; real returns; deposit-takers;
statutory protection; risks, interest rate risk and institutional risk; credit
risk assessment of deposit taking institutions; foreign currency deposits;
costs, charges and penalties

1.1.4   Analyse the factors to take into account when selecting between
different types of cash deposits, accounts and money market funds

1.1   THE ROLE OF CASH DEPOSITS

One of the key reasons for holding money in the form of cash deposits is **liquidity** – the ease and speed
with which an investment can be turned into cash to meet spending needs.

- Deposits held in **instant access** accounts are highly liquid – that is, access can be gained to them
immediately, so that they can be used to meet spending needs as and when they arise.
- Even money held on other forms of deposit – eg, seven-day notice accounts – can be accessed
reasonably quickly; and certainly more so than some other forms of investment.

We will look at various types of deposit, and consider how easy it is for the investor to gain access to
them, in a later section of this chapter. Most investors are likely to have a need for cash at short notice,
and so should plan to hold some cash on deposit to meet possible needs and emergencies before
considering more risky, and less liquid, investments.

The other main reasons are security, as a savings vehicle, and for the interest return that can be earned
on them.

- Accounts for holding cash deposits are generally characterised by a high level of **security**.
- **Capital** is very unlikely to be lost, at least in money terms. The purchasing power of capital held on
deposit will, however, be eroded by inflation.
- Against this, there is the reward of any **interest** receivable, and the rate of interest may exceed
inflation, resulting in a real rate of return for the investor.

A cash deposit account can serve as a vehicle for reaching a savings target; for example, when saving for
the cost of a major purchase, or for the deposit (part payment) on a house purchase.

1.2   INTEREST RATES

Cash deposits generally provide the investor with a return in the form of interest paid regularly, but
no capital growth. The exception is accounts which are held chiefly for transactional purposes, such as
chequing and current accounts: these generally do not earn interest; and we will ignore these for the
purposes of this chapter as they are not generally held for investment purposes.

Interest is normally paid as a percentage of the capital deposited. Generally speaking:

- Deposit-takers will pay higher rates of interest the larger the deposit. An account holding just £10 is likely to earn a lower rate of interest than one holding £100,000.
- Deposit-takers will also pay higher rates of interest for longer-term deposits. An account offering instant access is likely to earn a lower rate of interest than one where the money is tied up for a year.

This is not always the case – in some cases the market rate for long-term deposits can actually fall below that for shorter-term ones; but this is relatively unusual, and in most cases the depositor will earn more for having tied their money up for longer.

Interest rates may be variable or fixed at the outset. For instant access and notice accounts, they are usually variable, and for fixed-term deposits they are usually set for the entire period of the fix.

1.2.1   Gross and Net Interest Rates

If the interest rate quoted is described as **gross**, this means that it is the rate paid before deduction of income tax.

Normally, UK banks deduct basic rate income tax at source before crediting interest to a UK resident's account. However, those UK residents who are non-taxpayers – and overseas residents who are not liable for UK tax – can apply to HMRC to receive their interest gross on deposits with UK banks and building societies.

If the rate is quoted as **net**, this is the rate the investor will receive after deduction of basic rate tax. This means that the rate shows what the investor will receive, after the deposit-taker has deducted income tax at the savings rate of 20% on the amount of interest paid.

- If the depositor is a lower, or basic rate taxpayer, there will be no further tax to pay on the interest.
- If they are a higher-rate taxpayer, then a further 20% tax will be payable to HMRC (to make up the taxpayer's total 40% liability to tax on income).
- If they are an additional-rate taxpayer, then a further 30% tax will be payable to HMRC, bringing the total liability up to 50%.

It is rare to see the **net rate** of income tax for higher rate taxpayers quoted by a deposit-taker: usually, the rate is quoted net of basic rate tax, and higher rate taxpayers have to do their own calculations to work out what they will get. However, they will first have to establish the gross rate.

To calculate a net rate from a gross rate:

- For a basic rate taxpayer, take the gross flat rate and multiply it by 0.8 (this has the effect of deducting 20% from it). So, a rate of 4% gross will translate to 3.2% net of basic rate tax.
- For a higher-rate taxpayer, take the gross flat rate and multiply it by 0.6 (this has the effect of deducting 40% from it). So, a rate of 4% gross will translate to 2.4% net of higher rate tax.
- For an additional rate taxpayer, take the gross flat rate and multiply it by 0.5 (this has the effect of deducting 50% from it). So, a rate of 4% gross will translate to 2% net of additional rate tax.

1.2.2 Compounding

Historically, deposits have proven to give low returns compared with some other investments; but this is compensated for by a lower exposure to risk.

Where investors are attempting to compare the interest rates paid by one institution with those paid by another (or to compare the rates earned on a deposit with the returns on other forms of investment) they need to take account of **timing factors**.

Many institutions pay **tiered** interest rates – meaning that the larger the balance with them, the higher the rate of interest they will pay. But there may also be variations in when interest is paid – eg, monthly, quarterly, annually – and a higher rate of interest may be payable for interest paid less frequently. This may be an important consideration for an investor who is reliant on the interest for an income stream.

What it means is that, where two accounts have the same **nominal** historical rate of interest, but Account A credits interest more regularly than Account B, Account A will give the investor a better return (and more frequent income distributions).

EXAMPLE

Both accounts pay 4% per annum interest; but Account A pays it quarterly and Account B pays it annually. The investor leaves the interest in the account to roll up (ie, he doesn't take it out and spend it).

For a £10,000 account:

Account A pays 1% (ie, a quarter of 4%) at the end of Q1, taking it up to:
£10,000 x 101% = £10,100.00.

At the end of Q2, another 1% interest is paid – on the new total of £10,100.00:
£10,100.00 x 101% = £10,201.00.

At the end of Q3, 1% is paid on the total of £10,201.00:
£10,201.00 x 101% = £10,303.01.

At the end of Q4, 1% is paid on the total of £10,303.01:
£10,303.01 x 101% = £10,406.04.

The account has grown by £406.04.

Account B has capital of £10,000 at the end of year 1, and pays interest at 4%:
£10,000 x 4% = £10,400.00.

There is a difference of £6.04, or a small advantage with the account that pays interest more frequently at the same nominal rate, with the interest earned being rolled up into the capital.

The improvement has come about because the depositor has earned interest on his interest – the interest credited in the first quarter is added to the capital on which interest is calculated at the end of the second quarter, and so on. This effect is called **compounding**.

Of course, if the investor who has Account A doesn't leave his quarterly interest payments in the account (ie, he takes them out and spends them), he will not get the compounding effect: but he will get access to income he can spend earlier than he otherwise would with Account B.

So it is clearly very important to look at not just what the headline rate of interest is, but also how frequently this is calculated and applied to the account – and whether it is a flat or a compound rate.

1.2.3   Comparing Like with Like – the Annual Equivalent Rate (AER)

Clearly, there are different ways in which institutions can show their current and historic interest rates – and this could be very confusing for many depositors and their advisers. So, in the UK, every advertisement for a savings or deposit account should also show the quoted interest rate along with what used to be called the compound annual interest rate (CAR), and is now usually referred to as the **annual equivalent rate (AER)**.

The AER provides the depositor with a true rate of return, taking account of how often interest is credited to his account during a 12-month period. It therefore lets them compare one account with another on a like-for-like basis. The AER is usually quoted gross, ie, before any tax is deducted, though it can be quoted net too. It means that a depositor can compare two flat rates, without the complication of trying to work out the effect of one deposit-taker applying interest more often than another.

AERs only apply where interest is left in the account for the period; if the depositor draws it out (for example, to spend) it will no longer be meaningful.

1.2.4   Real Returns

The performance of cash deposits as an investment can be measured as a real rate of return by comparing the interest rate with the rate of inflation. The **headline** interest rate is also known as the **nominal** rate.

Approximately:

Nominal rate of interest – rate of inflation = real rate of return

For example, if annual interest is paid at a nominal rate of 5%, and the rate of inflation is 2%, then the real rate of return is approximately 3%. The purchasing power of the cash investment is increasing at 3% per year.

Interest rates on cash deposits will generally move approximately in tandem with rates of interest on borrowing; deposit-takers obtain income from the difference (the **margin**) between the deposit rates they pay, and the rates they charge to borrowers.

1.2.5   Interest Rates on Accounts with Variable Rates

Rates on accounts with variable rates of interest also generally move in line with the short-term **base** rate of interest set by the Bank of England's Monetary Policy Committee (MPC). This is set at a level which the MPC believes will help it in achieving its inflation rate objectives. If the economy appears to be **overheating**, with people finding credit and borrowing easy to obtain and afford, interest rates may be raised to discourage borrowing and limit economic activity.

Deposit-taking institutions are in competition with one another, and so the interest rates set on different deposit products reflects these competitive market conditions.

1.3   DEPOSIT-TAKERS

The principal UK deposit-takers are banks and building societies.

The FSA is responsible for the supervision of banks and building societies, in terms of their financial soundness and the way in which they carry on their business.

National Savings & Investments (NS&I) – a government agency backed by the HM Treasury and previously called National Savings, is one of the largest saving organisations in the UK that takes deposits. As a government agency it is not required to be authorised by the Financial Services Authority (FSA). We will look at NS&I products in Section 1.7 of this chapter.

1.3.1   Building Societies

A building society is a mutual organisation, which means that it is owned by its members. The members are the investment account holders and borrowers; as members, they have voting rights in the running of the organisation. Thus, the organisation's customers are also – in the main – its owners. This contrasts with the situation for banks, as we will see in Section 1.3.2.

Many former building societies have **demutualised** and turned themselves into banks, and some have subsequently been bought by banks. On demutualisation or acquisition of the society, members may be entitled to a **windfall** payment, reflecting a share of the reserves of the organisation that have been built up over its life. However, most of the remaining building societies now require new account-holders to waive their rights to such windfall payments, often by signing over the entitlement to charity. This is intended to prevent people opening accounts speculatively in the hope of gaining a windfall.

1.3.2   Banks

Banks are limited companies, owned by their shareholders. Their shares are almost invariably listed on the stock exchange. Thus, while a bank customer may also be a shareholder (and, therefore, an owner), this is by no means always the case.

The rights of account-holders are dealt with by reference to the terms and conditions of the account, and by contract law. The account-holders do not have voting rights over how the bank is operated.

1.4   RISKS

Deposits are generally regarded as low-risk investments, but they are not entirely risk-free.

The risks associated with them are:

- **Capital risk** – capital may be lost if the deposit-taker defaults (ie, becomes insolvent and cannot repay its depositors).

- **Inflation risk** – if the prevailing rate of inflation exceeds the interest payable on the account. This is the case where the account is a fixed-interest account: while an investor is locked in at fixed interest rates, inflation could accelerate, due to unforeseen economic conditions, and the purchasing power of the investor's capital will be eroded in real terms.
- **Interest rate risk** – the risk that the rate of interest paid on the deposit is less than could be obtained on other low-risk investment products, or the investor is locked in at a fixed rate for fixed terms, when he might otherwise have been able to take advantage of rising interest rates available in the market.
- **Operational risk** – the risk that the bank or building society gives poor service to the depositor, so that he suffers some form of loss because of this. For example, it does not move his money on to a fixed-rate account when he has asked it to.

1.5   REGULATION

In the UK, deposit taking is a regulated activity, and deposit-takers have to apply for and receive authorisation from the **Financial Services Authority (FSA)**, the UK financial services regulator. Authorisation is only granted if the deposit-taker meets certain standards, including its levels of 'solvency' (financial soundness).

Nonetheless, even with regulatory supervision, deposit-takers can get into difficulties – as the customers of Northern Rock can attest, following the events which stemmed from an announcement that Northern Rock required liquidity support in September 2007, culminating in its nationalisation in February 2008.

The FSA not only grants authorisations – it supervises authorised businesses and requires that they maintain certain standards of financial strength on an ongoing basis. The FSA derives its powers to carry out these functions under the Financial Services and Markets Act 2000.

However, recognising that things can and occasionally do still go wrong, other statutory protections are also in place to protect depositors. We will look at these in Sections 1.5.1 to 1.5.3 below..

1.5.1   Statutory Protections

Depositors can check out the financial strength of UK banks and other deposit-takers by researching their **credit ratings**. These are independent assessments carried out by credit rating agencies such as Fitch IBCA, Standard & Poor's and Moody's. They show the rating agency's opinion of the deposit-taker's financial standing, and how likely it is to be able to meet its liabilities to depositors when they fall due. The agencies all have their own rating systems, but they are generally quite similar; typically, a credit rating of AAA or AA is regarded as very strong, with lower ratings of A, BBB, BB, B and C and below reflecting progressively less strong finances. The agencies may use pluses and minuses (eg, AA–, B+) as indications of gradings within a rating band.

1.5.2   The Financial Services Compensation Scheme

If a UK deposit-taker fails, the depositor will have recourse to the **Financial Services Compensation Scheme (FSCS)**, which is administered by the Financial Services Authority (FSA).

The FSCS will pay compensation of up to £85,000 for each account-holder who is an eligible claimant, in each of the authorised savings institutions where an account is held, following default by a UK-regulated bank or building society.

The FSCS compensation limits apply:

- only to UK sterling deposits held at a UK branch of the deposit-taker;
- to each depositor, and not to each individual account;
- separately to each joint account holder; therefore, two joint account holders each could receive up to £85,000 each for a joint account, bringing compensation up to £170,000 for the couple.

The FSCS provides a valuable safety net for many depositors: but those with very substantial deposits will not, of course, receive compensation for their full losses. The ceiling on compensation available through the FSCS leads many investors to consider spreading their capital among a number of banks and building societies in order to reduce the overall risk. This may result in their earning a poorer rate of interest – as smaller deposits tend to command lower rates – but nervous depositors may regard this as a small price to pay.) The benefit of spreading the risk in this way should be weighed against the possible disadvantage of less interest being earned, because of the investor missing out on the higher rates offered for larger deposits.

1.5.3   The Financial Ombudsman Service (FOS)

Where a depositor suffers because the deposit-taker gives them poor service, they may have recourse to the Financial Ombudsman Service. The FOS acts to resolve complaints against regulated financial services providers, including banks and building societies, where these cannot be sorted out between the customer and the provider directly.

The FOS will investigate the complaint, looking at evidence from both customer and provider, and make a decision which is then binding on the provider.

The FOS can award a maximum of £100,000 (excluding any interest and costs) in compensation. Where a depositor believes they have suffered losses greater than this, they may be well advised to take the provider to court instead.

1.6   FOREIGN CURRENCY DEPOSITS

Deposits can be held with many UK deposit-takers in currencies other than sterling. Depositors may choose to hold accounts in foreign currencies for any of the following reasons:

- They have transactional needs in foreign currencies (eg, overseas income from earnings, or overseas spending needs such as on a property abroad) and wish to hold balances as a result.
- More importantly, for the purposes of this text, they may hold them for investment purposes:
  - An investor may choose to hold cash in foreign currency because the interest rates earned on that currency exceed those which they can obtain on sterling. They run the risk, however, that the currency depreciates against sterling and that the additional income they earn is more than outweighed by a loss in capital value when the deposit is converted back to the home currency.
  - Alternatively, they may hold the foreign currency for speculative reasons – ie, they believe that the currency is due to appreciate against the pound, and that they may, therefore, make capital gains. They run the risk, of course, that they are wrong and the currency depreciates against the pound instead.

Currency movements are notoriously difficult to predict, and the risks mentioned above are not trivial. In addition, a UK bank holding foreign currency deposits may apply higher charges because of the greater administrative burden on it, and these may offset some of the additional returns that might otherwise be earned.

1.7   THE MAIN TYPES OF DEPOSIT ACCOUNT

LEARNING OBJECTIVE

1.1.1   Understand the main types of deposit account: current; instant access; National Savings & Investment products; notice; fixed rate; term; money market

Banks and building societies offer a wide range of account types in which savers and investors can hold their cash. The key elements, in terms of account type and features, are:

*   **How money can be paid in**. Some types of deposit impose no restrictions on the amount that can be paid in; others have maximum and minimum balances, and minimum amounts that can be added after the account is opened (say, £30). This might be for commercial reasons; for example, the deposit-taker is aiming at high net worth customers and does not deal with customers of more modest means. With most fixed-term deposits you cannot add a further amount once the deposit has begun; you will need to open a second, separate deposit account.
*   **Withdrawals**. Most providers will include rules as to when, how easily and how quickly amounts can be taken out. For a current or **instant access** account, the depositor may be able to take money out at any time – though again there may be minimum withdrawal amounts so that the provider does not have to administer very small transactions. For notice accounts, the depositor must give a set amount of notice before he can take any money out. This might be anything from one week upwards (so we might talk about a **90-day notice account**, which means the depositor has to give around three months' forewarning if he wants some or all of his money back). With a fixed-term deposit, usually no withdrawals are permitted until the end date of the fixed period (so if a depositor takes out a one-year fixed deposit, his money is tied in for the whole period). If a depositor realises he has miscalculated, and needs his fixed deposit money back early, the deposit-taker may agree to release the funds – but often only after deducting a substantial penalty for **breaking** the deposit.
*   **How interest is paid**. Interest rates may be variable or fixed at the outset. For instant access and notice accounts, they are usually variable, and for fixed-term deposits they are usually set for the entire period of the fix. Many institutions pay **tiered** interest rates – meaning that the larger the balance held with them, the higher the rate of interest they will pay. There may also be variations as to when interest is paid – eg, monthly, quarterly, annually – and a higher rate of interest may be payable for interest paid less frequently. This may be an important consideration for an investor who is reliant on the interest for an income stream.

The following are some of the key account types you may encounter, and their features:

- **Current accounts** are typically used for transactional purposes, and allow the holder to get at his money as and when he needs it. They may come with a cheque book so that the holder can access his money simply by writing a cheque; alternatively or additionally they may come with a plastic card for the same purpose. At one time it was common for current accounts to earn interest, and there was some competition between providers on the basis of the interest rate paid; however, many providers have now stopped paying interest on current accounts.

- **Instant access accounts** also allow the holder to get his money when he wants, but do not usually carry a cheque book (or, if they do, may limit the number of times it can be used within a given period). Typically, where they earn interest, it is at a variable rate.

- **Notice accounts** require that the holder gives a certain period of notice before withdrawing all or part of his deposit. A 90-day notice account will thus require that the depositor give 90 days' advance warning before they can have their money back. Where the deposit-taker allows this to be waived, it may apply a penalty to compensate itself. These generally earn interest at variable rates (ie, the provider will link the interest paid to the base rate).

- **Fixed-rate accounts** earn a set rate of interest over their entire life; they are invariably for fixed terms as well. Interest is generally credited at the end of the term.

- **Term (or fixed-term) accounts** are tied up for a set period – for example, one month, or three months. They generally earn a fixed rate of interest over their life, which is added to the account at the end of the term, ie, on maturity).

- **Money market accounts**. To understand money market accounts and money market funds, it helps to know the difference between the two. **Money market** is simply a generic name used to describe the market wherein banks and other financial institutions lend, borrow and trade money, certificates of deposit (CDs) and other financial instruments. We will cover money market funds later in this chapter (see Section 1.8).

  A money market account is basically a premium account, or a high interest savings account. A money market account should not be mistaken for a money market fund. A money market fund is an investment strategy with larger returns than a premium savings account. A money market account can be opened very simply at almost any bank. The money you keep in such an account will be invested, but the bank or other institution does the investing and collects the return.

  Your money is usually put into investments like CDs, T-bills (a nickname for Treasury bills) or other safe financial instruments. Each of these are low-risk, short-term investments. Your reward for allowing the financial institution to use your money is a premium interest rate, which may be up to twice as high as a typical passbook account.

  While a money market account makes a decent low-risk investment, keep in mind that, because it is an investment, there are certain restrictions. Your money will not be as liquid as it is in a regular savings account, and a money market account usually requires a minimum deposit, as well as a minimum balance. While you can make withdrawals from a money market account, there is a limit to how many you can make.

- **National Savings & Investments (NS&I)**. Formerly called 'National Savings'. NS&I products are offered by the government and, as such, are regarded as **risk-free** investments.

1.7.1   National Savings & Investments (NS&I)

NS&I is an executive agency of the Chancellor of the Exchequer, and is accountable to the Treasury. It provides deposit and savings products to the investing public, and in doing so raises funds on behalf of the UK government. An investor holding an NS&I product is in essence lending to the government).

NS&I offers a wide range of products, from easy-access savings accounts to longer-term investments and, of course, premium bonds. As the products are **underwritten** by the government, they are regarded as effectively free from the risk of default. None of NS&I's products is subject to capital gains tax, but some products are subject to income tax. The following are its key products.

Savings Accounts

NS&I offers a range of products aimed at savers, including:

*   **Investment account**. This is in effect a passbook-style savings account. Savers can operate it over the counter at their post office, by mail or by standing order. It pays variable rates, tiered interest rates and has no set term. The minimum deposit is £20 and the maximum is £1 million. Interest is taxable and paid gross.

*   **Easy-access savings account**. This account also has no set term. It earns variable interest, at tiered rates, and the minimum and maximum deposits are £100 and £2 million. Interest is taxable and paid gross.

Income-Providing Products

NS&I's products aimed at the investor who is seeking interest income include:

*   **Guaranteed income bonds**. These provide a guaranteed monthly income. The minimum holding is £500 and the maximum total holding £1 million. The bonds are available for one-, three- and five-year terms. Interest is taxable and paid net.
*   **Income bonds**. These pay monthly income, and have no set term: the holder can withdraw his money without notice. Interest is variable, tiered, taxable and paid gross. The minimum holding is £500 and the maximum is £1 million.

Growth Products

NS&I's growth schemes include:

*   **Index-linked savings certificates**. These pay a return which is guaranteed and linked to the inflation rate as measured by the retail prices index (RPI). The minimum holding is £100, and the maximum is £15,000 per issue. Certificates can be bought for terms of either three or five years. Returns are tax-free.

*   **Fixed-rate savings certificates**. These pay a fixed rate of return over a period of time, such as two and five years currently. The returns are guaranteed for the term and are tax-free on maturity. The minimum holding is £100 and maximum is £15,000 per issue.

*   **Guaranteed growth bonds**. These provide a guaranteed return on your investment. The minimum holding is £500 and maximum is £1 million. Choice of terms are one, three and five years, with access available before maturity subject to a loss of 90 days' interest. Interest is taxable and paid net.

- **Guaranteed equity bonds**. These also provide a guaranteed return on your investment, linked to the performance of the FTSE 100 index over a set term. If the FTSE 100 index grows over the term, you will benefit from that growth. If it falls, you will still get back 100% of your original investment – guaranteed. The FTSE 100 index measures share prices only, so the investor will not benefit from dividends. This means that they may not get as high a return as they would with a direct stock market investment. The returns on NS&I's guaranteed equity bonds are subject to averaging and are liable to UK income tax on maturity. Although the capital is fully guaranteed, inflation may reduce the true value of the money over the investment term.

Tax-Free Products

Certain of NS&I's products provide returns free of tax (although the returns on these products are not generally high, reflecting also the fact that they are regarded as very safe). They include:

- **Premium bonds**, which carry no capital risk (the holder can withdraw his capital in full when he wishes). Instead of earning interest, bonds are entered into a monthly draw in which they could win their holder up to £1 million (or one of many smaller amounts). The minimum holding is £100 and the maximum is £30,000.

- **Direct ISA**. This account is NS&I's version of the individual savings account – a type of scheme whereby the holder can earn a return free of capital and income taxes. For 2011/12, investors can pay a maximum of £5,340 in a tax year into NS&I's Direct ISA, earning variable-rate interest on this free of income tax. There are no withdrawal restrictions.

- **Savings certificates**. NS&I offers a range of savings certificates, some of them paying fixed interest and some variable-rate. The returns on all of these are tax-free in the hands of the investor.

- **Children's bonus bonds**. These run for a period of five years and offer a guaranteed rate of interest (paid daily) from the outset. Returns are tax-free with no tax liability on the parents. The minimum investment per issue is £25 and maximum is £3,000. A bonus payment is made on the fifth anniversary. Access is allowed during the term, subject to loss of the bonus payment, and no interest is credited if the bond is cashed in during the first year.

1.8　MONEY MARKET FUNDS

LEARNING OBJECTIVE

1.1.3　Analyse the main characteristics, risks and returns of money market funds: cash assets only; near-cash assets; pricing, liquidity and fair value; costs, charges and penalties

1.8.1　What Are Money Market Funds?

Money market funds are investment funds that invest in cash assets or near-cash assets, which are generally viewed as low-risk and liquid.

Near-cash assets include short-term debt instruments such as commercial paper and government bonds close to expiry (short-term gilts and Treasury bills), while cash assets include short-term bank deposits.

Funds provide the benefits of pooled investment, as investors can participate in a more diverse and high-quality portfolio than they otherwise could individually. Like other mutual funds, each investor who invests in a money market fund is considered a shareholder of the investment pool, a part-owner of the fund. Money market funds are actively managed within rigid and transparent guidelines to offer the safety of principal, liquidity and competitive sector-related returns.

There are two basic types of money market funds: **constant net asset value** and **accumulating net asset value**. Shares in constant net asset value funds are issued with an unchanging face value (such as £1 per share). Income in the fund is accrued daily and can either be paid out to the investor or used to purchase more units in the fund at the end of the month. Accumulating net asset value funds, known alternatively as roll-up funds, operate under the same investment guidelines as constant NAV funds and income is accrued daily. However, unlike constant net asset value funds, income is not distributed. Instead income is reflected by an increase in the value of the fund shares.

1.8.2   Industry Origins

Money market funds were first offered in the US in the early 1970s, and now money market funds are widely used across the financial world in both the institutional and retail sectors. Money market funds were first exported to offshore European centres in the late 1980s. The principal providers of money market funds in Europe formed a trade association, the Institutional Money Market Funds Association (IMMFA).

1.8.3   Fund Ratings

Money market funds have the preservation of capital as their primary objective. Liquidity and competitive, sector-related returns are other key objectives. The rating process methodically identifies, assesses and weights each fund in terms of its ability to deliver on these objectives.

The rating criteria broadly comprise four main areas of analysis that systematically address a fund's operating principles: its credit quality, portfolio construction, fund management and regular post-rating inspection. These are described in more detail below.

Credit Quality

Credit quality is evaluated on three levels: what the fund can buy, whom it can do business with (including the exact nature of business) and whom it can appoint to keep its assets safe. The rating criteria, therefore, stipulate the fund's asset range and restrictions (such as quality, type and currency), acceptable counterparty risk (for all transaction-based investments) and acceptable choice of custodian.

Portfolio Construction

The most complex part of analysing a money market fund is judging a fund's sensitivity to changing market conditions and, therefore, gauging a measure of its ability to shield investors from adverse market swings. All money market securities (rated or otherwise) are subject to price fluctuations – based on interest rate movements, maturity, liquidity and the supply and demand for each type of security. Quantifying the cumulative effect of these is crucial to assessing overall portfolio performance.

Capital preservation is expressed in terms of the stability or constant accumulation of the fund's net asset value per share. As such, both formats are scrutinised for potential deviation in the fund's market value. Determination of market value, or portfolio price exposure, starts with the examination of susceptibility to rising interest rates. A critical component of this is the fund's weighted average portfolio maturity, which is specifically restricted by rating category.

Fund Management

The rating process requires an assessment of a fund manager's operations – in common parlance, the front, middle and back offices. Key areas of interest are the fund manager's level of experience, the stated investment objectives, portfolio management techniques, risk aversion strategies, operating procedures and internal controls, including disaster recovery. Owing to the precision necessary in running a money market fund successfully, every aspect of the fund's management must be able to withstand close scrutiny and demonstrate effective, ongoing integrity of operation.

Portfolio Inspection

Owing to the constraints of the rating criteria and the extremely low margin of error permitted at the level of fund valuation, rated money market funds are contractually obliged to supply all portfolios for periodic rating agency inspection. This is called fund surveillance. Any infringement or potential concern is communicated to the fund and timely rectification is required.

1.8.4   Benchmarks

Money market funds use different benchmarks to compare the performance of funds, as demonstrated through short-term indicative interest rates. The main indices are those shown below.

London Interbank Bid Rate (LIBID)

The London Interbank Bid Rate (LIBID) is the rate at which banks take deposits from each other. It is normally one-eighth of a percentage point lower than the London Interbank Offered Rate (LIBOR) – the rate at which banks lend to each other). LIBOR is calculated daily by the British Bankers' Association (BBA), and, while the BBA does not compile indicative LIBID rates, historic LIBOR rates can be found at www.bba.org.uk/bba/jsp/polopoly.jsp?d=141&a=627.

Sterling Overnight Interbank Average (SONIA)

The Sterling Overnight Interbank Average (SONIA) is the weighted average rate of all unsecured sterling overnight cash transactions brokered in London between midnight and 4.15pm with all counterparties in a minimum deal size of £25 million.

Euro Overnight Interbank Average (EONIA)

The Euro Overnight Interbank Average (EONIA) is the weighted average rate of all unsecured euro overnight cash transactions brokered in London between midnight and 4.00pm with all counterparties.

SONIA and EONIA are weighted average overnight deposit rates for each business day. Both indices are published at 5.00pm each day. Details of daily SONIA and EONIA rates can be found at www.wmba.org.uk/indices.php.

1.8.5 Types of Funds

Triple-A-rated money market funds invest in high-grade money market instruments. Typically these instruments include certificates of deposit, commercial paper, floating-rate notes, repurchase agreements, short-term government securities and time deposits. Managers have strict credit criteria applying to their selection of these instruments.

Commercial paper consists of short-term debt issued by a wide variety of corporations, such as domestic and foreign banks, finance companies, and specific issuers of commercial paper. Any commercial paper purchased by a money market fund must have received a high investment grade rating from a credit rating agency, in order for the fund to maintain its triple-A-rating.

About half of the commercial-paper market is now made up of **asset-backed commercial paper**. This is short-term debt backed not by the name and assets of an entire company but by a designated pool of specific assets, such as credit card debt, car loans and mortgages, including subprime mortgages, of course.

Traditionally, companies have used this paper to finance operations, borrowing cash they need to meet a payroll or buy inventory. They borrowed short-term money because it gave them flexibility and because it was cheaper than long-term debt most of the time. To extend the maturity of this short-term debt, effectively turning short-term debt into long-term debt at short-term interest rates, all they had to do was roll over the debt when it matured. And traditionally, commercial paper was backed by the credit of the entire company.

Asset-backed commercial paper offered big advantages to both the issuers and buyers of debt. It opened up the commercial paper market to a whole new level of companies that had not been creditworthy enough to tap this source of funding before. A company with a credit rating so low that tapping the commercial paper market was difficult could now put together a package of credit card receivables – the debt that card borrowers had run up doing business with the company. Because that paper was backed by a predictable flow of credit card payments, that issue of asset-backed commercial paper would find ready buyers.

For buyers, the advantage of asset-backed commercial paper was very simple: it paid more than traditional commercial paper did. The difference wasn't much, perhaps 0.1 or 0.2 percentage points, but, to managers of money market funds clawing for market share and investors, adding a fraction of a percentage point to a fund's yield can make a huge difference.

The closing of the market for some asset-backed securities has placed constraints on the liquidity of some of the money market funds that had holdings of these instruments. This, together with falling market values for these instruments, has led to some funds delivering negative returns. Investors in these funds were often unaware that such incidences could occur.

2. GOVERNMENT SECURITIES AND CORPORATE BONDS

LEARNING OBJECTIVE

1.2.1   Know the main issuing institutions and purposes for issuing fixed income securities: sovereign states and governments; public authority; corporate; credit institutions; supranational

1.2.3   Analyse the characteristics and differences between the main types of fixed income securities: fixed rate bonds; floating rate notes; zero coupon bonds; inflation-linked bonds; other index-and asset-linked bonds; asset-backed securities; convertible bonds; subordinated bonds; perpetual bonds; eurobonds and foreign issuer bonds

2.1   GENERAL FEATURES

Bonds (also known as debt securities) are a form of loan instrument. The person who invests in the bond is the lender, and the organisation issuing the bond is the borrower. The name derives from the original use of the word **bond** – a tie or commitment (as in the saying 'my word is my bond'). A bond is so called because it represents a promise to repay the capital borrowed at some defined point in the future and also, in most cases, a certain amount of interest in the intervening period.

At original issue, bonds may be sold as an open offer for sale directly to a smaller number of professional investors: this is called a private placing. In an **offer for sale**, a syndicate of banks with one bank as lead manager will buy the bonds en bloc from the issuer and resell them to investors. In this way, they underwrite the issue since, if the investors don't buy, the banks will be forced to keep them. Needless to say, they charge fees for this risk. If the lead bank buys all the bonds and sells them to the syndicate (usually called the **bought deal**), the syndicate members may themselves then sell the bonds at varying prices. More commonly these days, the lead manager and the syndicate buy the bonds simultaneously and agree to sell at the same price for a period – the **fixed price reoffering**. This is very common in the US and now in the so-called **euromarkets**. Less frequently (apart from the governments bonds), there may not be a syndicate but the bonds are sold by competitive auction.

There are several types of bond according to the issuer:

- government bonds;
- public authorities bonds;
- mortgage- and other asset-backed bonds (please note: "US Regulatory Bill May 'Flash Freeze' Asset-Backed Market, Industry Says" – http://www.bloomberg.com/news/2010-07-21/u-s-regulatory-bill-may-flash-freeze-asset-backed-market-industry-says.html);
- corporate bonds;
- supranational bonds;
- foreign bonds;
- high-yield bonds.

Corporate bonds may also be debentures, or convertibles, and there is a hybrid type of instrument, the preference share or participation stock.

There is another denomination for foreign bonds: the domestic issues by non-residents – bulldogs in the UK, yankees in the US, matadors in Spain, samurai in Tokyo and kangaroo bonds in Australia. Notice that these bonds are domestic bonds in the local currency; it is only the issuer who is foreign. They should be not confused with international bonds (eurobonds), which are bonds outside their natural market.

To help us become more familiar with some of the concepts associated with bonds, we will now examine some of the most common types.

2.2   GOVERNMENT BONDS

Government bonds seem to dominate the bond markets, with modern governments running a budget deficit which leads to large-scale issues of bonds. Sometimes the secondary market is run on stock exchanges (France, Germany, UK) and sometimes outside stock exchanges (US).

2.2.1   UK Government Bonds

Governments are regular issuers of bonds; it is one of the key ways in which they raise money to pay for the various activities they carry out.

Since 1998, the UK Debt Management Office (DMO) has issued bonds on behalf of the HM Treasury. Bonds issued by the UK government are known as gilt-edged stocks – or gilts, for short. This name derives from the fact that, originally, the certificates representing such investments were printed on paper which had a gold (gilded, or gilt) edging, something which was intended to represent the high level of safety associated with the government. Even today, you may hear people talk about a gilt-edged opportunity, meaning something that they perceive as being a very safe bet.

In the case of gilts, then, the borrower is the UK government, which uses the money raised in this way in order to fund the central government net cash requirement (CGNCR). The CGNCR represents the shortfall between:

* the central government's revenues (what money it takes in, in the form of taxes, duties, and the like); and
* what it spends on running the country (on things like paying state benefits and infrastructure projects such as road-building).

As such, it is a component of the public corporations net cash requirement (PSNCR) (see box below), which we will look at in Chapter 2.

The PSNCR is equal to the sum of:

* the CGNCR;
* the Local Government Net Cash Requirement (LGNCR); and
* the PCNCR.

That is, the total shortfall for central government, local authorities, and public corporations. Gilts are used to fund the first of these; but local governments and various public corporations can often issue bonds themselves (for example, local authority bonds).

New gilt issues also help the government meet the cost of repaying existing gilts that are due for redemption.

As with any loan, a gilt pays a rate of interest – known as the **coupon**. This may be fixed or variable; when it is variable, it is calculated by reference to a specific index – in this case, the Retail Prices Index (RPI). Such gilts are known as **index-linked gilts**.

The interest paid will depend on the terms of the gilt, and is usually shown in the gilt's title (eg, with a gilt whose title is 5% Treasury Stock 2014, the coupon, ie, the nominal interest rate, is 5% per annum).

Interest on most types of gilt is paid out twice yearly, although for some types it is paid quarterly.

Gilts are usually repayable by the government (ie, the capital is paid back to the holder of the gilt at the time, and the loan ceases) on their **maturity** or **redemption** date. The redemption date may be:

- **Fixed** – ie, if we looked more closely at the treasury stock we considered before, 5% Treasury Stock 2014, we'd find that the date in full was 7 September 2014. So, on 7 September 2014, whoever is the holder of the gilt at that time can expect it to be redeemed.
- Repayable between two set future dates (the choice of exactly when being up to the government). Such gilts show the two dates in their titles, and so are called **dual-dated gilts**. An example is '7¾% Treasury Stock 2012–2015'. It is rare for the government to issue dual-dated gilts these days, and there are now only three left outstanding.
- **Undated** – ie, there is no fixed redemption date, and the loan continues to run until the government decides it wants to redeem it. Although there is no obligation for the government to redeem, it may do so at its discretion. Again, the government does not issue new gilts of this type any more. The ones that are still running are among the oldest issues, some going back to the late 1800s. Undated gilts do not usually include a redemption date, eg, Consolidated 2½%. However, a few carry the abbreviation 'Aft' (eg, 3% Treasury 1966 Aft). This implies the government has the right to redeem the gilt in 1966 or at any time after.

Types and Classifications of Gilts

There are various different types of gilt. At one time, their different titles (such as Treasury, Exchequer, Funding and War Loan) gave an indication of the reason for their being issued; the issues of War Loan, for example, were made in 1914 and 1915 to help the government pay for the costs to the nation of the Great War. Nowadays, most gilts are issued with the name treasury, unless they have some other name reflecting their investment features, eg, conversion. There is a wide range of coupons (nominal interest rates) and redemption dates (the date on which the loan is repaid) from which investors can choose.

This wide choice, coupled with the fact that gilts (being backed by the government) are regarded as very safe, makes them popular investments not only with private investors, but also with institutional ones such as pension funds, insurance companies and fund managers.

Conventional gilts carry a fixed:

- rate of interest, shown in the title of the gilt;
- redemption date, the year of which is also shown in the title.

They cannot be encashed before the final redemption date (ie, you cannot ask the government to repay the debt early); but they can be bought and sold on the stock market, or via the Government Debt Management Office's 'purchase and sale service'.

Other gilt types include:

- **Index-linked gilts** – both the interest rate and the capital redemption on these gilts is calculated by reference to the inflation rate as measured at a set point before the pay date.
- **Dual-dated gilts (with two dates)** – the government has the option to redeem after the first date, but no later than the last date.
- **Convertible gilts** – the owner has the right to convert the gilt into predefined amounts of a different gilt at some time in the future. Convertibles are usually short- to medium-term bonds which may be converted into a longer issue at the discretion of the investor. In the FT, they are identifiable by the abbreviation 'Conv' in the title, eg, 'Conv 9% 2009'.
- **Floating rate gilts** – these are unusual in that they pay variable coupons, and in that they pay four times a year instead of semi-annually. The coupon is set by reference to LIBID at the beginning of each interest payment period (LIBOR – x% may also be used as a reference date), and they tend to trade at around their par (nominal) value. The DMO) does not issue floating rate gilts.

Gilts are classified in terms of how long they have to run before they will be redeemed (ie, before the government repays the capital). There are two different conventions used. One, the *Financial Times (FT)* method, is probably more familiar to retail investors who may use the FT to follow their holdings' prices. The FT classifies gilts as:

- shorts: under 5 years to run to redemption;
- mediums: 5–15 years to redemption;
- longs: over 15 years to run.

However, market convention – ie, that used between gilt dealers on the London Stock Exchange by the DMO which issues them, and by professionals, is to classify them as follows:

- shorts: 1–7 years to run to redemption;
- mediums: 8–15 years to redemption;
- longs: over 15 years to run.

In 2005, the DMO was given permission to issue a new range of **ultra-long gilts**. It has already done so by way of a 50-year issue, Treasury 5.25% 2055. This has widened investor choice even further. The new gilt is the longest-dated 'sovereign debt' issued anywhere in the world. The sole ultra-long issue is categorised along with the 'longs'; it doesn't have a separate category all to itself.

Features and Characteristics of a Gilt-Edged Security

In order to familiarise ourselves further with the features of a gilt, we will take as an example **5% Treasury Stock 2014**. Look at the following example certificate to see if you can identify the various bits of information on it.

> Reference no: 1234 Transfer no: 13/123456 Certificate no: 0001020304 Amount of Stock: £1,000.00
>
> ### HM TREASURY 5% TREASURY STOCK 2014
> #### Redemption at par on 7 September 2014
> #### Interest payments half yearly on 7 March and 7 September
>
> **MRS CATHERINE TURNER 1 WOODLANDS CLOSE WESTMINSTER LONDON SW1H 0XX**
>
> **THIS IS TO CERTIFY** that the above-named is/are the Registered Holder(s) of one **thousand pounds**
>
> 5% TREASURY STOCK 2014
>
> **Given under the Signature**
> **On 3 November 2004**
> **Secretary to the Treasury**
>
> This certificate must be surrendered before any transfer of the whole or part of the shares herein mentioned can be registered. Registrar and Transfer Office: Computershare Investor Services plc, PO Box 2411, The Pavilions, Bristol, BS3 9WX
>
> **You can check your holding at www.computershare.com**

This is an example of the information which you will find on the certificate which evidences your holding, if you hold £1,000 nominal of this stock.

The first thing to note is that every gilt has a name, to distinguish it from other gilts in issue.

The name gives you lots of information about the terms of a gilt, being made up of:

- The **name of the issuer** (in this case the Treasury Department of the UK government, although in fact nowadays the DMO handles the procedures and practicalities of issuing gilts). The name of the gilt serves no purpose other than to act as an identifier. Examples of gilt names include: Treasury, Exchequer, Funding, Conversion, Consolidated, War Loan. All new gilts are now called **Treasury gilts**. In general, gilts are registered securities, with the register of owners being held and maintained by Computershare Investor Services plc.

- The **coupon** – in this case, 5%. This is the amount of interest that an investor will earn each year on the nominal value of the gilt. So, in our example, you will earn £5.00 for every £100 nominal you own of the gilt each year. Interest is paid on most gilts half-yearly (ie, in this case 2.5% will be paid to the holder, twice a year).

The quoted coupon of a gilt represents the annual amount of interest paid per £100 nominal value. The nominal value is effectively the original amount borrowed by the government, and in the UK it is market convention to talk about gilts in terms of £100 nv when calculating the return on the investment on their price. Coupons are generally paid semi-annually, on fixed days, six months apart. Note, however, that the 2.5% consolidated gilt and floating rate gilts pay a quarterly coupon. Coupons are taxable (subject to income tax for individuals); however, tax is not normally deducted from the coupon payment and this is referred as to being a **gross** coupon. An individual taxpayer can choose to have income tax at the rate of 20% deducted from the payment of their coupon. This is referred to as **electing for withholding tax** to be deducted. For instance, if an individual holds £100 nv of the 6.5% gilt and they elect to have tax deducted, their next coupon receipt would be calculated as follows:

£100 nv x coupon rate x 6/12 (semi-annual coupon) x 80% (to take account of the 20% tax deduction) = next coupon receipt. £100 nv x 6.5% x 6/12 x 80% = £2.60. The gross coupon is £3.25 and the net coupon is £2.60.

- The **interest payment dates** are not in the title of the gilt – but you can find them on the certificate (in this case, they are 7 March and 7 September each year) and, if you were researching a gilt prior to buying it, your stockbroker would be able to provide you with the dates. In addition, interest payment dates for gilts are shown in the *Financial Times*. A few gilts pay their interest quarterly, instead of half-yearly.

- The **redemption date** – in this case, the year 2014. This is the year in which the government will repay the nominal sum held by the investor who holds the gilt at that time, to that investor. In effect, the government is repaying its loan.

  Some gilts show two dates in their title – eg, 7¾% Treasury Stock 2012–2015. This means that the government can choose to repay the gilt at any time from 2012 onwards, by giving three months' notice to investors – but it must repay it by 2015 at the latest. It is important to bear in mind, that the choice of when to repay the gilt is the government's and not the investor's. The government will make this decision based on what interest rates are doing in the market at the time. If the gilt represents cheap borrowing to it, it will likely let it run for as long as it can, but if it can replace it with cheaper new borrowings, it will probably repay it as early as is possible.

  The redemption date is the specified date on which the capital is repaid by the DMO. Normally, redemption is at par, ie, £100 for each £100 nv held. All remaining stock must be repaid on the redemption date. The remaining maturity of the gilt is used for categorisation purposes and the time to redemption is calculated from today's date until the maturity date. For instance, a 20-year bond starts off as a long when initially issued, but five years later it becomes a medium, and eight years later a short. Remember that the *Financial Times* classifies shorts as having redemptions up to five years, medium between five and 15, and longs as more than 15 years.

- The **nominal value** held (in this case, £1,000). This reflects the face value of the gilts that the holder owns – rather like the number of shares held in a company, or units in a unit trust, in that it is different from the value (despite being expressed in pounds and pence). It is also the value that the government will repay to the holder on the redemption, or maturity date. .

You will also see that the gilt certificate shows the holder's details, and a certificate number and transfer number.

Gilts are marketable securities – so, while you cannot encash one before its redemption date by going to the government and asking it to repay your loan, you can buy and sell gilts before their redemption dates.

However, whereas when a conventional gilt is redeemed by the government you know what you will get back – £100 per £100 nominal – when you buy and sell in the market you will get the price that is ruling at the time. This may be more than you paid for it, or less – so you could make a profit or a loss on it.

In other words, the value of the nominal holding is not the same as the current value of the stock. To calculate this, we need to know the current market price of the stock. This is expressed as an amount per £100 nominal of the gilt. Let us assume that the market price of 5% Treasury Stock 2014 is £105.95, so every £100 nominal of the stock is worth £105.95. Put another way we could also say that for every £1 nominal of the gilt we buy, it will cost us £1.0595.

So an investor wanting to buy £30,000 nominal of this gilt will have to pay (ignoring costs like stockbroker commissions and any accrued interest):

$$£30,000 \times £105.95 / £100 = £31,785.00$$

Note, there are a few conventional gilts that are not priced and quoted in sterling but in euros. We will look at the features of foreign-currency-denominated bonds, including gilts, in Section 2.2.2.

Because there is a ready market for gilts, people who want to hold them don't have to wait until the government issues a new one (though they can do this if they wish). Generally, the market for gilts is very 'liquid' – that is, they can be bought and sold quickly and easily at their ruling market price, so they are easy to turn into cash again.

There are a number of specialist firms known as Gilt-Edged Market Makers (GEMMs), whose main function is to ensure that there is a liquid market in stock. GEMMs deal with professional investors such as pension funds and insurance companies, and with stockbrokers (but not generally with personal investors, who will usually deal either with the DMO or through a stockbroker).

It is the GEMMS that ensure that gilts are as easily marketable as they are.

2.2.2 Foreign Government Bonds

We have already seen that there are a wide variety of gilts issued in the UK market by the UK government, but UK gilts and overseas government bonds act in different ways. Government bonds are usually referred to as risk-free bonds because the government could raise taxes or simply print more money to redeem the bond at maturity. Many governments issue inflation-indexed bonds, which protect the investor against inflation risk. The general features of overseas government bonds and the markets they trade in vary from country to country. Some examples are listed below:

*   Bonds may be issued by the central bank of the country (US, Germany, France), by the Ministry of Finance (Netherlands, Japan), or by the DMO on behalf of the government (UK, Ireland, Sweden, Portugal, New Zealand).
*   The issue may be to specialist dealers (US, UK, France, Germany and Italy) or to syndicates of banks (Switzerland).

- Bonds may be bearer (anonymous, with no register of holders) or registered form (Germany and UK respectively).
- Some markets pay interest semi-annually (US, UK, Italy, Japan), others once per year (France, Germany, Netherlands, Spain, Belgium).
- Bond prices may be quoted in fractions (US, eg, down to 1/32) or decimal (rest of the world).
- Note that in Germany the Bundesbank acts as market maker for Bunds.
- US T-bonds are all issued in registered dematerialised form, with a life in excess of ten years. All US T-bonds are issued with a coupon. There are no zero coupon T-bonds when first issued and they are issued by dutch auction.

Examples of government bonds, and the names by which they are often known, include:

- **T-bonds**: the name given to bonds with a maturity of ten years or more, issued by the US and Canadian governments.
- **T-notes**: as for T-bonds, but with a maturity of two–ten years.
- **Bunds**: issued by the German government, with a maturity of anything up to 30 years.
- **OATs** (Obligations Assimilables du Trésor): issued by the French government, with a maturity from four–30 years.
- **BONOs** (Bonos del Estado): issued by the Spanish government, may have almost any maturity period.

You could think of all of the above bonds as the overseas equivalent of a UK gilt: that is, a bond issued by the government of a country, in its domestic market.

- The **US** and **Canada** have registered T-bonds with a maturity of greater than ten years, T-notes between two and ten years; two-year Treasury notes are sold every month, while five- and ten-year Treasury notes and 30-year Treasury bonds are sold every quarter. They are sold by auction, on regular dates, to some 40 primary dealers.
- **Germany** has bearer Bunds with a maturity of greater than ten years (ten to 30), and medium-term notes such as Bobls between three to five years and Schatz two years. The ten-year issues are the popular ones (rather than of longer duration) and most are fixed-rate, although there is the occasional floating rate bond. All are issued by the Bundesbank and they are dealt by 70 primary dealers, contrasted with the 40 primary dealers in the US.
- **France** has bearer OATs (Obligations Assimilables du Trésor) with a maturity of four–30 years and shorter dated two- to five-year BTAN issues called Treasury bills rather than bonds (Bons du Trésor à Intérêts Annuels). Short-term T-bills are BTF – Bons du Trésor à Taux Fixe. French government bonds (OATs) are sold on a regular monthly auction basis (on the first Thursday in each month) and they are sold to primary dealers who have an obligation to support the auction. They must take up 3% of annual bond issuance and trade 3% of secondary market turnover. The primary dealers are spécialistes en valeurs du trésor (SVTs). However, at each auction the offerings are usually more of existing bonds rather than offering new ones each time. BTANs are sold on the third Thursday in each month. In the past, some fixed-rate bonds have been issued which are convertible later into floating rate, and floating rates convertible into fixed. Also in the past, some zero-coupon bonds called **felins** have been issued (only nine in recent years). After not issuing bonds at floating rate for several years, the Bank of France announced proposals in 1996 to issue new floating rate bonds with the interest paid quarterly and linked to a new benchmark for the yield of ten-year OATs called TEC10 (Le Taux de l'Echéance Constante).

- **Italy** has bearer variable-dated bonds: BTPs (Buoni del Tesoro Poliennali) if fixed rate with two–ten years in maturity, CCT (Certificati Credito del Tesoro) if floating with a similar maturity. Both are sold by the central bank to 20 primary dealers on fixed dates every month. There are also six-year bonds which buyers can sell back after three years, called CTO (Certificati del Tesoro con Opzione).
- **Spain** has its BONOs (Bonos del Estado) with maturities of three and five years, but the ten-year maturity is called Obligaciones del Estado. The central bank sells these on a regular date each month.
- **Japan** has JGBs with a normal maturity of ten years or a superlong one of 20 years. They are sold by the Ministry of Finance. 40% are sold to a bank syndicate in agreed proportions, and 60% are sold by the auction method. Two, four, five, six and ten-year bonds are sold monthly and 20-year bonds are sold quarterly. Government, municipal and public sector bonds are 60% of issuance and dominate the market.
- Although it is not commonly seen in the UK, France and more recently in Thailand and China, the respective governments have issued ultra-long bonds in 50-year maturities. These 'ultra-long-dated' bonds have been issued to meet the need from insurance and pension funds for high-duration securities.

2.2.3 Index-Linked Bonds

We have noted that most bond issues pay interest at rates which are fixed; hence they are known as **fixed-interest securities**. However, some pay interest rates which fluctuate. Sometimes, this is in relation to a given measure of current market interest rates. However, one other key form of bond is the **index-linked bond**: here, interest payments – and indeed the capital repayment at maturity – vary in accordance with changes in inflation rates. A key issuer of index-linked debt securities in the UK is the UK government, by way of index-linked gilts.

Index-linked gilts pay a rate of interest and a redemption value based on the change in the Retail Prices Index in the same period. Other governments that offer index-linked bonds are Australia, Canada, Iceland, Israel, New Zealand, Sweden and, more recently, the US and France. The UK linked-sector is much the biggest of these.

Consumer Prices Index (CPI) – We have already seen that the Bank uses this to measure inflation for some purposes (eg, targeting what it wants to keep the level of inflation at). The CPI uses a slightly different basket of goods and services, and is a relatively new index. It was introduced in the UK because it is more in line with the way other countries in the European Union measure inflation; as the UK is a member of the EU, it needs to be able to measure inflation on a like-for-like basis. The government has said, however, that it has no plans at present to switch from using the RPI for calculating payments on index-linked gilts.

Retail Prices Index (RPI) – this is an index used by the Bank of England to measure the rate of inflation and is discussed in greater detail in Chapter 2. The RPI measures changes in the prices of a basket of different goods and services which the average person is assumed to spend their money on.

Index-linked gilts were first issued in 1981, initially for institutional investors such as pension funds only. Subsequently, they were made available to private investors. Like conventional gilts they are regarded as low-risk, in that they are backed by the government and have clearly defined terms for interest and redemption payments.

However, they differ in that both interest and redemption payments are protected against inflation, which – as we've already noted – can at times dramatically erode the value of investments.

As with conventional gilts, investors receive two interest payments a year and they get a redemption payment based on the nominal or face value of their gilt holding. But these payments are adjusted to take account of what inflation has done since the gilt was issued.

The key points to remember are:

- The coupon quoted is much lower than would be the case with a conventional gilt (typically, of the order of 2–5%). This is because each interest payment is adjusted upwards to reflect the change in the RPI since the gilt was issued. So the total payment will – almost always – be greater than the nominal coupon unless the reference index is flat or falls.
- The capital redemption payment made at the gilt's maturity is also adjusted upwards, in a similar manner.

For the purposes of calculating interest and capital payments on index-linked gilts, the government measures the RPI as at three months prior to the relevant pay date (ie, for an interest payment due on 1 June, the payment will be adjusted by reference to the RPI for April that year).

It compares this RPI measure with that which was in place three months prior to the RPI when the gilt was issued – and adjusts the interest payment accordingly. So if inflation is strong, a holder's interest payments will rise, protecting his income.

Note: you should be aware that until 2004, the government used to calculate gilt interest and redemption payments by adjusting these payments using the RPI **eight months** prior to the relevant reference date. It has not changed the basis of calculation for old index-linked gilts issued under these terms – but new index-linked gilts have the use of the more up-to-date RPI figures built into their terms and conditions.

Investors need to remember that, since the RPI can go down as well as up, their income payments from an index-linked gilt can fall as well as rise.

Also, there is no deflation 'floor', ie, their final redemption payment could be less than £100 per £100 nominal, if there is a general fall in the level of prices in the UK.

The amount of capital that the investor will get back on redemption will depend on what inflation does up until a point three, or eight, months before the stock is redeemed. The amount of capital redemption will then be worked out in the same way.

2.2.4 Treasury Bills

Treasury bills, like gilts, are issued by the UK government through its DMO, as part of its work in managing the government's funding and cash management.

They are an example of zero coupon debt securities (see Section 2.3.2), and pay no interest; instead, they are issued at a discount to their face value and redeemed at par (that is, £100 per £100 nominal). The investor receives his return by way of the increase in price between the issue price and the eventual redemption price.

This does not mean, however, that an investor cannot lose money if they decide to sell their treasury bill before its maturity date: the price of treasury bills fluctuates in the market, as with any tradeable instrument, and could fall to below what they bought it at before rising again to par at maturity.

Treasury bills can be issued with maturities of:

- one month (approximately 28 days);
- three months (approximately 91 days);
- six months (approximately 182 days); and
- in theory, 12 months (up to 364 days), although to date no 12-month tenders have been held.

Members of the public wishing to purchase treasury bills at the tenders will have to do so through one of the treasury bill primary participants and purchase a minimum of £500,000 nominal of bills.

2.2.5 Local Authority Bonds

These are loan stocks issued by UK local authorities; they are often referred to collectively, especially by those dealing in them on the London Stock Exchange, as **corporation stocks**.

They are usually secured by a charge over the assets of the issuing authority – that is, if the local authority cannot repay the interest or capital of the loan as it falls due, from the cash it has available at the time, then those assets could be sold to raise the money – thus securingthe borrower's position.

They may also be guaranteed by the Public Works Loans Board, giving them extra safety. That said, and while local authorities might seem pretty sound, it is not unheard of for a local authority to go broke. Investing in local authority issues is not quite as safe as investing in, say, gilts, because the local authorities themselves are separate from central government and the issue may or may not be guaranteed.

The Public Works Loans Board is a statutory body which operates within the Debt Management Office.

Mainly, the PWLB's job is to lend money from the National Loans Fund to local authorities and other prescribed bodies, and to collect the repayments. In addition, however, it may also guarantee loans being raised direct by those bodies. See the PWLB section of the DMO website dmo.gov.uk if you would like more information.

Interest is paid to investors net of basic rate tax, ie, tax has already been deducted from the interest payment before it is forwarded to the investor, and will be sent to HM Revenue & Customs for him by the local authority.

Local authority issues are divided into:

- **Local Authority Fixed Stocks** – also known as local authority bonds, or sometimes town hall bonds or town hall mortgages. They are fixed-rate investments, whose capital cannot usually be redeemed early by the investor unless a penalty charge is paid. Interest is paid net of tax at source, but the tax can be reclaimed by non-taxpayers. These stocks are not marketable – ie, once an investor has bought a holding in the initial issue of stock, he cannot sell it on in the market – he must hold it until the maturity date, unless the local authority is willing to redeem early.
- **Local Authority Negotiable Loans (Yearlings)** – also often issued by local authorities. They have a life of no longer than two years, are issued at par, and are marketable. Again, interest is paid net of basic rate tax.

2.3 CORPORATE BONDS

Corporate (company) loan stock, or corporate bonds, are issued by companies. They may or may not be backed up with security taken over a specific asset owned by the issuing company.

Interest is paid at specific intervals which will be set out in the bond's terms – for UK corporate loans, this is usually half-yearly. It is paid net of basic rate tax. As with gilts, capital gains tax is not chargeable – provided the corporate bond is a **qualifying** corporate bond. Broadly, a qualifying corporate bond is one which is interest-paying, rather than a convertible.

Some bond issues carry guarantees with them; this means that the issuing company's parent, or occasionally some other third party, is undertaking to repay the capital and interest if the issuer cannot itself meet the repayments.

Corporate loan stocks may also be unsecured (ie, no specific asset is identified which will be sold to meet the repayments if the issuer does not have the money, and there is no separate guarantee).

The corporate bond market is a very strong one too, especially in the US, and growing significantly in Europe recent years. In Germany there is a big tradition of reliance on bank finance as opposed to either bonds or equities. Very large European corporates may, in any case, find it easier to issue the bond in London as a eurobond rather than as a **domestic bond**. A domestic bond refers to one in which the nationality of the issuer, the denomination of the bond and the country of issue are the same – for example, a sterling-denominated bond issued in London by a UK company.

An **international bond** is a bond issued in a non-domestic currency – for instance any non-sterling denominated bond issued in London or any non-dollar bond issued in the US.

Debentures are corporate bonds which are backed by security, for example, land or buildings. If the issuer goes into liquidation, these assets must be sold to pay the bondholders. Because they are more secure, however, the rate of interest is less.

A **convertible** is a bond which is converted later, either into another type of bond (for example, convertible gilts, see Section 2.2.1) or into equity. The difference between the implied conversion price of the equity and the market price is called the **premium**.

2.3.1 Permanent Interest-Bearing Shares

Permanent Interest-Bearing Shares (PIBS) are issued by building societies (which, as you should remember, are not companies). They are a form of fixed-interest security, and are traded on the London Stock Exchange. As with other interest-bearing securities, they meet the needs of many investors who seek income; they offer a higher return than investments such as gilts, but carry a higher risk than gilts.

PIBS have the following features:

- Interest is paid (gross) at a fixed rate, half-yearly. However there is no obligation on the building society to pay the interest in any one year. If it does not pay it, it is under no obligation to roll it over to the next year (ie, the shares are **non-cumulative**). It is highly unlikely that a building society would not pay the interest, but it could happen in times of severe financial pressure.
- PIBS are irredeemable, and thus have no redemption date. The only time they will be repaid by an issuing building society is on liquidation, in which case the PIBS holders will be the last creditors to be repaid.
- PIBS holders are members of the building society and will normally qualify for distributions on demutualisation.

If a building society demutualises, PIBS are automatically converted into **perpetual subordinated bonds (PSBs)**. The name comes from the fact that they will be low down in the order for payment compared with other loans, if the issuer were to get into financial trouble.

PIBS and PSBs are fairly illiquid, and an investor may find it difficult to trade when he wishes. The illiquidity of the market can lead to relatively large spreads (the difference between the buying and selling prices), adding to transaction costs. The market is relatively small, currently worth under £1 billion.

As with all fixed-interest securities, if interest rates rise, the prices of PIBS/PSBs will fall, as the fixed interest they pay becomes less attractive compared with other options.

An ordinary investor in a building society is protected by the **Financial Services Compensation Scheme**, but PIBS/PSB holders are not.

PIBS have been of interest to some so-called **carpetbaggers** who hold a minimum investment in the hope of a windfall on demutualisation of the building society, because PIBS-holders have membership rights.

Interest on PIBS/PSBs is paid gross and is taxable. Tax is collected through the investor's tax assessment. No capital gains tax is paid on sale because the shares are classified as qualifying corporate bonds.

PIBS and PSBs are bought and sold on a stock exchange, and can be traded through a stockbroker. They can only be traded in round amounts varying from 1,000 to 50,000 shares.

2.3.2 Zero Coupon Bonds

Zero coupon bonds pay no interest. Instead, the investor makes his return by virtue of the fact that the bond is issued at a price well below its eventual redemption price (the latter usually being 'par' – another way of saying £100 per £100 nominal). For example, a zero coupon bond might be issued at £60 per £100 nominal, with an eventual redemption price at £100 per £100 nominal.

Thus the return looks, on the face of it, more like a capital gain than an income stream. The holding's value is likely to rise gradually towards the redemption price, as it nears its maturity date.

It should, however, be noted that in most cases, tax authorities will deem the investor to have received a notional amount of income each year and tax them on that, so as to avoid the possibility of investors abusing zeros as a way to obtain the certainty of return of a fixed-interest instrument, without the income tax liabilities.

2.3.3 High-Yield Bonds

High-yield bonds are those which are regarded as being below 'investment grade' – that is, their issuer has a poor credit rating and there is a higher probability of their defaulting on either the interest payments, or the capital repayment. Because of this they tend to trade at lower prices compared to more secure debt issues, and so their yields (assuming the interest payments can be kept up) are high. High-yield bonds tend to have higher coupons.

Generally, a bond with a credit rating of BBB– and above is considered worthy of investment grade, and those below as junk bonds.

2.3.4 Convertible Loan Stock

As well as the straight corporate bonds we looked at above, corporate issuers may also issue **convertible loan stocks**. These behave, for much of their lives, like ordinary loan stocks, but have the potential to be converted into shares instead. Governments and local authorities don't offer this type of bond since they are not companies and do not issue shares.

The main features of convertibles are:

- The loan stock itself generally carries a fixed-interest coupon.
- The stock's terms include the right for stockholders to convert their holding into a predetermined number of ordinary shares, on or between set dates in the future.
- The conversion terms are usually expressed in such a way that a set number of shares will be received in return for each £100 nominal of loan stock converted.
- The conversion period may be on a set date, or a series of set dates, or between certain dates: there will usually be an expiry date, after which the stock cannot be converted. If the stock has not been converted, it then reverts to behaving like an ordinary loan stock (a straight loan stock), with the same coupon and maturity dates as were originally attached to it.
- Usually, convertibles are first made available to existing shareholders to give them the opportunity to avoid the dilution of their existing stake in the company.

- The conversion price – the effective price of the shares to an investor who acquires them by exercising his conversion option instead of buying them in the market – can be calculated by dividing the current market price per £100 nominal of the loan stock, by the number of shares that can be acquired for that £100 nominal. If the conversion price is lower than the current market price at the exercise date, then it will make financial sense to exercise it.

Companies issue convertibles for a number of reasons:

- Convertibles are attractive to many investors because they combine the certainty and predictable income streams of a loan stock with the potential for growth that shares offer.
- Because of their appeal, a company issuing a convertible (instead of a straight bond) may have a better chance of raising capital than it otherwise would.
- Conditions in the market may make it inadvisable, or impossible, to raise capital by way of a rights issue – something that we will look at later. A convertible issue may, however, be a better option.
- Interest on a company's loan capital is paid before tax – ie, the company's tax liability is calculated on the basis of the profits after deduction of interest which makes it a lesser net cost to the company than the payment of dividends (which are paid after tax).

2.3.5 Eurobonds

Eurobonds were created following World War II when companies wished to raise dollar financing outside the US due to legal constraints in the US. The term eurobond does not have anything to do with the euro currency and eurobonds do not have to be denominated in euros. A market was established in Europe allowing companies to issue dollar bonds outside the US. These are commonly known as eurodollars. Yen borrowed outside of Japan are called euroyen borrowings.

A eurobond is therefore defined as a bond issued outside the home country of its issuer, and in a currency other than that of the issuer's home currency. Eurobonds fall outside the regulatory jurisdiction of any one country. Their main features are:

- They can be issued in any major currency.
- They are issued outside the country of the currency in which they are denominated.
- They can be held by investors in almost any country.
- They are available in a very wide range of structures and with varying terms, to suit market conditions and their target investor base.
- They are not subject to withholding tax – ie, interest on them is paid gross to the holders.
- They are issued in bearer form – that is, the investor's name does not appear on a register held by the issuer.

The term 'eurobond' thus covers a wide variety of bonds, which include, among others:

- **Medium term notes (MTNs)** – typically these have a maturity of between two and ten years (although in practice they are not required to have a truly medium term, and you may come across issues with longer or shorter durations). They are often dealt in, and settled, in a rather different way to other debt securities, being treated for these purposes as more akin to commercial paper.
- **Euro-convertibles** – these are convertible into the equity of the issuer, as with the domestic convertible bonds we looked at earlier.

2.3.6 Supranational Bonds

These are bonds issued by institutions such as the European Investment Bank (EIB) and the World Bank. As with government bonds, they are regarded as the safest bond investments and have a high credit rating.

2.3.7 Floating Rate Notes

A floating rate note (FRN) is a form of security, created in the euromarkets and adopted elsewhere, that carries a variable interest rate which is adjusted regularly (at one- to six-monthly intervals – whatever is preferred by the issuer) by a margin against a benchmark rate such as LIBOR.

Issued for three years or longer, FRNs are popular during periods of increased volatility in interest rates, when lenders may be reluctant to lend funds cheaply at a fixed period for a fixed rate.

For example, the issuer might agree that their FRN will pay 50 basis points (0.5%) over the rate of LIBOR. So if LIBOR is 6% per annum over a six-month period (it is usually worked out as an average), the FRN will pay 6% per annum plus the 0.5% spread, or 6.5% per annum in total over the six-month period.

2.3.8 Asset-Backed Securities

Asset-backed securities are bonds issued on the security of a stream of specific income flows, eg, mortgage payments to a bank, out of which interest payments are made to investors.

2.3.9 Convertible Bonds

Convertible bonds give the holder the option to exchange the bond for a predetermined number of shares in the issuing company. They offer a slightly lower interest rate than corporate bonds because they can be changed into stock and so benefit from a rise in price of the underlying stock. If the stock performs poorly there is no conversion and the investor is left with a lower return than a non-convertible corporate bond would provide. This is the trade-off between risk and return.

2.4 THE INVESTMENT RETURNS ON DEBT SECURITIES

LEARNING OBJECTIVE

1.2.2   Analyse the main sources of investment risk and return associated with fixed income securities: capital return; interest or yield; liquidity; rates of interest; real returns; credit ratings; credit enhancements

The term **yield** generally refers to the return an investor makes on a particular investment. The income yield is the annualised income return on an investment, expressed as a percentage of the capital invested or current price.

Sometimes, however, it is the total return – the **yield to maturity** – which is of more interest. This will include the annualised capital growth or loss which will be made on the investment, if it were held to maturity.

Yields may be quoted gross or net of tax. Yields are useful for comparing one investment with another, to see which is more attractive to the investor.

Taking gilts as our example, the yield on a gilt will depend on:

- the gilt's coupon; and
- its market price.

The two main influences on the price of a gilt are:

- interest rates, as set by the Bank of England; and
- how long the gilt has to run until maturity.

The price of a gilt (and therefore its yield) will also be affected by demand in the market. As with most markets, when there are more buyers than sellers the price will rise; and conversely, when there are more sellers than buyers the price will fall. But of course, one of the key factors that influences investor demand is the attractiveness of a gilt compared to other investments – and this is why interest rates play a leading role in how much demand there is.

In addition, movements in the sterling exchange rate can affect foreign demand. If sterling is weak, UK gilts may look comparatively good value to an overseas investor; and if it is expected to strengthen then they may see a holding of a UK gilt as a good way to reap the currency gain while holding a secure investment.

Let's look at some different ways of assessing a gilt's yield, taking account of its current market price.

2.4.1   Running Yield

The running yield (also known as the interest yield) on a gilt expresses the income received on it, as a percentage of the investor's outlay.

It is calculated by dividing the coupon rate by the market price, and multiplying the result by 100.

$$\frac{\text{Gross coupon}}{\text{Market price}} \times 100 \ = \ \text{Interest yield (also known as 'running yield')}$$

Using as an example 12% Exchequer Stock 2009, trading at a price of £114 per £100 nominal, we have:

$$\text{Interest yield} = \frac{12}{114} \times 100 = 10.53\%$$

In other words, for every £100 actual which the investor invests in the above gilt, he will receive £10.53 per annum, gross, by way of interest. The interest yield is usually expressed gross (ie, as a rate before deduction of income tax).

2.4.2   Capital Returns

The running yield does not, however, tell the whole story for the investor. It does not reflect any capital gain or loss that will be incurred.

As the rates in the market change, the prices of the bonds will rise and fall, hence the investor may incur a capital loss or gain if he resells the bond. He could, of course, hold until redemption, in which case we know for sure that £100 will be received for every £100 nominal stock. The capital return will depend on the purchase price. If he bought his holding at a price above par – that is, he paid more than £100 per £100 nominal – he will incur a capital loss on the sale. If he paid less than par, he will make a gain on the sale.

$$\text{Holding period return} = \frac{\text{(Price received at maturity – Price purchased)}}{\text{Price purchased}}$$

The annualised capital gain/loss in terms of a return measure can be represented by:

$$\text{Annualised return from capital gain/loss} = \frac{\text{Holding period return}}{\text{Number of years to maturity}}$$

An estimate of these capital returns to redemption can be calculated, and incorporated into the overall return the investor will make should he hold the bond until maturity. The redemption yield, which we will look at next, reflects this capital loss, or gain, in addition to the interest payments that will be received.

2.4.3 Yield to Redemption

The Gross Redemption Yield (sometimes also written as Gross Yield to Redemption or Yield-to-Maturity (YTM)) assumes that the investor will hold the bond to its redemption date. He will receive this return annually on the bond investment if held to maturity. The assumption is that any coupons received will continue to be reinvested at a rate that is the same as the redemption yield.

To determine an approximate measure of the YTM from the coupon, bond price and the maturity of the bond, we can calculate the return in two parts: the interest yield component of the return plus the capital appreciation component of the return.

As far as the capital appreciation component of the bond return is concerned, the investor will (generally) make either a capital gain or a loss, depending on whether he bought the holding above par (at a premium) or under par (at a discount).

Clearly, then, to calculate this estimate of the redemption yield from the price and the coupon on a particular bond, we first need to work out the difference between the bond's current price and par, as well as the number of years it has to run. This procedure is outlined in this section.

Having determined the current yield earlier, we now calculate the return due to capital appreciation on the bond by using the formula presented above.

As already stated, the annualised return from capital gain/loss can be represented by:

$$\frac{\text{Holding period of return}}{\text{Number of years to maturity}}$$

- If the market price of the gilt is trading at a discount (below the par value of £100) then there will be a positive element of capital gain per annum to be added to the interest yield.
- If, on the other hand, the gilt is trading at a premium (market price of the gilt is above par) then the resulting return due to capital loss will need to be deducted from the interest yield, to arrive at the approximate redemption yield.

EXAMPLE

Let us consider the redemption yield that would have applied for 12% Exchequer 2009, price £114, in the year 2002.

1. **Recall from Section 2.4.1 that the running yield for this bond is 10.53%.**
2. **Holding period return is 100–114/114 = –0.1228.**
3. **Return due to the annualised loss on capital to redemption is –0.1228/7 = –0.0175 or –1.75%.**

So the approximate yield to redemption is a combination of yields in 1 and 3:
10.53% (the interest yield, as calculated before) –1.75% = 8.78%.

The approximate yield to redemption stated above is a gross yield, because no account has been taken of the income tax the investor will pay on it. Remember, there is no capital gains tax payable on gains realised on disposals of gilts.

To calculate a figure which shows the yield to redemption after tax – the **net redemption yield** – we need to take account of what income tax rate the investor will actually pay.

To do this, the interest yield needs to be adjusted by the investor's applicable tax rate, ie:

- 0% (non-taxpayers);
- 20% (basic rate taxpayer);
- 40–50% (higher-rate taxpayers).
- Net Redemption Yield (after-tax) = Gross Redemption Yield (1 – tax rate).

2.4.4   Volatility and Risk

There is an inverse relationship between the prices of bonds and their yields. The price variability of a particular bond that has some time left to maturity will change depending on interest rate expectations. Rising rate expectations will increase the redemption yield and push prices down and, conversely, falling yield expectations will lift bond prices. The variability of each bond price across the maturity range will depend on a number of factors. In general, longer-dated bonds are more sensitive to interest rate change, while coupons modify the variability of the bond.

The price variability of a bond depends on the interest rate change and risk characteristics of each bond – its '**duration**'. The duration is a function of the combined effect of a coupon and the maturity characteristics of each bond. An increase in yields will lower prices and a bond with a higher duration will be more sensitive to the same change in yields than a lower-duration bond.

In general, we expect greater volatility in:

*   bonds of a lower credit-quality. Junk (non-investment grade) bonds are more volatile because of their greater risk and speculative nature as compared with investment grade bonds.
*   lower coupon bonds, because a small change in current interest rates represents a proportionately greater change as a percentage of a low coupon than of a high coupon.
*   longer-dated bonds, because current interest rate expectations have a relatively greater impact on the overall return to maturity than for shorter-dated bonds.

Duration is a measure that can be used to estimate the price sensitivity of a bond to small changes in yields. The simplest measure for duration is called Macaulay's duration. When it is adjusted by dividing with a yield relative, it is called modified duration.

2.4.5   The Yield Curve

It can be useful to display graphically the yields available on bonds of differing maturities. A graph showing this, usually based on gilt yields and shown against the time they have left to maturity, is called a yield curve.

Normal Yield Curve

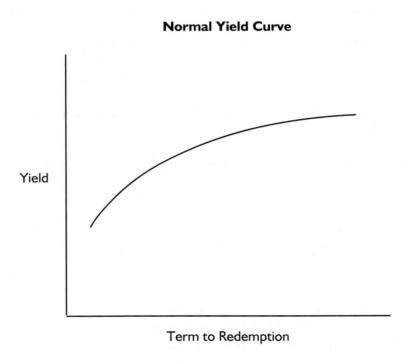

A yield curve does not show yields on securities at different points in time; it shows the yields at the same point in time, on securities with different lengths of time to maturity.

The shape of the yield curve provides important information to bond market participants about rate expectations in the capital markets. We shall not go into details of the financial theories developed to explain the yield curve or their rate term structures here. Hence a simpler interpretation is provided at this stage of the learning process. There are three common types of shapes of yield curves can be identified – normal, flat and inverted.

A **'normal' yield curve** has a positive (upward) slope, reflecting the fact that securities with more time remaining to maturity have a slightly higher yield than shorter-dated securities. Interpretation of the term structure of rates is a specialised activity. However, more broadly, an upward-sloping yield curve depicts the **time value of money**. Investors will generally require a higher yield, or a premium over shorter-maturity bonds, for tying up their invested capital for longer. This observed term premium is due to **greater uncertainty over longer future periods**. The yield curve is not static but dynamic, and is continually changing shape over time as new information about future rates arrives and is priced into the market. The emerging news can lead to complex changes in the shape of the yield curve.

At other times, the yield curve may start to look much **flatter**:

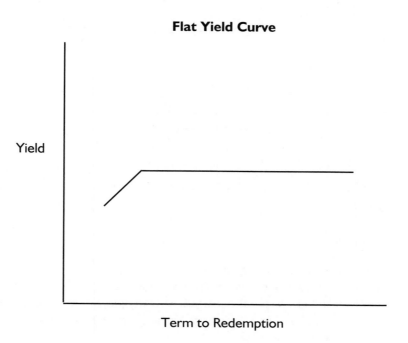

Flat Yield Curve

Yield

Term to Redemption

A flat yield curve is characterised by level rates across a range of maturities and this curve may reflect a relatively stable outlook for the economy. Alternatively, this flattening-off (in comparison with the normal yield curve) can reflect expectations of a gradual future decline in interest rates. A curve-flattening development is normally observed during an economic downturn phase in the cycle, also accompanied by moderating inflationary pressures.

When short- and long-term bonds are offering the same yields, investors may choose the bond with the least amount of risk. However, an investor's wish to have the certainty of holding bonds until maturity to meet a long-term obligation may put a high priority on choosing bonds with maturities matching dates when the investor wishes to realise funds.

Inverted Yield Curve

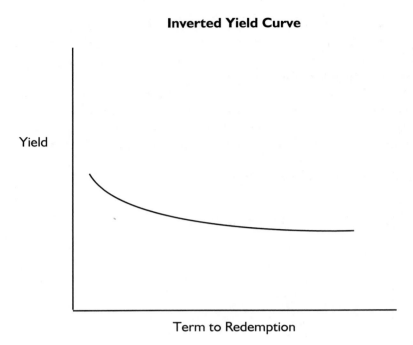

The yield curve may also sometimes be **inverted**, with yields on longer-dated securities being lower than on shorter-dated securities.

An inverted yield curve may reflect:

- expectations that interest rates will fall in the future;
- expectations that inflationary pressures in the economy will reduce dramatically in the future;
- lower supply and higher demand for gilts in the market; for example, a decrease in issuance of gilts by the DMO and/or increased demand from investors for long-dated gilts will cause the longer-dated gilt prices to rise and their yields to fall.

2.5   INVESTMENT RISK AND DEBT SECURITIES

LEARNING OBJECTIVE

1.2.2	Analyse the main sources of investment risk and return associated with fixed income securities: capital return; interest or yield; liquidity; rates of interest; real returns; credit ratings; credit enhancements

In the following sections we will consider various factors which can affect the riskiness of a debt security, and its performance – including liquidity, interest rates, real rates of return, issuing institutions and credit ratings, and methods of credit enhancement. These factors combine to affect the risk attaching to a debt security.

Bonds are, generally, **negotiable** or **marketable** securities – that is, they can be bought and sold (although there are, as we have seen, some bonds that cannot be sold prior to maturity, but they have to be held until their redemption dates; these include some local authority issues).

An investor considering holding bonds needs to consider the factors that will influence prices in the bond markets. As with any market (and as we saw earlier with specific reference to gilts) this is driven by supply and demand. The following factors affect the supply of, and demand for, bonds in the market:

*   Levels of interest rates in the home currency.
*   Changes in the credit rating of the issuer.
*   Changes in the economic environment – in particular:
    *   in the UK, the public sector net cash requirement has a large effect on the gilt and domestic bond market; in other countries, the local equivalent is also likely to be influential;
    *   levels of gross domestic product and gross national product, seen as barometers of the productivity and economic health of a country;
    *   unemployment figures, since these are also seen as indicative of the health of the economy – and may spark some interest rate movements if the government is trying to take action.
*   The coupon and redemption date of the bond.

Sentiment in the bond market often has an effect on equities, as well, in part because the economic events that impact on the one also affect the other, and in part because bonds are often seen as a safe haven when the equity markets are doing badly. This is due to the fact that bond prices are generally much less volatile (less prone to going up and down) than equities, because of their relative certainty of return.

Other factors are considered below.

2.5.1   Liquidity

As with other investments, bonds can carry liquidity risk – the risk that the bond is hard to sell quickly, or can only be sold quickly at a price which does not reflect a fair market value.

Liquidity risk is not a problem for large issues, or issues where there is a guaranteed market such as UK gilts. However, it can be a much greater problem for smaller issues and those where the creditworthiness of the issuer is less sound.

2.5.2   Rates of Interest

Interest rate risk is the risk that market rates rise. The consequence of this for holders of fixed-interest securities is that:

*   the coupon becomes comparatively less attractive than it was before, relative to rates in the market;
*   consequently the price of the bond falls, as demand for it dries up and/or investors sell in order to free money up to lock into higher rates elsewhere.

Thus the investor suffers a 'double hit': he is locked into a bond paying rates which could be bettered elsewhere; and the price of his holding has also fallen, in line with the market.

2.5.3   Real Returns

The returns on fixed-interest securities can, as with the deposit-based investments, be eroded by inflation; indeed if inflation reaches very high levels, the real return on the bond could be negative.

Of course, index-linked bonds – which we looked at earlier in Section 2.2.3 – provide protection against inflation risk in that both income and capital are adjusted for changes in the RPI.

2.5.4 Issuer Risk

Issuer risk is the risk that the issuer of the bond gets into financial difficulties and cannot keep up the interest payments, or defaults on the capital. Generally speaking, investors regard bonds as less risky than equities, because:

*   If the issuer has poor profits (or no profits at all) in a given year, it must still pay interest on its debt. Dividends on the other hand are paid from profits, so may be at risk in a poor year.
*   If an issuer goes into liquidation, then the order of pay-out is such that bondholders will be repaid before shareholders, and, if there are not enough assets to go around, shareholders may therefore get nothing at all. This is because, in the course of a liquidation, assets are sold off to raise the cash to pay off debts – and there is a legally prescribed order in which that cash is distributed. Shareholders are not debtors, but owners of a company, and as such are last in the pecking order for distributions.

That said, of course, much depends on the financial status of the issuer itself. Equities issued by a large, financially sound and well-run company may in fact be a safer investment than debt issued by a company whose finances are in a poor state and which may default on its liabilities.

Still, it is fair to say that when looking at a single issuer, debt instruments issued by it are likely to be more secure than shares issued by it.

The price debtholders pay for this additional security is, of course, the fact that their rewards are limited to the payment of interest and repayment of loan capital, on the terms originally specified. If the company does very well indeed, they will not get any extra profit, whereas shareholders can hope to see their shares rise in price, and to receive rising dividends each year.

The riskiest bond issuers are those falling into the junk category; junk bond issuers suffer a relatively high rate of defaults, for which they are compensated by relatively high yields, providing that the issuer can keep up the repayments.

2.5.5 Credit Ratings

A number of issues may affect a bond's safety, in terms of the likelihood of its being repaid. Clearly, an investor in any form of bond is going to be keen to know what the issuer's creditworthiness is, so as to assess whether the returns are worthwhile in light of the risk to his interest and capital.

Generally speaking, bonds issued by governments are regarded as the most secure – although it is not unheard of for governments to default on their debts. In any event, it can be hard for an investor to assess the creditworthiness of either a government or a company. In order to help them do so, a number of specialist agencies provide credit ratings using standardised scales, to bond issues. Among the most well known are:

*   Moody's;
*   Standard & Poor's; and
*   Fitch IBCA.

If an issuer wishes to be rated (and many do, because some investors will simply not buy debt which does not have an independent credit rating attached to it), then they will invite the rating agency to inspect its financial status and operations. The agencies then assign a rating to the issuer, and often different ratings to individual debt issues from the same issuer, depending on the seniority or otherwise of the specific issue.

The rating agencies consider the following main areas:

- the issuer's current financial strength;
- the financial and commercial management of the organisation;
- the economic and political background in the environment in which the organisation operates;
- competition in the industry in which the organisation operates.

An issuer's rating can change from time to time, with its own fortunes and those of the environment in which it operates. Ratings generally use a series of letters and numbers, which are available for investors to refer to so they can understand what they are seeing.

For example, Standard & Poor's most secure credit rating is 'AAA' (or 'triple A'), with AA being somewhat less secure, and A and A– being progressively less secure yet. The permutations are too numerous to set out here, but you should be aware that (for example):

- AAA-rated debt is more secure than AA-rated debt;
- A-rated debt is more secure than B-rated debt;
- B-rated debt is more secure than C-rated debt.

2.5.6   Credit Enhancements

In order to make their bond issues more attractive to investors, by reducing the risk of default, many issuers whose finances are not in good shape arrange for another organisation (generally one with very strong finances) to **guarantee** the debt. This means that, if the issuer cannot pay the interest or capital from its own resources, the 'guarantor' (the organisation issuing the guarantee) will make the repayments.

The investor therefore relies on the creditworthiness of the guarantor, as opposed to that of the issuer, for his security. An example of this is a lesser-known company arranging for its debt to be guaranteed by a major bank or insurance company.

2.5.7   Secured/Unsecured Status of the Debt

Bond issuers can issue debt in secured or unsecured form.

- **Secured debt** involves the identification of certain of the issuer's assets, so that, if the issuer defaults, the bondholders will have a prior legal claim over that asset.
- **Unsecured debt** leaves the investor with no certainty as to the payment of interest or repayment of capital, excepting for the issuer's promise to repay.

If a company which has issued debt goes into liquidation, then any bonds it has issued are ranked in order of seniority.

> **Liquidation** – occurs when a company is 'wound-up', with its assets being sold off to repay its outstanding debts, and the surplus (if there is any) is distributed to the shareholders.

This ranking determines the order in which they will be repaid – with those ranking last being at greatest risk of there not being enough money to go round. The ranking will depend on whether the bond is:

- secured or unsecured (if it is secured, then the bondholders can rely on the proceeds of the specific asset designated as security);
- described as **subordinated** or **unsubordinated**. Unsubordinated bonds carry an unconditional promise that they will be repaid before the creditor's other obligations. Unsubordinated bonds are also sometimes described as **senior** debt. Subordinated bonds rank after them for repayment, and are sometimes known as **junior** debt.

2.6 DEALING IN DEBT SECURITIES

LEARNING OBJECTIVE

1.2.4 Understand how fixed income securities are traded and settled: primary and secondary markets; decentralised market; clearing, settlement and safe custody; pricing, liquidity and fair value; coupon; nominal value; market price; clean and dirty prices; redemption date; transaction costs and charges;

2.6.1 Costs of Purchase and Sale

Like shares and other stocks, bonds can be bought and sold through a **stockbroker**. Investors will pay the broker a commission, which may vary from broker to broker and will also depend on the size of the deal. (Usually, for larger deals, stockbrokers will charge commissions based on a lower percentage of the deal size. Some brokers will also offer investment advice as to which gilt may suit the investor's needs best, and on conditions in the market.

Where an investor buys a bond through a stockbroker, they will pay the current market price; they can, however, give their broker special instructions – for example:

- to buy **at best** (ie, at the best available price in the market);
- to buy at a **limit** (ie, not to pay more than a certain amount for the stock; if the broker cannot complete the deal at the limit or better, he will not place it at all).

Gilts can also be bought directly from the:

- DMO's Gilt Purchase and Sale Service (operated by Computershare);
- DMO at gilt auctions.

Directly from the DMO's Gilt Purchase and Sale Service

Since 2003, private investors have been able to deal in gilts which are already in issue, directly with the DMO, on an **execution-only** basis (that is, no advice is given and the investor must make their own decisions). The service is called the Retail Gilt Purchase and Sale Service, and it is operated by a firm called Computershare.

To be able to use Computershare, investors have to first go through a process which means they become approved investors. This is very similar to the anti-money laundering procedures. It is how the DMO and Computershare satisfy the UK anti-money laundering requirements with regard to each investor. Once an investor is an approved investor, they will not then have to provide evidence of his identity and address every time they want to use the purchase and sale service (nor will they have to do so if they invest via a gilt auction, see below).

Once an investor has been accepted as a member of the approved group, they are able to use the gilt purchase and sale service on an execution-only basis, to buy and sell holdings of gilts. Commission charges on deals made this way (particularly smaller ones) may be less than those levied by stockbrokers and banks for the same sized deals, so this service can be attractive to retail investors.

The investor needs to complete the appropriate dealing form (which they can obtain directly from Computershare). When Computershare sends them the form, it will also include a list of gilts available for purchase. The investor then sends the form, with the appropriate payment (in the case of gilt purchases) directly to Computershare.

The application should show the gilt they want to buy and the amount in money terms they want to invest (ie, **not** the nominal amount of the gilt they want to buy – since they will not know the exact price at which the deal will be carried out when they post their dealing form).

The price at which the deal is done will depend on conditions on the date that Computershare has the form, cleared funds and any other information it needs to proceed; that is, an investor cannot say 'I would like to deal at XX price or better' (as he could if dealing through a stockbroker). They get the prevailing market price, as determined by the DMO, at the time the deal is placed. Thus, the benefit of potentially cheaper dealing costs is to some extent offset by this lack of control.

Computershare sends the investor his gilt certificate, and a contract note setting out all the costs, approximately four days after the deal date.

Direct from the DMO at Auction

Members of the approved group can also deal direct with the DMO to buy gilts at auction. Many large gilt issues are first brought to the market in this way, and it can represent a very cost-effective route for an investor to buy into a new issue, since there is no bid-offer spread to pay, and no stockbroker's commission.

Even though the investor does not know the price at which he will eventually deal, he does at least know that there will be minimal dealing costs.

> **Bid-offer spread** – the difference between the prices at which a share, bond, unit trust or other investment can be bought and sold on the same day.

EXAMPLE

If an investor were to see a gilt described as having a price of £118–118.25, this would mean that the price at which £100 nominal of that gilt can be **bought** is £118.25. The price at which £100 nominal can be **sold** is £118.00, and the **bid-offer spread** is £0.25 per £100 nominal.

The DMO issues an auction calendar giving details of the gilts which it proposes to auction in the months ahead; this is usually published up to a year in advance, with finalised dates as to which gilts will in fact be auctioned, and on what dates, being announced at the end of each quarter.

Non-competitive bids. Private investors can bid on a non-competitive basis in a gilt auction for a minimum of £1,000 nominal of the particular gilt; the maximum they can bid for is £500,000 (conventional gilts) or £250,000 (index-linked).

The fact that they bid on a non-competitive basis means that any successful application will be met in full. That is, the investor gets as much stock as he requested, at the average accepted bid price for that particular auction (ie, the weighted average price paid by successful competitive bidders). So someone sending in a non-competitive bid has to accept that they will be allocated stock at whatever this price turns out to be. They do not know it in advance.

Competitive bids. Any application to bid for over £500,000 nominal (£250,000 in the case of index-linked) will be a competitive bid and must be submitted through a GEMM, stating the price the investor is willing to pay. Investors submitting a competitive bid price which is too low risk getting no stock, or only a proportion of the amount they originally bid for. Those who bid the highest prices will get as much stock as they have subscribed for, unless the issue is heavily oversubscribed, in which case it may be allocated on a pro rata basis across the highest bidders.

Usually, investors in this category are institutional investors, and sometimes they bid for very large allocations of stock.

As we have seen above, it is the competitive bids which are used to determine what price the non-competitive bidders will be allocated stock at.

2.6.2 Market Prices

Many bond prices, including those of gilts, are quoted in the *Financial Times* and some other newspapers.

The prices quoted are:

- the mid-point between buying and selling prices (called the **mid-market price**);
- **clean prices**, meaning that they take no account of **accrued interest** (explained in Section 2.6).

2.6.3   Clean and Dirty Prices

Interest on a bond is, as we have seen, paid at set periods. However, it accrues on a daily basis – that is, every day an additional 1/365th of the total annual interest becomes due to the owner. So someone selling (for example) a gilt between two coupon periods will normally be compensated for the interest that was due to them up to the settlement date of the sale, and the person buying it will have to pay for that accrued interest.

So the price paid for the gilt (the market price x the nominal amount being traded) is adjusted by an amount for the accrued interest to date. The accrued interest is calculated up to and including the settlement date of the deal – that is, for gilts, usually one working day after the deal date.

EXAMPLE

Staying with gilts to illustrate the point, 5% Treasury Stock 2010 pays interest on 7 March and 7 September. Someone who bought a holding in it for settlement on 7 April 2009 (that is, a month after the previous coupon payment) was also buying 31 days of accrued interest. Having done this they will then become entitled to the next full interest coupon payment on 7 September.

The price the buyer pays will then (ignoring any stockbroker's commission) be the 'clean' market price for the gilt, plus an accrued interest adjustment of:

Half the coupon (as interest is paid twice yearly) x $\dfrac{\text{number of days since last payment}}{184 \text{ (ie, half a year)}}$

or, in the case of our example gilt,

5% / 2   x   31 / 184 = £0.421196 per £100 nominal of the gilt.

Seven working days before the interest payment date (or 10 working days in the case of War Loans), the price of a gilt goes **ex-dividend** (also written as xd). This may sound odd, as we usually use the term 'dividends' in connection with shares – it is just a convention, and in the case of gilts refers to the interest that will be paid.

Ex-dividend means 'without the dividend', and it means that anyone buying the gilt between now and the imminent interest payment date won't get that interest, unless they have bought it on **special terms**, which have been advised to the registrar, so that they know who to make the payment to.

Anyone who holds the gilt on the xd date will get the full interest payment.

Anyone who sells the gilt between the xd date and the pay date (ie, within the xd period) will receive the full interest payment – but will have to pay some of it back to the person who buys the holding, since they will have obtained a couple of days' interest to which they were not entitled.

Sometimes, people dealing in the xd period can agree to ask the registrar to pay the entire forthcoming interest payment to the buyer – even though, as we've seen, this is not the convention (these are the special terms referred to earlier in this subsection). This is called buying **cum-dividend** – cum is Latin for 'with'.

So, you may see the following adjustments quoted in respect of a gilt deal to ensure that an investor gets the exact number of days' interest that he has held the stock for:

- **Investor buys cum-div** – interest from the last payment date to the settlement date is added to the cost.
- **Investor buys ex-div** – interest from the settlement date to the next payment date is deducted from the cost.
- **Investor sells cum-div** – interest from the last payment date to the settlement date is added to the sale proceeds.
- **Investor sells ex-div** – interest from the settlement date to the next payment date is deducted from the proceeds.

So, as we've seen, **interest payments** are generally made to the holder who was registered **seven business days** before the interest payment date. After this date, the stock will be sold without interest (referred to as **ex-interest** or **ex-dividend**). The seller of the stock will receive the interest payment, generally for a full six months.

Sales at any time since the last interest payment up to this date are made cum-interest/cum-dividend (with dividend). In this case, the subsequent interest payment will be paid to the purchaser.

Accrued interest is the daily interest earned on the stock since the last interest payment date, which is paid and received at the time of a transaction, in addition to the clean price of the stock, to give the dirty price that the buyer must pay.

EXAMPLE

An investor pays £96 for a purchase of government stock with a coupon of 7%. He buys the stock 60 days after the last payment of interest. He will pay the dirty price as calculated below:

Clean price	**£96.00**
Interest	$60/365 \times £7 = £1.15$
Dirty price	**£97.15**

If a stock is sold ex-interest/ex-dividend, the buyer will be compensated for the fact that he receives no interest in respect of the time he has held the stock in the current interest period. Thus, the clean price will be adjusted downwards slightly to reflect this interest adjustment.

2.6.4 Redemption Date

Bonds and gilts are issued with a promise that investors' money will be repaid at a set future date - the redemption date. Redemption dates can be set at:

- short-term (within 7 years);
- medium (7–15 years);
- long-term (over 15 years).

The investment will then be repaid at the agreed date. Undated gilts, which have no fixed redemption date, are also available.

2.7   BOND INDICES

LEARNING OBJECTIVE

1.2.5   Understand the purpose and construction of the main bond indices,
and the considerations needed for less liquid markets

A bond market index is a composite listing of bonds or fixed-income instruments and provides a statistic that can be used to measure performance in the portfolio management process.

2.7.1   Types of Indices

Bond indices can be categorised based on their broad characteristics, such as whether they are composed of government bonds, corporate bonds, high-yield bonds or asset-backed securities. They can also be classified based on their credit rating or maturity date.

Bond indices are generally **total return indices** and are used mostly to view performance of a market over time. In addition to returns, bond indices also incorporate the combined yield, duration, and convexity of individual bonds.

Bond indices generally include more individual securities than stock market indices do, and are broader and more rule-based. This allows portfolio managers to predict which type of debt issues will be eligible for each index.

2.7.2   Weighting

Most bond indices are weighted by market capitalisation. Bond indices are usually based on market capitalisation, like the shares indices. If the index is of, say, the top 50 bonds (or companies, in the case of the shares indices), then **top** means biggest by market capitalisation. Sometimes the index is described as **weighted**. This simply means that a 1% change in the price of the largest bond/company in the index will have more impact than a 1% change in the price of the smallest. Since the bond/share price is always changing, it follows that all the top bonds/shares are not always the same. There is a provision for removing some bonds/shares and adding others, say, every quarter.

2.7.3   Indices and Passive Investment Management

Bond indices are harder to replicate, compared to stock market indices, due to the large number of issues. Usually, portfolio managers define suitable benchmarks for their portfolios, and use an existing index or create blends of indices based on their investment mandates.

They then purchase a subset of the issues available in their benchmark, and use the index as a measure of the market portfolio's return against which to compare their own portfolio's performance. Often the average duration of the market may not be the most appropriate duration for a given portfolio. Replication of an index's characteristics can be achieved by using bond futures to match the duration of the bond index.

2.7.4 FTSE Global Government Bond Indices

The FTSE global government bond Indices consist of central government debt from 22 countries denominated in the domicile currency, or euros for Eurozone countries. There is a euro aggregate index and the indices are organised by region: Asia Pacific (including China), the Americas and the Eurozone plus a European ex-Eurozone index. The indices are also available at the country level and by maturity band.

2.7.5 FTSE Covered Bond Indices

The FTSE covered bond indices consist of securitised issues from 14 countries, including Jumbo Pfandbrief from Germany. Each issue is comparable in structure and quality to the German Jumbo Pfandbrief market. The indices are available at aggregate, country level and by maturity bands.

2.7.6 FTSE Corporate Bond Indices

FTSE Euro Corporate Bond Index

The FTSE Euro Corporate Bond Index includes euro-denominated issues from global corporate entities. Each bond is classified under the Industry Classification Benchmark (ICB). The index constituents are investment grade debt with a minimum rating of BBB–. Sub-indices are structured by credit rating and maturity band.

FTSE Sterling Corporate Bond Index

The FTSE sterling corporate bond index consists of sterling-denominated corporate bonds of investment grade quality. Each bond is classified under the Industry Classification Benchmark (ICB). There are 11 industrial sector sub-indices including telecommunications, utilities and banking. The index has sector rating and maturity sub-indices. Telecommunications and non-financials (ie, the headline index minus Financials) are calculated as additional sub-indices.

The FTSE corporate bond indices have 14 additional sub-indices besides the maturity sub-indices.

Agency credit ratings have been grouped as follows:

Sub-Indices Rating Definition	Agency Equivalent Ratings		
	Fitch	S&P	Moodys
AAA	AAA	AAA	Aaa
AA	AA– to AA+	AA– to AA+	Aa3 to Aa1
A	A– to A+	A– to A+	A3 to A1
BBB	BBB– to BBB+	BBB- to BBB+	Baa3 to Baa1

2.7.7 Sub-Indices

All indices have the following five maturity sub-indices:

- 1–3 years
- 3–5 years

- 5–7 years
- 7–10 years
- over 10 years

2.7.8 Capital Index

The capital index of all the listed indices is calculated every day. Each Capital Index is an arithmetically weighted index based on the clean price, and weighted by the nominal amount outstanding.

2.7.9 Total Return Index

A total return index is calculated for all the indices. A total return index reflects the price changes and interest payments of each bond. What does total return mean? When measuring performance, it is the actual rate of return of an investment or a pool of investments over a given evaluation period. Total return includes interest, capital gains, dividends and distributions realised over a given period of time and it accounts for two categories of return: income and capital appreciation. Income includes interest paid by fixed-income investments, distributions or dividends. Capital appreciation represents the change in the market price of an asset.

2.7.10 Additional Calculations

In addition to the capital index and total return index, the following fundamentals of bond indices are also calculated:

- average coupon;
- average gross redemption yield;
- average time to maturity;
- average (Macaulay) duration;
- average modified duration;
- average convexity;
- the sum of the nominal value of all bonds in each index;
- the number of bonds in each index;
- the weight of the index in relation to its relevant aggregated index (when applicable).

2.7.11 Quality-Controlled Price Sources

The capital and total return indices are calculated using indicative pricing from the key dealer banks in each market. The design of the methodology and availability of the price sources ensures a single price for each bond in the index. The FTSE applies quality controls to ensure each single price in the index is unbiased and representative of the market.

The prices used for the calculation of the indices are based on data and real-time price quotations. To calculate the price, the arithmetic mean between bid and ask quotes (mid-prices) is used in the indices.

2.7.12 An Investable Index

These indices enable managers to develop successful investment strategies. The selection criteria of only including constituent securities of bonds which have a bid and ask quote means the indices are an accurate and neutral representation of the market for investors.

2.7.13 Eligibility of Bonds

The following types of bonds are included in the indices:

- all straight bullet bonds maturing in one year or more;
- zero coupon bonds;
- strippable bonds are included with their total volume and considered as being regular non-stripped bonds.

Excluded from the indices are:

- coupon strips and maturity strips (separated interest and capital repayment securities);
- partly-paid bonds;
- variable interest bonds (including floating rate bonds);
- index-linked bonds;
- callable, puttable and extendible bonds;
- convertible bonds;
- bonds with no final redemption date.

2.7.14 Historical Data

The indices' base dates are as follows:

- Global Government Bonds: May 1988.
- Covered Bonds: January 1996.
- Euro Corporate Bonds: July 1999.
- Sterling Corporate Bonds: March 2004.
- Euro Emerging Markets Bonds: December 1995.

2.8   SELECTING BONDS AND BOND FUNDS

LEARNING OBJECTIVE

1.2.6   Analyse the factors to take into account when selecting bonds and bond funds: bond characteristics; direct bond strategies; indirect investment; investing in bonds through funds; advantages and disadvantages of investing in bonds and bond funds

2.8.1   Bond Funds

Investment in bonds can be achieved in two ways, directly through a stockbroker (or the DMO), or indirectly through a fund managed by a professional fund manager and marketed to investors by a retail fund management group. Indirect investment is a simple and effective way of investing without getting involved in the effort and costs of buying and selling on your own account.

Money from a large number of investors is pooled and invested in a portfolio of bond stocks. These are selected and managed for the investor by a fund manager. The fund is divided into many small parts known as units. This is why it is often referred to as a **unit-linked** fund. The price of each unit will depend on the value of the underlying investments. So when you invest, the number of units you receive will depend on how much you invest and the buying price of the units at the time of your investment.

Bond funds are marketed by fund management groups to both private and institutional investors. The funds are managed according to a set mandate by a professional fund manager, who receives a fee for his efforts. A charge is levied for the annual management, and initial charges are applied when new investments are made into the fund. Bond funds will invest in a broad or a tightly focused range of debt securities, including many of those discussed in earlier paragraphs.

Bond funds can be used to provide access to the underlying securities at a more affordable cost, and to a much broader spectrum of investors. For example, Treasury bills are only available to new investments for sums in excess of £500,000, and are out of reach of most private investors.

Bond funds also provide greater liquidity to investors, as they retain an amount of cash within the fund to facilitate any redemption requests.

Using a broad spread of underlying securities can also help to diversify risk away from the investor, and so in this way the risk potential can vary between funds and is dependent on the type and number of securities held.

The performance of bond funds can be compared with sector indices and averages, and against the underlying performance of the individual securities themselves.

Factors to consider when selecting a suitable bond or bond fund for inclusion within a portfolio include the:

- investor's preferences for income or growth;
- length of time they are prepared to keep their money invested;
- level of access required;
- amount of risk that they are prepared to take;
- tax consequences on sale.

A number of bond strategies can be employed to deliver income or capital returns to investors, which include duration positioning, yield curve positioning, asset allocation and security selection. Qualitative and quantitative market analysis can be used to provide a framework for bond investment decision-making. The investment grade of the debt can be used to determine the risk of capital loss to the investor, while providing opportunities to deliver increased returns over traditional gilts.

2.8.2 Advantages and Disadvantages of Investing in Bonds

Advantages of Bonds
- Bonds pay higher interest rates than savings accounts.
- Bonds usually offer a relatively safe return of principal.
- Bonds often have less volatility (price fluctuations) than stocks, especially short-term bonds.
- Bonds offer regular income.

- Bonds need less careful attention in management than other investments.

Disadvantages of Bonds

- Bonds offer no hedge against inflation because inflation causes interest rates to rise which then causes bond prices to fall.
- Even though they are generally less volatile than stocks, bond prices can be quite volatile because market interest rates vary after a bond is issued.
- Bonds over the long term have lower returns than stocks.
- Individual bonds do not compound their interest. However, this is possible with bond funds.
- Diversification is hard to achieve unless investing in bond funds.

3.   EQUITIES

3.1   WHAT ARE EQUITIES?

Companies raise their initial **capital** – the money to carry on their activities – in two ways; through share capital and through loan stock (bonds). In this section, we will consider share capital.

One important contrast to keep in mind is that people who hold loan stock are creditors of the company. The company owes them a debt, which they have to repay, but they have no ownership interest in the company.

On the other hand, the people who own shares in a company are its owners. An individual may only have a few shares out of many thousands (or even millions) issued by the company – nevertheless, that individual still owns a small part of the company and has the rights that attach to that ownership. The term 'equities' refers to the ordinary shares of companies. The directors of the company, who are tasked with running the company, have a duty of care to the shareholders, as they are responsible for looking after their capital.

However, this ownership means that shareholders bear a fair amount of risk compared to investors in bonds issued by companies.

Bondholders expect to receive a set sum in interest. (The exception, as you should remember, is where the bond pays a variable rate of interest – but even then the interest is determined by a set formula.) In addition, the bondholder normally expects to receive a nominal amount of capital back on maturity; there is generally no additional profit or gain if the company is doing very well. The only real risk is that of the company running into difficulties so serious that it cannot repay its creditors – thankfully, not a very regular occurrence, though it can happen.

Shareholders, however, generally have a much greater exposure to the financial fortunes of the company they have invested in. If the company does well, they may receive a rising income stream, and the value of their shares can also increase substantially (giving them capital growth); but if a company performs poorly it may, as we shall see, pay falling dividends – or no dividend at all. Its share price may also fall, potentially becoming worthless if the company gets into real trouble.

We will examine this concept in more depth as we progress through the chapter; for now, it is enough to remember that shares are generally characterised by the relative insecurity of both income and capital over the short term (some types more so than others), but they offer a much higher probability of producing real growth over time than, for example, cash and bonds.

There are different types of share in a company, with different rights and investment risks attached to them. We will look at these next.

3.2   THE DIFFERENT TYPES OF SHARE

1.3.1   Understand the characteristics and differences between the main types of shareholder equity: ordinary; redeemable; non-voting; preference; convertible preference

3.2.1   Ordinary Shares

As we have noted, ordinary shares are sometimes also called equities, because the people who own them are entitled to the equity in the company which has issued them.

> **Equity** – the value of a company's assets less its liabilities. Thus, the total interest in a company which is owned by its ordinary shareholders is sometimes known as the **shareholders' equity**; it represents the value they own in the company, after all its debts have been repaid.

From this it should be apparent that someone holding shares in a company has a stake in that company – they are its joint owner, along with all the other shareholders.

An ordinary shareholder can buy his holding in one of two main ways:

*   By buying them as new shares, when the company first issues them (an Initial Public Offering or IPO). A company does this in order to raise money to invest in its business (for example, to buy new premises, carry out new research or expand into new markets). This is called the **primary market** in shares.
*   By buying existing shares which are being traded on the stock market. The shares pass from buyer to seller, and the company does not itself receive any new funds from this activity. This is called dealing in the **secondary market**.

A company's ordinary share capital is an important part of the way in which it funds its activities – probably the most important part, in fact. It represents the owners' stake in the company and is generally pretty permanent in nature – it will not get repaid (in the way that loan stock will, on its maturity or redemption date) – unless and until the company is 'wound up', or some other fairly major event takes place.

People who hold shares do so in the hope that the company will do well, and that they will earn a return from them over and above what they originally paid for them. This might be in one of the following forms:

- **Capital growth**, in that if the company does well the price of its shares should go up. The investor hopes they can, eventually, sell the shares for more than they paid for them.
- **Income**, by way of dividends. Many types of company distribute much of the profits they make in any year to their investors (shareholders) by paying a dividend to them. In fact, companies generally pay dividends twice a year – an 'interim dividend' part-way through, and a 'final dividend' once final results are announced.

People who hold ordinary shares also generally have **voting rights**. These give them a vote over certain issues affecting how the company is run – for example, on things like the appointment of the company's directors and auditors. This does not mean that the ordinary shareholders exercise direct control over the company's day-to-day affairs. (This job is the responsibility of the **directors** of the company.) The shareholders do, however, have an indirect influence on a company's management – for example, if they are unhappy with the company's performance they may not support the directors' pay awards, when the time comes to vote on them.

Investing in shares involves **risk** – both in terms of whether the investor's shares will fall in price, and in terms of whether the company will make enough profits to pay steady, and rising, dividends.

If the company does not do well – or indeed if the stock market as a whole is performing badly – share prices may fall. When this is so, an investor who has to sell his shares at that point may make a loss. Thus, shares are really only appropriate investments for people who can stand the risk of some loss – and who are able to tie their money up for a reasonable period (usually regarded as being five years or more).

If a company is 'wound up' – put into liquidation, with all its assets being sold to pay off its liabilities (debts) – the ordinary shareholders are the last people in line for any pay-out. Thus, there is the possibility there may not be enough money left to give them a pay-out at all: all the money might be spent on paying off the company's creditors (including, of course, its bondholders).

So, just to reiterate, ordinary shareholders suffer from a fair degree of **risk**, in that:

- they rank last for any surplus remaining after liquidation of the company; and
- while a share entitles the owner to share equally in any disbursements of profits made by the company – dividends – the company is under no legal obligation to make any such distributions, and, if it does not make decent profits, there may be nothing to distribute anyway.

Their reward for taking on this level of risk is that if the company does very well, they may make handsome capital gains – with (theoretically at least) no cap on how high these could be; and if profits remain strong, they should receive stable and rising dividends.

Companies can issue ordinary shares of different 'classes', or types. The difference between classes usually relates to the rights their shareholders have compared to one another, and means that each class may appeal to a different type of investor (as they may help them satisfy different investment objectives).

Usually, these distinctions are determined by the voting or dividend rights attached to the share. Holders of 'straight' ordinary shares will have full voting rights, and will be entitled to any dividends declared and paid by the company. A few examples of others are set out below.

Redeemable Shares

A public listed company or even a private company can create a variety of ordinary shares that confer different voting rights on the shareholders. These forms of shares give the company directors more flexibility to make decisions about managing the long-term growth of the firm.

Usually there are two ways that a company can repurchase its shares: buy them back from the market, or retire shares by redeeming shares of a certain class.

Along with ordinary shares, **redeemable shares** are issued by a company, with an agreement to buy back these issues from the shareholders after a certain date or at some specified future date. These shares cannot be used as a single financing method, and must form part of a package of ordinary shares containing non-redeemables.

Often a company can only issue redeemable shares if its Articles of Association provide for it. Also, all the details of the redemption, including the date of redemption and the price to be paid for the shares at that date, will be contained in the Articles.

The exact nature of such issues is determined by the directors and laid out in the shares' terms of issue. The shares can be redeemed at the directors' discretion from distributable profits or from the issue of new shares to the public. Redeemed shares are retired and reduce the share capital of the firm.

Dual-Class Shares

Redeemable shares should not be confused with **dual-class shares**. Companies (often newly listed as IPOs) sometimes create another class of common stock that has limited voting rights and a preferential claim to the firm's profits. There are two forms of this dual class: **class A** shares and **class B** shares.

Class A type shares may have non-voting rights or may carry one vote. Type A shares, common to the UK offer no voting rights and may have the same dividend paid as ordinary shares. A 'one vote' share, issued in the US, usually comes with a higher dividend rate than B class shares.

In the UK, class B shares, also sometimes called **accumulating ordinary shares**, rank equally with ordinary shares. Instead of a cash dividend payment, the shareholders will receive a share dividend in the form of a free issue of shares on a pro-rata basis. Type B class shares in the US allow the bearers to cast multiple votes, such as three, five or ten votes per share, and their dividend is lower than class 'A' shares.

In most of the dual classes of common stock, the controlling group of shareholders represent founding families or their descendants. The dual-class shares may also be created in dual-class recapitalisations that form a part of a wider corporate restructuring process. In this case, the management of the firm will want to consolidate its control in order to carry out long-term programmes and avoid short-term pressures to show good results.

Deferred Dividend Shares

Holders of these shares have full voting rights, and rank equally with the other ordinary shareholders if the company is liquidated. However, the payment of dividends to them is deferred until some specified date. Again, these usually trade at a lower price than the 'ordinary' ordinaries; they may also, during the deferral period, suit investors who are more interested in capital growth than income (perhaps because they are higher-rate income tax payers, or because they already have enough income from other sources).

Deferred Ordinary Shares

These are also sometimes called **founder shares**. Holders of them usually receive no dividend until that paid to the ordinary shareholders has hit some minimum level.

3.2.2 Preference Shares

Preference shares give their holders superior rights and security, over and above those of ordinary shareholders.

The price that holders pay for this additional safety, however, is that the returns a holder can earn are generally limited – whereas in theory, if a company does spectacularly well, there is no limit to the returns the ordinary shareholders might receive.

These additional rights relate mainly to the:

- payment of dividends; and
- repayment of capital if the company should be wound up (ie, go into liquidation).

Since preference shares are not, technically, equity capital (ie, their holders do not participate fully in the risks of the business), they are not referred to as equities.

The main features of preference shares are as follows (you may wish to compare them with the features of ordinary shares and, where possible, with those of bonds issued by companies:):

- The dividends on preference shares are generally fixed, and are expressed as a percentage of the nominal value of the shares.
- Preference shareholders get priority in the payment of their dividends over the ordinary shareholders. That is, the ordinary shareholders will not get their dividend paid at all unless and until the preference shareholders have received their dividends. If there is not enough profit to go round, the ordinary shareholders may go short.
- Preference shares may be expressed as being **cumulative** (see below).
- As we have already noted, preference shareholders usually also take priority when the company goes into liquidation. However, all they receive will be the nominal value of their shares (not the market value) and, if there is any surplus to be distributed, it will be distributed to the ordinary shareholders.

The exact rights that a preference share carries will vary from case to case; potential investors should ensure that they have investigated the precise terms and conditions before investing; their stockbroker can usually help them do this.

There are also various different types of preference share (just as there were with ordinary shares), and the type may determine what rights the shareholder has. The main types of preference share are as follows:

- **Cumulative** – if the company has not made enough profit to pay the preference shareholders' dividends in one year, then the unpaid dividend is **accumulated** and will be paid when the company does have sufficient profits. This may mean the ordinary shareholders have to wait for some time before they receive their dividend – ie, until any arrears on the preference dividends have been 'caught up'.
- **Non-cumulative** – where preference shares are non-cumulative, any unpaid dividend is not accumulated. The shareholder has to wait until the next dividend declaration to receive anything. The ordinary shareholders are therefore in a rather better position, since they do not have to wait until the preference shareholder arrears have been 'caught up'.
- **Participating** – participating preference shareholders receive a fixed dividend (as for traditional preference shares), but they also have the right to participate in surplus profits, along with the ordinary shareholders. The extent to which they participate in this way will vary from company to company.
- **Redeemable** – here the company has the right to redeem the shares at some point in the future. This may be on a fixed date, or at a time chosen by the company. When a company redeems shares, the shareholder returns them to the company – which pays him a sum of money for them and then cancels them, so that the company's total issued share capital is reduced.
- **Convertible** – the preference shareholders have the right to convert their shares at some point in the future to a specified number of ordinary shares.

Often, preference shares have a combination of these features – so you might see a share with a name like 'XYX plc £1 Cum. Red. Pref. shares'.

Usually, preference shares are taken to be cumulative unless there is something to the contrary in the title (eg, 'non-cum. Pref. shares').

3.3   PRIVATE EQUITY

LEARNING OBJECTIVE

1.3.2   Understand the characteristics and differences between the main types of private equity share capital

The private equity market provides capital to invest in unquoted companies, including public companies that are de-listed as part of the transaction. These investments may take the form of a purchase of shares from an existing shareholder (a buy-out if control is acquired) or an investment in new shares providing fresh capital to the investee company (development capital). Frequently both types of funding are provided in any given transaction.

The term 'private equity' has no consistently applied definition and is increasingly applied to any investor that is not quoted on a recognised financial market. Hedge funds, value funds and active funds and similar institutions have some similarities to private equity, but there are clear organisational and strategic differences that set them apart.

It is increasingly common to see private equity funds investing alongside other types of organisation and combining the industry knowledge of a trade bidder with the transactional and transformational skills of a private equity fund. The private equity market has two distinct components: venture capital, targeted at new and early stage companies, and development capital and buy-outs, targeted at mature businesses.

The most common investment strategies in private equity are leveraged buyouts (LBO), venture capital, growth capital, distressed investments and mezzanine capital.

3.3.1 Leveraged Buyouts

Leveraged buyouts involve a financial sponsor agreeing to an acquisition without itself committing all the capital required for the acquisition. To do this, the financial sponsor will raise **acquisition debt** which ultimately looks to the cash flows of the acquisition target to make interest and principal payments. Acquisition debt in an LBO is often non-recourse to the financial sponsor and has no claim on other investment managed by the financial sponsor.

Therefore, an LBO transaction's financial structure is particularly attractive to a fund's limited partners, allowing them the benefits of leverage but greatly limiting the degree of recourse of that leverage. This kind of financing structure leverage benefits an LBO's financial sponsor in two ways: the investor itself only needs to provide a fraction of the capital for the acquisition, and the returns to the investor will be enhanced (as long as the return on assets exceeds the cost of the debt).

3.3.2 Venture Capital

Venture capital is a broad subcategory of private equity that refers to equity investments made, typically in less mature companies, for the launch, early development or expansion of a business. Venture investment is most often found in the application of new technology, new marketing concepts and new products that have yet to be proven.

Venture capital is often subdivided by the stage of development of the company, ranging from early stage capital used for the launch of start-up companies, to late stage and growth capital that is often used to fund expansion of existing business (see Section 3.3.3).

Entrepreneurs often develop products and ideas that require substantial capital during the formative stages of their companies' life cycles. Many entrepreneurs do not have sufficient funds to finance projects themselves, and they must therefore seek outside financing. The venture capitalist's need to deliver high returns to compensate for the risk of these investments makes venture funding an expensive capital source for companies. Venture capital is most suitable for businesses with large up-front capital requirements which cannot be financed by cheaper alternatives such as debt. Although venture capital is often most closely associated with fast-growing technology and biotechnology fields, it has also been used for other more traditional businesses.

3.3.3 Growth Capital

Growth capital refers to equity investments, most often minority investments, in relatively mature companies that are looking for capital to expand or restructure operations, enter new markets or finance a major acquisition without a change of control of the business. Companies that seek growth capital will often do so in order to finance a transformational event in their life cycle.

These companies are likely to be more mature than venture-capital-funded companies, able to generate revenue and operating profits but unable to generate sufficient cash to fund major expansions, acquisitions or other investments. The primary owner of the company may not be willing to take the financial risk alone. By selling part of the company to private equity, the owner can take out some value and share the risk of growth with partners.

3.3.4 Distressed Investments

Distressed, or special situations, is a broad category referring to investments in the equity or debt securities of financially stressed companies.

3.3.5 Mezzanine Capital

Mezzanine capital refers to subordinated debt or preferred equity securities that often represent the most junior portion of a company's capital structure that is senior to the company's common equity. This form of financing is often used by private equity investors to reduce the amount of equity capital required to finance a leveraged buyout or major expansion. Mezzanine capital, which is often used by smaller companies that are unable to access the high-yield market, allows such companies to borrow additional capital beyond the levels that traditional lenders are willing to provide through bank loans. In compensation for the increased risk, mezzanine debt holders require a higher return for their investment than secured or other more senior lenders.

3.4 INVESTMENT RISK AND SHARES

LEARNING OBJECTIVE

1.3.3   Analyse the main sources of investment risk and return associated with equities: capital return; dividends; liquidity; credit ratings; corporate actions; company liquidation; market conditions

3.4.1 Characteristics, Risks and Performance

Investors generally hold shares in the hope of generating a return on them. However, the pursuit of these returns is not without its risks. These risks can affect:

*   the capital the investor has tied up – in that the share price may fall, or fail to rise in line with inflation or with the performance of other, less risky investments; and
*   their income – in that if the company is not as profitable as they had hoped, the dividends it pays may not keep pace with inflation; indeed they may fall or even not be paid at all. This is called **passing** a dividend.

The past performance of shares can be assessed through reference to the movement in the price of the actual share, and the amount and frequency of the dividend payment. Always remember that past performance is not an indicator of future performance.

In the following sections we will consider various factors which can affect the riskiness of investment in shares, and their performance – including liquidity, growth, volatility and issuing institutions. These factors can combine to affect the risk attached to shares.

3.4.2 Liquidity

In addition to other risks, investors have to consider whether (regardless of how the company has performed, and whether its shares have risen in value) those shares can actually be traded.

Private companies, whose shares are not listed on a stock exchange, may be very difficult to deal in. Further, there may be conditions in the company's constitutional documents (its Memorandum and Articles of Association) which mean that those wanting to sell their shares must first offer them to their co-shareholders, or restrict their ability to sell at an acceptable price. This is in addition to the difficulty in actually determining what is a fair price, since there is no market mechanism to set this.

Even shares which are listed may be illiquid and hard to deal in: some listed shares are not actively quoted and may be dealt in very infrequently. It may be difficult for a broker to find a willing buyer/seller, and then only at a price which is unattractive to the investor.

Liquidity risk is rarely an issue, however, for blue chip companies – eg, those in the FTSE 100, where there is a deep and liquid market – that is, many potential buyers and sellers, and no difficulty in dealing quickly at the current market price.

For this reason, investors who are considering investing in the shares of private companies, or those which have small issues or are infrequent dealers, should ensure that they can afford to run the risk of being unable to unload their holding promptly, or at what they see as a current fair market price.

3.4.3 Growth

Many investors' objective in buying shares is to secure capital growth, through an appreciation in the share price. Others invest for income, but usually also hope for this to grow too – so that their income keeps pace with inflation.

But investing for growth involves risk. Will the investor's shares rise (or fall) in price and will the company make enough profits to pay steady and rising dividends?

As covered in Section 3.2.1, if a company doesn't do well or if the stock market as a whole is performing badly, share prices may fall and an investor who has to sell his shares at that point may make a loss. Thus, shares are really only appropriate investments for people who can stand the risk of some loss and who are able to tie their money up for a reasonable period (usually regarded as being five years or more).

If a company is wound up, the ordinary shareholders are the last people in line for any pay-out and so there might not be enough money left to give them a pay-out at all.

Ordinary shareholders therefore suffer from a fair degree of **risk**, in that:

*   they rank last for any surplus remaining after liquidation of the company; and

- while a share entitles the owner to share equally in any disbursements of profits made by the company – dividends – the company is under no legal obligation to make any such distributions and if it doesn't make decent profits there may be nothing to distribute anyway.

Their reward for taking on this level of risk is that if the company does very well, they may make handsome capital gains with theoretically at least no 'cap' on how high these could be. If profits remain strong, they should receive stable and rising dividends.

3.4.4 Volatility

Volatility is the term used to describe the degree to which an investment is prone to swings in pricing. Even an investment which appreciates dramatically in price can carry unacceptable levels of volatility, if the investor wants to hold something which performs steadily and does not give him sleepless nights!

It is possible to measure the (historic) volatility of a given share, by looking at the price swings it has undergone in the past. This can then be compared with the returns the share has also historically provided, and these can be looked at against the risk and return of other investments – for example, against the returns available on investments regarded as virtually risk free. Professional investment managers do this to assess whether the additional returns, which they believe an investment may offer, are worth the additional volatility (risk) to their investors: shares that are volatile are regarded as higher risk because their performance can change, quickly and in either direction, in a short period of time.

Key volatility measures include **standard deviation** – a statistical measurement of a share's volatility (ie, of that share's tendency to rise or fall in value in a short period of time). The standard deviation of a share thus measures the average return made on it over a period of time by showing the degree to which its price fluctuates in relation to its **mean return**.

If share A had given a consistent four-year return of 3%, for example, it would have a **mean**, or average, of 3%. The standard deviation for share A would then be zero – because its return in any given year had not differed from its four-year mean of 3%.

On the other hand, if share B had, in each of the last four years, returned 5%, 17%, 2% and 30%, it would have a mean return of 11% – on the face of it, more rewarding than share A. It would also have shown a high standard deviation, however, because each year its return differed from the mean return. This share is therefore more risky because the returns fluctuate more widely within the four-year period.

Volatility is only one possible way of measuring the riskiness of a share – and a share with a relatively stable past performance is not necessarily guaranteed to continue in this way. Unforeseen market factors can influence volatility, and a share that this year has a standard deviation close or equal to zero may behave differently next year.

Investors can compare the returns they are receiving against the volatility of the shares they hold. Of two shares with similar returns, the one with the lower standard deviation will have a better risk-reward ratio.

3.4.5 Issuing Institutions

Shares are issued by companies and their performance is linked to the fortunes of those companies. Different companies are subject to different business risks determined by, among other things:

- **The nature of the industry they are involved in.** For example, some companies are established to operate in tried-and-tested fields, and their business model is well established. Others are involved in new areas, such as research and development, where much of their activity is speculative and could result in excellent profits – or in total loss.
- **The cyclicality of that industry.** Some companies are involved in providing goods and services which people only want at certain stages of the economic cycle; others, in goods which people want more of in a downturn; and still others in things that people need no matter what the state of the economy.
- **The competence of the management.** No matter how good a company's business model or products, its prospects cannot be good if it is being run by inexperienced or lax management.
- **The financial soundness of the company.** A company which is, for example, over-geared can suffer disproportionately if interest rates rise, for example.

3.4.6 Market Conditions

It is not only factors relating to the company itself that can affect the price of its shares; factors affecting the market as a whole will also impact, since an individual share is unlikely to buck the trend (though it may move by a greater or lesser degree relative to the rest of the market). Thus, when conditions are such that the market as a whole is rising strongly, the share prices of even poorly performing companies are likely to benefit to some degree. As one commentator has noted, 'even turkeys can fly in a hurricane'. Conversely, when the market falls steeply even sound blue chip companies will suffer with it. Factors affecting the market as a whole include:

- The performance of other companies – especially, but not only, those in related or similar industries.
- Political events, especially where a change in government policy will affect conditions for the economy and business.
- Economic news – interest rates, inflation, exchange rates and unemployment are all relevant to sentiment about the market as a whole.
- Price movements on other world stock markets.
- Factors affecting how much investors have in the way of investable funds (eg, changes in interest rates or tax).
- Buying and selling activity on the part of large institutions. For example, one or two large investors moving their asset allocations away from equities and into cash or bonds can have a noticeable impact on the price of the market as a whole.

3.5   CORPORATE ACTIONS

LEARNING OBJECTIVE

1.3.3   Analyse the main sources of investment risk and return associated with equities: capital return; dividends; liquidity; credit ratings; corporate actions; company liquidation; market conditions

3.5.1   The Impact of Corporate Actions

Corporate actions is the collective term for a range of actions a company can take which affect the holdings, benefits or rights of its shareholders. Many corporate actions have a direct impact on the number and/or value of shares in issue. We will take a look at some of the more common corporate actions here, being capitalisation issues, share splits and rights issues. Dividend payments are also technically corporate actions, but we will look at the impact of these separately later in this chapter.

3.5.2   Capitalisation Issues (also described as Bonus Issues or Scrip Issues)

Sometimes, companies which have their shares listed on the Stock Exchange want to increase the number of shares in issue without raising new money; one way they can they do this is by issuing new shares and allocating them to existing holders.

Companies do this in part because it may make their balance sheet simpler and cleaner, and in part because having more shares in issue can improve their marketability. We will examine both those reasons in a bit more depth in a moment: first, let's consider what actually happens in practice.

If company ABC plc has a capitalisation issue, the number of its shares in issue will increase – but, as we have said, no new capital will be raised. The new shares are allocated to existing shareholders, on a 'pro rata' basis.

> **Pro rata** – a Latin term meaning 'in proportion'. Thus shareholders will be allocated new shares in proportion to their previous holdings.

For example, with a 1-for-4 capitalisation issue, the shareholder will be given one new share for every four previously held.

Capitalisation issues have an effect on a company's accounts. Some of the company's 'reserves' (eg, its share premium account, reserves from the revaluation of assets, and retained profits which have not been distributed to shareholders) are converted into share capital, thereby increasing the number of shares in issue. The effect can be to simplify the company's balance sheet.

A before and after example shows what the effect of the 1-for-4 issue we discussed above could be:

	Before cap issue	**After cap issue**
	£	**£**
Ordinary shares	200,000	250,000
Share premium reserve account	60,000	10,000
Reserves	140,000	140,000
Net worth (net assets)	400,000	400,000
Number of ordinary shares	400,000 x 50p	500,000 x 50p

The total balance sheet is neither stronger, nor weaker, than it was before, because the total net worth (that is, the net assets) is still exactly the same.

> **Net assets** – the total of a company's assets (everything it owns), less the total of its liabilities (everything it owes).

All that has happened is that there has been a change in the way the shareholders' funds are shown.

The price of the shares in the market after the capitalisation issue (the ex-cap price) will, all things being equal, fall in direct proportion to the increase in share capital. So, in our example, if the company's shares were priced at 250p each before the 1-for-4 bonus issue, you could expect to see them fall to around 200p.

400,000 shares x 250p are worth	£1,000,000
100,000 shares are issued free	nil
Thus 500,000 shares are now worth	£1,000,000 + 0 = £1,000,000 or 200p per share

However, certain market factors might also affect the ex-cap price of the shares:

- the lower price per share might make the shares more marketable, since it is easier to deal in them; and
- capitalisation issues are normally seen as a sign that a company is successful, since it indicates that there are plenty of reserves (such as undistributed profits) to reallocate.

These factors may combine to encourage more investors to want to buy the shares, so the price may rise a little above the expected value.

When a capitalisation issue has been made, the existing shareholders will each receive a renounceable certificate, which shows the number of shares to which they are entitled. If a shareholder wants to sell any of them, all he has to do is sign the reverse. There is no need to also complete a share transfer form (as there normally would be).

3.5.3 Share Splits (also known as Stock Splits)

Share splits occur when a company reduces the nominal (par) value per share of its issued share capital, without altering the value of its total nominal share capital. (Contrast this with what we have seen with capitalisation issues in Section 3.5.2)

The effect of a share split on the market price may, in theory, be the same as for a capitalisation issue. Increased marketability may again cause the share price to settle above the theoretical price, however.

3.5.4 Rights Issues

Very often, a company will need to raise more capital once it is already up and running. It might want to do this in order to:

- pay off existing borrowings, especially if they are at interest rates which look high in comparison with current market rates;
- fund expansion;
- acquire funding to make new acquisitions (ie, take over other companies).

A company might raise this money by borrowing from the bank, or issuing a bond – but this could be expensive if interest rates are high or the company already has heavy borrowings.

An alternative is for it to ask its existing shareholders to invest more money in the company, by participating in a **rights issue**. In other words, the shareholders are asked to subscribe for (and pay for) a new **tranche** of shares.

The term 'rights issue' is used because the existing shareholders have a statutory (ie, legal) right to subscribe for these new shares if they choose to. This protects them from having their interest in the company diluted by other, new shareholders. They do not, however, have to take up these rights if they don't want to.

The main features of a rights issue include:

- New shares carry the same rights – to dividends, votes, etc – as the old shares already in issue. That is, they are described as ranking *pari passu* with the old shares.

> **Pari passu** – Latin for 'in a like manner', meaning they are treated similarly.

- The price to be paid for the new shares (the subscription price) will be below the current market value of the old shares.
- The number of new shares on offer to existing shareholders will depend on the terms of the issue and how much money the company is trying to raise; it is expressed as 'x' number of new shares, for every 'y' number currently held – eg, a 1-for-4 rights issue.

Companies will often arrange to have their rights issue underwritten by an appropriate financial institution, so as to ensure that the issue is successful.

Underwriting – in the context of a rights issue, a process whereby a specialist financial service organisation (usually a merchant bank, stockbroking house or similar) promises to take up any shares which the existing shareholders do not choose to take up themselves.

The issuing company is thus assured that if the issue is badly received (perhaps because of unexpected and unfavourable conditions in the market) it has not gone to all the expense of arranging the issue only for it to fail to raise any new money. For a fee, the underwriting house undertakes to take up the unwanted new shares at a set price, and it will then hold these shares in its own name. It will try to sell them in the market, preferably for a profit, when conditions improve. The underwriting fee is due to it whether or not the issue is successful; it is the price the issuing company pays for securing a guarantee that the issue can't fail.

You could think of this as an insurance policy – you pay premiums whether or not you make a claim, in return for the comfort you get that you are covered.

We can calculate the expected market price of the company's old and new shares, after the rights issue; this is known as the **theoretical ex-rights price**, and it represents what we would expect both lots of shares to start trading at, once the rights issue has been completed and the new shares are 'fully paid' – ie, the investors have paid for the ones they want to take up.

The theoretical ex-rights price is calculated as in the following example.

EXAMPLE

An investor holds 40 shares in **ABC Ltd**, at a current market price of £4.50 each – thus the total value of his holding is £180.00.

There is a rights issue at £3 on a 1:2 basis (1-for-2).

Thus, he can expect rights to 20 new shares to be allocated.

After taking up the rights – 20 new ones at £3 each – the investor now owns 60 shares, total cost value £240.00. This is calculated as follows:

	£180.00	cost of original shares
plus	£60.00	cost of new shares
=	£240.00	

£240.00 divided by the number of shares the investor now owns (60) is £4.

£4 per share is therefore the new level at which all the shares in issue will now trade (other things being equal) – that is, it is the **theoretical ex-rights price (TERP)**.

What this also tells us is that we can expect:

*   the price of the old shares to fall, from £4.50 each, to £4;
*   the price of the new shares to rise when they start trading, from the £3 they will cost to £4.

The investor will receive a **provisional letter of allotment** detailing the extra shares he is entitled to receive in accordance with the terms of the rights issue. The letter will advise him of the deadline for making a decision; this is usually two or three weeks after it is issued. It will also set out the timetable of events (for example, when any payment will have to be made by).

The investor must then consider what to do – ie, whether to:

- take up the allotment in full;
- sell the rights;
- split the allotment so that part can be sold to raise money to take up the balance; or
- let the rights lapse.

Many investors take professional advice before deciding on what action to take (for example, from their stockbroker). The types of thing they will take into account are:

- the terms of the rights issue;
- what the company plans to do with the money – ie, the reason for the issue, and what market sentiment is towards it;
- how the company has been performing to date;
- how the share price has been performing and what effect the rights issue is expected to have on it in the near term.

We can contrast the effects of a bonus and a rights issue as follows:

Bonus issues:

- raise no new money for the company;
- increase the number of shares in issue;
- result in a lower share price, which may also make the shares more marketable.

Rights issues:

- raise new money for the company;
- increase the number of shares in issue, providing that the issue is successful or is underwritten;
- are made at a price below the current market price of the company's shares;
- may be used to finance specific activities such as expansion, financing the acquisition of another company (a 'takeover'), or paying off existing debt.

3.5.5 Liquidation

When a company ceases trading it is generally 'wound up' – put into liquidation, and then ultimately dissolved. Part of this process involves turning its assets into cash, so that its debts can be paid off and the surplus paid out to the owners (the shareholders). In some, rare, cases, the shareholders are given assets instead of cash.

Depending on the reasons for the winding-up, there may be enough money to go around – or there may not. If there is not enough money to repay the company's creditors, it is referred to as being **insolvent**.

On liquidation and winding-up, there is a strict order of priority as to how the assets are distributed. Those first in the order of priority are clearly much more likely to get a full payout. There may well be insufficient money to pay those lower down the list.

Certain creditors take precedence over investors (for example, the liquidator's fees, HMRC). Looking purely at the order in which investors in a company are repaid, the order is as follows:

- secured bondholders and debenture holders stand at the head of the queue, followed by:
- the unsecured bondholders;
- the preference shareholders; and finally
- the ordinary shareholders.

Within these broad categories, there can be some further subdivisions. For example, there can be different levels of seniority of debt, which determines which of a company's several issues takes precedence in the event that there is not enough to repay all of the issues.

An announcement that a company is going into liquidation will invariably have some effect on its share price; it is, after all, as major an event as the company can undergo. The market's reaction will depend on whether the company is:

- **solvent** (can pay its debts, and will presumably have some money left over for the shareholders); or
- **insolvent** (unable to pay its debts);

and whether the liquidation is:

- **voluntary** – because the company has carried out the activity it was set up for and is now ready to pay out the proceeds to its owners; or
- **involuntary** – perhaps because the company is insolvent, and its creditors have petitioned the court for it to be wound up.

In cases where a company is insolvent and an order is made for its winding-up, its shares – if they are listed – are likely to have been suspended by the market on which they trade; so investors may find they are 'locked in' to their holdings, and cannot sell even if they wanted to.

3.6   LISTING AND TRADING OF EQUITIES

LEARNING OBJECTIVE

1.3.4   Understand the issues involved in dealing for clients in equity markets: regulated and designated investment exchanges; OTC and alternative trading platforms; access to markets; principal and agency trading; listed and unlisted securities; quoted and unquoted securities; admission to trading

3.6.1 Listing of Shares

Companies may seek to list their shares for one of several reasons – for example:

- In order to raise capital for further growth.

- In order to put an objective value on the business.
- To create a market in the company's shares, or increase liquidity in them – so as to give existing shareholders the opportunity to realise the value of their shareholdings (an exit route).
- To allow the company to acquire other companies – both as a result of greater access to the necessary capital to fund the takeover, and as a result of being able to issue shares with a market value as a means of funding the acquisition.
- To enhance the company's credibility, which can improve its business prospects.
- To enable the company to provide for employee participation in its ownership, increasing their long-term commitment to the business and improving the recruitment and retention of good staff.
- To improve efficiency. This happens because listing requires high levels of disclosure and transparency over the company's affairs, which are likely to lead to improved internal controls and management structure – and, usually, greater operating efficiency for the business as a result.

The term 'listed' means that a company's shares have met a range of criteria which allow them to be traded on a particular stock market. The body which sets these criteria is known as the Listing Authority. The UK's listing authority for the London Stock Exchange (LSE) is the Financial Services Authority (FSA).

Not all listed companies' shares are admitted to trading, however; being listed simply means that the company has met the requirements of the Listing Authority, and its shares are permitted to trade. Where a company's shares are actually available for trading, and prices are available, they are referred to as **'quoted'**.

3.6.2   Stock Exchanges

A stock exchange is an organised marketplace for issuing and trading securities by members of that exchange. Each exchange has its own rules and regulations for companies seeking a listing, and continuing obligations for those already listed.

Historically, stock exchanges have operated as national monopolies from a central location, or physical marketplace, mainly catering for the needs of domestic investors and domestic issuers. As mainly mutually owned, or not-for-profit, organisations, many stock exchanges had become bureaucratic, parochial and resistant to change and, ironically, had restricted access to new capital for fund development, investment in new trading and settlement technology and facilitation of expansion into new markets. However, recently, in an attempt to meet the challenges posed by competing trading systems and the globalisation of financial markets in an increasingly price-sensitive and competitive global marketplace, many have sought to become more dynamic and cost-efficient and have striven to create new markets. Indeed, stock exchanges have been taking their lead from the radical changes recently undertaken in the derivatives markets. These have included abandoning restrictive mutual ownership by exchange members to become shareholder-owned listed companies, operating as electronic trading networks as the move to electronic trading has gathered pace, and creating new markets through strategic mergers and alliances with other exchanges.

The motivation behind many of these mergers and alliances has been a realisation that financial markets have integrated to such a degree that the shares of most multinational companies, rather than just being listed on their domestic stock exchange, are instead listed on those stock exchanges that best reflect the global distribution and capital requirements of their business. Listing on an overseas stock exchange also enhances the liquidity and marketability of companies' shares and can also build the company's brand. In effect, a global capital market has been created through the globalisation of markets and economies.

3.6.3   The London Stock Exchange (LSE)

The LSE began life in 1773 when traders who regularly met to buy and sell the shares of joint stock companies in Jonathan's Coffee House voted to change the name of the coffee house to that of the London Stock Exchange. The LSE is Europe's largest stock exchange, accounting for over 35% of European stockmarket capitalisation, about 10% of world stock market value and over 50% of foreign equity trading on world stock exchanges. Despite this, the LSE continues to evolve in a very competitive global marketplace.

The LSE is a **recognised investment exchange (RIE)** and, as such, is responsible for:

- providing a primary and secondary market for equities and fixed interest securities;
- supervising its member firms;
- regulating the markets it operates;
- recording all transactions, or bargains, executed on the exchange;
- disseminating price sensitive company information received by its regulatory news service (RNS) and distributed through commercial quote vendors, also known as secondary information providers (SIPs).

The LSE operates both a primary and secondary market for:

- Domestic plcs. These include:
  - companies with a full listing;
  - smaller UK plcs admitted to AIM;
  - exchange-traded funds (ETFs) and other innovative investments on its extraMARK exchange.
- International equities.
- Domestic bonds:
  - gilts;
  - local authority fixed-interest securities;
  - corporate bonds.

Companies across the world come to the London Stock Exchange looking to raise money to develop and grow their businesses. The UK markets cater for companies large and small, from start-ups to global brands.

Main Market

The main market is Europe's most prestigious and effective listings venue for established companies, a proven way to raise capital and gain profile.

Alternative Investment Market (AIM)

The alternative investment market (AIM) is the London Stock Exchange's international market for smaller growing companies. On AIM you will find a wide range of businesses ranging from young, venture capital-backed start-ups to well-established, mature organisations looking to expand. Since its launch in 1995, over 2,500 companies have joined AIM, raising more than £34 billion in the process, both through Initial Public Offerings (IPOs) and further capital raisings. This capital has helped AIM-quoted companies of all kinds to fund their development and pursue their ambitions. Many companies have made the transition to the exchange's main market following their success and positive experience on AIM.

To join AIM, companies do not need a particular financial track record or trading history. There is also no minimum requirement in terms of size or number of shareholders. This more flexible approach reflects the fact that AIM was designed specifically for smaller growing companies, and has helped AIM to become the leading global growth market.

International Companies

The London Stock Exchange is a global marketplace. Around 350 companies in 54 different countries use a London listing to gain the profile and access to capital they need to grow into truly global companies. Similar markets exist overseas, including NASDAQ and the NYSE in the US, the Hang Seng in Hong Kong, and the Shenzen in China.

3.6.4 Alternative Trading Systems (ATSs) and Over-the-Counter (OTC)

Alternative Trading Systems (ATSs) are also known under the Markets in Financial Instruments Directive (MiFID) as **Multilateral Trading Facilities (MTFs)** and have risen in importance in several financial markets around the world as an alternative to traditional exchanges, or as a complement to voice broking and bilateral over-the-counter (OTC) trading. The UK is host to over 20 ATSs, active in markets for equities, bonds, financial derivatives and commodities. It also hosts a number of firms that are affiliated with overseas-based ATSs. This has allowed market participants to adopt new trading strategies such as posting limit orders or crossing trades.

Over-the-counter (OTC) or **off-exchange** trading is used to trade financial instruments such as stocks, bonds, commodities or derivatives directly between two parties. This contrasts with exchange trading, which uses facilities constructed for the purpose of trading (ie, exchanges), such as futures exchanges or stock exchanges.

An OTC contract is a bilateral contract in which two parties agree on how a particular trade or agreement is to be settled in the future. It is usually from an investment bank to its clients directly. Forwards and swaps are prime examples of such contracts. It is mostly executed via the computer or the telephone.

3.6.5 Agency and Principal Dealing

When an investor buys a stock from someone who is acting as an **agent**, it means they do not own the stock that you are buying. Instead, they are buying it from a dealer and then reselling it to the investor.

When the agent buys the stocks, they will pay the dealer's 'mark-up'. However, the agent cannot then pass another mark-up on to the investor. The agent is obliged to get a price for the stock (which is what he has to pay the dealer) and then pass that price on to the investor. However, the agent has to make a living, and they do this by charging a fee for facilitating the transaction.

Buying stocks from someone who is acting as **principal** means that they have actually purchased the stock themselves and are holding it in their inventory. The principal therefore takes more risk than an agent because, while the principal is holding the stock, they are exposed to any movement in the stock price, and could lose money if the price drops.

The principal does not charge a fee, and instead charges a mark-up. A principal can provide investors with a 'bid' and 'ask' quote. The bid is what he is willing to pay to buy stock from an investor, and the ask is the price he requires in order to sell stock to you. The difference between the bid and the ask is called the 'spread' or 'mark-up' and represents the profit to the principal.

3.6.6 Unquoted Shares

Shares in some companies, often smaller ones, are not traded on any stock exchange.

Companies might not be quoted (or listed) because they prefer to run their businesses in relative privacy, or because they do not meet the listing requirements, such as minimum market capitalisation; in other words they are too small to join a stock market. The London Stock Exchange requires companies to have a trading record of three years and sets a minimum market capitalisation.

3.6.7 Admission to Trading

A differentiation is made between the terms 'listing' and 'admission to trading' – the latter takes place without prior listing procedure.

Company	London Stock Exchange Notice
TIDM	
Headline	Admission to Trading - 07/04/2010
Released	08:00 07-Apr-2010
Number	7906J08

RNS Number : 7906J
London Stock Exchange Notice
07 April 2010

CISI
CHARTERED INSTITUTE FOR
SECURITIES & INVESTMENT

**NOTICE OF ADMISSION TO TRADING ON
THE LONDON STOCK EXCHANGE**

07/04/2010 8:00am

The following securities are admitted to trading on the LSE with effect from the time and date of this notice.

PXP VIETNAM FUND LTD

| 12,000,000 | Ordinary Shares of USD0.05 each fully paid | (B5W0SC0)(KYG7301W1033) |

If you have any queries relating to the above, please contact Issuer Implementation at the LSE on 020 7797 1614.

This information is provided by RNS
The company news service from the London Stock Exchange

3.7   DEALING IN SHARES AND SHARE PRICES

LEARNING OBJECTIVE

1.3.5   Understand how equity securities are traded and settled: liquidity, pricing and fair value; cost of purchase and sale; nominal value; market price; cum- and ex-dividend; transaction costs and charges

3.7.1   Factors Affecting Share Prices

Most investors who buy equity-based products are familiar with warnings such as '*the price of shares can fall as well as rise, and you may get back less than the amount you originally invested*'. Such warnings are required by the regulators, and serve to remind investors that their capital is at risk when they invest in the stock markets.

Memorable stock market crashes in which share prices fell dramatically and where many investors lost significant proportions of their savings include the 1987 crash, the worldwide stock market falls that happened in the early part of this century and the more recent financial crisis.

Equity prices have always been volatile – that is, prone to swinging up and down rather than providing steady returns. This is mainly because:

- the value of a share should, all other things being equal, reflect how well a company is doing – and this can vary tremendously, depending on the management's skill, the economic environment, and often a degree of luck; and
- share prices are driven by supply and demand. If people feel optimistic about a share, or about the stock market or economy as a whole, there will be more buyers than sellers and the price will rise. Conversely, if they are pessimistic, the price will fall.

Even companies which are regarded as stable, well-run and unlikely to suffer badly in an economic downturn (the so-called 'blue chip' stocks) have been known to fall significantly in value – and occasionally to become insolvent. It is this uncertainty that investors have to bear in mind when they are considering buying equities for their long-term growth prospects.

We will next look in detail at one of the main factors that can affect prices.

Supply and Demand

As stated above, the price of shares is driven by **supply and demand**. As, in most cases (with the exception of certain collective investment schemes), the number of shares in issue is fixed and the supply of shares must come from people willing to sell their existing holdings (although, as was explained in Section 3.5, certain types of **corporate actions** can also affect supply).

If there are more investors keen to sell their shares than there are new investors looking to buy, the price of the shares will fall; where the converse is true, they will rise.

The appetite of investors to buy or sell a company's shares will depend on a range of factors, including:

- good (or bad) financial results, or indeed expectations of results;
- recommendations from stockbrokers to buy/sell a given stock;
- rumours that a company may be the subject of a takeover bid or merger;
- the skill (or otherwise) of the management team;
- the political climate, since government policy can make life harder for some types of company;
- the economic climate, including such factors as interest rates, inflation, exchange rates and unemployment;
- the price movements on other world stock markets, which can affect global sentiment towards shares;
- whether investors have funds available to commit to the markets;
- buying and selling activity on the part of large institutions.

3.7.2   Share Dealing

Listed shares and – often – unlisted shares too, are bought and sold through a stockbroker. The broker can deal for the client in one of three ways:

- **Execution-only dealing service.** In this case the stockbroker simply carries out the client's instructions.
- **Advisory or non-discretionary service.** In this case the stockbroker makes recommendations but the client makes the final decision.
- **Discretionary service.** In this case, the stockbroker will have authority to buy and sell without reference to the client. A legal agreement will set out the parameters for the transactions that can be taken on behalf of the client – for example, the amount of risk the client wishes to take or the types of securities he wishes to consider.

If the stockbroker is acting on an **execution-only** basis, this means that the client has agreed that he will not receive advice on his investments. He makes his own investment decisions and will give instructions to the broker to buy and sell shares.

The broker placing the deals will generally use either the **Stock Exchange Electronic Trading System (SETS)** or the **Stock Exchange Automated Quotation System (SEAQ)**.

SETS is the single platform for the trading of constituents of the FTSE All Share Index, exchange-traded funds (ETFs) and exchange-traded commodities along with over 180 of the most traded AIM and Irish securities. SETS offers market making in all stocks, including those deemed to be 'liquid' under MiFID. This is an order-driven system, unlike SEAQ which is quote-driven. Investors submit orders to the SETS system via stockbrokers, who are LSE member firms. The information is transmitted electronically, and orders are automatically executed where possible. SETS sends out information (orders, transactions, other messages) via a broadcast public feed.

SEAQ operates for trading the fixed-interest market and AIM-listed shares not traded on SETS.

The market comprises **market makers** and **brokers**:

- **Market makers** are a type of stock exchange member firm who promise to give buy and sell prices in a given range of securities – so that there is always a market in those securities (hence their name, 'market makers'). Market makers are in competition with each other for business, and the broker will choose the best price offered when executing his client's order (the principle of **best execution**), taking into account a range of factors.
- **Brokers** act as their client's agent, and place deals with the market makers in those securities their clients wish to deal in.

Some firms are allowed to act in dual capacity as market maker and broker, and many large banks do just that.

The settlement system now used for shares in most larger companies is called **CREST** (Certificateless Registration of Electronic Stock and Share Transfers).

The standard market convention is for equity trades to settle on a three-day settlement period (T+3). This means that the proceeds of a sale, or costs of a purchase, and the stock, must change hands within three business days of the deal date. Settlement can be delayed beyond T+3 by agreement between the parties and is commonly seen where private investors sell shares in certificated form – that is, a stock transfer form has to be completed and deposited along with the paper share certificate which takes much longer, hence the need for a longer time period.

3.7.3 Liquidity

Liquidity is the ease and speed with which a holding in a share is turned into cash at the prevailing market price. For the most liquid shares, orders can be quickly executed via SETS at prevailing market prices.

Less liquid shares, or very large deals (outside normal market size) may not be able to be placed so quickly. The broker may only have one or two market makers to choose from. Indeed if the share is unlisted and there is no market maker for it, there may be considerable delay before a matching buyer can be found.

As we have already learned, the term 'liquidity' refers to the ease with which a company's shares can be turned into cash, ie, sold. Some shares are more liquid than others; those blue chip shares of the very largest companies that make up the FTSE 100 share index are the most liquid, as there will generally be a number of market makers willing to set both bid and offer (buying and selling) prices for them.

Where shares are less liquid, their prices may be more prone to big swings. They are referred to as being more volatile than other shares.

3.7.4 Costs of Purchase and Sale

The costs of investing in shares can be broken down as follows:

- **Purchase cost.** The purchase cost includes a **spread** which is the difference between the bid and offer price of the share. The spread, from which market makers make their profits, could be 0.5% for a liquid share or 5% or more for a less easily traded share.
- **Broker's commission.** A typical charge would be, say, 1.5% on a deal up to £7,000, with a minimum charge of £25. Execution-only services, including online brokers, are generally cheaper than this, ranging from around £10 per deal upwards.
- **Stamp duty and Stamp Duty Reserve Tax (SDRT).** SDRT of 0.5% is payable on the value of purchases of UK equities settled through CREST, rounded up to the nearest penny. Stamp duty of 0.5% is payable on purchases of UK equities not settled through CREST, rounded up to the nearest £5. Stamp duty on stock registered in Ireland is charged at 0.1%.
- **Panel of Takeovers and Mergers (PTM) Levy.** The PTM levy is a flat £1 on either sales or purchases in excess of £10,000.

3.7.5 Nominal Value and Market Price

The number of shares which a company issues is determined by the:

- amount of share capital which is being raised; and
- par or nominal value of the shares.

For example, ABC Company may aim to raise £500,000 (to invest in expanding its operations and investing in new premises and machinery). It could do so by issuing:

- 500,000 ordinary shares with a par value of £1 each;
- 1,000,000 shares – each with a par value of 50p – to raise the same amount of capital.

The latter option may suit some companies. By making more shares available to potential shareholders, their marketability may be improved.

It is quite possible for companies to sell their shares, when they are initially issued, for more than the stated par value. For example, a company may issue 100,000 ordinary shares of £1 par value, launching them into the market for £1.30. The additional 30p is known as a **premium**.

> **Premium** – in the context of a share issue, the excess price per share that the company raises, over and above the par value of those shares.

The par, or nominal value of a share, is usually shown in its name. So:

- someone might have a holding of 1,000 £1 ordinary shares in XYZ Co plc;
- but the shares might be trading at £2.30 each on the stock market;
- the value of his holding would therefore be £2.30 x 1,000 = £2,300.

We can also talk about the total market capitalisation of a company, by reference to the total number of shares in issue, multiplied by its current share price. If XYZ Co plc has 1,000,000 shares in issue, then, its total market capitalisation is:

$$1,000,000 \times £2.30 = £2,300,000$$

Nowadays, the regulators in many countries let companies issue shares of no par value (NPV), and you may see this in a share's title: for example, ABC Company ordinary shares NPV.

Remember that the price of a company's shares in the market will bear no relation to their 'par value' – and an investor will be more interested in what the market value of his shares is, rather than in what their par value is. The market price of a share need bear no relation to its nominal value; it is determined by supply and demand, based on the various factors – company performance, market sentiment, economic environment – that we have looked at so far.

3.7.6 Cum- and Ex-Dividend Prices

As we have noted, many companies pay dividends twice a year (interims part way through the company's financial year, and then a final dividend when the full-year profits are declared).

Companies which raise money from the public, eg, by issuing their shares on the stock market, are obliged to ensure that the dividends they declare are paid on the due dates. On the '**declaration date**', the company will announce the:

- amount of the dividend;
- dividend payment date; and
- record date.

The **record date**, is important. To be eligible to receive the dividend, a shareholder must be on the share register, as the registered owner of the shares, as at the record date. The record date usually falls on a Friday.

> **Record date** – this is the cut-off date, selected by the company, to determine which shareholders will receive the imminent dividend payment.

The record date and payment date can, in theory, fall on the same day, but usually the payment date falls some time after the record date.

Investors who want to buy and sell shares in the run-up to a dividend payment need to be aware not only of the record date, but also of the **ex-dividend date**.

This date is determined by the stock exchange, and in accordance with guidance issued by the London Stock Exchange in its Dividend Procedure Timetable, usually falls on the Wednesday immediately prior to the record date, giving the company's registrar time to compile an accurate list of eligible shareholders. On this date a company's share price will be quoted with the letters 'xd' after it, to indicate that anyone buying the shares after this point will not be eligible to receive the next dividend.

Because buyers of ex-dividend shares do not qualify for the forthcoming dividend, the **price falls** (by roughly the amount of dividend per share) to reflect this.

A share which is not ex-dividend is described as **cum-dividend** or **cum-div** – ie, the buyer buys them with the right to the next dividend to be declared. Shares are assumed to be cum-dividend unless otherwise indicated.

3.8   EQUITY INDICES

LEARNING OBJECTIVE

1.3.6   Understand the purpose and construction of the main equity indices, and the considerations needed for less liquid markets

Stock market indices may be classed in many ways. A **world** or **global stock market index** typically includes large companies, without regard for where they are domiciled or traded. Two examples are MSCI World and S&P Global 100.

A **national index** represents the performance of the stock market of a particular nation, and reflects investor sentiment on the state of its economy. The most regularly quoted market indices are national indices composed of the stocks of large companies listed on a nation's largest stock exchanges, such as the American S&P 500, the Japanese Nikkei 225, and the British FTSE 100.

The concept may be extended well beyond an exchange. The Dow Jones Total Stock Market Index, as its name implies, represents the stocks of nearly every publicly traded company in the United States, including all US stocks traded on the New York Stock Exchange (but not American Depositary Receipts (ADRs)) and most traded on the NASDAQ and American Stock Exchange.

Specialised indices exist that track the performance of specific sectors of the market. The Morgan Stanley Biotech Index, for example, consists of 36 American firms in the biotechnology industry. Other indices may track companies of a certain size, a certain type of management, or even more specialised criteria.

Some indices, such as the S&P 500, have **multiple versions**. These versions can differ based on how the index components are weighted and on how dividends are accounted for. For example, there are three versions of the S&P 500 index: price return, which only considers the price of the components; total return, which accounts for dividend reinvestment; and net total return, which accounts for dividend reinvestment after the deduction of a withholding tax.

An index may also be classified according to the method used to determine its price. In a **price-weighted index** such as the Dow Jones Industrial Average, the price of each component stock is the only consideration when determining the value of the index. Thus, price movement of even a single security will heavily influence the value of the index.

In contrast, a **market-value weighted** or **capitalisation-weighted index** such as the Hang Seng Index factors in the size of the company. Thus, a relatively small shift in the price of a large company will heavily influence the value of the index.

In a **market-share-weighted index**, price is weighted relative to the number of shares, rather than their total value.

Traditionally, capitalisation- or share-weighted indices all had a full weighting, ie, all outstanding shares were included. Recently, many of them have changed to a float-adjusted weighting which helps indexing.

A **modified market-cap-weighted index** is a hybrid between equal weighting and capitalisation weighting. It is similar to a general market cap with one main difference: the largest stocks are capped to a percentage of the weight of the total stock index, and the excess weight will be redistributed equally amongst the stocks under that cap.

3.9 MEASURING THE PERFORMANCE OF SHARES

LEARNING OBJECTIVE

1.3.7 Analyse equity securities and equity funds using the following valuation measures: price earnings (PE) ratio; earnings per share; dividend yield; dividend cover; borrowings; net asset value; past performance

In this section we will look at some of the key measures that enable investors to compare the performance and value of shares, against each other or against other types of investment.

3.9.1 Earnings Per Share (EPS)

Not all of a company's profits are distributed to its shareholders by way of dividend. Some of them are retained for reinvestment into the business. It is important that this happens, if a company is to grow and remain competitive, and if its share price is to remain strong over the long term.

Investors who are not reliant on their dividend stream to live on may therefore be more interested in a company's overall earnings, instead of just the element it distributes by way of dividend.

Steady growth in a company's earnings should – in theory – ensure that the ordinary shareholders can continue to receive stable and rising dividends in future. So the earnings yield calculation can be a good indicator of one company's comparative strength of earnings against that of another. The formula is as follows:

$$\text{Earnings yield (\%)} = \frac{\text{Earnings per share (gross)}}{\text{Market price of share}} \times 100$$

3.9.2   Price/Earnings Ratio

The price/earnings ratio (or P/E ratio) of a company is simply the current market price of its shares, divided by the annual earnings per share:

$$PE \ ratio = \frac{Current \ market \ price \ of \ share}{EPS}$$

Some of the main reasons why the P/E ratio is a useful tool for investors in equities are:

- **Relevance** – it may be more relevant to analyse a share's performance on the basis of its earnings than its dividend record.
- **Comparisons** – P/E ratios can be useful for comparing the shares in different companies, particularly those in similar industries.
- **Risk** – a company's P/E ratio can show how risky the market believes an investment in the company to be:
  - a low P/E ratio may indicate a high perceived level of risk (or poor prospects for profit growth);
  - a high P/E ratio may indicate a relatively low perception of risk, or an expectation of good profits growth.

A company with a P/E ratio which is lower than the average for its sector or industry could, however, have the potential for an upward correction in its price, providing that the market expects its profits to improve in the future (ie, you could regard its shares as 'cheap').

Alternatively, a low P/E ratio could indicate that the company is in difficulties and that prospects for its recovery are seen as uncertain (ie, you could regard its shares as cheap, but for a good reason!).

P/E ratios are not without their difficulties as predictors of a company's future share price performance. In part this is because a company's earnings can fluctuate significantly from one year to the next, meaning that reliance on historic figures can be risky. For this reason, P/E ratios can be calculated on a historic basis – or on a projected basis, based on assumptions as to what the company's earnings per share will be in the future.

3.9.3   Dividend Yield

One common comparison is the dividend yield. This is the ongoing distribution of profits that investors are receiving from a company. The yield is simply the income earned by the investor on his holding, as a percentage of the prevailing share price.

Gross Dividend Yield

Yields are often calculated on a gross basis (ie, before any tax has been deducted) so that investors can assess them based on whatever their own personal tax rate is.

For UK equities, this is based on the cash dividend paid per share plus any associated tax credit, and the formula is as follows:

$$Gross \ dividend \ yield = \frac{Gross \ dividend \ paid \ in \ year}{Current \ market \ price \ of \ share} \times 100$$

The gross dividend yield is based on all the dividends paid by the company to the ordinary shareholders in respect of the preceding financial year. It is therefore a historical measurement – ie, it is based on past events which may not, of course, be repeated in the future.

Sometimes, therefore, investors will calculate a prospective yield based on a forecast of what the dividends will be for the current financial year.

When a company declares quarterly or interim dividends, it is usual to continue reporting the dividend yield on the basis of the dividend for the previous year; the dividend is not updated to reflect the current year's part performance to date.

Net Dividend Yield

Many companies state their net dividend yield instead, on the basis that for the average personal investor, this is most likely to reflect his actual tax status.

The net dividend is the amount of dividend actually received by the investor, after 10% income tax has been deducted from it, at source, by the company.

Some Considerations for Investors in Respect of Dividend Yields

Dividend yields on equities generally vary by the type of business the company is in, and the investment risk associated with the company. Companies that are perceived as operating profitably, and with good prospects, usually have lower yields than those in depressed industries or with higher risk factors. This lower return is the price the investor pays for the lower level of risk he is perceived to be taking on.

A company which is not regarded as so secure will tend to have a lower share price. Therefore its dividend yield will be higher as a percentage. This is the investor's reward for the additional risk he is incurring by investing in the company.

A **high dividend yield** is therefore nearly always an indication of an **above-average level of risk**.

Investors generally expect their dividends to rise over time, ideally at a rate which exceeds inflation so as to preserve their income in real terms. Of course, where this happens, and healthy dividend growth is seen, share prices will generally also rise, because investors are happy with the company's performance and there is good demand for the shares. However, rising share prices will have an impact on the calculation we looked at above and will, in turn, tend to depress the overall dividend yield of the share – a cyclical effect.

3.9.4 Dividend Cover

Dividend cover is calculated by dividing the total profits attributable to a company's ordinary shareholders by the total amount of dividend actually paid to them.

Profits attributable to ordinary shareholders are the total of profits after tax and preference share dividends have been deducted.

You could think of dividend cover as being a way of showing the number of times that the dividend could theoretically have been paid out to shareholders, from available profits. Thus, shareholders' dividends are safer if there is a high level of dividend cover (there is plenty of money available to pay their dividends). High dividend cover is also a good indication that the company is retaining earnings in the business – which should bode well for the share price in future, too. Dividend cover of 1.5 times or lower is usually considered as low by investors and analysts and could be a cause for concern.

Companies are permitted to (and often do) pay dividends not just from the current year's profits, but also by using previous years' retained profits. This means that a company which has made a loss in the current year may still be able to pay a dividend to its ordinary shareholders. However, when a company pays a dividend which exceeds this year's profits attributable to shareholders, it is described as paying an '**uncovered dividend**'.

3.9.5 Borrowings

A company which has raised a high proportion of its capital through borrowings (as opposed to by issuing shares) is described as being **highly geared**. Ideally, a company will not rely too heavily on such sources of funds. This is because:

- A company reliant on borrowings may have problems if its lenders decide not to roll over the debt, and the company cannot easily pay it back.
- The company's business strategies may become distorted, because it has to focus more on the short-term need to generate cash (to make interest payments and repay the capital of the loan) than on longer-term planning.
- If interest rates rise, the company may struggle to find the cash to keep up interest payments – but must do so, even if its profits are poor or non-existent.

The ratio of a company's equity to its debt is known as the **gearing ratio**. When times are good, highly geared companies may be expected to do better than those of their competitors with little or no borrowings. Their profits will increase, but they are still only committed to the same fixed levels of interest repayments (unless they have issued floating-rate debt); thus the surplus profits are available for shareholders. Conversely, however, when times are bad and profits are poor or non-existent, they must still service their debt; and as a consequence will suffer a disproportionately high downturn in profits.

3.9.6 Net Asset Value Per Share

The net asset value (or NAV) of a company is, in essence, everything it owns, less everything it owes – thus:

$$\text{Net asset value} = \text{assets} - \text{liabilities}$$

We can calculate the **net asset value per share** of a company by calculating the total net asset value of the company and dividing this by the number of shares in issue:

$$\text{NAV per share} = \frac{\text{assets} - \text{liabilities}}{\text{shares in issue}}$$

The importance of the NAV per share of a company depends on the type of business it is in. For those companies whose resources are mainly made up of the people skills they possess (for example, architects' practices, advertising agencies or law firms), most of the value of the business may be tied up in the skills and knowledge their employees possess, and the relationships and ideas they have. There is relatively little in the way of physical or financial assets. For other companies, however, with most of their resources committed to plant, property and equipment, such assets may be more valuable. In this case, an investor who buys a share at 100p may be interested to know that the NAV of the company is 130p, because if the company goes into liquidation there is, in effect, a 30p buffer supporting that share price.

NAV is particularly important for investors in investment trust companies, a type of investment company which invests into the shares of other companies.

3.9.7 Past Performance

In assessing whether to invest in a share or not, investors will invariably consider its past performance (despite repeated warnings that past performance may be no guide or guarantee to the future!).

However, the past performance of a single share in isolation does not tell the whole story. Investors should consider this in the light of the following factors:

- The **performance of the market** as a whole – for example, by measuring how the share has performed against the performance of the market as a whole. This can be done by looking at the performance of an appropriate **benchmark**. For example, an appropriate benchmark for blue-chip shares might be the FTSE 100 index.
- The share's **total return** – that is, not only the capital growth (or loss) that has been obtained, but also the dividends that have been received. This is because a company's share price falls when it declares a dividend in favour of its shareholders, since it is paying away part of its value to those shareholders. Investors should be careful, when comparing one share with another, to consider the total returns of each; a share that pays out dividends may appear to have performed badly on a purely capital basis, when compared with one that had a policy of paying no dividends to its investors.
- The **volatility** of the share – we have looked at this in Section 3.4.4, but in essence it is important to consider not only how well the share has done, but also the bumpiness of the ride the investor has experienced in the process!

3.10　SELECTING EQUITIES AND EQUITY FUNDS

1.3.8　　　Analyse the factors to take into account when selecting equities and equity funds: equity fund strategies – growth, income, market capitalisation, sector, region, customised; growth/dividend prospects; direct versus indirect investment; advantages and disadvantages of investing in equities; cost, turnover, liquidity and ease of trading

To select a suitable equity or equity fund for investment you must first understand the investor's requirements in terms of income or growth, their tolerance and attitude to investment risk, and their need for liquidity and access. Investors may, for example, wish to avoid certain sectors such as utilities or transport, while others may express a wish to invest in a socially responsible or ethical way.

The past performance of the equity or fund and the various performance measurement methods discussed earlier (P/E ratio, dividend cover) should be used to help assess the performance of the equity or fund relative to its peers.

In the case of an equity fund, the experience of the manager and his team should be taken into account. The fund strategy should be assessed to ensure that it matches the investor's needs (income or capital growth) using an active or passive management style.

3.10.1 Growth Investing

Growth investing is a relatively aggressive investment style. At its most aggressive, it simply focuses on those companies whose share price has been on a rising trend and continues to gather momentum as an ever-increasing number of investors jump on the bandwagon. This is referred to as **momentum investing**.

Buying **growth at a reasonable price (GARP)** investing is a less aggressive growth investment style where attention is centred on those companies that are perceived to offer above-average earnings growth potential that has yet to be fully factored into the share price.

True growth stocks, however, are those that are able to differentiate their product or service from their industry peers so as to command a competitive advantage. This results in an ability to produce high-quality and above-average earnings growth, as these earnings can be insulated from the business cycle. A growth stock can also be one that has yet to gain market prominence but has the potential to do so: growth managers are always on the look out for the next Microsoft.

The key to growth investing is to forecast future earnings growth rigorously and to avoid those companies susceptible to issuing profits warnings. A growth stock trading on a high P/E ratio will be savagely marked down by the market if it fails to meet earnings expectations.

3.10.2 Income Investing

Income investing aims to identify companies that provide a steady stream of income.

Income investing may focus on mature companies that have reached a certain size and are no longer able to sustain high levels of growth. Instead of retaining earnings to invest for future growth, mature firms tend to pay out retained earnings, as dividends, as a way to provide a return to their shareholders. High dividend levels are prominent in certain industries, such as utility companies.

The driving principle behind this strategy is to identify good companies with sustainable high dividend yields to receive a steady and predictable stream of income over the long term. Because high yields are only worth something if they are sustainable, income investors will also analyse the fundamentals of a company to ensure that the business model of the company can sustain a rising dividend policy.

3.10.3 Value Investing

In contrast to growth investing, value investing seeks to identify those established companies, usually cyclical in nature, that have been ignored by the market but look set for recovery. The value investor seeks to buy stocks in distressed conditions in the hope that their price will return to reflect their intrinsic value, or net worth.

A focus on recovery potential, rather than earnings growth, differentiates value investing from growth investing, as does a belief that individual securities eventually revert to a fundamental or intrinsic value. This is known as **reversion to the mean**. In contrast to growth stocks, true value stocks also offer the investor a considerable safety margin against the share price falling further, because of their characteristically high dividend yield and relatively stable earnings.

3.10.4 Geographic and Regional Spread

A well diversified portfolio should include exposure to different stock markets around the world. A global asset allocation will help give weighting to markets that may generate the returns that the investor is seeking, and also provide the right balance of risk and reward to meet their objectives.

3.10.5 Market Sectors

As well as looking at the geographical spread, an adviser or investment manager may also consider specific market sectors that they expect to outperform in a particular economic cycle, eg, banking, oil, pharmaceuticals and telecoms.

3.10.6 Market Capitalisation

Consideration should also be given to the market capitalisation of stocks and further diversity achieved through selecting between large-cap, mid-cap and small-cap stocks.

In stock market terminology, a company's value is measured by calculating how much its shares are worth in total. If a company has 1,000 shares in issue and each is worth 100p, for example, the company is capitalised at £1,000. If the share price rises to 150p, the company will be capitalised at £1,500. This is often referred to as a company's market cap. The biggest companies on the London Stock Exchange are often known as **large caps**; those in the FTSE 250 can be described as **mid caps** and the smallest shares are known as **small caps**.

Large caps are sometimes referred to as blue chip shares and many hold certain characteristics. Typically they are more heavily traded than smaller stocks, which make it easier for investors to buy and sell them. Technically speaking, they are more 'liquid', which essentially means they are easier to trade. Smaller company shares, by contrast, can be less liquid, which means their shares are traded less regularly.

3.10.7 Direct and Indirect Investment

Equities clearly have a major part to play in the investment portfolio of all investors; this can be achieved either by direct investment in shares, indirectly through investment funds, or by a combination of both.

Appreciating the need to diversify and having regard to the client's objectives, it is unlikely that a single investment fund or one individual security will meet a client's requirements. As an alternative to direct investment, or to complement direct holdings, investors can also utilise the wide range of equity investment funds or exchange-traded funds that are available.

Fund Costs

The direct purchase and sale of equities involves a variety of costs including, dealing transaction costs, commissions, stamp duty, and the PTM levy.

Some investment funds, eg, open-ended investment companies (OEICs), make charges for undertaking the management of the fund and the types of charges that can arise include:

- **Initial charges** – investment funds may impose an initial charge for investing in a fund and that is expressed as a percentage of the amount invested. The range of charges varies widely from fund to fund and depending upon whether the investor deals direct with a manager or uses a fund supermarket or platform. Because of investor dissatisfaction with the high level of initial charges, a number of fund groups have dispensed with these and instead moved to a basis of charging exit fees, if the investor disposes of their holding within a specified period of time.
- **Ongoing charges** – a fund will incur costs and expenses for the running of the fund such as dealing commissions, audit fees and custody fees. The fund management group will also make a charge for the management of the fund, and this is usually expressed as a percentage of the funds under management.
- **Performance charges** – performance fees may also be charged in certain funds over and above the annual fee providing that specified levels of growth over a benchmark have been achieved.

Charges vary from fund to fund, but the charging structure must be detailed in the fund's prospectus. Institutional investment in funds is clearly going to be significantly larger than any retail investment.

Exchange-Traded Funds (ETFs)

Exchange-traded funds (ETFs) are a type of open-ended investment fund that are listed and traded on a stock exchange. They typically track the performance of an index and trade very close to their NAV. Some of their distinguishing features include:

- They track the performance of a wide variety of fixed-income and equity indices as well as a range of sector and theme-specific indices and industry baskets. Some also now track actively managed indices.

- Some ETFs are more liquid, or more easily tradeable, than others depending upon the index they are tracking.
- The details of the fund's holdings are transparent so that their NAV can be readily calculated.
- They have continuous real-time pricing so that investors can trade at any time. They will generally have low bid-offer spreads depending upon the market, index or sector being tracked.
- They have low expense ratios and no initial or exit charges are applied. Instead, the investor pays normal dealing commissions to his stockbroker.

The returns of ETFs include both price movements and any income from the underlying index components. The index can be composed by: equities (developed, emerging, sectors or/and themes), bonds (government bonds, corporate bonds, money market), alternatives (commodities, private equity, hedge funds), or short/leverage (short-term trading/hedging instruments, eg, day trading).

With exchange traded products (ETPs), a distinction can be made between:

- **ETFS** – exchange-traded funds as a diversified basket of securities, UCITS-regulated;
- **ETCs** – exchange-traded commodities as single-commodity or diversified basket of securities, futures or physically backed, typically collateralised;
- **ETNs** – exchange-traded notes as single-commodity or diversified basket of securities, typically uncollateralised, issuer credit risk

ETFs can be used by retail and institutional investors, hedge funds and private wealth managers. In this way, they can work together towards an efficient way to gain index exposure. They can be used by retail and institutional investors for a wide range of investment strategies, including the construction of core-satellite portfolios, asset allocation and hedging.

3.11 ADVANTAGES AND DISADVANTAGES OF INVESTING IN EQUITIES

LEARNING OBJECTIVE

1.3.8   Analyse the factors to take into account when selecting equities and equity funds: equity fund strategies – growth, income, market capitalisation, sector, region, customised; growth/dividend prospects; direct versus indirect investment; advantages and disadvantages of investing in equities; cost, turnover, liquidity and ease of trading

Advantages

- Equities typically provide the best returns of any asset class over the long term.
- Equities traditionally provide a hedge against inflation.
- It is possible to participate in international as well as domestic opportunities in a broad variety of different industries, helping to achieve a great degree of diversity and reduce risk within the portfolio.
- Equities offer improved liquidity when compared to other forms of investment such as direct property or alternative investments like art, diamonds, gold and vintage cars.

Disadvantages

- Share prices fluctuate, which short-term-orientated investors may find disconcerting.
- Companies may suffer financial problems and possibly even go bust, resulting in the loss of the investor's capital.
- Unlisted or small-cap stocks are potentially riskier and may even prove difficult to trade in certain market conditions.

3.11.1 Turnover

Turnover refers to the rate at which the individual equities within a portfolio, directly or indirectly held, are bought and sold. Whether an investor holds equities directly or indirectly through a fund, the frequency of purchase and sale transactions within the portfolio may impact on the eventual rate of return experienced by the investor, particularly if the level of trading is significant. This is a result of the costs discussed in Sections 3.7.4 and 3.10.7.

3.11.2 Liquidity

Unlisted stocks may be difficult to trade in certain market conditions and could, therefore, be termed illiquid. Indirect investment in equities may offer greater liquidity by comparison, due to the ability of the fund manager to repurchase an investor's interest in the fund, using cash held for this purpose.

3.11.3 Ease of Trading

One of the benefits of holding equities directly is that they can be very easy to trade. A number of well-known stockbrokers offer dealing facilities via the internet, allowing retail investors the ability to trade online, at minimal cost, once the account opening process has been completed.

Purchasing indirect equity holdings, through an OEIC for example, usually requires a little more administration. In the past, this would have involved the completion of an application form to purchase 'units' in a particular fund, which would then be submitted to the manager with a cheque for the investment amount. However, it is now possible to open an account with a **fund supermarket** or **platform** and buy and sell OEICs in much the same way as direct equities through a stockbroking account. This ongoing development in IT back office systems and their integration with the internet is enabling investors even greater access to investment opportunities, reducing both cost and administration.

4. PROPERTY

LEARNING OBJECTIVE

1.4.1   Understand the differences, characteristics, risks and returns of the main property markets and sectors: residential and buy-to-let; commercial – retail space, hotel, office, industrial/warehouse

1.4.2   Analyse the main sources of investment risk and return associated with property investment, both direct and indirect: capital growth; yield; location and quality; occupancy rate; tenant creditworthiness, tenancy and rental agreement; term and structure of lease; asset liquidity; market volatility and risk; sector risk

1.4.3   Understand how the direct residential and commercial property markets operate: ownership and lease structures; conveyancing, buying and selling; costs – transactional, management; property valuation; finance and gearing; investment performance measurement and the role of the Investment Property Databank

As an asset class, property has consistently provided positive real-long-term returns, allied to low volatility and a reliable stream of income. An exposure to property can provide diversification benefits, owing to its low correlation with both traditional and alternative asset classes.

However, property can be subject to prolonged downturns and, if invested in directly, its lack of liquidity and high transaction costs on transfer only really make it suitable as an investment medium for the long term. The availability of indirect investment, however, makes property a more accessible asset class to those portfolio managers running smaller diversified portfolios.

4.1   RESIDENTIAL VERSUS COMMERCIAL PROPERTY

Over the past decade, investment in property has proliferated as people saw the value of properties rise, and has led to greater interest in this asset class. Property has a role to play in a well diversified portfolio and an investment manager needs to consider whether exposure to the residential or commercial sector is appropriate for the portfolio they are managing. It is therefore important to understand the differences between the two.

Some of the key differences are: shown below.

	Residential Property	**Commercial Property**
Direct Investment	Range of investment opportunities including second homes, holiday homes and buy-to-let	Size of investment required means direct investment in commercial property is limited to property companies and institutional investors
Tenancies	Typically short renewable leases	Long-term contracts with periods commonly in excess of ten years
Repairs	Landlord is responsible	Tenant is usually responsible
Returns	Largely linked to increase in house prices	Significant component is income return from rental income

4.1.1 Characteristics of the Residential Property Market

The UK has a relatively high level of owner-occupation of residential property, compared with some other countries. Home ownership has been promoted by tax incentives, including exemption from capital gains tax for the taxpayer's own principal private residence. The rented sector also saw the rise of buy-to-let (BTL) ownership by many new private landlords during the 1990s and early 2000s. More easily obtainable mortgage finance, and rising house prices, together with increasing knowledge on the part of private property investors, have fuelled the buy-to-let boom.

The economic downturn experienced in 2008, and the subsequent lack of high loan-to-value mortgages, reduced demand for new investment properties. However, this lack of suitable mortgage product also meant that individuals who were unable to purchase would instead rent, and so rental demand in certain regions did not diminish significantly.

Inexperienced landlords who bought properties at the top of the market, with the expectation of making a short-term gain, may now find themselves with an asset that has diminished in value. Coupled with any breaks in letting these properties, many may now find themselves forced to sell in a less than receptive market.

4.1.2 Characteristics of the Commercial Property Market

Commercial property is divided into three main sectors: retail, offices and industrial. The types of underlying property contained in each sector are:

- **Retail** – shopping centres, retail warehouses, standard shops, supermarkets and department stores.
- **Offices** – standard offices and business parks.
- **Industrial** – standard industrial estates and distribution warehousing, or logistics facilities.

A breakdown of the UK investment market based on mainstream institutional property is monitored by Investment Property Databank. It covers only the three main sectors and its reports show:

- London and the southeast have the lion's share of commercial property investments.
- Retail property is more evenly distributed across regions than offices or industrial. Shopping centres, retail warehouses, department stores, supermarkets and standard shops are found in most towns of any size throughout the country and, with the exception of standard shops, come in large lot sizes.
- The office market is heavily skewed towards London and the southeast. London alone accounts for more than 66%, with concentrations in the City and West End.
- Industrial property is also concentrated in London and the southeast.

Investment in commercial property has tended in the past to be dominated by insurance companies and pension funds. These institutions may, in the course of their investments, act as property developers and, once a property is built, the landlord. In recent years, more private investors have been making direct investment in commercial property, including wealthy individuals from overseas.

Commercial property is typically let on long leases. In the past this could be as long as 99 years. Now it is likely to be a maximum of 25 years, with three- or five-year rent reviews. Offices, factories and warehouses tend to produce the highest yields in the property sector, and retail typically produces the lowest yields.

The value of commercial property is generally assessed as a **multiple of the rental income**. For example, a property might be purchased at a price which equates to 20 years' multiple of the annual rent.

The owner of an investment property hopes that the:

- rental income will increase (a rising income return);
- property will increase in value as well (a capital return).

A property price set at a high multiple may reflect expectations of strong future rental growth.

With the exception of auctions, there is obviously no formal public market in commercial property and transactions are agreed between buyers and sellers often using the services of specialised agents. This lack of a formal exchange means that valuers are used to estimate the likely selling price of a commercial property. This process combines financial information about the property with market data to come to a balanced, evidence-supported assessment of its value using the RICS Appraisal and Valuation Standards (known colloquially as the Red Book).

As with other types of property, sales and purchases are both time-consuming and expensive. The costs of buying a property are significant when compared with other assets and average 1.7625% for agents fees and legal costs plus stamp duty land tax.

The following is taken from the IPF Summary Report published in November 2011 and cites some interesting characteristics of property investments.

'UK property has delivered positive long-run real returns. However in most cases it is not always a perfect hedge against inflation. Nominal returns may not always keep in line with inflation or inflation expectations. In comparison, equities tend to be a far better hedge against inflation. At the same time, property does hedge against economic growth and, consequently, is useful for matching future assets to liabilities where future liabilities are nominal GDP related (ie, wages).'

The three key factors for property investments in terms of performance are position in the cycle at purchase, GDP growth and inflation, in that order. Inflation is an important driver of nominal returns but not the dominant one. As income provides all of the real total returns over most years and sub-periods, looking at returns in real terms emphasises the need to maintain and protect income.

Total returns to the different sectors and to alternative assets, and their relative volatility, behave differently in the face of changes to inflation and GDP growth.

- **Best scenario for property** – high-growth low-inflation stage of the economic cycle associated with the non-inflationary consistent expansion (NICE) era.
- **Worst scenario** – high-inflation low-growth (stagflation) stage. This implies that cost-push inflation, such as when commodity prices are rising faster than retail inflation, is not favourable.
- **Beneficial scenario** – high GDP growth, unless it is also accompanied by high inflation. This means that the demand-pull scenario combination (when strong economic growth causes competition for resources and rising prices) does not imply a higher property allocation, except for investors prepared to take on high risk.
- Property should be preferred to equities when low inflation is expected, except for the low inflation-low growth combination where equities should be preferred.

4.2   OWNERSHIP AND LEASE STRUCTURES

In England and Wales, an interest in property can either take the form of a freehold or a leasehold interest.

- **Freehold** – the freeholder of a property has the right to use or dispose of the property as they wish, albeit subject to legislation, local planning laws and any covenants that specifically apply to the property.
- **Leasehold** – the freeholder can create a lesser interest in the property known as a leasehold interest. The leaseholder, or tenant, to whom this interest is conferred, has the right to use the property for a specific period, subject to the terms of the lease and the payment of rent. Unless prevented from doing so under the terms of the lease, the leaseholder can also create a sublease and act as the head lessee to a sub-tenant.

Some leases include break clauses that can significantly impact on the investment value of a property as they can give the landlord and the tenant the option to end the lease before its expiry date. The standard convention is to assume that a tenant's break option will be exercised and that it will negatively impact as the income from the property can change or even disappear at this point.

On the other hand, landlords' break options can have a positive impact as they give the opportunity to re-let at a higher rent, find a better tenant or refurbish the property. When a commercial property is rented out, a rent review period is agreed between the landlord and the tenant and set out in the terms of the lease. Typically, commercial rents in the UK are reviewed every five years and the revised rent is based on what rents can be achieved in the open market for comparable properties. Leases often provide for upwards-only reviews, where the new rent cannot be lower than the rent that the tenant is currently paying.

4.3   BORROWING

Given the substantial value of most properties, and the fact that they can make excellent security for lending purposes, most property investments are made with help from borrowed funds. The investment is **geared**.

The gearing effect of borrowing for property purchase can be severe if prices start to fall, and **negative equity** can result if the loan is a high percentage of the property value.

4.4   RETURNS FROM RENT

Property which has been let produces an income return, in the form of rent paid by its tenants to the owner (the landlord). This is true both of private residential property lettings to households, and of commercial properties let out to businesses.

Research shows that, over the long run, investment in property has provided real returns ahead of the returns on cash and gilts and slightly below that of equities. The commercial property market has, however, suffered from crashes from time to time; for example, between 1989 and 1992, following a period of significant levels of speculative development in London, some office rent levels halved.

The residential property market tends to move in cycles which are different from those of the commercial property market, and it is influenced by economic factors such as disposable incomes and interest rates. A major slump in the residential market followed substantial rises in interest rates in the years following 1989. A shortage of building land and planning restrictions contributes to rising prices in some areas, particularly the south of England. The declining affordability of homes for many people means that they have to rent (unless they have some alternative, such as living with parents), and this keeps demand for rental property – and therefore rents – relatively high.

The rental income on property will depend on a variety of factors, including:

*   supply and demand;
*   the quality of the property itself and how appealing it is to tenants; and
*   the terms that have been agreed. Depending on the nature of the lease or letting agreement, there may be restrictions on how often and by how much the rent can be adjusted.

For residential properties, rental income is taxed as business income. It is treated as a single business, even if the investor has bought and lets out more than one property. A residential property investor who lets out several properties can offset losses from one against profits from another.

Note:

*   there are some differences in the tax treatment for residential and holiday lettings; and
*   very low rental income (up to £4,250 pa) under the rent-a-room scheme – where someone lets out a room in their own home – is tax-free.

The rent on commercial property is also treated as business income. Because of this, there are various capital allowances and expenses which can be offset against it, potentially reducing the investor's overall tax burden.

The **rental yield** from a property investment can be calculated as:

$$\text{Rental yield} = \frac{\text{Gross rent} - \text{expenses}}{\text{Cost of property, including purchase costs}}$$

Gross rent should be adjusted by excluding estimated void periods (ie, times when there is no tenant), which can generally only be estimated in calculating the yield for a future period.

Expenses include agents' charges, buildings insurance (and contents insurance, if furnished) and the cost of renewals of furnishings and appliances. Total expenses are likely to be between 20% and 25% of the gross rent.

Purchase costs include legal fees, the cost of surveys or valuation, stamp duty land tax and the initial cost of furnishings. Agents' fees may be incurred on the transaction if an agent has been employed to search for the property, but usually only the seller incurs agents' fees.

Note that the costs of loan interest have not been included in expenses. The rental yield is the rent after expenses as a proportion of the capital cost of the investment. The rental yield income can be compared with the rate that the investor is paying for a loan to purchase the property.

4.4.1 Quality of Tenants

The quality of tenant in a let property is important to its overall investment return. Poor-quality tenants may:

- not be able to pay their rent. Evicting and replacing them can (depending on the terms of the tenancy) be costly and time-consuming. It may also result in rental voids.
- also fail to meet their obligations in terms of maintaining the property in good order, resulting in expense to the landlord in bringing it back to lettable standard once they depart.

The ideal tenant is one of good financial standing who is likely to have an interest in maintaining the condition of the property on an ongoing basis.

4.4.2 Occupancy Levels

When the property is unlet (void periods), no income is being earned. A prospective investor should understand the local rental market and what factors influence local levels of demand, in order to estimate what void periods can be expected and build these into estimates of rental income. The location of the property and its overall condition and character can affect the incidence of void periods.

4.5 CAPITAL RETURNS

Over time, property values can be seen to increase, generally in excess of inflation (providing a real return). However, the property market is cyclical and can fall sharply.

Commercial property, to a greater extent than residential property, can be vulnerable to influences on overseas investment. Factors such as the value of sterling and how foreign investors are taxed on UK commercial property can affect prices. In addition, since much of the commercial property market is owned by large institutional investors, it means it must compete with other asset classes such as equities and bonds.

Effects such as interest rate moves can have a significant effect on the property market due to the market's leverage through borrowing. This can affect the cost of servicing any debt taken on. Higher rates can have a negative effect, while lower rates can be positive.

4.5.1 Depreciation

Property prices can be affected by the condition of the property. If it is deteriorating and no remedial action is taken, it may depreciate steadily as the costs involved in restoring it continue to rise. Eventually it may fall to a level where the only real value is the land on which it stands – and this must be offset against the costs of levelling the property and rebuilding.

4.6 COSTS

4.6.1 Transaction Costs

Property transactional costs are relatively high compared to other financial instruments. This is another reason why property should be seen as a longer-term investment.

- In addition to agents' and legal costs, property purchases are subject to stamp duty land tax.

- Often, property transactions are protracted and the vendor may incur expenses during this period.

Stamp duty land tax (SDLT) is payable on purchasing property. The tax is rounded up to the next multiple of £5.00. No SDLT is chargeable for transfers on divorce, or for transfers to charities if the land is to be used for charitable purposes.

SDLT is charged as a percentage of the amount paid for property or land when it is bought or transferred – unless there is a relief or exemption. SDLT rates are progressive. The amount payable can also vary depending whether the property is being used for residential or non-residential purposes, and whether the property is sold as a freehold or leasehold. The rates for residential buyers are set out in the tables below, and full details of SDLT rates and thresholds can be found at www.hmrc.gov.uk.

Residential Land or Property SDLT Rates and Thresholds

Purchase price/lease premium or transfer value	SDLT rate
Up to £125,000	Zero
Over £125,000 to £250,000	1%
Over £250,000 to £500,000	3%
Over £500,000 to £1 million	4%
Over £1 million	5%

Source: *HMRC*

If the value is above the payment threshold, SDLT is charged at the appropriate rate on the whole of the amount paid. For example, a house bought for £130,000 is charged at 1 per cent, so £1,300 must be paid in SDLT. A house bought for £350,000 is charged at 3%, so SDLT of £10,500 is payable.

Non-Residential Land or Property SDLT Rates and Thresholds

Purchase price/lease premium or transfer value (non-residential or mixed use)	SDLT rate (includes first time buyers)
Up to £150,000 – annual rent is under £1,000	Zero
Up to £150,000 – annual rent is £1,000 or more	1%
Over £150,000 to £250,000	1%
Over £250,000 to £500,000	3%
Over £500,000	4%

Source: *HMRC*

Note that for the above purpose the annual rent is the highest annual rent known to be payable in any year of the lease, not the net present value used to determine any tax payable on the rent.

Properties Bought in a Disadvantaged Area

If the property is in an area designated by the government as disadvantaged, a higher threshold of £150,000 applies for residential properties.

Purchase price/lease premium or transfer value	SDLT rate	SDLT rate for first-time buyers
Up to £150,000	Zero	Zero
Over £150,000 to £250,000	1%	Zero
Over £250,000 to £500,000	3%	3%
Over £500,000 to £1 million	4%	4%
Over £1 million	5%	5%

Source: *HMRC*

First-time buyers of residential property can apply for SDLT relief if the:

- effective date is on or after 25 March 2010 and before 25 March 2012;
- consideration given is £250,000 or less.

4.6.2 Maintenance Costs

Various costs in maintaining a property, include:

- **Ongoing repairs and maintenance** – these may fall to the landlord or the tenant, depending on the terms of the rental agreement; it is important to factor this in when calculating the net return on the property.
- **Insurance** – which again may fall to the landlord or tenant, depending on terms.
- **Rates and council taxes** are payable on the property. These will vary by local authority.

Where the property is commercially let, there may be legal requirements to ensure certain standards of access, security and safety, which can increase costs.

4.7 CONVEYANCING

Conveyancing is the legal process of transferring property rights from seller to buyer (for a sale/purchase), or switching a mortgage from one lender to another (for remortgaging).

A conveyancing solicitor acts on behalf of either the buyer or seller and represents their interests in the property transaction. They ensure that the terms and conditions of the contract for sale are fair and reasonable and that all financial information is correct. The process differs depending upon whether they are acting for the buyer or the seller.

The seller's conveyancer will first request a copy of the **land registry** entry for the property. This is sometimes referred to as the office copies. They then prepare a **contract** for sale, incorporating the land registry plan and details, before forwarding it to the buyer's solicitor.

The buyer's solicitor will apply for the **searches** from a variety of bodies including the local authority, and will assess the contract for sale that has been received from the seller's lawyer. Additionally, if the buyer is borrowing money on a mortgage, the solicitor will need to receive a copy of the formal mortgage offer and be satisfied that the buyer has sufficient funds available to complete the transaction.

If there are items in the contract for sale that the buyer's solicitor is not happy with, they will raise a query with the seller's solicitor. Once these have been resolved, the searches have been completed and proof of funds provided, both parties exchange contracts.

Exchange of contracts is the point of no return for both parties and is a legally binding agreement. At any time up until this point, either party can withdraw from the process with no penalty other than any monies incurred to date.

At exchange of contracts a **completion date** is normally agreed when the transfer will be finalised. On the day of completion the monies are transferred between the parties and ultimately, the keys are handed over.

4.8 LIQUIDITY

Direct investment in property (whether commercial or residential) is generally pretty illiquid:

- Property can take some considerable time to sell.
- It is generally indivisible – if the investor wants to realise a small part of his portfolio he cannot sell, say, only the bathroom of one of his residential properties. He could perhaps sell one flat in a block of flats he owns, but this might be uneconomic in terms of breaking up the value of the block as a whole.

Property should not be recommended to investors who have immediate or near-term liquidity needs (see also Section 4.12.4).

4.9 PERFORMANCE MEASUREMENT

Performance in the property market is measured by reference to the various indices and analysis offered by, chiefly, the Investment Property Databank (IPD) (see Section 4.10.6).

4.10 VALUATION MEASURES

LERANING OBJECTIVE

1.4.4   Analyse property and property funds using the following valuation
          measures: cash flow and average yield; capitalisation rate; rental value,
          review; reversionary value; average repair costs; comparative analysis;
          market indices and trends

4.10.1 Cashflow and Average Yield

Like the economy, the property market goes through cycles: periods of growth leading to oversupply and market weakness, followed by stabilisation, absorption and then growth, leading to shortage of supply and so on.

The simplest yardstick of property value is initial yield. This is the current annual rent divided by the value of the property, including purchase costs. The average initial yield across the whole property market fluctuates over time and may reflect a general economic cycle and/or specific changes in attitude towards property.

4.10.2 Capitalisation Rate

The capitalisation rate or cap rate is a ratio used to estimate the value of income-producing properties. Put simply, the cap rate is the net operating income divided by the sales price or value of a property expressed as a percentage. Investors, lenders and appraisers use the cap rate to estimate the purchase price for different types of income-producing properties.

A market cap rate is determined by evaluating the financial data of similar properties which have recently sold in a specific market. It provides a more reliable estimate of value than a market gross rent multiplier since the cap rate calculation uses more of a property's financial detail. The GRM calculation only considers a property's selling price and gross rents. The cap rate calculation includes a property's selling price, gross rents, non-rental income, vacancy amount and operating expenses, thus providing a more reliable estimate of value.

In a property transaction, the seller is trying to get the highest price for the property or sell at the lowest cap rate possible, while the buyer is trying to purchase the property at the lowest price possible, which translates into a higher cap rate.

Investors expect a larger return when investing in high risk income properties. The cap rate may vary in different areas of a city due to desirability of location, level of crime and general condition of an area. You would expect lower cap rates in newer or more desirable areas of a city and higher cap rates in less desirable areas, to compensate for the added risk.

In a property market where net operating incomes are increasing and cap rates are declining over time for a given type of property such as office buildings, values will be generally increasing. If net operating incomes are decreasing and cap rates are increasing over time in a given marketplace, then property values will be declining.

4.10.3 Reversionary Value

The reversionary value of a property is the expected value at the end of the term of the lease.

It is in the nature of leasehold tenancy for a property's value to diminish as the lease expires, and a long lease is generally worth more on the open market than a short lease.

In enfranchisement cases, when the enfranchising leaseholders have the opportunity to grant themselves lease extensions, it can generally be assumed that the action will achieve some improvement in the value of the individual properties.

The amount of this improvement will be heavily dependent upon the length of the unexpired term before extension and there are no hard and fast rules as to how much the value will increase. A valuer will assess this and make an estimate, based on research into similar properties in the local area.

If a leaseholder has made improvements to the property which affect its value, these must be disregarded for the purposes of the valuation. If the improvements are substantial, the valuer will have to calculate the additional value they give to the property and then discount this from the estimated present value of the property.

For the purpose of calculating the reversionary value, a value must be ascribed to the property representing what it could be sold for when the current term expires.

Most long leaseholders have statutory protection to revert to assured tenancies on the expiry of their existing leases. In the valuation of leasehold interests subject to protected occupancy, the improved value is sometimes discounted by a percentage to reflect the fact that the landlord will not receive a vacant property on expiry, but a paying tenant.

4.10.4 Rental Value Review

The rent review period is agreed between the landlord and the tenant and set out in the terms of the lease. Typically, commercial rents in the UK are reviewed every five years.

In general, a rent review is decided by negotiation between the tenant and landlord, and by referring to the rents achieved in the open market for comparable properties. Once agreed, the tenant is committed to pay the landlord a rental income which is effectively fixed (subject only to further reviews) until the lease is terminated.

UK commercial leases have traditionally provided for upwards-only reviews. This means that the new rent negotiated on review cannot be lower than what the tenant is currently paying, even if the market rents in the area have fallen below that level. In this case, the tenant and landlord usually agree to continue with same rent the tenant currently pays.

Although upwards-only reviews are traditional, it should be noted that UK leases can specify a different basis for reviewing rents. Leases which spell out an annual amount or percentage by which the rent will increase, or link the increase to the RPI, are becoming more common. In addition, but less frequently, a rent review may state the exact properties to be used as comparables. If the landlord and tenant cannot agree a rent review, they can ask an independent expert or arbitrator (often appointed by the Royal Institution of Chartered Surveyors) to decide the matter.

4.10.5 Average Repair Costs

During the credit crisis, the capital value of UK commercial property fell about 45% from its 2007 peak and at the same time, expenditure on repair and maintenance also plunged. Commercial property maintenance is generally the responsibility of the tenant. However the impact of the recession meant that this slipped further down a tenants' list of priorities. Underinvestment in essential maintenance work can have a serious impact for landlords and lead to large and unexpected repair bills, falls in asset values and, in some cases, legal liability if there have been breaches of health and safety legislation.

Value of Repair and Maintenance in Commercial Property

The recession has already affected asset values and rental yields, and now a further impact may be experienced with greater dilapidation costs. Pressures on cash flow and the continuing reluctance of banks to lend, mean that tenants may be less diligent with property maintenance. The cost of neglect can be substantial for landlords, who may struggle to let dilapidated properties once leases have expired.

Lack of maintenance could impair assets values even further and, as property owners become less able to secure finance to fund the remedial work due to their weaker financial position, they are forced to delay repair work even longer.

One option for landlords is to prepare carefully programmed maintenance schedules which set out accountability and tenant obligations for maintenance under the terms of their leases. To ensure this is effective, landlords should consider monitoring procedures and outline the remedial activities that could be invoked.

The recession has meant that many properties are now only partially occupied, leaving the landlord liable for the cost of maintaining the empty parts of the building. Landlords can avoid this situation, by optimising the maintenance schedule – and ad hoc repairs – to coincide with periods of full occupancy.

4.10.6 Comparative Analysis, Market Indices & Trends

Commercial property investors need to be able to measure the returns they achieve on their investment and compare performance. The IPD (Investment Property Databank), produces objective, reliable property benchmarks and indices for 18 countries and is the world leader in performance analysis for the owners, investors, managers and occupiers of real estate. The IPD started in the UK in 1985 and began to compile data from leading commercial property investors, eventually creating the UK's first reliable index of commercial property returns. The IPD maintains various databases, which hold records of properties owned by investors, managed by portfolio managers, and occupied by businesses and government. They contain detailed financial and descriptive information on each of the individual buildings, leases and tenants. The IPD measures the financial performance of real estate for fund managers and insurance, pension and private investment companies across the world..

However, performance is not measured on the basis of transaction data, but by records from portfolio valuations.

IPD's annual database is the most comprehensive benchmark of direct property performance in the UK. It monitors 12,137 properties in 278 funds with a total value of £192 billion, equivalent to 49% of the UK investment market. These properties are valued annually, but two subsets are valued more frequently.

The quarterly index, launched in 2006, values 8,003 properties, £122 billion worth in December 2006, held in 187 separate funds. the monthly index compiles a database of 67 portfolios (4,249 properties). This latter provides a fast-moving indicator of current market conditions. The monthly index covers 15% of the UK investment market, but differs in composition from the annual index. For example, it contains few large portfolios and fewer higher-value assets, such as shopping centres and central London offices. A summary of the end-month results is published in the Companies & Markets section of the *Financial Times*.

The analysis carried out by the IPD enables investment managers to measure the performance of their real estate portfolios and to benchmark themselves against their peers. The various indices and measures available help to highlight the strengths and weaknesses of a property fund's performance

In 2006, another index series, the FTSE UK Commercial Property Index, was launched. It differs from the IPD indices in several important respects. Most significantly, it is based on the indirect property holdings of a Guernsey-listed real estate fund. This fund is invested in a range of property vehicles and is structured so that its holdings mimic the UK commercial property investment market.

The headline FTSE UK All Property Index has three additional sector indices, giving investors daily performance data on the retail, office and industrial sectors of the UK commercial property market. It is available by subscription.

There are also the UK Pooled Property Fund Indices, compiled by IPD and sponsored by the Association of Real Estate Funds and HSBC. These measure the quarterly performance of £3 billion worth of commercial and residential property held by some 60 collective investment schemes offering indirect exposure to UK property.

The performance of UK quoted real estate company shares is tracked as part of the FTSE Actuaries All Share Index for UK equities, published daily in the Companies & Markets section of the *Financial Times*.

It is important to understand that property indices are based on valuations and not transaction prices. Therefore, they tend to underestimate the true volatility of the market. Nevertheless, even after adjusting to allow for valuation smoothing and lag, property's volatility is still lower than that of other assets.

4.11 INDIRECT PROPERTY INVESTMENT

LEARNING OBJECTIVE

1.4.5   Analyse the factors to take into account when selecting property and property funds: property shares, OEICs, REITs, bonds, trusts, funds, fund of funds, limited partnerships; property fund strategies; growth/ dividend prospects; direct versus indirect investment; pricing, liquidity and fair value; advantages and disadvantages; costs and ease of trading

You should be aware that collective investment schemes offer the investor the benefit of indirect exposure to a variety of asset classes.

A number of these can include property – generally commercial, but sometimes also residential. We will take a look at a few of the options available.

4.11.1 Property Company Shares

A variety of property development and property investment companies are listed on the London Stock Exchange. They invest in a wide variety of properties, some undertaking the development of property projects and some simply seeking to identify and invest in undervalued properties. Where the properties are let, the company may pay a dividend income to its investors; others, however, which invest in development opportunities, may pay no income at all.

The price of the shares will move with supply and demand and may diverge from the value of the underlying asset values. Gearing (borrowing) by the company can increase the share price volatility.

The share price can be affected by systemic factors affecting the stock market as a whole, as well as factors specific to the company or the property sector.

Compared with direct investment in property, a significant advantage of this means of investing in property is liquidity. The investor can realise his investment in a listed property company easily through a stockbroker, since there are market makers who quote prices for all listed stocks.

4.11.2 Unit Trusts

Originally, unit trusts were prohibited from directly investing in property and could only invest indirectly via property shares. Nowadays, they can invest directly into commercial property. At the launch of such a fund, the manager must be confident that he will attract sufficient funds to make adequate property purchases to establish a well spread portfolio.

There are, however, restrictions on the proportion of the fund that can be invested in leases with less than 60 years to run, or in unoccupied property. There are also restrictions on holding mortgaged property, which limits gearing. No more than 15% in value of the fund assets can be invested in a single property.

Additionally, there are unit trusts that invest in property company shares.

As with unit trusts and open-ended investment companies (OEICs) generally, the investment will be redeemed at net asset value. However, if many investors choose to sell at one time, the unit trust or OEIC may need to invoke its right to postpone encashment of units/shares until property can be sold. This possible restriction in accessibility makes property funds potentially less liquid than other funds (though still more liquid than an investment directly into property). This happened during the 2007/2008 economic crisis.

There is no capital gains tax charged to the fund itself for unit trusts, OEICs and investment trusts. Investors may be subject to capital gains tax on gains when they sell the units or shares.

Authorised property unit trusts are regulated by the FSA. Like all authorised funds, they can be sold direct to retail investors. They pay corporation tax on their income but do not pay capital gains tax within the vehicle.

There is a wide variety of property unit trusts, from specialist funds (eg, urban regeneration and residential) to general commercial property. Most have a wide commercial property base, thus offering investors a sufficient variety of underlying assets to give them exposure to a diversified portfolio of property investments. There is also a wide range of authorised unit trusts investing into property company shares and (increasingly) real estate investment trusts (REITs), a vehicle which we will look at in Section 4.11.4.

Such vehicles can surmount some of the liquidity issues that face investors investing directly in property; for example, if a unit trust holds shares in a listed property fund, it can sell those shares on the stock market to realise cash to meet its investors' redemption needs. Each open-ended property unit trust will have predetermined redemption procedures (which differ from trust to trust), so the investor should ensure that he understands these before investing.

In addition, there is a developing secondary market that allows the transfer of units between investors on a matched bargain basis; in some cases this can provide an exit route, where the individual trust's terms are more restrictive and an investor needs to sell his units promptly.

4.11.3 Open-Ended Investment Companies (OEICs)

Similarly, UK OEICs can invest in property and property vehicles (and provide a similar range of advantages).

There may be some differences in the tax treatment of property AUTs and property OEICs. Both vehicles are currently tax-effective investments for UK taxpayers. They are not particularly tax-effective investments for non-taxpaying investors, however, such as registered pension schemes and ISA investors.

Under new proposals, property OEICs holding a certain percentage of their assets in property or in UK REITs will be able to avoid taxation. This is payable by investors. This would enable a non-taxpaying investor to avoid the impact of tax on the rental income earned by the OEIC. This option is not available to AUTs, so OEICs may – from a tax perspective at least – become a viable option for property investment for non-taxpayers.

Both types of open-ended property fund (that is, AUTs and OEICs) will continue to be exempt on capital gains on the sale of properties.

4.11.4 Real Estate Investment Trusts (REITs)

REITs are a relatively new investment vehicle in the UK. They can provide investors with tax-efficient and diversified exposure to rental properties. REITs are tax-transparent property investment vehicles. Initially introduced in the US, they have been adopted by other countries including Japan, the Netherlands and France and were launched in the UK in January 2007.

Tax-transparent property investment vehicles, such as REITs, distribute nearly all of their taxable income to investors. Providing they do this, they are exempt from capital gains and corporate taxes. Investors pay tax on the dividends and capital growth at their own marginal tax rates, thus avoiding the double taxation that would otherwise affect investors in UK property companies.

Companies qualifying to become UK REITs must be resident in the UK and listed on a recognised stock exchange. Their income and gains from property will be exempt from tax. They must distribute at least 90% of their tax-exempt profits, and the distributions which are tax-exempt are paid net of tax. These distributions are taxed as property rental income at the holder's marginal tax rate; other distributions will be taxed in the same way as normal dividends.

The following further conditions apply:

- no single shareholder may hold 10% or more of the share capital or voting rights;
- the ratio of interest on loans funding the tax-exempt property business to rental income must be less than 1.25:1.

REITs can be held in ISAs and Child Trust Funds. A number of UK property companies have chosen to convert to become REITs.

4.11.5 Life Assurance Property Bonds

Life companies offer bonds. These are not a debt security of the type we have already looked at, but rather a type of life policy giving investment exposure to a variety of asset classes. Property is among the range of asset classes to which exposure can be obtained through a life policy or insurance-based pension product. The value of the benefits paid under the life policy is directly linked to the net asset values of the properties held. A life fund is not permitted to borrow.

In addition, most 'with profits' funds operated by life companies include an element of property exposure in their portfolios.

Although life products are more liquid than direct investments in property, life companies retain a right to postpone the encashment of units (and therefore the payment of benefits under the policy). This could come into effect if many investors wished to encash their bonds at the same time, necessitating the sale of properties – a process that could take some time. This condition was invoked by several life companies during the crisis in 2008.

Income and capital gains are subject to tax within the fund at 20%. This cannot be reclaimed by non-taxpayers, and higher-rate taxpayers will pay additional tax. The tax treatment of holdings accessed through a policy is thus different from that for collective investment schemes and listed property shares.

In addition, the policy carries insurance benefits for the policyholder.

4.11.6 Offshore Funds

Many property funds are established in offshore or international financial services centres such as the Isle of Man, Cayman and Dublin. This may provide certain tax advantages (though offshore vehicles are not advantageous for every investor, and some can be positively disadvantageous); in many cases it is because of the more relaxed regulations in those jurisdictions, which may mean that the fund has to comply with fewer rules in terms of diversification and the levels of liquidity it has to maintain, or in terms of how the assets are held.

4.11.7 Investment Trusts

Investment trusts are listed, closed-ended vehicles which are traded on the stock market. A number of these invest in the shares of property companies.

Property investment trusts are, therefore, closed-ended, pooled investments – but they are only permitted to invest in shares and securities of property companies, not in property directly. They are permitted to borrow, which can increase the risk for the investor as well as the potential return.

The share price of the trust will fluctuate with supply and demand for the shares of the trust and may be at a discount or a premium to the net asset value.

4.11.8 Funds-of-Funds

One of the investee funds in which a fund-of-funds invests may well focus specifically on the property market. This provides the investors in the fund-of-funds vehicle with a measure of exposure, and access to specialist expertise, in this asset class.

4.11.9 Limited Partnerships

In some cases, the fund vehicle for investment in the property market may be established as a partnership vehicle (as opposed to a unit trust or company). Such vehicles are usually aimed at direct investment in the property market, and are targeted at the wealthier or more experienced investor. Their tax treatment is rather different from that of trust or corporate-based vehicles, since the HMRC 'looks through' the vehicle to a greater extent.

4.12 COSTS AND EASE OF TRADING

4.12.1 Valuation

Auctions aside, there is no public market in commercial property investments. It is primarily a private market, made principally by agents who seek to match buyers and sellers with buildings. Sellers typically engage an agent to market their property. The buyer will usually recognise the agent's role in introducing the property to them, either by retaining the agent to act on the purchase or simply by paying an introductory fee.

With the advent of e-commerce, many agents now market properties for clients via websites and there are several platforms that seek to create electronic market places. Property auction houses also sell commercial lots for sellers. In recent years the auction market has grown steadily, driven by the growing demand from private investors. Two factors fuelling this demand are that initial yields on properties in the auction room have been higher than finance rates and that there has been a ready supply of debt finance.

4.12.2 Costs

The costs of buying a property are significant when compared with acquiring interests in other assets. In large part, they stem from the fees associated with the necessary due diligence. The market norm is 1.7625%, which reflects fees, plus VAT for the following services:

- Agents' advice on the purchase, which may sometimes, but not always, include fees for valuation, building surveys, environmental audits and mechanical and engineering tests.
- Legal transaction fees.
- Stamp Duty Land Tax (SDLT).

See Section 4.6.1 for details of SDLT rates.

4.12.3 Pricing and Fair Value

Unlike other financial assets, most commercial real estate does not trade in an exchange with openly quoted prices. Professional valuers are used to estimate the likely selling price of an asset. This process combines financial information about the property with market data to come to a balanced, evidence-supported assessment of its price. The valuer uses their expert knowledge and experience of the market to make a judgment.

The RICS Appraisal and Valuation Standard is the national valuation practice standard in the UK. It is used by RICS members, who value most of the investment property in the UK, and their clients. But even when these standards are used, the valuation of a property and the price it sells for can be different.

To some extent this reflects the imperfect nature of market information, ie, the seller may know more than the buyer, or vice versa. It can also reflect different views about the future prospects for the property itself and how the market is likely to perform.

4.12.4 Liquidity

Investors often cite a lack of liquidity as a key disadvantage of commercial property. However, research published by the IPF in 2004 found that the UK market average holding period for an investment is seven years. It also found that the holding period has been shortening over time, suggesting steady gains in liquidity.

Nevertheless, turnover is relatively low compared to that in the equities and gilts markets. Two reasons for property's 'stickiness' are that it takes longer and is more expensive to execute a deal. Although the property industry has taken steps to streamline transactions, it can take several months from initial marketing to completion of contracts. This time lapse clearly represents an opportunity cost for investors.

5.   ALTERNATIVE AND SPECIALIST INVESTMENTS

LEARNING OBJECTIVE

1.5.1   Understand the purpose, characteristics, risks and returns of the main types of alternative investments: gold and other metals; commodities; art; antiques; forestry

1.5.2   Analyse the factors to take into account when investing in alternative investments: direct versus indirect investment; investment time horizon; features – quality, durability, provenance; transaction, delivery and ongoing costs; pricing, liquidity and fair value; advantages and disadvantages of investing in alternatives

Alternative investments are those which fall outside the traditional asset classes of equities, property, fixed interest, cash and money market instruments.

They include physical assets, which is what we will focus on here; you may also hear them referred to as 'chattels'. Chattels are tangible, moveable things. When used for investment purposes, they are sometimes also referred to as 'collectables'.

While assets of this type tend to be popular with collectors, they do also have the potential to appreciate substantially in value. They are not exclusive to wealthy clients and due to the wide variety of options available, even modest investments are possible; many people have a collection of coins or stamps, for example, and can find to their surprise that they have amassed a portfolio of reasonable value over time.

Some chattels can make good investments – they may go up in value. However, there may be disadvantages:

- They often suffer from illiquidity and can be difficult to sell quickly if funds are required for other purposes.
- They can be difficult to value due to the size of the different markets.
- Prices can change rapidly as markets are subject to trends and fashions. The art and antiques markets, for example, can be very volatile and are specialist areas.
- These objects rarely generate income (unless they can be hired out to museums and the like).
- Dealers' charges tend to be quite high.
- Special and secure storage may be required, again at a cost.
- There is the risk of fire, theft, damage or flood to be insured against.
- It may be hard to get a true valuation, as this may be a matter of the valuer's opinion unless and until the object comes to be sold.
- There is little or no regulation in the market for chattels.
- The item may prove to be a forgery, and next to worthless.

Alternative investments include (but are not limited to) the following:

- Jewellery.
- Antiques.
- Books.
- Art.
- Classic cars.
- Autographs.
- Posters.
- Coins.
- Stamps.
- Comic books.
- Toys (which can eventually be worth four to five times more than their original price, if they are in good condition and in the original packaging).
- Racehorses.
- Fine wine.
- Precious metals.
- Memorabilia (eg, commemorative items).

Alternative assets are becoming increasingly popular in the UK, and with alternative investments there is fun is choosing your items, such as works of art and items of antique furniture, which can brighten your home as well as providing a potential profit.

As well as the potential for growth, there is the pleasure to be had from owning a rare object. Investment in chattels should generally be seen as an area for specialist or wealthy investors only.

These are high-risk sectors and the value can go down as well as up, as fashions and demand change. Research and careful selection of pieces are a must.

5.1 ART

Investing in art sounds so civilised: perusing the catalogues of the country's best-known auction houses looking for a personal masterpiece, or hunting through flea markets in the hope of hidden treasures. But the world of art is not an easy one for amateurs to navigate. For one thing, it's immense, and knowing what you are looking for can be incredibly difficult, even for experts.

Getting to grips with artists, with movements, with genres and periods is one part of the problem, and becoming competent at choosing where to invest can take a very long time. And it's not just the artists you need to get to know. The subject matter is key to a painting, or indeed a photograph's, value. A brilliantly painted portrait of the artist's wife, for example, could not rival a less impressive portrait of Winston Churchill in terms of value.

Similarly, photographs of famous people, places and events will often be more saleable than more obscure, albeit attractive, scenes. Unfortunately, buying a new artist's work and hoping it will be worth more when they hit the big time cannot be directly compared with investing in a small company early and cashing in later.

Young, talented artists will often have a dealer, and that dealer will make sure the prices are set at the right level. Tactics such as driving up the bidding at auction can often make finding a bargain difficult.

Fairytale-like stories of paintings being bought at auction for next to nothing and sold on for a fortune make auctions more alluring. But not everyone is that lucky, and buying at auction is expensive, with fees to be paid to the auction house by both the buyer and seller, sometimes at up to 20% of the price. A painting will have to appreciate substantially in value if one is to make money from it.

The main trouble with investing in art is that it is very difficult to get an accurate valuation. At auction, rival bidders who want the same piece can quickly push the sale price beyond all estimations, which can clearly work in an investor's favour if they are the seller.

5.2 ANTIQUES

Antiques are among the most tangible alternative assets, and like works of art they are collected for their aesthetic appeal as much as their value. Investing in antiques, like investing in art, is a medium-to-long-term venture. The trick is to choose a style and period you like best and stick to it, because collections of similar pieces are more likely to increase in price than a mishmash of items.

Assets should be examples of fine craftsmanship and be in good condition. To maximise profit, investors should seek to acquire items that they feel may become popular in the future, rather than buying items that are already fashionable and expensive.

Indirect investment in art and antiques can be achieved by investing in businesses who operate in these markets.

5.3   PRECIOUS METALS

During times when inflation has soared, currencies have weakened, and stock markets have plummeted (such as during the current period of instability), precious metals have been seen as more attractive. The degree of their attractiveness seems to directly correspond to the level of fear in the markets.

Gold, of course, has always been regarded as intrinsically valuable, accepted internationally and negotiable. Many investment portfolios have a small percentage invested in gold. But investing in precious metals can be complex. Gold prices are dependent on the wider conditions of market for bullion. Gold prices can fluctuate due to political and international events and changes in specific countries. They are open to speculation, as well as changes in technologies involving gold, such as usage in the automobile industry. Depending on how the investor chooses to invest in gold, there may be costs of ownership too. Banks, for example, may apply holding charges for precious metals, and there are no dividends to be earned from gold investment *per se*.

Investment in precious metals is also open to fraud, with investors advised to purchase their precious metals through banks or reputable dealers. Investment in gold can catch out unwary investors, with large quantities being stolen by criminal gangs, involved in fraud or otherwise being of dubious origin or purity. Demand for gold is variable and subject to fluctuations influenced by the factors discussed above.

Because of their volatility, precious metals should represent only a small portion of an investor's portfolio. The most conservative way to go into precious metals is through a unit trust or OEIC fund. This will be professionally managed, diversified and often particularly well suited to new investors. The drawback to holding precious metals is that they increase in value only when the price per ounce goes up. By contrast, stocks and bonds can pay dividends and offer other income sources. If conditions for gold are poor, it can sit for years doing virtually nothing.

There are five principal ways to invest in gold and precious metals: tangible coins and bars; certificates; precious metals mutual funds; stock in mining companies; and gold and metals futures.

5.4   COMMODITIES

For those keen to invest in commodities, there are several options open. They can spread-bet on moves in the relevant index, although this is not for the faint-hearted as potential losses incurred are unlimited and may exceed the initial investment. They can invest in individual companies, eg, Rio Tinto, although, unless they have a lot of money to play with, they are not really going to be able to spread their risk adequately. A UK-listed collective fund specialising in natural resources or commodities may be more appropriate.

5.5 FORESTRY

During the 2007/2008 credit crisis, fund managers were looking for alternatives to plunging stock markets and a property slump. At this time forestry investment seemed to buck the trend and offered valuable opportunities to reduce risks and to underpin falling returns. The IPD reported that the UK Forestry Index returned 31.6% in 2007, compared to an annualised return of +5.3% in equities, +6.4% in bonds and −3.4% in commercial property in the year. Over the last 30 years the asset has proved to be a useful investment, as it has not only delivered diversification benefits to a conventional long-only bond/equity portfolio, but it has outperformed financial assets. Moreover, it has offered a secure hedge against rising inflationary pressures over the years by delivering higher returns in real terms.

Timber is a renewable resource, oxygenating and absorbing excess carbon dioxide from the planet. From this perspective its future role as an ecological asset is appealing. The natural product has a variety of uses ranging from firewood and carton packaging material to high-quality veneers. With developing countries manufacturing products for the global economy, timber in its various forms has continued to experience constant demand. These are not the only advantages offered by timber and forestry products as, in general, income from timber sales is free from both income and corporation tax, and the growing of timber on forestry land for commercial gains is also free from capital gains tax.

As the value of timber increases on the land supporting the forestry business, a listed share of stock of a company that owns commercial timber and land should experience an appreciation in its share prices. This is an appealing investment for discerning ethical investors who want to see more funds directed towards sustainable forestry products. Although timber is loosely connected with the environmental sector, investments are not regulated by financial authorities. Some land and plantations in the UK and abroad are approved for investment through a Self-Invested Personal Pension (SIPP).

Plantations in South Scotland delivered the highest return in 2009, at 21.0%, as well as over the three, five and 18 years to 2009, returning 20.9%, 20.6% and 7.7%, respectively.

There is a distinction between forestry or timber land and timber. Timber is grown on the land and is sold and renewed with three components making up the value of the timber product sold: yield of wood per acreage; size and quality of trees; and the market price of the species of forest products.

The land on which the timber is grown clearly affects the product quality. Substantial price differences can occur by geographic region and climatic factors that produce the timber. Finally, management competence and strategies can impact greatly on returns. The price of timber is a function of the relative size of the trees grown on the land. Small trees provide the lowest prices because they are useful mainly only for firewood or paper pulp, while slightly larger trees can be used for small carpentry products or furniture. As trees get much larger they can be used for sawn timber and planks that provide much higher prices to a supplier. The largest trees are in the veneer class and are used for high-quality furniture applications.

Forestry product risks can be classified into biological and economic risks. Biological risks are losses due to natural events. Disease and insect damage are usually uninsurable, as is fire, drought and windstorm damage. Fortunately, such risks are mitigated by good land management practices. Management risk can be exacerbated by poor management practice and can seriously erode the value of timber. The non-fungible character and the long lead time required to grow the trees can generate liquidity risk or shortages for some types of timber.

Despite these risks, forestry investment is set to grow further as it allows portfolio managers opportunities to reduce their portfolio risks. Pension funds looking to fill the pension fund gap are expected to invest more in this asset class. The correlation benefits are clearly there and have been demonstrated in a number of US studies of timberland prices over the period from 1960–2002. These results show that correlations between timberland and financial assets are close to zero or negative. The correlations are also negative with the stock markets.

6. CORRELATION OF ASSET CLASSES

LEARNING OBJECTIVE

1.6.1   Analyse combinations of asset classes based on: historical returns; index and benchmark comparisons; correlation of performance between asset classes; advantages and limitations of relying on historical data

6.1 DIVERSIFICATION AND CORRELATION

Correlation is a measure of how the returns from two different assets move together over time, and is scaled between +1 and −1. Assets with a high level of correlation (close to 1) tend to move in the same direction at the same time. Assets with a low correlation (close to 0) tend to move independently of each other. Assets with strong negative correlations (close to −1) tend to move in opposite directions.

Diversification and risk reduction is achieved by combining assets whose returns have not moved in perfect step, or are not perfectly positively correlated with one another.

Only when returns are perfectly negatively correlated, in that they move in the opposite direction to one another at all times and in the same proportion, can they be combined to produce a risk-free return. Where there is zero or imperfect correlation, there are still diversification benefits from combining securities that give this result. In fact, a perfectly positive correlation, when security returns move in the same direction and in perfect step with each other, is the only instance when diversification benefits cannot be achieved. It should be noted, however, that correlations can arise from pure chance and so past correlation coefficients of investment returns are rarely a perfect guide to the future.

In modern portfolio theory, combining securities into a diversified portfolio means that the overall risk will be less than the risk inherent in holding any one individual stock and so reduces the combined variability of future returns.

6.2 ASSET CLASS CORRELATION

Assets with a low or negative correlation are attractive to investors, in that when one asset is performing badly, the other asset is hopefully rising in value.

Asset classes are an important concept for all investors to consider. Each asset class is differentiated by three factors that characterise its investment performance. These are the:

* historic level of return that the asset class has delivered;
* historic level of risk that the asset class has experienced;
* level of correlation between the investment performance of each asset class.

Each asset class has a different level of risk and return. They may also have a low level of correlation to each other. Investors can use these differences to consider how likely their investments are to meet their objectives and appetite for risk. It can be possible to even out investment performance over time, by spreading investments across different asset classes.

For example, returns from **UK equities** and **overseas equity markets** are highly correlated, reflecting the increasing globalisation of equity markets. While investors may look to invest overseas to gain exposure to different industries and companies, most major equity markets now rise and fall together in response to global news.

Cash and property are negatively correlated. At times when interest rates are high and returns on cash deposit accounts become more attractive, property investors will be hit by the increased cost of borrowing.

For many years, the only three generally recognised asset classes were cash, equities and gilts. In recent years there has been a general trend to recognise a range of alternative asset classes that show particular and different investment performance. However, many of these asset classes are either esoteric or not open to most investors. In parallel, **property** has become recognised over the past 20 or 30 years as showing alternative characteristics to the three historic asset classes. As property has gained in popularity, it has become recognised as a core asset class in its own right. Recent events in the sector have diminished this.

The table below shows the correlation of returns between the major asset classes over the 20-year period from 1988 to 2007.

	UK Equities	Overseas Equities	Property	Fixed Interest Gilts	Index Linked Gilts	Cash
UK Equities						
Overseas Equities (unhedged)	0.87					
Property	0.29	0.44				
Fixed Interest Gilts	0.41	0.35	0.08			
Index Linked Gilts	0.55	0.50	0.21	0.84		
Cash	0.16	0.03	−0.36	0.15	0.19	

6.3　HISTORICAL ASSET CLASS RETURNS

Historical Returns from Different Asset Classes

Year	UK Equities %	Overseas Equities %	Commercial Property %	Fixed Interest Gilts %	Index-Linked Gilts %	Corporate Bonds %	Cash %	RPI %
1988	11.5	30.6	29.5	9.4	13.5		10.1	6.8
1989	36.1	31.1	15.4	5.7	15.2		14.1	7.7
1990	−9.7	−33.1	−8.4	4.2	3.5		15.5	9.3
1991	20.8	23.2	−3.1	18.6	4.4		12.2	4.5
1992	20.5	16.3	−1.6	17.0	17.5		9.8	2.6
1993	28.4	24.9	20.2	34.4	23.0		5.9	1.9
1994	−5.8	0.6	11.9	−12.2	−9.1		5.1	2.9
1995	23.9	19.7	3.6	17.4	12.9		6.4	3.2
1996	16.7	1.1	10.0	9.0	6.4		6.0	2.5
1997	23.6	19.0	16.8	22.9	13.7		6.6	3.6
1998	13.8	22.0	11.8	29.6	19.9	14.8	7.2	2.8
1999	24.2	31.0	14.5	−0.4	4.4	−0.2	5.2	1.8
2000	−5.9	−4.1	10.5	8.0	4.2	10.2	5.7	2.9
2001	−13.3	−14.2	6.8	−0.9	−0.5	6.9	4.8	0.7
2002	−22.7	−27.5	9.6	9.9	8.2	9.5	3.7	2.9
2003	20.9	20.3	10.9	1.2	6.6	5.7	3.5	2.8
2004	12.8	7.5	18.3	8.4	8.5	6.7	4.3	3.5
2005	22.0	24.6	19.1	11.0	9.0	9.0	4.6	2.2
2006	16.8	5.5	18.1	0.0	2.9	0.8	4.6	4.4
2007	5.3	9.7	−3.4	2.7	8.5	1.8	5.6	4.0
Return (%pa)								
10 years	6.2	5.9	11.4	6.6	7.1	6.4	4.9	2.8
20 years	10.9	8.7	10.1	9.3	8.4		7.0	3.6
Volatility/Risk (%pa)								
10 years	16.2	18.4	6.7	9.2	5.4	4.7	1.1	1.1
20 years	15.6	18.7	9.4	11.1	7.4		3.5	2.1

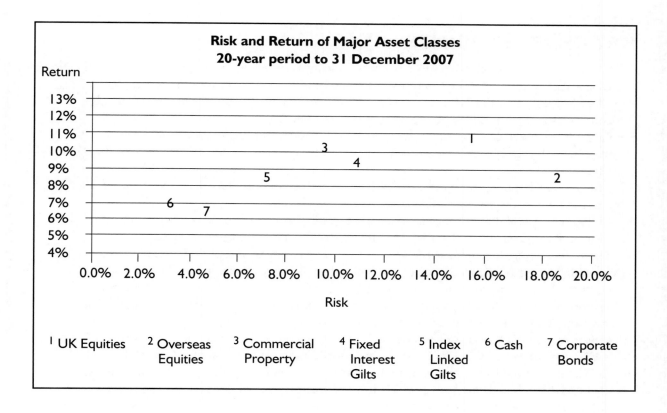

Risk and Return of Major Asset Classes
20-year period to 31 December 2007

¹ UK Equities	² Overseas Equities	³ Commercial Property	⁴ Fixed Interest Gilts	⁵ Index Linked Gilts	⁶ Cash	⁷ Corporate Bonds

6.4   ADVANTAGES AND LIMITATIONS OF HISTORICAL DATA

Historical data can be useful when considering the performance of the individual asset classes during the construction of an investment portfolio. Correlation and volatility experienced by each asset class can be considered at different moments in time, when various economic conditions persist. This enables the investment manager to form a view as to how a particular investment strategy may respond if similar conditions are experienced in the future.

However, there can be no certainty that the same outcome will be experienced if those economic conditions are repeated in the future. Past performance is only ever a guide.

KEY CHAPTER POINTS

- Fixed-interest securities carry more risk than holding money in a deposit account because their capital value varies. Changes in interest rates and other economic factors can affect bond prices.
- Fixed-interest securities include those issued by governments (called gilts in the UK) and by companies and other corporate bodies (corporate bonds).
- Bonds from lower-quality issuers (companies with poor credit ratings) will have higher yields than those from higher-quality issuers (such as governments), reflecting the different levels of default risk.
- If held to redemption, the investment cash flows of fixed-interest securities are known, assuming that the bond issuer does not default.
- Ordinary shares and preference shares differ in their dividend rights, in the rights they give over control of the company and in their priority of entitlement to assets on a liquidation.
- There are risks in holding shares; investors should be willing to accept total loss of capital. Diversification can help to reduce the risk, but equities are not suitable for all investors.
- Futures and options are derivatives which allow various sophisticated investment and risk-hedging strategies to be implemented. Many people participate in equity investment through pooled investment schemes such as unit trusts, OEICs and investment trusts.
- Unit trusts and OEICs are open-ended collective investments, and so their price closely reflects the underlying net asset value. OEICs are Investment Companies with Variable Capital (ICVCs).
- Unit trust and OEIC investments carry the risks of their underlying investment class – for example, equities or bonds – but provide a vehicle for diversification within asset classes and sectors.
- Buy-to-let is a form of direct investment in residential property. Returns can vary widely between different regions and timescales.
- Property should be selected with care. All costs and possible void periods should be fully evaluated.
- Most property investors invest for capital gains, but gearing means that a downturn in the market could affect equity severely.
- Commercial property is a different market and some exposure may be considered by investors seeking to diversify across various asset classes.
- Indirect or pooled investment in property allows relatively small sums to be invested in a diversified portfolio of properties and there is much more liquidity than with direct investment.
- Life assurance companies offer a range of policies known as 'bonds', which can provide investment returns as well as insurance benefits. These include unit-linked policies and with-profits bonds.
- Offshore life companies also offer a similar range; in addition, some offer portfolio bonds – where the policyholder can tailor the investments to which his benefits are linked – and capital redemption bonds, where there is no life assured.
- A variety of specialist investments, such as collectables, can prove rewarding but are higher-risk, often illiquid or hard to value, and usually only suitable for experts.

CHAPTER TWO

THE MACRO-ECONOMIC ENVIRONMENT

This syllabus area will provide approximately 6 of the 80 examination questions

1. LONG-TERM GLOBAL DEMOGRAPHIC TRENDS

LEARNING OBJECTIVES

2.1.1   Understand the main long-term global trends and the effects of technological changes/advancements: ageing population; rising living standards; access to education; growth of the service sector; changing patterns of the economy; productivity of capital and labour; wealth and income distribution

1.1   INTRODUCTION

We will begin by considering a variety of features relating to the UK population – predominantly, social, demographic and economic factors. These are, of course, interrelated, and the reason that we begin with them is to help us understand people's investment needs, which result from the socio-economic environment in which they live, and the trends that they may be subject to.

The term 'demography' means the study of populations using statistics, based on numbers collected through census returns and other surveys. In the UK, a full census of the population is carried out every ten years. The latest took place in 2011. The UK government originally conducted its census as a simple head-count of the population; however, more recently, additional information about the population has been obtained.

The UK government publishes various statistics every year. Two examples are:

* the Annual Abstract of Statistics; and
* Social Trends.

Both contain information on the population as a whole, but Social Trends goes into more detail about the way people live. Summary census information can also be viewed at www.statistics.gov.uk (as can the entire texts, both of the Annual Abstract and of Social Trends). Some data comparisons from the past and projections into the future are given in the comments below (source: www.statistics.gov.uk).

The statistics cited may appear to be somewhat out of date, but at the time of drafting were the most up to date available. This highlights the difficulty in collecting, collating and analysing demographic data for an entire population.

1.2   POPULATION SIZE

The population of the UK as a whole grew significantly during the 20th century, but this growth is expected to level off during the 21st century.

In every year since 1901 (with one exception – 1976) there were more births than deaths. Until the mid-1990s, this natural increase was the main driver of population growth. Since the late 1990s, there has been a continuing natural increase, but net international migration from other countries has also been an increasingly important factor. The increase is projected to continue – and in the year to mid-2005 there was the biggest annual increase since 1962. In the main it was attributable to immigration from other countries.

1.3   AGE STRUCTURE AND THE AGEING POPULATION

As seen above, the population of the UK is growing in size, but it is also becoming increasingly older. 'Ageing' refers both to the ageing of the population and the increasing number of people reaching older age. Over the period 1983 to 2008 the number of people aged 65 and over in the UK increased by 18% to 9.9 million, the number of people aged 85 and over doubled to 1.3 million, and the percentage aged under 16 fell from 21% to 19%. In 1983 women and men had median ages of 36 and 33 years respectively, a difference of three years. The difference in median ages for women and men decreased to two years in 2008 and is projected to remain at this level until 2033.

Population ageing will continue for the next few decades. By 2033 the number of people aged 85 and over is projected to reach 3.2 million and represent 4% of the total population, and the population aged 65 and over will account for 22% of the total population, while the proportion of the population aged between 16 and 64 is due to fall from 65% to 59%.

The age structure of the population is of particular interest to the government (for planning) and to businesses. This is because people make different contributions to the economy, or are more burdensome to it, at different stages in their lives.

In past decades, age structure depended chiefly on birth rates and death rates: not only, of course, on the current birth rate, but also on that of previous years. For example, there was an increase in the number of births immediately following the Second World War and another, as these baby boomers themselves had children, in the 1960s. In very recent years it has also been increasingly affected by net immigration figures. Since people do not tend to be as geographically mobile in their later years and the majority of people moving to the UK are of working age, we may see some changes to the ageing trends (though perhaps not enough to reverse them) in the coming years.

The effect of greater life expectancy is that a larger proportion of the population will be senior citizens (65 years or over) and unlikely to be working, although the normal retirement age is being increased gradually, so that there will be more people carrying on in work past the age of 65. This trend is offset, but only to an extent, by the number of younger immigrants moving to the UK.

1.3.1 The Implications of an Ageing Population

Generally, it is the working population that has the burden of generating a country's economic wealth. As a greater proportion of the population reaches retirement, the percentage that is working will fall. Thus, the percentage of people who are not in employment – and who are therefore dependent on the working population – will be higher than in earlier times.

The same could, of course, be true in a country where there was a high percentage of people who were so young as to be below working age.

These factors place an extra burden on the working population, which must pay, through taxes, for expenditure on:

- state-funded old age pensions;
- state-funded health care provision;
- state education and training of the young or out-of-work.

In the UK, while the working population as a percentage of the total population has been fairly constant, there has been a shift in the relative proportion of elderly to young dependants. This has been occurring since 1961 and continued into the 1990s. This long-term shift is important for the following reasons:

- Elderly dependants have different needs (for long-term health provision, for example) from younger people, whose main requirements from the state are for education. Planners must take this into account when allocating resources for social provision.
- The elderly, as a market segment, are becoming increasingly dominant. For this category of the population, retirement planning is a key concern.
- The falling numbers of young people will mean that organisations might have to change their recruitment policies or production methods. There will be fewer people of what is currently regarded as working age, and employers will have to compete for them.

1.4 OTHER IMPORTANT DEMOGRAPHIC AND SOCIAL CHANGES

Demographic information is also used to map the social units in which people live (eg, family size). Some trends in the UK are as follows:

- Between 1971 and 2007, the number of households in Great Britain rose by 5.8 million to 24.4 million.
- In Great Britain in 2007 the proportion of people living alone (12%) was double that of 1971.
- In 2005 there were just under 284,000 marriages in the UK, around 27,000 fewer than in 2004, and 197,000 fewer than in 1972, when the number of marriages peaked at 480,000.
- Over the last 20 years, the proportion of unmarried men and women aged under 60 cohabiting in Great Britain rose from 11% of men and 13% of women to 24% and 25% respectively.
- One in ten men and one in four women forming a civil partnership in the UK in 2006 had been in a previous legal partnership, in nearly all cases a marriage.
- Married women giving birth for the first time were, on average, age 30 in England and Wales in 2006, compared with age 24 in 1971.

1.5 THE EFFECTS OF CHANGING DEMOGRAPHICS ON THE FINANCIAL LIFE CYCLE

The financial life cycle is a concept that is used when considering what people's financial needs might typically be at various stages in their lives. Although not everyone's life follows this pattern, many people's do – so it can be a useful tool for predicting what products and services will be in most demand as the population's demographic (in terms of age) changes.

Particular products and services can be target-marketed at people who occupy specific stages in the cycle. For example, the following stages might be identified:

- **Childhood** – characterised by dependence for most needs on adult carers. Financial needs are usually few, though a child may have a need for a savings account, and perhaps a cashpoint card.
- **Single young adulthood** – usually at this stage, the person is either in further education or in their first job. Income may still be relatively low, but the individual may also have few financial commitments as yet and a reasonable amount of disposable income. The thought of saving for the future may not be a high priority.
- **Young couple, no children** – at this stage there may be two incomes coming into the household and, with no children, again no major financial commitments. However if the couple are attempting to get on the property ladder, then saving for a deposit will be a priority: if they have already bought, then the right mortgage will be important.
- **Parents with dependent children** – usually in a couple, but, as we have seen, lone parents are becoming increasingly common. At this stage, disposable income is likely to fall: in addition the parent(s) may have less time for leisure activities. Saving for a larger property or for school fees may be a priority.
- **Empty-nesters** – this is the term used for parents whose children have left home and are independent. Such people may suddenly find that they have more disposable income than they have had for a long time. In addition, their careers may be well advanced so that their incomes are reasonably high, and if they are fortunate they may also have paid off a large proportion of their mortgages and be living in a property which has increased in value. However, for many this stage has not been so easy – their property may have fallen in value, and because of the difficulty of getting on the property ladder their adult children may still be living at home!
- **Retired** – an increasing proportion of the population, as we have seen. Retirees who have been in employment or otherwise managed to save for much of their lives may have accumulated a reasonable amount of capital; in addition, if they are homeowners, they may have capital locked up in the value of their homes. Their financial needs may centre on ensuring that this capital generates enough income for them to live on; on provision of long-term care when their health is not so good; and perhaps on how they may best leave any surplus assets to their intended beneficiaries on death.

This traditional pattern is, however, changing – for a variety of reasons:

- Our empty-nesters may find that, rather than caring for their children, they are now caring for their elderly parents – which places an additional financial and time burden on them. This pattern is likely to continue, and indeed increase, as the population ages.
- The increasing longevity of people means that the issue of paying for care into old age is gaining in importance – especially if the adult children of the elderly population are unwilling or unable to shoulder this burden.

- Affordability issues – brought about by the fact that wage inflation has not kept pace with house price inflation – means that many people who would in earlier decades have been on the housing ladder are now renting or – increasingly – remaining in the family home until well into adulthood. This means that would-be empty-nesters may, in some cases, have both their own parents and their adult children living with them.

1.6 EARNINGS GROWTH AND RISING LIVING STANDARDS

In the early years of the 21st century, growth in earnings for the UK has been more subdued relative to the late 1990s. For example, the Average Earnings Index grew by 3.8% in 2002 and 3.1% during 2001, compared with 5.5% for 1999 and 4.5% for 2000. However in the year to December 2008 it had reduced to 3.2%.

Growth in earnings can vary widely between sectors. 2001/02 was the first sustained period since 1993 in which public sector (government) employees' earnings growth was higher than that of the private sector. Since then, private sector earnings growth has outstripped public sector earnings growth in some, but not all, years.

In considering trends in household income over time, it is important to strip out the effects of inflation to establish the change in 'real' incomes. If people's real incomes are increasing and the population is more or less stable, this increase in real incomes is reflected in growth in national output.

As real incomes rise, in periods of economic growth, people can buy more goods and services. Their living standards – in an economic sense, at least – are rising. During a recession (the definition of which we will look at in Section 4), living standards are likely to fall. Of course, even in a recession there will be some whose incomes increase, although the overall impact will be a loss in living standards.

1.7 CHANGING PATTERNS OF THE ECONOMY

A distinction can be made between the primary, secondary and tertiary sectors of the economy. As we will see, these sectors can change in importance over time:

- The **primary sector** of the economy consists of industries that **produce** raw materials such as crops and minerals. These are sometimes called extractive industries. Over the long term, this is a shrinking sector in the UK.
- The **secondary sector** consists of industries that **process** raw materials – largely, the manufacturing industry. This sector normally grows rapidly during the early stages of economic development. In the UK, this is also in decline – mainly due to falling manufacturing (the part of the sector most heavily involved in international trade), as opposed to construction, energy and water. The decline in the secondary sector has led to falling employment in this area. This has created some severe unemployment problems in regions which were previously heavily dependent on particular industries.
- The **tertiary sector** is made up mainly of goods **distribution and service industries**. It is often referred to as the service sector of the economy. This sector has become the predominant provider of employment and output in the UK economy. A major reason for the continuing growth in this sector has been the rapid expansion in the banking, finance and insurance sectors, many of which are well placed to capitalise on recent technological advances (see Section 1.10).

1.7.1 Growth of the Service Sector

Within the tertiary (service) sector, the rising share of banking, finance and insurance reflects a number of factors:

- London has built on its reputation as one of the leading financial centres of the world and in many areas (for example, currency trading) it is pre-eminent, despite increasing competition from other centres. The strong position of the City (the London financial community) makes it a large exporter of financial services.
- Increasing affluence and changing social factors (eg, increasing levels of owner-occupation of housing) have increased domestic demand for financial products of various kinds (eg, current accounts, mortgages and insurance products).
- Events such as the abolition of exchange controls in 1979 and the deregulation of financial markets during the 1980s served to widen supply as well as intensify competition in this subsector.

1.8 PRODUCTIVITY

Economists identify four factors of production in the economy: land, labour, capital (ie, machinery and plant) and enterprise. These factors are combined in various ways, in order to produce goods and services.

Productivity is a measure of the efficiency with which factors of production are used. It can be calculated as the total output divided by the number of units of a factor of production, for example, the number of persons employed (to measure the productivity of labour) or the number or value of machines used (to measure the productivity of capital).

Substitution between factors of production (for example, between labour and capital) may take place if it is feasible; for example, machines can be made to do work previously carried out by labour, or people can provide labour to do work that would otherwise be done by machines. It is most likely when the price or productivity of one factor of production rises relative to another. If wages go up, the marginal cost of labour will rise and firms will want less labour at this higher cost. Labour will also become more expensive in relation to capital, and there will be some substitution of capital for labour. The net result of an increase in wages will be a reduction in the quantity of labour employed, unless the productivity of labour can be increased at the same time, to strengthen the demand for labour.

Increases in productivity create greater economic wealth and boost real household incomes. By producing more with the country's factors of production, there are more goods and services available for people to use and consume.

In general, the service sector has higher profitability than the manufacturing sector; this reflects the fact that the manufacturing sector is more capital-intensive and so involves more capital expenditure on fixed assets.

1.9 WEALTH AND INCOME DISTRIBUTION

Wealth is not evenly distributed throughout households in the UK: roughly speaking, the top fifth of households are some four times better off, in income terms, than the bottom fifth.

In 2005/06, the **original income** (that is, income like wages and pensions – before allowing for taxes and benefits) of the top fifth of households in the UK was fifteen times greater than that for the bottom fifth (£72,900 per household per year compared with £4,900). However, after this had been redistributed through taxes and benefits, the ratio came down to four-to-one (an average final income of £52,400 compared with £14,400).

The Office of National Statistics points out that some types of household gain more than others from the redistribution of income through tax and benefits. For example:

- retired households pay less in tax than they receive in benefits and so gain overall;
- of non-retired households, single adult households with children also gain;
- most other non-retired households pay more in tax than they receive in benefits;
- however, households with children do relatively better than households without children due to the cash benefits and benefits in kind (including health and education services) which are received by these households.

Cash benefits like Income Support, Pension Credit, Child Benefit, Incapacity Benefit and the State Retirement Pension play a big part in reducing income inequality, as they are paid mainly to households with lower incomes. Cash benefits make up 57% of gross income for the poorest fifth of households, 38% for the next group, falling to 2% for the top fifth of households.

Income can be related to occupational groupings; for example, nearly half of the households in the richest 20% by income are headed by people in professional or managerial occupations.

Wealth – the amount in assets that people have – is also related to social structure. In the UK, a large proportion of wealth is held as property, and so increases or falls in property prices can affect wealth significantly. According to data from HM Revenue & Customs (HMRC), in 2003 1% of the population owned some 21% of the country's wealth. The results are even more skewed if housing is excluded from the estimates, suggesting that house ownership helps even up the distribution of wealth in the UK.

Wealth is considerably less evenly distributed than income, and family/personal life cycle effects tend to ensure that this keeps on being the case. Overall, people tend to build up assets during their working lives (with some blips if they raise children) and then draw them down during the years of retirement, leaving anything left over to others when they die.

1.10   TECHNOLOGICAL CHANGES AND ADVANCES

The development of new technology is behind many of the increases in productivity that have helped create economic growth. New technologies can produce significant leaps forward in economic conditions.

For example, the dawn of mass production made possible by the Industrial Revolution of the late 18th century was fuelled by technological advances – specifically, in the spinning of cotton and the development of steam power. Electrification and the development of motorised transport were further major technological changes.

More recently, computerisation has made major changes to the economy and to how businesses organise their operations. **Interconnectedness**, by way of the internet and advanced telecommunications, is having a further effect in terms of how information and data are transmitted, how businesses and people communicate and how, when and where people work.

The availability of fast and efficient telecommunications enables a shift to new ways of employing staff resources and of reaching customers. In the past, workers may have had to relocate to where employers delivered their services. Now, a bank, for example, may outsource many staff functions involving communication with customers to overseas centres; extensive branch networks have become a thing of the past for many financial services companies, and many functions have been centralised.

2. GLOBAL TRENDS AND THEIR IMPACTS

LEARNING OBJECTIVE

2.1.2   Understand the impact of the following on global trades and asset classes: international markets; globalisation of business and finance; market failures

So far, we have thought about the effects of various local factors, such as demographics, on the UK economy. But a country's economy does not exist in isolation; it is also affected by what is happening in the rest of the world. In many ways the effect of world events on countries' local economies and social environments is increasing; we call this effect **globalisation**.

2.1   INTERNATIONAL MARKETS

The financial markets in the UK are regarded by many as the main world markets for dealing in a variety of assets such as securities and derivatives: equities, warrants, fixed income, currencies, money markets, contracts for difference (CFDs), options, futures, and other linked investment products. But these UK-based markets face stiff competition from other financial centres, which try to compete for international business by introducing innovative financial instruments, ensuring speedier or more secure settlement, or making dealing cheaper and quicker. However, as competition can improve efficiency and global education, we should regard this as a positive outlook in the long term.

In addition to these longer-term considerations, financial markets in the UK are affected on a daily basis by what is going on overseas. Just as events in other countries affect the UK economy, so they do the UK stock market. Rates of growth in the rest of the world are especially important for economies (like the UK's) that have a large foreign trade sector. If trading partners have slow growth, the amount of exports a country can sell to them will grow only slowly. This limits the country's own opportunities for investment and growth.

Different national economies may be at different stages of the business cycle at any one time. However, with increasing globalisation of trade and investment, there is a tendency for their economic cycles to become increasingly **correlated** (tied in with one another). In particular, the large size and economic wealth of the economy of the US exerts a significant influence on the economies of other countries, particularly its major trading partners such as the UK.

The importance of the US in the world economy means that investment markets, such as equity and bond markets, often react most closely to what is happening in the economy and markets of the US. If there is an economic recovery in the US, it is anticipated that this recovery will soon affect other economies, as US consumers and companies will demand more goods and services available on world markets. The stimulus to other countries will have knock-on effects in those countries as companies' earnings are boosted and employment rises.

To summarise:

- The price of assets dealt in on UK markets is affected by events on foreign markets. If events in the US mean that its stock market falls sharply, then other world markets invariably suffer as a result. (As the old adage has it, if the US stock market sneezes, the whole world catches a cold.) A good example of this was seen in the immediate aftermath of the 9/11 terrorist attacks. Shares in the US plummeted and were quickly followed down by shares on other markets, to such an extent that most markets were suspended until orderly trading could be restored.
- Many multinational companies have their shares traded on more than one stock market. Events affecting the shares in one place will affect the prices at which they are quoted on others, through arbitrage activity. Arbitrage is activity which aims to take advantage of the different prices at which an asset might be traded on different markets; it has the effect of bringing those prices back into balance.
- Many companies quoted on the London Stock Exchange have operations around the world – so economic events in other countries affect their value and profitability.
- Events affecting other countries' currencies can (as we will see in Section 5.9) have a significant effect on UK markets, through the economy and interest rates.

Because of these and similar factors, the wealth of UK people and businesses, which is tied up in shares or other investments, can be affected by what is happening in the international markets.

As well as monitoring the growth of individual economies, we can measure growth and output for larger regions – and, indeed, for the world as a whole. The International Monetary Fund (IMF) publishes a *World Economic Outlook* twice a year.

2.2 GLOBALISATION OF BUSINESS AND FINANCE

In terms of business and finance, the term 'globalisation' tends to be used in several ways.

- It is often used to describe the increasingly interrelated and interconnected nature of business and financial systems. Businesses which were once essentially local now increasingly cross borders: banks offer services to people and businesses in many different countries; and businesses find their raw materials, and sell to customers, much farther afield than used to be the case.
- It is also used to describe the way in which various things (products, processes and, in some cases, lifestyles) are becoming more similar around the world – as people and businesses become more mobile, taking their ways of doing things with them, and as international standards are established to make it easier for international trade and activity to take place.

You can probably think of some examples pretty easily: McDonald's is a good example of a retail business which provides a pretty similar consumer experience, wherever you are in the world; and there are few countries without a McDonald's. In the world of finance, HSBC (which provides banking, investment and a host of other services) has some 7,500 offices in 87 countries and describes itself as 'the world's local bank'; perhaps in an attempt to show that, while it may be truly global, it also makes an effort to reflect local business practices wherever it operates. A customer of HSBC, or any other global banking organisation, could probably move from one country to another without having to change the banking group with which he/it dealt.

The pace at which trade and finance becomes globalised, and the rate of flow of goods, services and money around the world as a consequence, has also been helped by the efforts of governments and many multinational organisations such as the World Trade Organisation (WTO) and the Organisation for Economic Co-operation and Development (OECD).

- The **WTO** deals with the rules of trade between different nations and among its aims are the liberalisation of trade laws between countries. It provides a forum in which governments can negotiate the basis on which their countries will trade with one another.
- The **OECD** describes itself as 'an international organisation helping governments tackle the economic, social and governance challenges of a globalised economy'. Among other things, it aims to help contribute to world trade, and to support sustainable economic world growth.

Another international forum working on liberalising trade, this time within a specific block of countries, is the European Union (EU), which is covered in Section 2.3.

Globalisation is seen by some as good (for example, where it enables poorer countries to participate in international trade) and by others as bad (for example, where it results in the loss of national identities and an increasingly homogeneous world – or where it results in the rise of huge multinationals, which are so big that they are seen as being beyond the control of governments and regulators). Whatever your view, it is an increasing fact of life.

2.2.1 Impacts of Technology

We have already noted that technology has had a huge impact on the way businesses interact, and on how profitable they are. A number of issues arise from this, in the context of global dynamics:

- As we have seen in Section 1.10, some businesses – including financial services firms – have found that they can outsource or 'offshore' certain activities (typically call centres and computer programming) to countries where appropriately skilled labour is cheaper, such as India.
- For some types of businesses – including in financial services – the internet has been a key factor in this development; it is easy for buyers and sellers to find one another, and electronic communications – coupled with increasing clarity on the law regarding electronically concluded agreements – has speeded up the pace at which they can do business across borders.
- Where one country has access to new technologies which have not yet been adopted, or cannot be afforded, in another, it can give the first country a significant economic advantage.

2.3   EUROPEAN ECONOMIC AND MONETARY UNION

The European Union (EU), initially called the European Economic Community (EEC), was set up after the Second World War, with the aim of integrating the various countries and helping them rebuild their economies. The process of European integration was launched on 9 May 1950, when France officially proposed to create 'the first concrete foundation of a European federation'.

Six countries (Belgium, Germany, France, Italy, Luxembourg and the Netherlands) joined from the very beginning. Today, after several waves of accession, the EU has 27 member states.

The EU works towards **single European markets** in various trade sectors, finance being one of the most important. The aim is to remove barriers to international trade by, among other things, ensuring that similar regulatory rules are in place throughout the EU. From a financial services perspective this should mean that, in terms of investor protection, it makes no difference to a customer whether he buys a financial product from a provider in his home state, or from a neighbouring state.

Many of the measures by which the EU is working towards this come under an initiative called the Financial Services Action Plan, which aims to introduce similar laws and regulations in various areas of financial services. Many of these are already in place, and the UK itself has implemented a number of them. This means that it is easier for UK financial services firms to sell their products into Europe – but also that it is easier for EU firms to sell their products into the UK (meaning more local competition for UK firms).

A further aim of the EU is to achieve monetary union across as many member countries as is possible, through the process of substituting the euro for their existing home currency. Countries have to satisfy certain economic conditions before they can do so, but many believe that the benefits of meeting those conditions are worthwhile. To date the UK has not joined, and there is much debate about whether it would be good for the economy as a whole, and for the financial industry in particular. This has been tempered by recent events as some peripheral members of the Eurozone have sought bailouts from EU member states and the International Monetary Fund (IMF).

The impact of joining the euro is different for different participants in the economy. For example, some individuals may perceive the main impact as being that they do not need to exchange sterling for euros when they travel to EU states on holiday. On the other hand, businesses may find that their exchange rate risks are reduced if they buy raw materials from Europe, or sell goods and services to Europe.

Those in favour of joining the euro say it would be good for the economy because:

- it would make it easier for UK companies to trade with their European partners, because exchange rate risk would no longer be a factor in each deal; everyone would be buying and selling in euros;
- this would boost trade both for those businesses buying raw materials from Europe and those selling goods or services into Europe;
- there would be less likelihood of volatility in exchange rates and also in interest rates – which would give stability and help businesses and government plan for the future;
- generally, the euro seems so far to be associated with steady and low inflation, which is regarded as good for an economy;
- a stronger sense of European identity would be good for Britain as a whole and joining the euro would help with this;

- the pound sterling is not, in any case, a particularly major currency any longer, given the importance of the US dollar and the euro;
- the UK is part of the EU, and to join the euro would make it more properly a member of the 'euro-club'.

Those against argue that:

- in giving up sterling for the euro, the UK would be giving away important aspects of the control of its own economy: for example, domestic interest rates would no longer be set by the Bank of England, but by the European Central Bank – and so a key tool in influencing inflation and other aspects of the economy would be lost. In effect, only fiscal measures (taxes and government spending) would be left – and these tools can take much longer to affect economic activity than can changes to interest rates;
- if the euro collapsed because of problems in other EU countries, the UK would suffer along with them;
- the UK might end up supporting the economies of weaker EU countries;
- the British public is sentimentally attached to the pound sterling and would not support such a move.

2.4 MARKET FAILURE

Market failure occurs when freely functioning markets fail to deliver an optimum allocation of resources. This prevents equilibrium – a situation where demand for products and services does not equate to the quantity supplied and, as a result, economic and social welfare may not be maximised and eventually lead to economic inefficiencies. Under such circumstances, there is a clear economic case for government intervention in markets that is required to redress the economic balance and to restore equilibrium.

Government can justify their interventionist policies by stating that they are acting in the best interests of the public when markets cannot achieve market efficiency. This is especially true if, for example, there is a Pareto sub-optimal allocation of resources in a market/industry.

The main causes of market failure are as follows.

Externalities

This is where private and social costs and/or benefits diverge. The social optimum output or level of consumption diverges from the private optimum. They are defined as third party (or spill-over) effects arising from the production and/or consumption of goods and services for which no appropriate compensation is paid. Externalities can cause market failure if the price mechanism does not take into account the full social costs and social benefits of production and consumption.

Public Goods

The characteristics of pure public goods are the opposite of private goods. In fact, most are services rather than goods. These services are clearly in demand but must be provided collectively by the government for two main reasons:

- **Non-excludability** – goods cannot only be confined to those who have paid for them. However, there is always the problem that non-payers can take a free ride and enjoy the benefits of consumption of the goods.
- **Non-rivalry in consumption** – consumption by one person does not reduce the availability of the same goods to others.

Some examples of public goods/services include police services, flood defence systems, street lighting, public parks and beaches and national defence. Public goods are not normally provided by the private sector in an economy and because of their nature, the private sector is unlikely to be willing and able to provide public goods. The government therefore provides them for collective consumption and finances them through general taxation.

Merit Goods

Merit goods are those goods and services, the provision of which the government regards as necessary to avoid under-consumption. The government feels obliged, therefore, to subsidise or provide the good/service free at the point of use.

Both the public and private sector of the economy can provide merit goods and services. Consumption of merit goods is thought to generate positive externality effects where the social benefit from consumption exceeds the private benefit (for example, health services, education, work training, public libraries, citizen's advice, inoculations).

Monopoly

Agents operating in a market can gain market power, allowing them to prevent other mutually beneficial gains from trades occurring. This can lead to inefficiency due to imperfect competition. Agents may artificially fix prices higher and moderate output when compared to free-functioning competitive markets where there are many suppliers.

Inequality

Market failure can also be caused by the existence of inequality throughout the economy. Wide differences in income and wealth between different groups within the economy can lead to a wide gap in living standards between affluent households and those experiencing poverty. Society may come to the view that too much inequality is unacceptable or undesirable.

In this case, the government may decide to intervene to reduce inequality through changes to the tax and benefits system and also specific policies such as the national minimum wage.

Government intervention may seek to correct the distortions created by market failure and to improve the efficiency in the way that markets operate as follows:

- pollution taxes to correct for externalities;
- taxation of monopoly profits (the windfall tax);
- regulation of oligopolies/cartel behaviour;
- direct provision of public goods (defence);
- policies to introduce competition into markets (de-regulation);
- price controls for the recently privatised utilities.

3. NATIONAL INCOME

3.1 NATIONAL INCOME, GROSS NATIONAL PRODUCT AND GROSS DOMESTIC PRODUCT

The simple diagram below shows how income is generated and circulates in an economy:

*   In order to make the goods and services they provide, firms must use labour provided by households (remember from Section 1.8 that labour is one of the factors of production). They have to pay those households for the labour they provide, thus providing the households with income.
*   Households must pay firms for the goods and services they need. The income of firms is thus the sales revenue from the sale of goods and services.

This creates a **circular flow of income** and expenditure; income and output are different sides of the same coin. This diagram assumes a **closed economy**, ie, there is no leakage of income to overseas providers.

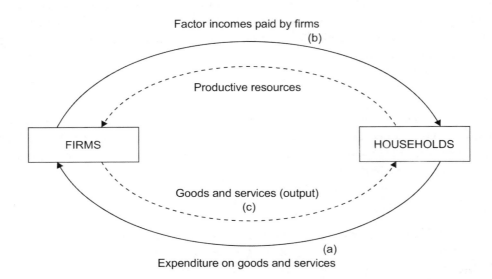

We can measure the activity shown in the above diagram in the economy, in different ways. The measure chosen will depend on which aspect of the above flow we are focusing on. Three key measures of economic activity are:

*   national income (NI);
*   gross national product (GNP);
*   gross domestic product (GDP).

3.1.1   National Income (NI)

'UK national income is defined as "the sum of all incomes of residents in the UK which arise as a result of economic activity, from the production of goods and services". Such incomes, which include rent, employment income and profit, are known as factor incomes because they are earned by the so-called factors of production: land, labour and capital.' (Office for National Statistics)

National income is also called **net national product**. As noted above, the terms 'income' and 'product' are two different aspects of the same circular flow of income around the economy. The term 'net' means after deducting an amount for capital consumption or depreciation of fixed assets from the gross figure.

Although technically national income has a particular definition, generally you will find all of the three measures given above (NI, GNP and GDP) loosely referred to as **national income**.

Measuring national income is useful for the following purposes:

* measuring the standard of living in a country (national income per head);
* comparing the wealth of different countries;
* measuring the change in national wealth and the standard of living;
* determining long-term trends;
* assisting central government in its economic planning.

3.1.2   Gross Domestic Product (GDP)

National income is largely derived from economic activity within the country itself. Domestic economic activity is referred to as total domestic income or domestic product. It is measured gross. The term gross domestic product (GDP) refers (in the UK) to the total value of income/production from economic activity within the UK.

3.1.3   Gross National Product (GNP)

As we noted above, the diagram showing the circular flow of income in the economy assumes that it is closed. In reality:

* some of the UK's national income arises from overseas investments; and
* some of the income generated within the UK is earned by people who are non-residents.

The difference between these items is **net property income from abroad**. The sum of gross domestic product plus net property income from abroad is the gross national product.

We can, therefore, show the relationship between GDP, GNP and national income like this:

	GDP
Plus	Net property income from abroad
Equals	GNP
Minus	Capital consumption
Equals	National income (net)

3.1.4   Injections and Withdrawals

In addition to using total incomes in the circular flow, as a measure for national income, we can use a method that measures total expenditure in the economy.

We add a number of injections to, and withdrawals from, the circular flow. These arise from:

- savings by consumers (a withdrawal from the cycle, since the money is no longer circulating if it is being saved);
- investment flows into firms (an injection, since it represents money the firms can now start using in their economic activity);
- imports (a withdrawal, since the money goes overseas to pay for goods and services bought from abroad);
- exports (an injection, since overseas buyers make payments into the UK to pay for goods and services);
- government spending (an injection, since the government adds to the revenues of firms providing it with goods and services); and
- taxation (a withdrawal, since it reduces the income households have available to spend on goods and services).

You should be able to see that we are moving away from – or at least building on – the simplified, closed-economy model that we started this section with.

The gross domestic product is made up of:

$$C + I + G + (X - M)$$

This measure gives us one way of looking at the level of national economic activity. It also shows us that if a government wants to influence levels of activity, it may be able to do so by influencing one or more of the components of the formula above. For example, it could:

- try to increase consumer expenditure – that is, spending by households, or 'C' above;
- take steps to increase private investment in firms (I);
- increase its own spending (G);
- try to improve the balance of payments (X – M).

From the above you should be able to see that it is possible to measure the amount of economic activity, or output, in a national economy. This is done by aggregating (adding together) all the incomes generated, to give a total figure for national income.

The bigger the national income in a country, the more its average income. A rising level of income means more spending on the output of firms, and more spending means more output of goods and services. Providing that such increases are not simply due to the effects of inflation, then the resulting increases in income should lead to a rise in the standard of living.

Rising national income (economic growth) is an economic policy objective of most governments. It is better if this growth is stable and steady, rather than uncontrolled and erratic.

Most UK national income is derived from economic activity within the UK. The measure of economic activity within the UK is referred to as total domestic income or domestic product. It is measured gross, ie, before deducting an amount for capital consumption or depreciation of fixed assets, to give the GDP, referring to the total value of income/production from economic activity within the UK.

4. ECONOMIC AND BUSINESS CYCLES

LEARNING OBJECTIVE

2.1.3   Understand the main stages of economic, financial and stock market cycles, including: trade cycles; business cycles; asset price bubbles; economic shocks; difficulty in forecasting national and international trends

4.1   THE TREND RATE OF GROWTH

Although there are many sources from which economic growth can emanate, in the long run the rate of sustainable or **trend rate of growth** ultimately depends on the:

*   growth and productivity of the labour force;
*   rate at which an economy efficiently channels its domestic savings and capital attracted from overseas into new and innovative technology and replaces obsolescent capital equipment;
*   extent to which an economy's infrastructure is maintained and developed to cope with growing transport, communication and energy needs.

This trend rate of growth also defines an economy's **potential output** level or full employment level of output – that is, the sustainable level of output an economy can produce when all of its resources are productively employed.

When an economy is growing in excess of its trend growth rate, actual output will exceed potential output, often with inflationary consequences. However, when a country's output contracts – that is, when its economic growth rate turns negative for at least two consecutive calendar quarters – the economy is said to be in recession, or entering a deflationary period, resulting in spare capacity and unemployment.

4.2   THE ECONOMIC CYCLE

Unlike in micro-economics, where the establishment of a market-clearing price in a single market brings supply and demand into equilibrium, in macro-economics the interaction of individual markets and sectors may cause the economy to operate in a state of disequilibrium, often for significant periods of time. This is considered in Sections 6.2 and 6.3y. The fact that actual growth fluctuates and deviates from trend growth in the short term gives rise to the **economic cycle,** or business cycle.

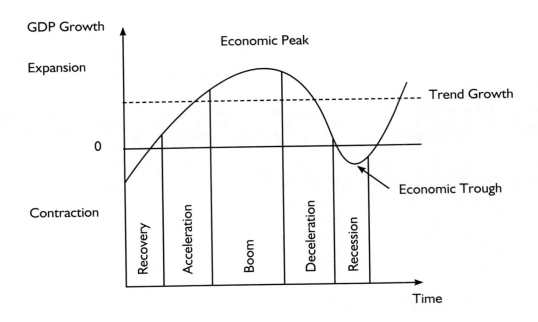

Economic cycles describe the course an economy conventionally takes, usually over a seven- to ten-year period, as economic growth oscillates in a cyclical fashion. The length of a cycle is measured either between successive economic peaks or between successive economic troughs. Although cycles typically assume a recovery, acceleration, boom, overheating, deceleration and recession pattern, in practice it is difficult to identify exactly when one stage ends and another begins, or, indeed, to quantify the duration of each stage.

Where an economy is positioned in the economic cycle also determines the performance of the various asset, or investment, classes (see Section 7.2). Finally, empirical evidence shows that if the short term peaks and troughs of conventional cycles are ignored, economic cycles of 50 years or so pervade economies. These so-called Kondratieff cycles (or super-cycles) flow from the benefits of innovation and investment in new technology.

The economy tends to experience different trends which may feature boom, slump, recession and recovery.

- **Boom** – a period of fast economic growth. Output is high due to increased demand and unemployment is low. Business confidence may be high, leading to increased investment. Consumer confidence may lead to extra spending.
- **Slump** – a period when output slows down due to a reduction in demand. Confidence may begin to suffer.
- **Recession** – a period where economic growth slows down and the level of output may actually decrease. Unemployment is likely to increase. Firms may lose confidence and reduce investment. Individuals may save rather than spend.
- **Recovery** – a period when the economy moves between recession and a boom.

What Happens in a Boom?

- Businesses produce more goods.
- Businesses invest in more machinery.

- Consumers spend more money. There is a high level of consumer confidence.
- Less money is spent by the government on unemployment benefits.
- More money is collected by the government in income tax and VAT.
- Prices tend to increase due to extra demand.

What Happens in a Recession?
- Businesses cut back on production.
- Some businesses may go bankrupt.
- Consumers spend less money. There is a fall in consumer confidence.
- Individuals may lose their jobs.
- More money is spent by the government on unemployment benefits.
- Less money is collected by the government in income tax and VAT.
- Prices start to fall.

4.3   BUSINESS CYCLES

As explained, over the long term, economies usually display an underlying positive rate of growth, sometimes known as the trend growth rate. This is likely to reflect, among other factors, the average level of investment. Investment also plays a key role in the business cycle, sometimes known as the **trade cycle**, the pattern of fluctuations around the trend.

A variety of different economic indicators shows cyclical movements of expansion and contraction in economic activity over time. Some of these indicators rise in periods of economic expansion. See Section 5 for more on these.

4.4   ASSET PRICE BUBBLES

A bubble is 'a sharp rise in price of an asset or a range of assets in a continuous process, with the initial rise generating expectations of further rises and attracting new buyers – generally speculators, interested in profits from trading in the asset rather than its use or earning capacity'. This definition implies that, in a bubble, the price of the asset deviates from its fundamental value and that a reversal of expectations and a sharp decline in prices (a crash) would usually occur.

4.5   ECONOMIC SHOCKS

An economic shock is defined as an event that produces a significant change within an economy, despite occurring outside it. Economic shocks are unpredictable and typically impact supply or demand throughout the markets. An economic shock may come in a variety of forms. A shock in the supply of staple commodities, such as oil, can cause prices to skyrocket, making it expensive to use for business purposes. The rapid devaluation of a currency will produce a shock for the import/export industry because a nation will have difficulty bringing in foreign products.

4.6   TREND FORECASTING

Governments and international organisations try to look forward and influence not only the short-term economic outlook, but also to learn from analysing longer-term trends, and to influence these as well. Even quite small changes in growth, year-on-year, can have a considerable cumulative effect over a longer period.

The UK government, for example, has a stated aim of increasing long-term growth (known as the **trend growth rate**) – through strategies aimed at increasing employment opportunities and productivity, by promoting economic stability and by way of its wider economic policies.

5.   KEY ECONOMIC INDICATORS

LEARNING OBJECTIVE

2.1.4   Interpret key economic and business indicators: gross domestic product; interest rates; consumer price and inflation indices; retail sales; unemployment rate; industrial production; stock market indices; money supply changes; foreign exchange indices; leading, lagging and coincident indicators; pro-cyclic, counter-cyclic and acyclic indicators

A variety of different economic indicators shows cyclical movements of expansion and contraction in economic activity over time. Some of these indicators rise in periods of economic expansion. They are known as 'pro-cyclic' indicators and include the rate of growth of consumer spending, job vacancies and investment. An increase in a pro-cyclic indicator such as GDP will be reflected in a strong economy. If GDP instead were to decrease, it would mean that the economy could be headed for a recession. Other indicators (the so-called counter-cyclic indicators) fall in periods of economic expansion, such as unemployment and the number of bankruptcies. An acyclic indicator has little effect on the economy

5.1   GROSS DOMESTIC PRODUCT

We have looked at the concept of gross domestic product in the context of the national income. GDP refers, in the UK, to the total value of income/production from economic activity within the UK. Its measurement is important in understanding the growth, and trends, in the UK economy and output.

5.2   INTEREST RATES

When you hear talk of the Bank of England (BoE) adjusting interest rates, it means that the BoE is adjusting the rate at which it lends money to banks, known as the base rate. Usually, other interest rates – such as the rates on a credit card or a variable mortgage – will follow the BoE's adjustments, because banks pass on the extra costs of borrowing to the end consumer.

Investors watch changes in interest rates very closely. An increase in interest rates not only slows down consumer spending, but will also hit the future performance of companies. Higher interest rates make it more expensive for firms to expand their business operations by borrowing money or issuing debt, because they will have to pay a higher interest rate on their loans. High interest rates have a secondary effect of encouraging investors to switch out of equities and into low-risk cash instruments, thereby further depressing share prices.

5.3 INFLATION INDICES

'Inflation' is the name given to a general increase in price levels. (Another way of describing a general rise in prices is as a decline in the purchasing power of money.)

Inflation is an important concern for investors, as well as for borrowers; for investors, inflation erodes the value of their investment if the growth in the investment does not keep pace with it.

Inflation is measured by reference to an **index**, made up of a notional basket of all the things the 'average' person is assumed to spend their money on. However, in reality different people spend their money on different things – so there are several inflation indices, reflecting different ways of calculating the general rise in price levels and the cost of living. These are known collectively as **consumer price indices**.

They may be used for several purposes – for example:

*   as an indicator of inflationary pressures in the economy;
*   as a benchmark for wage negotiations; and
*   to determine annual increases in government benefits payments.

The **Retail Prices Index (RPI)** measures the percentage changes, month by month, in the average level of prices of the commodities and services, including housing costs, purchased by the great majority of households in the UK. The items of expenditure within the RPI are intended to be a representative list of items, current prices for which are collected at regular intervals.

In December 2003, the standardised European inflation measure, the **Harmonised Index of Consumer Prices (HICP)**, began to be used as the basis for the UK's inflation target. In the UK, it is more commonly known as the **Consumer Prices Index (CPI)**. The CPI excludes most housing costs. However, pensions and benefits and index-linked gilts continue to be calculated on the same basis as previously, using the RPI.

The current rate of UK inflation (as at March 2011) is:

*   CPI: 4.0%.
*   RPI: 5.3%.

The term **underlying rate of inflation** is sometimes used to refer to the RPI, adjusted to exclude mortgage costs and sometimes other elements as well (such as the local council tax). The effects of interest rate changes on mortgage costs help to make the RPI fluctuate more widely than the underlying rate of inflation.

High levels of inflation can cause problems:

*   Businesses have to continually update prices to keep pace with inflation.
*   Employees find the real value of their salaries eroded.
*   Those on fixed levels of income, such as pensioners, will suffer as the price increases are not matched by increases in income.
*   Exports may become less competitive.

- The real value of future pensions and investment income becomes difficult to assess, which might act as a disincentive to save.

There are, however, some positive aspects to high levels of inflation:

- Rising house prices contribute to a feelgood factor (although this might contribute to further inflation as house owners become more eager to borrow and spend).
- Borrowers benefit, because the value of borrowers' debt falls in real terms – ie, after adjusting for the effect of inflation.
- Inflation also erodes the real value of a country's national debt and so can benefit an economy in difficult times.

5.4   RETAIL SALES

Retail sales are an indicator of household consumption. They are an important economic indicator because consumer spending drives much of our economy. Think of all of the people and companies involved in producing, distributing, and selling the goods you use on a daily basis like food, clothes and fuel. When consumers open their wallets, the economy tends to grow steadily. Retail shelves empty and orders are placed for replacement merchandise. Plants make more gadgets and order raw materials for even more.

However, if consumers feel uncertain about their financial future and decide to hold off buying new refrigerators or blue jeans, the economy slows down. This is why politicians may resort to tax cuts to give the economy a boost. By putting cash in consumers' hands, they hope consumer spending will help the economy move out of a recession.

5.5   UNEMPLOYMENT

The unemployment rate measures the number of people available for work and seeking employment. Labour statistics offer a general sense of the state and direction of the economy as a whole. If unemployment is on the rise or few new jobs are being created, it is a sign that companies themselves are not expanding their businesses and the economy may be slowing down. On the other hand, tight labour markets and large-scale job creation indicate a growing, or even overheated, economy.

The reaction of markets to news about unemployment can often seem paradoxical. If the economy is doing well, investors will fear that a fall in unemployment (which you would think would be good news) will be inflationary (more people in work and spending money). Very low unemployment can also be a sign of labour shortages. On the other hand, a fall in unemployment when the economy is in recession is good news for the markets as it suggests an improvement in the overall state of the economy.

5.6   INDUSTRIAL PRODUCTION

Industrial production measures the change in output for the industrial sector of the economy. The industrial sector includes manufacturing, mining and utilities. Although these sectors contribute only a small portion of GDP, they are highly sensitive to interest rates and consumer demand. This makes industrial production an important tool for forecasting future GDP and economic performance. Industrial production figures are also used by central banks to measure inflation, as high levels of industrial production can lead to uncontrolled levels of consumption and rapid inflation.

5.7   STOCK MARKET INDICES

A variety of different indices are used to measure the performance of stock markets. The main indices are:

- The **FTSE 100 index** measures the combined performance of the hundred most highly capitalised blue chip companies listed on the LSE. In doing so it represents about 81% of the UK market. It is used extensively by portfolio managers to benchmark their performance, and has been in existence since 1984.
- The **FTSE 250 index** was introduced in 1992, and is made up of mid-capitalised companies which fall outside the FTSE 100. It represents approximately 15% of UK market capitalisation.
- The **FTSE All Share index** is the oldest of these three examples, having been introduced in 1962 (it was then known as the FTSE Actuaries All Share Index).

Indices can also be calculated using different mathematical formulae – for example, in terms of the weightings given to different shares and their price movements. Some are calculated so that the shares are arithmetically weighted according to capitalisation, ie, the larger the company, the bigger its weighting in the index. Others are calculated using the geometric mean and are unweighted: each share counts equally, no matter what its market capitalisation.

5.8   MONEY SUPPLY CHANGES

Later in this chapter (Section 6.4) we will look at various ways of measuring the money supply (also known as **money stock**). This is the total amount of money circulating in an economy. We will also look at narrow money and broad money and at the more formal definitions of M0 and M4. The amount of money in circulation, and changes in that amount, are important to the economy – chiefly because of the impact this is assumed to have on prices (and, therefore, on inflation).

5.9   FOREIGN EXCHANGE RATES

These are the rates at which one country's currency may be exchanged for that of another country. So an exchange rate is the price of one currency, in terms of another. You may see a foreign exchange rate quoted as a single figure – for example, the rate for US dollars against sterling was quoted by Bloomberg as \$1.6297 (that is, \$1.6297 = £1.0000) at close of business on 5 April 2011. This price is the **mid price** because it is the average rate calculated from the bid and ask closing prices on the day.

The foreign exchange rate quoted by dealers for a particular country is a pair of FX rates. The lower one is the **bid**, which is the dealer's buying price, and the higher is the **ask**, which is the dealer's selling price. The dealers make their profits by selling to one customer at the ask price and simultaneously buying the currency from another customer at the bid price. The difference between the bid-ask spread is the dealer's profit from the deal. Commissions are additional costs borne by the buyers and sellers.

A country's currency exchange rate with other countries is important for the health of its economy. For example, we saw that changes in the exchange rate can affect the competitiveness of UK goods abroad, and thus can have a major impact on the balance of payments. For the UK pound sterling, exchange rates with the euro, the US dollar and the Japanese yen are key rates, as Europe, the US and Japan are major trading partners.

The foreign exchange (**forex**) markets are worldwide and the main dealers are banks. Their customers include companies and individuals who are buying or selling goods and services abroad; they also include investment inflows and outflows, as investors trade currencies in the hope of making a gain on any exchange rate movements, or buy currencies which offer higher rates of interest. However, investors buying a high-yielding foreign currency in the hope of benefiting from the high interest rates earned on it also need to beware of the fact that, if that currency declines in value, they may make a capital loss on the exchange rate.

5.10   LEADING, LAGGING AND COINCIDENT INDICATORS

Leading indicators are indicators that usually change **before** the economy as a whole changes. They are therefore useful as short-term predictors of the economy. Stock market returns are a leading indicator: the stock market usually begins to decline before the economy as a whole declines and usually begins to improve before the general economy begins to recover from a slump. Other leading indicators include the index of consumer expectations, building permits, and the money supply.

Lagging indicators are indicators that usually change **after** the economy as a whole does. Typically the lag is a few quarters of a year. The unemployment rate is a lagging indicator: employment tends to increase two or three quarters after an upturn in the general economy.

Coincident indicators are those which **change at approximately the same time** as the whole economy, thereby providing information about the current state of the economy. An example is personal income. There are many coincident economic indicators: GDP, industrial production and retail sales are coincident indicators. A coincident index may be used to identify, after the fact, the dates of peaks and troughs in the business cycle.

5.11   DIFFICULTIES IN FORECASTING NATIONAL AND INTEREST RATE TRENDS

Forecasting national and economic trends in a single country and on a global scale is a highly specialised and challenging activity for econometricians. With regards to forecasting, www.cabinetoffice.gov.uk offers the following pointers.

Essentially, forecasting as an activity aims to identify and track past trends and then extrapolate into the future. A series of economic data such as interest rates, economic growth or inflation data is tracked regularly over a historic time period. The data is obtained in the form of a time series that is then projected forward by using statistical/econometric techniques. As well as quantitative (statistical methods), it also includes the use of more qualitative (judgmental) methods.

As looking into the future naturally involves a varying degree of uncertainty, sometimes a distinction is drawn between forecasting and projections. In certain contexts, particularly economic ones, forecasting is used to refer to short-term extrapolations associated with a reasonable degree of certainty. Projections are considered to be longer term, more sophisticated, but also less reliable. This distinction does not always hold true, for example demographic projections can be very reliable over the time span of a generation.

There are two main types of trend analysis – quantitative and qualitative analysis.

5.11.1 Quantitative Analysis

Quantitative trend analysis is probably the most common forecasting method. It relies on the statistical analysis of historical data – in other words it is relatively objective. Quantitative techniques include extrapolation (such as moving averages, linear projections against time or exponential smoothing) and econometric methods (typically using regression techniques to estimate the effects of causal variables). This type of analysis is commonly used to forecast demographic and economic changes where extrapolating over time is believed to have some validity.

Other techniques for short- to medium-term analysis and forecasting include:

*   **Modelling** – modelling is an extremely useful tool for quantitative analysis.
*   **Estimation** – one of the key difficulties in conducting forecasting is a lack of available data. If this is the case, estimation may be suitable.
*   **Triangulation** – when developing a model, data is often incomplete or approximate. In other instances you may have several sources of data that conflict. One way of developing a base to work from is to triangulate the available information to develop a defensible average.

5.11.2 Qualitative Analysis

Qualitative trend analysis is more subjective and is concerned mainly with social, institutional, commercial and political themes (ie, things which may not be linearly related to the past). For example, qualitative trend analyses deal with issues such as:

*   What is the future of trade unions?
*   What is the future of political parties or NGOs?
*   What is the future of the entertainment business?

One of the most common forms of qualitative trend analysis is the identification of 'megatrends' – driving forces which can change society in all spheres, eg, politics, economics, technology, values and social relations. Other tools include scenarios and analogies.

Qualitative analyses can be applied to most areas, but work best when focusing on real change. Megatrends apply to all areas, within the defined time and setting. It is important, though, to be aware that megatrends may themselves produce powerful counter-trends – and that they may interact with each other.

Strengths

*   Quantitative forecasts are usually more objective, relatively inexpensive and easy to use (contingent upon some knowledge of statistics).
*   Qualitative forecasts can be valuable predictors of new trends by using the creativity and good judgement of experts.

Weaknesses

- Quantitative forecasts can be misleading. The past is not always predictive of the future and such forecasts do not take into account unpredictable changes or discoveries (eg, discovery of new natural resources) or 'wild cards' (eg, unexpected acts of terrorism).
- When using qualitative techniques to identify possible new trends, it will always be the case that some or maybe even all of the results are eventually disproved. It is particularly difficult to distinguish between short term fads and long term trends.

6. THE ROLE OF GOVERNMENT

LEARNING OBJECTIVE

2.2.1   Understand the role of government and central banks in fiscal and monetary policy: interest-rate-setting process; money market operations; fiscal easing; other interventions

6.1 GENERAL ECONOMIC POLICY AIMS

As well as providing a legal and regulatory framework for economic activity, the government plays a role in managing the economy. Among the aims of a government's economic policy may be the following:

- To achieve **sustainable growth** in national income per head of the population. Growth implies an increase in national income in real terms (remember, 'real' means after stripping out the effects of inflation). National income grows through the expansion of economic activity: more goods and services become available for people to consume. The idea of sustainable growth implies that major fluctuations in the business cycle are avoided, and that output grows on a steady upward trend. This is generally seen as the most important goal of a government's economic policy.
- To **control inflation** in prices. This has become a central objective of economic policy in many countries in recent years.
- To achieve **full employment**. Full employment does not mean that everyone who wants a job has one all the time, but it does mean that unemployment levels are low, and involuntary unemployment is generally short-term.
- To achieve a **trade balance** – that is, a balance between exports and imports. The wealth of a country relative to others, a country's creditworthiness as a borrower and the goodwill between countries in international relations all depend on the achievement of an external balance over time. Deficits in external trade, with imports exceeding exports, might also be damaging for the country's prospects for economic growth.

6.2 FISCAL POLICY

Fiscal policy is government policy on taxation, public borrowing and public spending.

- **Direct taxation** is taxation of incomes and, in some cases, wealth (as with inheritance tax).
- **Indirect taxation** is taxation of products and services, for example, Value Added Tax.

The amount that the government must borrow each year is now known as the **Public Sector Net Cash Requirement (PSNCR)** in the UK. The PSNCR is the annual excess of spending over income for the entire public sector – not just for the central government.

A government might intervene in the economy by:

- spending more money and financing this expenditure by borrowing;
- collecting more in taxes without increasing spending;
- collecting more in taxes in order to increase spending, thus diverting income from one part of the economy to another.

A government's fiscal stance may be expansionary, contractionary or neutral, according to its overall effect on national income.

- Spending more money and financing this expenditure by borrowing indicates an **expansionary** fiscal stance. Spending will increase and so national income will tend to rise, either in real terms, or in terms of price levels only; that is, the increase in national income may be real (ie, there is growth even after the effects of inflation are stripped out), or it may be simply inflationary.
- Collecting more in taxes without increasing spending indicates a **contractionary** fiscal stance. A government may deliberately raise taxation to take inflationary pressures out of the economy.
- Collecting more in taxes in order to increase spending, thus diverting income from one part of the economy to another, indicates a broadly **neutral** fiscal stance. We saw in Section 1.9 that the government can redistribute wealth (as measured through net income) through such activity.

If government raises taxes and spending by the same amount, so that its overall budget remains in balance, there will be an increase in aggregate monetary demand. This is because taxpayers would otherwise have saved some of the money they pay in increased tax; but instead the government spends all of it within the economy. The net effect is that more money gets spent, albeit by a different party (in this case the government itself). This effect is called the **balanced budget multiplier**.

Since government spending or tax reductions may be inflationary, and higher domestic prices make imports relatively cheaper and exports less competitive in foreign markets, fiscal policy has possible implications for the balance of payments (discussed in Section 6.5).

Fiscal policy can also be used in an attempt to reduce unemployment and stimulate employment. For example:

- more government spending on capital projects, on which people are employed to work;
- government-funded training schemes;
- taxation of companies on the basis of the numbers and pay levels of employees.

Government spending, however, might create inflationary pressures, and inflation tends to create more unemployment. Fiscal policy must therefore be used with care, even where the aim is to create new jobs.

The impact of changes in fiscal policy is not always certain, and fiscal policy to pursue one aim (eg, lower inflation) may create barriers to the pursuit of other aims (eg, employment) for a while. In addition, the effects of fiscal changes can take a very long time to feed through into the economy, by which time other factors may have changed, complicating the overall outcome.

Government planners also need to consider how fiscal policy can affect savers, investors and companies.

- The tax regime, for example, affects different savings instruments and/or property ownership, and this affects investors' decisions.
- Companies will be affected by tax rules on dividends and profits, and tax breaks for certain activities. They may take these rules into account when deciding on dividend policy, or on whether to raise finance through debt (loans) or equities (by issuing shares) and other activities.

One feature of fiscal policy is that a government must **plan** what it wants to spend, and so how much it needs to raise, either in income (through taxation) or by borrowing. It needs to make a plan in order to establish how much taxation there should be, what form the taxes should take and so which sectors of the economy (firms or households, high-income earners or low-income earners) the money should come from. This formal planning of fiscal policy usually follows an annual cycle. In the UK, the most important statement of changes to policy is the Budget, which takes place in the spring of each year. The Chancellor of the Exchequer also delivers a Pre-Budget Report each autumn. The Pre-Budget Report formally makes the government's spending plans available for scrutiny.

Because of the annual planning cycle of government finances, and because there is usually a considerable time-lag before businesses and people act upon changes brought about through tax and government spending, fiscal policy is not very responsive to shorter-term developments in the economy. For shorter-term fine-tuning of the economy, the government may need to use monetary policy.

6.3   MONETARY POLICY

Monetary policy is concerned with changes in the amount of money in circulation – the **money supply** – and with changes in the price of money – **interest rates**. These variables are linked with inflation in prices generally, and also with exchange rates – the price of the domestic currency in terms of other currencies.

Later (in Section 6.4) we will look at how the supply or stock of money in an economy affects inflation and other economic variables.

Until the 1970s, the tools for implementing monetary policy also included direct controls (exercised through the Bank of England) on the amount of lending that banks were allowed to undertake. In the 1980s, most monetary policy implementation centred on trying to control the overall supply of money in the economy. Targets were set for the growth of money (notes, coins, bank deposits), and interest rates were varied accordingly. However, measures of the amount of money in the economy did not always prove to be a reliable guide to demand and inflation. As a result, by the mid-1980s monetary policy came to be based on an assessment of a wider range of economic indicators rather than a single measure of money supply growth.

Since 1997, the most important aspect of monetary policy in the UK has been the influence over interest rates exerted by the Bank of England, the central bank of the UK. The **Monetary Policy Committee (MPC)** of the Bank of England is charged with the responsibility of setting interest rates with the aim of meeting the government's inflation target of 2% based on the Consumer Prices Index (CPI).

The UK inflation objective was formalised in the 1998 Bank of England Act. This Act states that the Bank of England is expected 'to maintain price stability and, subject to that, to support the economic policy of HM Government including its objectives for growth and employment' (Bank of England Act 1998).

If the inflation target is missed by more than one percentage point on either side for three successive months – in other words, if the annual CPI inflation rate is more than 3% or less than 1% – the Governor of the Bank of England, as Chairman of the MPC, must write an open letter to the Chancellor explaining why, and what the Bank proposes to do to ensure inflation comes back to the target.

The MPC influences interest rates by deciding the short-term benchmark **repo rate** – the rate at which the Bank of England deals in the money markets. This is known as the Bank of England's base lending rate, or the **base rate** for short. (A repo contract is a sale and repurchase agreement: securities are sold but must be repurchased later.) The base rate affects the commercial rates which financial institutions then set for the different financial instruments they offer or deal in; so when the MPC changes the base rate, commercial banks generally react quickly by changing their own deposit and lending rates.

However, a government does not have an unlimited ability to have interest rates set how it wishes. It must take into account what rates the overall market will bear, so that the benchmark rate it chooses can be maintained.

6.3.1   The Interest-Rate-Setting Process: The Monetary Policy Committee

Setting UK interest rates was once the Chancellor's responsibility. The system was subject to abuse. Chancellors periodically overruled the advice of Treasury experts, especially when an election approached.

For this reason, following Labour's May 1997 election victory, one of the Chancellor's first actions was to de-politicise the rate-setting process. Responsibilities for setting interest rates were assigned to the Monetary Policy Committee (MPC) of the Bank of England.

The MPC has operated in an extremely able and transparent manner over the last few years. It announces each decision to change rates or keep them unchanged precisely at 12 noon on the day each meeting ends. Gone are the days when sudden and unexpected rate announcements would spook investors.

Composition of the MPC

The Bank's MPC is made up of nine members – the Governor, the two Deputy Governors, the Bank's Chief Economist, the Executive Director for Markets and four external members appointed directly by the Chancellor. The appointment of external members is designed to ensure that the MPC benefits from thinking and expertise in addition to that gained inside the Bank of England. Members serve fixed terms, after which they may be replaced or reappointed. Compared to other government rate-setting agencies in Washington and Brussels, the MPC is a model of openness.

Each member of the MPC has expertise in the field of economics and monetary policy. Members do not represent individual groups or areas. They are independent. Each member of the Committee has a vote to set interest rates at the level they believe is consistent with meeting the inflation target. The MPC's decision is made on the basis of one person, one vote. It is not based on a consensus of opinion. It reflects the votes of each individual member of the Committee.

A representative from the Treasury also sits with the Committee at its meetings. The Treasury representative can discuss policy issues but is not allowed to vote. The purpose is to ensure that the MPC is fully briefed on fiscal policy developments and other aspects of the government's economic policies, and that the Chancellor is kept fully informed about monetary policy.

MPC Meetings

The MPC meets every month to set the interest rate. Throughout the month, the MPC receives extensive briefing on the economy from Bank of England staff. This includes a half-day meeting – known as the pre-MPC meeting – which usually takes place on the Friday before the MPC's interest-rate-setting meeting. The nine members of the Committee are made aware of all the latest data on the economy and hear explanations of recent trends and analysis of relevant issues. The Committee is also told about business conditions around the UK from the Bank's Agents. The Agents' role is to talk directly to business to gain intelligence and insight into current and future economic developments and prospects.

The monthly MPC meeting itself is a two-day affair. On the first day, the meeting starts with an update on the most recent economic data. A series of issues is then identified for discussion. On the following day, a summary of the previous day's discussion is provided and the MPC members individually explain their views on what policy should be. The Governor then puts to the meeting the policy which he believes will command a majority and members of the MPC vote. Any member in a minority is asked to say what level of interest rates he or she would have preferred, and this is recorded in the minutes of the meeting. The interest rate decision is announced at 12 noon on the second day.

Public Accountability: Explaining Views and Decisions

The MPC goes to great lengths to explain its thinking and decisions. The minutes of the MPC meetings are published two weeks after the interest rate decision. The minutes give a full account of the policy discussion, including differences of view. They also record the votes of the individual members of the Committee. The Committee has to explain its actions regularly to parliamentary committees, particularly the Treasury Committee. MPC members also speak to audiences throughout the country, explaining the MPC's policy decisions and thinking. This is a two-way dialogue. Regional visits also give members of the MPC a chance to gather first-hand intelligence about the economic situation from businesses and other organisations.

In addition to the monthly MPC minutes, the Bank publishes its Inflation Report every quarter. This report gives an analysis of the UK economy and the factors influencing policy decisions. The Inflation Report also includes the MPC's latest forecasts for inflation and output growth. Because monetary policy operates with a time-lag of about two years, it is necessary for the MPC to form judgements about the outlook for output and inflation.

The MPC uses a model of the economy to help produce its projections. The model provides a framework to organise thinking on how the economy works and how different economic developments might affect future inflation. But this is not a mechanical exercise. Given all the uncertainties and unknowns of the future, the MPC's forecast has to involve a great deal of judgement about the economy.

6.3.2 Money Market Operations

The Bank of England's framework for its operations in the sterling money markets is designed to implement the MPC's interest rate decisions while meeting the liquidity needs of, and so contributing to the stability of, the banking system as a whole.

The Bank of England is the sole issuer of sterling central bank money, the final risk-free settlement asset in the UK. This enables the Bank to implement monetary policy and makes the framework for the Bank's monetary operations central to liquidity management in the banking system as a whole and by individual banks and building societies.

The Bank's market operations have two objectives, stemming from its monetary policy and financial stability responsibilities as the UK's central bank. They are to:

- Implement monetary policy by maintaining overnight market interest rates in line with Bank Rate, so that there is a flat risk-free money market yield curve to the next MPC decision date, and very little day-to-day or intra-day volatility in market interest rates at maturities out to that horizon.
- Reduce the cost of disruption to the liquidity and payment services supplied by commercial banks. The Bank does this by balancing the provision of liquidity insurance against the costs of creating incentives for banks to take greater risks, and subject to the need to avoid taking risk on to its balance sheet.

The framework has four main elements: reserves-averaging scheme, operational standing facilities, a discount window facility, and open market operations.

Reserves-Averaging Scheme

Eligible UK banks and building societies undertake to hold target balances (reserves) at the Bank on average over maintenance periods running from one MPC decision date until the next. If an average balance is within a range around the target, the balance is remunerated at bank rate.

Each reserves maintenance period runs between the monthly scheduled MPC meetings. Reserve-scheme members undertake to maintain a level of reserves within a +/−1% range around a target that they choose, averaging across reserve balances at the end of each calendar day over the maintenance period as a whole.

Reserves are remunerated at the Bank's official rate. Interest penalties are applied if, at the end of the maintenance period, scheme members fail to achieve the reserves target by holding an average level of reserves higher or lower than the specified range. Settlement banks also pay a penalty if their reserve account is overdrawn at the end of any day.

Subject to meeting the monthly target balance and avoiding overnight overdrafts, reserve balances can be varied freely to meet day-to-day liquidity needs. For example, funds can be moved on and off reserve accounts up to the close of the Clearing House Automated Payment System (CHAPS) in order to accommodate unexpected end-of-day payment in/outflows. In this way, reserve balances can be used as a liquidity buffer. Within the Bank's ceilings on reserve targets, reserve banks can also change their reserve target from month to month in response to, for example, variations in the size or uncertainty of their payment flows.

Operational Standing Facilities

Operational standing deposit and (collateralised) lending facilities are available to eligible UK banks and building societies. They may be used on demand. In normal circumstances, the lending/deposit rates are 25 basis points higher than bank rate and 25 basis points below Bank Rate respectively.

The purpose of the operational standing facilities is to stabilise expectations that overnight market interest rates will be in line with bank rate; and, to that end, to give banks a means to manage unexpected 'frictional' payment shocks that could otherwise take their reserves accounts either below zero or to a level where they would otherwise be unremunerated. The Bank will seek to satisfy itself that use of the facility is consistent with these purposes.

On each day in a monthly maintenance period, the rate charged on the operational standing lending facility is 25 basis points above bank rate; and the rate paid on the operational standing deposit facility is 25 basis points below bank rate.

The operational standing deposit facility is uncollateralised. The operational standing lending facility is for overnight reverse repo against eligible collateral. The operational standing facilities are available all day subject to operational constraints arising from deadlines in payments and securities settlement systems.

A Discount Window Facility (DWF)

The purpose of the DWF is to provide liquidity insurance to the banking system. The DWF is not intended for firms facing fundamental problems of solvency or viability. Eligible banks and building societies may borrow gilts, for up to 30 days, against a wide range of collateral in return for a fee, which will vary with the collateral used and the total size of borrowings. Institutions eligible to participate will be banks and building societies that are required to pay cash ratio deposits (CRDs) and which otherwise meet the requirements for eligibility, as determined by the Bank, for the Bank's sterling monetary framework facilities.

Open Market Operations (OMOs)

OMOs are used to provide to the banking system the amount of central bank money needed to enable reserve-scheme members, in aggregate, to achieve their reserves targets. OMOs comprise short-term repos at bank rate, long-term repos at market rates determined in variable-rate tenders, and outright purchases of high-quality bonds.

Short-term OMOs are held weekly, with an overnight-maturity fine-tune on the final day of the maintenance period. The size of the weekly OMO is varied to offset expected weekly changes in banknotes in circulation and other sterling flows across the Bank's balance sheet (so-called autonomous factors). Day-to-day, reserve averaging absorbs the short-term fluctuations that occur across the Bank's balance sheet. The Bank currently provides long-term financing to the banking system through long-term repos at market rates determined in monthly OMOs; and through monthly OMOs to purchase conventional gilts. The Bank plans in due course to inject reserves via the purchase of high-quality foreign currency bonds, with the cash flows swapped into sterling (outright purchases).

In normal circumstances, the Bank's weekly short-term OMOs take place on Thursdays and have a maturity of one week. They are conducted at bank rate. On the days when the MPC makes scheduled interest rate decisions, the Bank undertakes its weekly short-term OMO at 12.15pm, in order to follow the MPC's noon announcement. On days when there are no scheduled interest rate announcements, the Bank undertakes its weekly, short-term OMO at 10.00am. Short-term OMOs are settled same day.

The Bank conducts, as a matter of routine, an overnight-maturity fine-tuning OMO at the end of each reserves maintenance period (ordinarily the Wednesday preceding the Thursday MPC decision) to ensure that the banking system's net need for central banking money, taking into account the amount required for reserve-scheme banks to achieve their aggregate reserve targets, is provided as precisely as possible. These operations take place at 10.00am. They are for same-day settlement. The Bank is prepared either to provide or drain central bank money at the Bank's official rate in this operation and both are equally likely on the assumption that errors in the Bank's liquidity forecast are unbiased.

The Bank conducts long-term repo OMOs monthly, usually at 10am on a Tuesday mid-month. The Bank may lend at three–, six–, nine– and 12-month maturities. These OMOs are variable-rate tenders open to the Bank's OMO counterparties. The Bank is therefore a price-taker and allocates the funds offered to successful bidders at the rate(s) that they tender. Settlement of long-term repo operations takes place on the day following the OMO (T+1). The Bank conducts OMOs to purchase gilts monthly, normally on a Monday towards the end of the month. These are likewise competitive tenders in which the Bank is a price-taker and buys gilts from those making successful offers at the price they offer.

6.3.3 Fiscal Easing and Other Interventions

Quantitative easing (QE) is a way of pouring money into a cash-starved banking system. The banks get cash in exchange for government bonds, helping them to build up their reserves – and the hope is that they then lend some of it out to families and businesses.

During the 2007/2008 global credit crisis, the US was the first country in recession to turn to QE to unblock the credit freeze in the banking sector and the wider economy. To stimulate economic growth and to encourage banks to lend to the retail sector the US Federal Funds Rate (a key US reference rate) was slashed. By December 2008 the Fed Funds rate stood at 0.25% (compared to a cycle high of 5.25% in September 2007). Ben Bernanke, chairman of the Federal Reserve, followed this rate cut move with QE in the spring of 2009 by purchasing billions of dollars' worth of assets, including mortgage-backed assets.

QE is not new and was used by Japan when it faced deflation – a period of falling prices – from 2001 until 2006. Along with the US Fed, the UK BoE also actioned the QE programme. In March 2009, the MPC announced that, in addition to setting the base rate at 0.5%, it would start to inject money directly into the economy in order to meet the inflation target and to ward off the dangers of deflationary pressures. In a bold move, the instrument of monetary policy shifted towards the quantity of money provided rather than its price (bank rate).

Significant reductions in bank rate to a record low of 0.5% had provided the large stimulus to the economy that the Bank wanted. With interest rates not far from zero, the MPC needed to provide additional stimulus to support demand in the wider economy. So the MPC boosted the supply of money by purchasing assets like government and corporate bonds. Thus, the Bank supplied extra money directly into the economy to unfreeze the credit markets – but this did not involve printing more banknotes. Instead, the Bank paid for these assets by creating money electronically and crediting the accounts of the companies it bought the assets from. This extra injection of billions of pounds was intended to support more spending in the economy and to restore future inflation back to the target.

The effect of the record low base rate set by the MPC, combined with QE, was to boost the UK stocks markets and reduce medium- and long-dated gilt yields.

6.4   THE MONEY SUPPLY AND ITS EFFECTS

LEARNING OBJECTIVE

2.2.2   Understand how the money supply affects: inflation; deflation; disinflation; interest rates; exchange rates; relationship between money supply, inflation and employment

The term 'money supply' is used to describe the total amount of money circulating in an economy – and, as with many concepts in economics, there are different ways of measuring it. For example, economists often talk about narrow money and broad money.

- **Narrow money** – used to describe the total sum of all financial assets (including cash) which meet a pretty narrow definition of money; for example, they must be very liquid and available to finance current spending needs. A deposit which was fixed for a long period would not, therefore, meet this definition.
- **Broad money** – used to describe the total sum of a wider range of assets, including some which are not as liquid as those falling within the definition of narrow money. It might include, for example, money held in savings accounts which are not instant-access accounts.

When governments attempt to affect the economy, one of their tools (as we have already seen – but will examine in more detail) is the **money supply**. This is measured by reference to the **monetary aggregates** – of which there are four, all published by the Bank of England.

The most important of the four are known as M0 and M4:

*   **M0** is the measure of notes and coin in circulation outside the Bank of England, plus operational deposits at the Bank of England. (This is, therefore, quite a narrow definition of money.)
*   **M4** is the measure of notes and coin in circulation with the public, plus sterling deposits held with UK banks and building societies by the rest of the private sector. (This is thus a broader definition.)

6.4.1   How Money Supply Affects Inflation, Deflation and Disinflation

Inflation measures the general rise in prices in an economy. As we have seen in Section 6.3, the Bank of England is charged with taking steps to keep inflation within a certain range. Interest rates are the main, and most effective, tool it has at its disposal for doing this; but the money supply is also a factor. In this section we will look at why this is so.

This makes some intuitive sense, if money is regarded as being held mainly for transactional (spending) purposes; an excess of money will mean that more money is chasing the same amount of assets, and therefore pushing their prices up. Conversely, if there is less money in supply, there is less to be spent – so asset prices will fall correspondingly. This theory works better in some economic environments than in others.

Deflation describes a general fall in the level of prices, and **disinflation** is a reduction in the rate of inflation (ie, a slowing of price growth – as opposed to a fall in prices). Using the quantity theory of money, price growth can, in theory, be slowed (disinflation) or even reversed (deflation) through changes to the money supply.

6.4.2   How Money Supply Affects Interest Rates

Money supply is also important to interest rates.

We can think of interest rates as being the 'price' of money. If a bank lends us money it is the price we are willing to pay that bank for the use of its cash (and the price the bank is willing to accept for having to forgo the opportunity to use the money for other, potentially more lucrative, activities). Conversely, if we place our cash on deposit with a bank, the interest we earn on it is what the bank has agreed to pay us.

Monetary economic theory states that interest rates are largely determined by the demand and supply of loanable funds. That is, if the money supply increases, and there is no increase in the demand for money (eg, for investment purposes) then this increases the amount of loanable funds available (eg, for savings). As there is more money available for savings this acts to depress interest rates.

6.4.3 The Relationship between Money Supply, Inflation and Employment

The monetarist explanation of inflation operates through the Fisher equation.

$$MV = PT$$

where:

M = money supply

V = velocity of circulation

P = price level

T = transactions or output

There is a direct relationship between the growth of the money supply and inflation, as monetarists assume that V and T are fixed. The mechanisms by which excess money might be translated into inflation are examined below. Individuals can also spend their excess money balances directly on goods and services. This has a direct impact on inflation by raising **aggregate demand**. The more inelastic the aggregate supply in the economy, the greater the impact on inflation.

The increase in demand for goods and services may cause a rise in **imports**. Though this leakage from the domestic economy reduces the money supply, it also increases the supply of pounds on the foreign exchange market, thus applying downward pressure on the exchange rate. This may cause imported inflation.

If excess money balances are spent on goods and services, the increase in the demand for labour will cause a rise in money wages and unit labour costs. This may cause **cost-push inflation**. Cost-push inflation occurs when there is a reduction in aggregate supply. This inflation is bad news as it means that real national income will fall and prices will rise.

Inflation can be bad for businesses: their costs will rise because the amount they have to pay for goods will go up. Their sales may fall as consumers will not want to buy as much because the prices have gone up. Exports will fall as UK prices rise in comparison to other countries' prices. Inflation can also cause a disruption of business planning; uncertainty about the future makes planning difficult and this may reduce the level of investment. Budgeting becomes a problem as businesses become unsure about what will happen to their costs. This may have a knock-on effect on employment.

However, it is possible that some businesses will benefit from inflation as consumers carry on buying their good or service at the higher price. This will lead to an increase in the business revenue.

6.5   THE BALANCE OF PAYMENTS

2.2.3   Understand the impact of surpluses and deficits on business and the economy

2.2.4   Understand the composition of the balance of payments, and the factors behind and benefits of international trade and capital flows: current account; imports; exports; effect of low opportunity cost producers

The **balance of payments** in an economy measures the payments between that country and others. It is made up of the country's exports and imports of goods, services and of transfers of financial capital. It measures all the payments received, and money owed, from overseas parties, less all the payments made, and debts owed, to people overseas.

6.5.1   Current and Capital Accounts

The accounts used to measure the UK's balance of payments are:

* the current account; and
* the capital and financial account.

The balance of payments figures also include a 'balancing item' to correct any statistical errors and to make sure the accounts 'balance'.

The **current account** measures flows in relation to trade in goods and services, income from investment and compensation of employees and current transfers (eg, private sector gifts to people overseas, or government aid to abroad). The current account balance is usually seen as the most important component of the balance of trade, because it has the greatest impact on other economic factors such as output and employment.

The **capital and financial account** measures inward investment, foreign investment, foreign currency borrowing by, and deposits with, UK banks, and changes in official reserves.

The **balancing item** is included to deal with errors and omissions in the accounts; if more currency flows into the UK than is recorded in actual transactions, then the balancing item will be positive, and vice versa.

6.5.2   The Impact of Imbalances on Exchange Rates

The balance of payments between the UK and other countries is important for a number of reasons, not least the impact that it may have on UK exchange rates (and therefore on the competitiveness of UK exports and of imports into our economy).

A **deficit** on the current account means that the country is not matching its overseas expenditures with its current overseas income. How much this matters depends on the size of the deficit and on how persistent it is. A small negative balance, or one which only persists for the short term, may not be regarded as too serious. It can be financed by the country running down its reserves, or capital inflows. However, a deficit lasting longer has to be financed. A country's reserves are not infinite, so cannot be run down indefinitely. The alternative is to increase overseas borrowing to finance the deficit. To do this to too great an extent is not in the country's interests either, since the larger the UK's debts to the outside world, the greater are the servicing requirements (repayment of interest and capital) on that debt.

One method of correcting a current account deficit may be to allow sterling to fall in value against other currencies. This tends to make foreign goods and services more expensive for UK buyers and so will encourage consumers to 'buy British' instead. In addition, it makes UK goods and services cheaper for overseas customers, helping UK exports. Both these factors will help to restore a positive current account balance.

However, if the current account is also being financed by rising overseas debt, this can create concerns about the stability of the economy, which may lead to government action to raise interest rates (so as to prevent an outflow of investment funds). You should remember that higher interest rates can encourage foreign investors to invest in sterling assets – pushing up the exchange rate as they buy sterling to do so. Rising interest rates may well lead to a strengthening of the currency – which is clearly at odds with the strategy outlined above, of trying to manage the current account through a low exchange rate.

Persistent surpluses and deficits on the balance of payments can create a considerable headache for a government and can impact on exchange rates, interest rates and consequently other activity in the economy.

7. MARKET BEHAVIOUR

The economy as a whole has a great influence on the financial markets.

- In a recession and at the start of a recovery, inflation and interest rates are typically low or falling. Low interest rates mean that the coupons on yields on fixed-interest securities will look relatively attractive; so investors will be prepared to pay higher prices for such securities.
- Conversely, the higher interest rates generally seen in a boom period will result in lower prices for fixed-income securities. That is, investors will not be willing to pay a high price to secure the fixed coupon attached to the security. (We will look at this idea in Section 7.2.2.)

The prices of equities (company shares) also tend to reflect market sentiment about prospects for the economy and so are influenced by the stages of the economic cycle. The main share price indices, such as the FTSE 100 Index in the UK and the S&P 500 Index in the US, serve as barometers for the market.

Share prices can be sharply influenced by changes in sentiment, and these themselves can happen quickly – for example, because of news that a particular economic indicator has been announced as being significantly different from what was expected. If there is a new expectation of an economic recovery, for example, share prices may rise in anticipation. People will expect that the recovery will mean better prospects for companies, higher profits, and therefore increasing share prices and dividends. Investors will be prepared to pay a premium for those shares – and the expected rise in prices becomes self-fulfilling.

A situation of persistently rising share prices is often called a **bull market**. If expectations about economic recovery are dented – for example, because there are reports of rising unemployment or bankruptcies – then share prices may drop back again. If an economy is booming, higher interest rates or concerns that it might be coming to an end can reverse the general direction of share prices. A persistent downward trend in equities prices is often called a **bear market**.

In the long run, share prices benefit from a steadily growing economy, with rising output, where corporate earnings grow.

7.1 THE ROLE OF FINANCIAL INVESTMENT IN THE ECONOMY

LEARNING OBJECTIVE

2.2.5   Understand the role of financial investment in the economy: primary markets as introducers of new funds to business and government; secondary markets enabling investors to adjust investments to meet individual needs

7.1.1 Primary Markets

The term 'primary market' refers to the market for new issues of shares or other securities (for example, loan instruments).

Companies and governments need capital in order to carry on their activities (for example, to buy premises, invest in machinery and so on). In order to raise this capital they may issue securities such as shares or loan stock. We will look at these securities from the investor's perspective in a later chapter. It is worth remembering that:

- Shares represent a share in the ownership of a company. Investors buy them in the hope of **capital appreciation** (the value of the company, and therefore the price of the share, goes up); or **income** (the company earns profits and pays them to its investors in the form of **dividends**).
- Loan instruments represent borrowings by the issuer, which must be repaid at some time. They therefore have a **capital repayment value** to the investor and (usually) a **coupon**, which represents the interest that will be paid periodically to the investor. An example of a loan instrument issued by a company is a debenture; an example of a loan issued by the UK government is a gilt.

In order to raise the money it needs, whether it be by way of share capital or loan capital, the issuer will offer the new securities on the primary market.

Primary markets are important both for new ventures – eg, a company which is just being established – and for existing ventures which are expanding and raising new capital, or which have been in existence for a while but are just introducing their existing shares to the public market for the first time.

For a new company, listing its shares on the London Stock Exchange (LSE) for the first time, the LSE acts as a primary market: the market through which it reaches its initial investors and raises a new tranche of capital.

The process of introducing shares or loan stock on to the market for the first time is known as **listing** them. Issuers have to meet certain standards before they can list their securities on the exchange:

- the size of the company;
- the value of securities they are introducing on to the market;
- the information available to potential investors in order to decide whether to invest;
- on an ongoing basis, the information companies must disclose to the market about activities or shares.

7.1.2 Secondary Markets

Once an investor has bought a holding in shares or loan instruments in the primary market, they may need to sell or reduce it due to a change in their circumstances or those of the company. They may need their money back, their investment objectives may change, or substantial capital gain can be realised.

The secondary markets offer a mechanism for them to do this and to invest in other listed securities.

The LSE acts as a secondary market in securities, among other exchanges. The secondary market is not capital raising but allows for trading of existing issues.

7.2 MACRO-ECONOMIC INFLUENCES ON ASSET CLASSES

LEARNING OBJECTIVE

2.3.1   Analyse the impact of macro-economic influences on each of the main asset classes: fixed income; alternative investments; cash; property; equities

In arriving at a suitable investment strategy it is worth considering the impacts of the wider economy on the individual asset classes. Armed with this information, it is possible to position a portfolio to potentially benefit from changes in the macro-economy.

In addition to using a suitable asset allocation model in order to diversify the portfolio and reduce risk by limiting exposure to any one sector or asset, the investment manager also needs to assess the macro-economic indicators and the position of the economy in the business cycle in arriving at a decision over when to make the individual investments within each asset class. As we will see in the following pages, each asset class may respond differently to changes at the macro-economic level.

The **investment clock** below describes the inter-relationship between the economic cycle and various sectors:

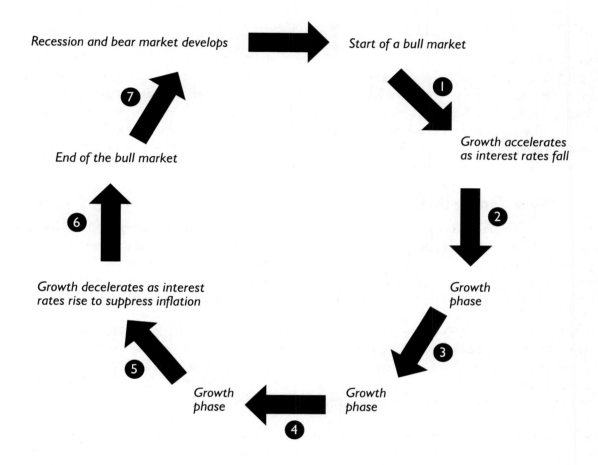

Sectors which may be in favour with investors at each point in the economic cycle include:

1. Bonds, interest-rate-sensitive equities – banks, house buildings.
2. Exchange-rate-sensitive equities – exporters, multinationals.
3. Basic industry equities – chemicals, paper, steel.
4. Cyclical consumer equities – airlines, automobiles, general retailers, leisure.
5. General industrial and capital spending equities – electrical, engineering, contractors.
6. Commodities and basic resources.
7. Cash; defensive equities – food, retail, pharmaceuticals, utilities.

However, the clock assumes that the portfolio manager knows exactly where in the economic cycle the economy is positioned and the extent to which each market sector is operationally geared to the cycle. Moreover, the investment clock doesn't provide any latitude for unanticipated events that may, through a change in the risk appetite of investors, spark a sudden flight from equities to government bond markets, for example, or change the course that the economic cycle takes. Each economic cycle is different, and investors' behaviour may not be the same as that demonstrated in previous cycles.

7.2.1 Cash

The returns achieved on traditional cash deposits are influenced by regional and international macro-economic factors such as inflation. Cash deposits, along with other money market instruments (such as T-bills and commercial paper) are an asset class having maturities of less than 12 months. These products provide investors with liquid investments that meet short-term needs.

Along with cash deposits, the returns provided by these investments also depend on the issuers' industry and firm-specific factors. The nominal rate of return on cash is made up of the real rate plus the inflation rate. Inflation erodes the value of capital and, if the real rate of interest being earned on the capital is less than the rate of inflation, then the value of a cash investment will diminish over time. Although interest rates may be increased by the Bank of England to control excessive inflationary growth in the economy, any investors holding time deposits will have to wait until the deposit matures in order to benefit from any changes in rates.

7.2.2 Fixed-Income Securities

Any changes that are made to interest rates as a result of macro-economic influences will also affect the value of fixed-income securities. These assets often have maturities of more than one year. An issuer of a fixed-income security raises funds from capital markets and, in return, an investor in this asset class receives regular coupon interest on the long-term loan that he has provided to the issuer, plus a redemption of the principal value of the investment at the maturity of the longer-term loan.

Yield-to-maturity (YTM) is a term used to identify the dynamic annualised return or rate that is provided to the investor for the entire period of the loan. There is an inverse relationship between the level of yield and the price of a bond. The yield on a particular bond is not static, but reacts instantaneously to fresh news as underlying factors or drivers start to influence market expectations. Typically, bond investments lose value when the whole interest rate cycle turns upward.

As an example, let us consider macro-economic influences on bonds. At the top of the growth phase in a normal economic cycle, inflationary pressures are likely to be increasing at an unacceptably high rate. Thus, interest rates may be increased. This rate increase will be necessary in order to control and moderate near- or long-term inflationary excesses in the economy. An increase in short-term rates can be transmitted across the whole yield curve, affecting bonds of longer maturities. This effect will diminish the value of existing fixed-interest holdings within the portfolio.

Alternatively, as the economy declines and begins to enter recession, interest rates may be reduced to stimulate the economy and to encourage consumption and spending. Falling money market interest rates and bond yields will lead to an increase in the prices and value of fixed-interest assets.

7.2.3 Equities

As an asset class, equity prices are affected both by macro-economic as well as company-specific factors. The price of a share is directly influenced by economic considerations. News that helps to boost company prospects, stimulate sales and lower costs of production and distribution will clearly be beneficial. Hence share prices increase on activity that translates into higher company cash flows and also raise expectations of higher dividends. When the economic growth cycle turns upward, investor confidence grows on expectations that increased spending and consumption in the economy will revive business activity. If this business confidence translates into visibly higher cashflows that strengthen a company's position in the marketplace, then increased investor demand for a company's shares will continue to lift share prices. Therefore, whereas bond returns measured in nominal terms are negatively impacted by rising inflation pressures, equities are seen as moderately good hedges against inflation.

7.2.4 Property

As an asset class, property or real estate is often considered to be a special type of alternative investment. Real estate provides access to tangible assets; often this is in commercial or retail property. This asset class has some unique features that are not common to equities or bonds. First, it is investment in a fixed unmovable object, ie, land or property located in a certain space. Second, one property is only approximately comparable to another, hence it is not fungible with another and presents challenges for valuers. Property is also not divisible, which makes it unique, and, finally, a property is illiquid due to its immovability and indivisibility.

In the last few years there has been increased interest from money managers to strategically include property in their portfolios. In addition to return opportunities, the asset allows managers to reduce risks through diversification and to provide inflation protection. Within a contemporary portfolio of bonds and equities, property provides good diversification benefits because of its lower correlations with other financial asset classes. As a result of this benefit it has become a common investment vehicle for pension funds and insurance companies worldwide.

Returns from property come from two sources: rental yield, and capital appreciation of the underlying property stock.

As with the common types of financial asset classes (money market, equity and bonds), the intrinsic value of real estate is affected not only by the key macro-economic factors (eg, GDP growth, inflation, interest rates and employment), but also by other asset-specific factors relating to the rental yields available to investors, the possibilities for capital appreciation, the availability of land, EU migration patterns, bank lending policy and taxation benefits and subsidies.

As an example, we can examine the impact of the response of the UK housing market to particular macro-economic events. During much of the earlier 2007 boom, the strength in the property market coincided with relatively low interest rates, strong equity market performances, high levels of consumer confidence, high employment rates across Europe, and loose credit card and bank lending policies. However, the onset of the mortgage crisis in the sub-prime mortgage market in the US in the autumn of 2007 triggered the first wave of a two-stage crisis. Combined with the ensuing credit crunch in the global capital markets, the resulting global economic recession and sharp drop in investor confidence lasted up until March 2009, when quantitative easing began. The outlook for growth was dampened not only by the drying up of credit by banks in the crisis, but also by outlooks for poor GDP growth in wider G7 economies.

Liquidity had dried up and a sharp credit squeeze in the commercial and the retail property market by banks triggered foreclosures in the US housing market. The contagion spread across the world, leading to the prominent bankruptcy of Lehman Brothers in the autumn of 2008 that further escalated the banking and housing market crises. The crisis was partially alleviated by large-scale central bank and government intervention in spring 2009. The co-ordinated intervention took the form of maintaining record low base rates in the UK and US, the privatisation of selected banks, monetary support to recapitalise the global banking system and further injections of liquidity via quantitative easing. All of these interventions were designed to stabilise the banking system, reduce the impact on the real economy and to stimulate and encourage the ailing banks to lend funds to households and companies.

The overall housing market performances as measured by the UK Nationwide Housing Price Index stood at 9738.6 in September 2007, its highest level since the quarterly index was created on 31 December 1952. The housing market plunged during the crisis of 2007/2008 to set a cycle dip by March 2009, and this reflected a housing market drop of 21% over an 18-month period.

This co-ordinated action at government level pump-primed the banking system and stabilised the capital markets. Stock markets recovered and, along with a moderating credit-squeeze, the property market regained composure, again stimulated by strong recoveries in the BRIC economies (Brazil, Russia, India and China). Low historic interest rates and stimulative quantitative easing policies continued to drive modest improvements in the commercial and retail property markets. However, during 2010 and early 2011, the rise has been tempered by high levels of unemployment across Europe, sluggish economic growth and tight government fiscal policy and record levels of budgetary deficits in some EU economies that have hampered recovery in the property markets.

Whereas the retail property market is more sensitive to employment conditions and the general health of household accounts, the commercial property market is not only dependent on economic drivers but also on external dependencies linked to global markets. In addition, most reputed developers prefer the leasing model and then to sell the leased-out property to investors. These are good options to buy, as they give the buyer a return on investment from the very beginning.

Real estate is a complex investment with its own unique benefits and disadvantages that each investor weighs differently. The possible benefits are as follows:

- Tax subsidy law allows mortgage interest, property taxes and other expenses to be tax deductible.
- Mortgage loans allow property borrowers to utilise more financial leverage than is available on shares or bonds. The loan-to-value (LTV) on a property in the UK has stabilised around the 75-80% mark even after the 2007/2008 credit crisis.

- Property investors have opportunities to add value to their property through renovation and restoration. This flexibility is not available to investors holding shares in companies.
- Multiple property investments in a portfolio with different geographical locations can provide diversification opportunities.
- Property can provide a good inflation hedge because there is positive correlation between inflation and property prices.

7.2.5 Alternative Investments

Over the last few years, many institutional investment portfolios have added a new class called **alternative investments** to their portfolios. They are often complex in nature, have limited regulations and can be relatively illiquid compared to their financial counterparts. Although not new, they fall into the following major classes: property (as discussed in Section 7.2.4); commodities; private equity and hedge funds.

Commodities

Even though households have been investing in gold and diamonds for centuries, commodities have found a useful place in the money manager's portfolio. The low correlation of these assets with financial assets such as equities and bonds has generated strong interest in these securities. Their appeal is based on the notion that commodities (ranging from gold to oil to wheat) are not financial investments but have intrinsic value that is dependent on other forces. These forces are not necessarily affected to the same extent by macro-economic conditions as financial assets. Their low correlation with other financial investments makes them useful as effective hedges against inflation.

Gold bullion, physical silver and oil have all received significant coverage in the press in recent years. Even before paper money existed, gold and silver were the currencies of choice as their portability and durability proved to be useful as a medium of exchange. Their scarcity value and safe-haven status during economic and political strife has proved that they deserve a strategic role in the institutional portfolio in order to stabilise returns.

Private Equity (PE)

Private equity investment developed rapidly in the 2000s. It is an asset class that involves professional funds that provide valuable financing for start-up companies, business acquisitions and company buy-outs. Essentially, it is an equity investment made by a select group of investors into a company or an asset not traded publicly in the capital market.

Both institutional and high net-worth individuals/families, called PE investors provide, the finance. These funds are pooled and channelled via a private equity group into a series of PE investments or projects. Risk for an investor may be reduced by diversification into a portfolio containing a range of PE projects.

There are four forms of private equity, namely: venture capital; corporate finance/buyout sector; mezzanine finance and distressed finance. The distinction between venture capital and PE has blurred in recent years. Investors pool funds and provide the money to invest in a variety of investment and projects in return for gains within a few years. The PE firm may be a Strategic Business Unit (SBU) within a larger financial institution. Funds-of-funds deliver diversification through investment in pools of different PE funds.

The private equity projects are managed by the general partner in a PE firm. The funds usually have an exit strategy and will liquidate their assets after a certain time (around five years on average) and move on to another financing project.

The investment characteristics of PE are:

- **Illiquidity** – investors tie up their funds for a long period until the fund realises its investment aims. Thus, such investments do not offer easy options to cash-out.
- **Lack of value transparency** – intrinsic value is difficult to determine due to limited availability of risk and return data. There is limited information to base estimates of project cash flows during the management period of the fund. The project may be moving through uncharted territory.
- **Specialised fund management skills** – general partners of PE firms have specialist skills and may also require assistance from advisers who can bring new experience to a complex investment as it goes through its development stages.
- **Exit strategies** – investors get their money back after the investment is liquidated. A venture capital investment, for example, may be liquidated through an IPO of shares to the public. Shares are allocated to private equity investors who sell them into the marketplace after the expiration of the lock-up period.

Hedge funds

Hedge funds or hedge funds-of-funds are managed by private fund managers who take investments from non-retail clients, often high net-worth individuals who have minimum investment amounts. Although amounts can be less nowadays, in the early days at least $1 million investment was required to participate in a hedge fund. There are also minimum lock-period requirements, and this may make it difficult for investors to get their money back if they need it in the short term. Hedge fund managers include their own funds as part of the fund they are running on a collective basis. Funds-of-funds are managed by professionals who invest in combinations of hedge funds to enhance return possibilities and to provide diversification.

An attractive feature of this investment is that fund managers are not constrained to a narrow range of strategies. They are not regulated to the same extent as mutual funds and can take a much higher level of risk by utilising a wide variety of investment strategies in their search for alpha. Hedge funds come with different investment styles and often combine high-risk investments such as derivatives and short-selling techniques in their approaches to delivering superior returns. Historically, hedge funds were subscribed by high net-worth individuals who met the minimum investment of $1 million. Their fees are high and they often charge '2 and 20' fees, which means that the initial management fee is 2% of the fund's net asset value (NAV), followed by a 20% performance (incentive fees) on the net profits made on the fund.

Please refer to Chapter 1 for more on the asset classes above.

KEY CHAPTER POINTS

- The UK population is increasing. In aggregate, the age structure is shifting towards a higher proportion of elderly people (though immigration is slowing this trend, to a degree).
- There is an increase in single person households, though most people still live as part of larger units.
- With more older people, and also more young children, the proportion of the population that is working reduces, and the proportion that is non-working, and dependent on the working population, increases.
- Living standards rise when incomes increase by more than the rate of inflation.
- The value of property is a significant part of personal sector wealth in the UK.
- Productivity is a measure of how much output is produced by factors of production. Factors of production are land, labour, capital and enterprise. Increases in productivity, for example those produced by technological developments, create economic wealth and enhance household incomes and therefore living standards.
- A major factor behind the growth in the tertiary (service) sector of the economy has been the rapid expansion of the banking, finance and insurance sectors – and of technology.
- A number of international factors influence UK markets and the local economy.
- Globalisation is an increasing factor, both in business and finance.
- The UK is part of the European Union, but has not yet joined into monetary union with the euro. There are advantages, and disadvantages, to doing so.
- Fiscal policy is the government's policy on taxation, borrowing and public (government) spending.
- Monetary policy is concerned with measures which affect the amount of money in the economy (the money stock or money supply) and the price of money (ie, rates of interest).
- A central bank acts for a government and typically has various functions, such as the issuance of banknotes, management of government finances, dealing in the money markets to set interest rates and acting as lender of last resort to the banking system. The Bank of England is the UK central bank, and the Monetary Policy Committee its interest rate-setting body.
- Economies go through cycles with identifiable phases and characteristics; governments try to stabilise the volatility of these cycles through various forms of intervention.
- The primary markets are the markets on which new funds are made available to enterprises and to government. Instruments are subsequently traded in secondary markets.
- Countries can suffer from trade imbalances when they import significantly more than they export, and vice versa.
- There are a number of economic and market measures or indices which can be used to gauge the direction and strength of changes in the economy, or of a market.

CISI
CHARTERED INSTITUTE FOR
SECURITIES & INVESTMENT

CHAPTER THREE

PRINCIPLES OF INVESTMENT RISK AND RETURN

This syllabus area will provide approximately 6 of the 80 examination questions

1. THE TIME VALUE OF MONEY

1.1 COMPOUND INTEREST

LEARNING OBJECTIVE

3.1.1   Understand the effects of compound interest and the time value of money

The idea of compound interest and the effect it can have on an investment takes account of the additional growth that arises when an investor leaves his interest invested with the main deposit (the principal) instead of withdrawing it to spend: he begins to earn interest on that interest, and his investment rolls up all the faster for it.

EXAMPLE

Suppose that £2,000 is invested at 10% interest. After one year, the original principal plus interest will amount to £2,200.

	£
Original investment	2,000
Interest in the first year (10%)	200
Investment at end of one year	2,200
Interest in the second year (10%)	220
Total investment at the end of two years	2,420

The second-year interest of £220 is made up of 10% earned on the original investment, and 10% earned on the interest earned in the first year.

Instead of performing the calculations shown above, we can calculate compound interest using a standard formula, as follows:

$$S = X(1 + r)^n$$

where:

X = the original sum invested
r = the interest/return rate, expressed as a proportion (so 5% is written as 0.05)
n = the number of periods over which we are compounding
S = the sum invested after n periods

Compounding effects may appear to be minimal over one or two periods, but over a long time they can make a considerable difference to the growth of an investment.

In the previous example, interest has been calculated **annually**, but this isn't always the case. Interest may be compounded **daily, weekly, monthly** or **quarterly**.

1.2   PRESENT VALUE

LEARNING OBJECTIVE

3.1.2   Calculate the present value of: lump sums; regular payments; annuities; perpetuities

The calculation of present value is used to determine how much to invest today, given a known rate of interest and frequency of payment, in order to achieve a required amount. The methods used to calculate present value are known as **discounted cash flow techniques** or **DCF**. The rate of interest that is to be received is known as the **discount rate**, and the amount that is required to be achieved is known as the **terminal value** or **future value**.

1.2.1   Present Value of a Future Sum Cash Flow

The amount that needs to be invested today in order to obtain a targeted future sum is determined through discounting. The procedure is a reverse process to compounding. Thus, the future amount required by the rate of interest earned over the period is calculated by rearranging the formula for compound interest as follows:

$$PV = \frac{FV}{(1 + r)^n}$$

where:

PV = present value (or value of sum invested)
FV = future value (or value at end of compounding period)
r   = interest rate expressed as an integer (eg, 5% = 0.05)
n   = number of periods being compounded (eg, 5 years)

We will use data from the compound interest formula to illustrate this. How much needs to be invested today at 5% per annum to generate £127.63 (to two decimal points) after five years?

The formula is:

$$PV = \frac{£127.63}{(1 + 0.05)^5}$$

$$= \frac{£127.63}{(1.05)^5}$$

$$= \frac{£127.63}{1.2763}$$

$$= £100$$

This can be proved by entering into a calculator $127.63 \div 1.05^5$ and can be checked in reverse using the compound interest formula: $100 \times 1.05^5 = 127.63$.

As the present value formula expresses future cash flows in today's terms, it allows a comparison to be made of competing investments of equal risk which have the same start date but different payment timings or amounts.

1.2.2   Present Value of an Annuity

The present value of an annuity refers to a series of equal cash payments that will be received over a specified period of time. As before, the present value of an annuity is calculated by discounting the future cash flows to today's value. The same formula can be used for regular payments.

We will first consider where payments are made in arrears. If we expect to receive payments of £100 over each of the next three years, we can calculate their present value assuming interest rates remain at 5%, using the formula above.

Year	Cash Flow	Discount Rate	Formula	Discount Factor	Present Value
1	100.00	5%	$100.00 \div 1.05$	0.9524	95.24
2	100.00	5%	$100.00 \div 1.05\,^2$	0.9070	90.70
3	100.00	5%	$100.00 \div 1.05\,^3$	0.8638	86.38
Total					272.32

So the present value of those future payments totalling £300.00 is actually £272.32. The table also shows how this converts into a discount factor, that is, by how much the future value is discounted in decimal terms.

Instead of calculating each present value, this can be calculated by using another formula:

$$\text{Present value (PV) of an annuity} = £ \times \left[\frac{1 - (1+r)^{-n}}{r} \right]$$

where:

$£$ = the amount of the annuity paid each year;
r = the rate of interest over the life of the annuity;
n = the number of periods that the annuity will run for.

Using the example above, the calculation is as follows:

Present value (PV) of an annuity $= 100 \times \left[\dfrac{1 - (1 + 0.05)^{-3}}{0.05} \right]$

$$= 100 \times \left[\dfrac{1 - (1.05)^{-3}}{0.05} \right]$$

$$= 100 \times \left[\dfrac{1 - (0.86384)}{0.05} \right]$$

$$= 100 \times \left[\dfrac{0.13616}{0.05} \right]$$

$$= 100 \times \left[2.7232 \right]$$

$$= £272.32$$

The present value of an annuity can be used for calculating such things as the monthly repayments on a mortgage and it can also be used in investment appraisal.

1.2.3 Present Value of Perpetuities

A **perpetuity** is a series of regular cash flows that are due to be paid or received indefinitely, which in practice is defined as a period beyond 50 years.

It is simply calculated using the following formula:

$$\text{Present value (PV) of a perpetuity} = \frac{A}{r}$$

where:

A $=$ amount of periodic payment
r $=$ interest rate

Although a perpetuity really exists only as a mathematical model, it can be used to approximate the value of a long-term stream of equal payments by treating it as an indefinite perpetuity.

So, for example, if you have a commercial property that generates £10,000 of rental income and the interest rate is 8%, then the formula can be used to calculate its present value by capitalising those future payments into its present value of £125,000.

$$\text{Present value (PV) of a perpetuity} = \frac{£10,000}{0.08} = £125,000$$

Perpetual Bond Calculations

A perpetual bond is a bond with no maturity date. Hence it pays coupons indefinitely and the bond is not redeemed. It is irredeemable. They are also known as consols. Some of the historically notable perpetual bond issues were made by the UK Treasury to pay off loans related to the Napoleonic wars (1814). There exist eight undated gilts, which make up a very small proportion of the UK government's debt. They have no fixed maturity date. These gilts are very old. The redemption of these bonds is at the discretion of the UK government, but because of their age, they all have low coupons, and there is therefore currently little incentive for the government to redeem them.

Perpetual bonds are priced using the following expression:

$$P = \frac{C}{Y}$$

where:

P = price of the bond.

C = annual coupon rate.

Y = yield to maturity of the bond.

Preference Shares and Calculations

Preference shares are equity instruments that are often considered to be a hybrid; having similar characteristics to a bond and a share. The shares pay a constant dividend indefinitely. Hence, as with a perpetual bond, they can be considered as securities offering fixed income indefinitely.

Preferred equity is priced by using the following expression:

$$P = \frac{D}{K}$$

where:

D = constant dividend set for the security.

K = return expected by the holder of the share.

1.3   FUTURE VALUE

3.1.3   Calculate the future value of: lump sums; regular payments

1.3.1   Future Value of Lump Sums

Future value refers to the future value of an amount invested now at a given rate of interest. We effectively already looked at future value when we considered compounding interest in Section 1.1. We saw that the future value of £100 deposited today at 5% per annum for a period of years was:

Year	Balance at the start of the year	Interest for the year at 5% per annum	Balance at the end of the year
1	100.00	5.00	105.00
2	105.00	5.25	110.25
3	110.25	5.51	115.76
4	115.76	5.79	121.55
5	121.55	6.08	127.63

To calculate future value, the formula is:

$$\text{Future value (FV)} = \text{Present value (PV)} \times (1 + r)^n$$

So to calculate the value in five years' time of £100 invested today at 5% per annum, we would enter this into a calculator as $100 \times (1.05 \char`\^ 5) = 127.63$.

Where interest is paid more frequently, the formula is adjusted so that if interest is instead paid half-yearly it would become:

$$FV = PV \times (1 + r/2)^{2n}$$

$$£100 \times (1 + (0.05 \div 2))^{2 \times 5} = £100 \times 1.025^{10} = £128.00845$$

In the example above the rate of interest for the half-year has been calculated first; namely, half of 5%, which is then expressed as a decimal, ie, 1.025. The term is then converted into the number of periods on which interest will be paid, in other words ten half-yearly interest payments.

1.3.2   Applying Compound Interest to Regular Payments

So far we have concentrated on establishing the final value of invested lump sums when compound interest is applied. We now move on to looking at how final values are established when a series of equal payments are invested either at the start or the end of each year. The former payments are known as being made in advance, whilst the latter are termed as being made in arrears.

If investing at the start of each year, then the following formula may be used:

$$FV = \text{Payment} \times \left[((1 + r)^n - 1)/r \right] (1 + r)$$

where:

FV = future value

r = interest/return rate

n = number of payment periods

EXAMPLE

£100 is invested at the start of each year for five years at a fixed rate of interest of 6% per annum compounded annually. What will the accumulated value of these series of payments be at the end of the five-year period?

Solution

$$
\begin{aligned}
FV &= £100 \times [((1.06)^5 - 1)/0.06](1.06) \\
&= £100 \, [((1.06)^5 - 1)/0.06](1.06) \\
&= £100 \, [(1.34 - 1)/0.06](1.06) \\
&= £100 \, [(0.34)/0.06](1.06) \\
&= £100 \, [5.6371](1.06) \\
&= £563.71(1.06) \\
&= £597.53
\end{aligned}
$$

The future value (FV) is £597.53.

We can check these figures using the following table.

Year	Deposit Paid	Balance at Start	Interest Rate	Interest Earned	Balance at End
1	100	£100.00	6%	£6.00	£106.00
2	100	£206.00	6%	£12.36	£218.36
3	100	£318.36	6%	£19.10	£337.46
4	100	£437.46	6%	£26.25	£463.71
5	100	£563.71	6%	£33.82	£597.53

If investing at the end of each year, then the following formula may be used.

$$FV = \text{payment} \times \left[((1 + r)^n - 1)/r \right]$$

EXAMPLE

£100 is invested at the end of each year for five years at a fixed rate of interest of 6% per annum compounded annually. What will the accumulated value of these series of payments be at the end of the five-year period?

Solution

$$FV = £100 \times [((1.06)^5 - 1)/0.06]$$

$$= £100 [((1.06)^5 - 1)/0.06]$$

$$= £100 [(1.34 - 1)/0.06]$$

$$= £100 [(0.34)/0.06]$$

$$= £100 [5.6371]$$

$$= £563.71$$

The future value (FV) is £563.71.

We can check these figures using the following table.

Year	Deposit Paid	Balance at Start	Interest Rate	Interest Earned	Balance at End
1	100	£0.00	6%	£0.00	£100.00
2	100	£100.00	6%	£6.00	£206.00
3	100	£206.00	6%	£12.36	£318.36
4	100	£318.36	6%	£19.10	£437.46
5	100	£437.46	6%	£26.25	£563.71

Table header: Future Value

Note: The difference between this and the earlier example, ie, (£597.53 – £563.71 = £33.82) is solely accounted for by one earlier payment being invested over the entire five-year period, ie, ((£100 × $1.06)^5 - 1$) = £33.82.

1.4   THE TIME VALUE OF MONEY

Both investor and adviser need to appreciate the implications of holding investments over a period of time, and the effect of inflation during the time period on returns from investments.

When considering the passage of time, understanding the **compounding** effects we have just considered is critical. The principle of **discounting** is rather like compounding in reverse, as it allows us to calculate, among other things, what rate of interest or return will produce a specific sum at a future date.

If a person has a choice between (A) £1,000 now, and (B) £1,000 in one year's time, then they will prefer for (A). If you have £1,000 now, you can invest it and earn interest, so that you would have more at the year-end. You might alternatively have other uses for the money.

This example shows that money has a **time value**. The option of having money now is of more value than the option of having money at a date in the future, because we can make it work for us from an earlier point. **Interest** can be seen partly as the return required by the lender to compensate for the time value of money that the lender is supplying to the borrower.

The formula we use to calculate the effects of compounding is, you will remember, that if we invest £X now for n years at r% interest per annum we should obtain £X $(1 + r)^n$ in n years' time.

Thus, if we invest £10,000 now for four years at 10% interest per annum, we will have a total investment worth £10,000 x $(1+10\%)^4$ = £14,641 at the end of four years (that is, at year 4 if it is now year 0).

The principle of **discounting** is that if we wish to have £S in n years' time, we need to invest a certain sum now (year 0) at an interest rate of r% in order to obtain the required sum of money in the future.

EXAMPLE

If we wish to have £14,641 in four years' time, how much money would we need to invest now at 10% interest per annum? (You could think of this as being a bit like the reverse of the compounding calculations we have already looked at.)

Using our compounding formula, $S = X(1 + r)^n$

where:

X	=	the original sum invested
r	=	10%
n	=	4
S	=	the sum we want to achieve = £14,641

£14,641 = $X(1 + 0.1)^4$

£14,641 = X times 1.4641

so X = $\dfrac{£14,641}{1.4641}$ = £10,000

We can see that £10,000 now, earning interest at 10% per annum, is the equivalent in value of £14,641 after four years. We can therefore say that £10,000 is the present value of £14,641 at year 4, at an interest rate of 10%.

1.5   INFLATION AND INVESTMENT RETURNS

LEARNING OBJECTIVE

3.1.4   Calculate real and inflation-adjusted returns: nominal returns; real or
inflation-adjusted returns; total returns

The **nominal return** on an investment is the return it gives, unadjusted for inflation. Thus, a bank
account paying 4% interest annually has a nominal return of 4%. The **real return** is the return it
provides an investor after stripping out the effects of inflation.

Thus, if inflation is running at 3% per annum, the above bank account would be providing a real return
calculated as follows:

Nominal return – Rate of inflation = Real return

4% – 3% = 1% real return

This rough calculation is useful for giving an approximation of the investment's real rate of return – but
if we need an exact measure, it is a little more complicated. To get a completely accurate figure, the
relationship between the **rate of inflation**, the **real rate of return** and the **nominal rate of return**
is as follows, with rates expressed as a decimal (eg, 5% is expressed as 0.05):

(1 + real rate of return) × (1 + inflation rate) = 1 + nominal rate of return

If the nominal rate of return is 12% per annum and the annual rate of inflation is 8% per annum, the
real rate of return is the return earned after allowing for the return needed just to keep pace with
inflation.

We may rearrange the equation above to find the real rate of return:

$$\frac{1 + \text{nominal rate}}{1 + \text{inflation rate}} = 1 + \text{real rate}$$

$$\frac{1.12}{1.08} = 1.037$$

The real rate of return is thus 3.7%.

It's not unusual for people to use the **approximate** measure we looked at first, however – ie, real
return as the difference between the nominal rate of return and the rate of inflation. In our last
example, this would be 12% – 8% = 4%.

It is possible for a real return to be negative; in the example above, if inflation were to run at 6% per
annum but a bank account continued to pay 4% per annum, then the real return on it would be around
–2%. Put another way, the purchasing power of a deposit held in that bank account would be falling at
2% a year.

This is important, because investors need to keep the effects of inflation in mind when planning their financial affairs. Even quite low levels of inflation can erode the purchasing power of someone's wealth over time.

You may also see the term **total return**. This means the return on an investment both from its income production, and any capital gains (or losses) it generates. The total return on an investment may be important to an investor when comparing one investment with another; but it may also be important to him to strip out the elements of that return which are attributable to capital gain/loss, and to income, since these may be treated differently for tax purposes.

You should remember that we looked at methods of calculating the redemption yield on a fixed-interest security in Chapter 2. The redemption yield takes account of both the interest to be paid, and any gain/loss if the security is held to maturity. It therefore calculates the annualised **total return** on that security, assuming it is held to maturity.

2. INVESTMENT RISK AND RETURN

2.1 RISK PREMIUM

Risk and **reward** are important aspects of investment decisions. It is true that low-risk investments generally generate a low return. To believe, however, that taking on a high level of risk is a sure way to produce higher returns is to misunderstand the meaning of risk. Risk is present when there is a possibility of poor performance. A risky investment can offer the possibility of relatively high rates of return, but the other side of the coin, from which the riskiness arises, is that the return might instead be low or negative.

We can say that **risk** and **potential reward** are generally positively correlated; investments with a higher potential return generally carry a higher risk.

Both financial advisers and their clients need to understand clearly the connection between risk and return:

- High-risk investments generally have the potential for a higher reward, plus a greater possibility of loss.
- Low-risk investments generally have a lower reward, with a lower possibility of loss.

An investment strategy that provides a way to invest money to produce the optimum rate of return for a given level of risk would clearly be valuable. The aim of a fund manager (or an individual investor) is to achieve higher returns than others, without incurring greater risks.

While it is almost impossible to avoid risk entirely, a holding in a UK government security (a gilt) is regarded as being virtually free from risk of default by the government. It is therefore used to give a benchmark for what is described as the **risk-free rate of return**. If we hold a gilt from now up to its redemption, or if it is an undated gilt which will never be redeemed, then we know exactly what return we will get if we continue to hold it. The risk-free rate of return will vary through time, just as interest rates generally vary.

The government's 4% Consolidated Stock, an undated or perpetual gilt, can be used for these purposes. There is no preset date for redemption at par, and the instrument is effectively a government promise to pay the owner £4 for each £100 of the stock each year, indefinitely. For example, when the stock is priced at around £80, it will give a yield of 5% indefinitely – which can be regarded as a virtually risk-free rate of return if we simply hold on to the stock. The yield on this undated stock indicates the market's view of the **long-term interest rate**.

The rates of return on other investments will differ from the risk-free rate, reflecting the additional return that is required by investors who are taking a risk on those investments. This additional return is the **risk premium**.

The idea of **risk premium** is relevant in various contexts:

- An **individual** may find that such a premium is required from them when taking out a mortgage, for example. The housebuyer seeks an investor (lender) from whom to borrow money. If the individual's mortgage proposal carries higher than average risk, they may find that they have to pay a higher rate of interest than if the risk were lower. If the individual's credit rating is below average, or if the amount to be borrowed is a relatively high percentage of the value of the property, then the individual may find that some lenders will not offer their most favourable terms. The borrower is effectively having to pay a risk premium in order to borrow the money.
- For **companies** seeking finance, the principle is the same. For example, loans to companies with relatively low credit ratings will generally carry higher rates of interest (carrying a risk premium relative to the interest rates that are available to companies with higher credit ratings).

For the UK during the 20th century, on average equities produced a return 5.6% per annum higher than the return from gilts, on average. This can therefore be treated as the **risk premium** from investing in **equities**. Equity holders run the risk that they may receive much lower returns – even below the rate on risk-free assets. The risk premium from investing in shares compensates them for taking that risk.

2.2　TYPES OF RISK

LEARNING OBJECTIVE

3.2.1　Analyse and explain the main types of risk and the implications for investors: systemic risk; market risk – asset price volatility, currency, interest rates, foreign exchange rates, commodity price volatility; concentration and diversification; long-term investment risk; liquidity, credit risk and default; gearing; fraud and financial crime; counterparty and institutional risk; market timing

Almost all investments carry a certain level of risk. As we have worked through different asset classes in Chapter 2, we have thought about the different risk levels attached to different types of investment.

However, a large element of the risk attached to any one investment can be 'mitigated' (reduced) through appropriate diversification. It is necessary to take a certain level of risk if you want to achieve any form of reward. There is a trade-off between increasing levels of risk, and the potential rewards your investment may give you.

You might think that some investments are not risky at all – in particular, the **liquid** and **interest-bearing** elements of a portfolio. Indeed, we even describe some investments as being **risk-free**, for comparison purposes. Even these investments, however (which include bank deposits and investments like gilts), carry some risk. They are subject to:

- **interest rate risk** – the risk that interest rates move against the investor. For example, they invest in an asset with a fixed interest rate of 4% over three years. Meanwhile, interest rates move up to, say, 8%, but they are still locked into the low rate. Or, they invest in a bank deposit paying a variable rate of interest and rates are reduced – so their income falls.
- **inflation** – a general rise in the level of prices, which means that a fixed sum of money won't buy as much at the end of the year as it did at the start – it's worth less because inflation has eroded its purchasing power.

To protect capital against these risks, people often invest in equities. The hope is that the companies will do well and their shares will go up in value, providing capital growth for the investor. However, shares can go down as well as up; when companies do very badly, their shares may even fall to a **nil** value. So this part of the portfolio may be considerably riskier than the liquid and interest-bearing elements.

Companies pay a large portion of their annual profits out to their shareholders in the form of dividends. If they do well, and make more profits each year, dividends will go up, so the investor gets rising income as well as capital growth. But again there is an element of risk. Falling profits could mean falling dividends, and sometimes companies do so badly that they pay no dividend at all.

So, to limit the risk involved in investing in equities, the investor needs to diversify by spreading their equity holdings across a number of different companies.

2.2.1 Systematic Risk

A systematic risk is one which affects the financial system as a whole – as opposed to any individual share – and is therefore likely to affect pretty much all investments.

Systematic risks tend to be outside the power of most investors to predict, and often of the investment manager to protect against; however, some types of investment are more vulnerable to systematic risk than others. They tend to be of the following types:

- **Liquidity** – the term can mean both the amount of cash in a portfolio, or, in connection with a given investment, how easily it can be converted into cash. If a specific type of investment or market is illiquid – ie, it is hard to sell the investment quickly for a fair price – there is little that can be done. Problems of illiquidity can be normal for a particular investment class (eg, property can be hard to sell in poor markets) – or they can arise suddenly, because of a particular event. For example, if one large bank were to fail, and other banks were owed a lot of money by it, there could be a liquidity problem in the banking industry.

- **Interest rates** – the outlook for interest rates, and the length of time at which they stay at a given level, has a great effect on most types of investment – certainly on fixed-interest securities and shares. If interest rates are high, businesses find it expensive to borrow to fund any expansion of their activities; even if they have additional funds, they may find it more profitable to put this on deposit and earn high rates of interest, instead of using it to trade. If economic activity is affected by recession as in recent years, some shares prices may fall, and vice versa. In addition, consumers are affected by high interest rates – their credit card or mortgage bills are likely to be higher – so they spend less, reducing the profits that companies can make from their consumer activities. Also, when interest rates are high, the prices of fixed-interest securities fall as their fixed-interest element becomes less attractive compared to current market rates.

- **Inflation** – a general rise in the level of prices (and so also is a general fall in the purchasing power of money). The level of inflation in an economy is a big indication of its overall health, and of the steps that are being taken by the government to tackle issues such as unemployment, and growth.

  High levels of inflation are often associated with high interest rates, and vice versa. If inflation is higher than the level of interest being earned on a deposit account, then that account is in effect worth less to its owner at the end of the year than it was at the start. Inflation can thus erode the real value of capital, even where investments are making reasonable returns.

  Currently we are seeing inflation at what are, historically, very low levels; in the UK it has been between 3% and 5% for some time. There are many who can remember inflation levels in the mid-teens during the 1980s (and interest rates to match). A gradual reduction in inflation, in the UK and other countries, over the past 15–20 years has led to the current environment of low interest rates, and has, to a degree, encouraged investors to seek higher returns by investing in stock markets rather than keeping their money on deposit with banks and building societies.

- **Currency** – currency risks apply to a range of investments. It might seem obvious that holding shares in a US company, priced in US dollars, carries some currency risk; but there is some currency risk if an investor holds shares in a UK company quoted in sterling.

  This is because most major UK companies have some exposure to foreign currencies themselves; either because they have branches and subsidiaries abroad, earning profits in foreign currency – or perhaps because they buy their raw materials abroad or sell their goods overseas. Thus movements in the price of one currency against another can have an effect on their profits, when translated back into sterling.

  A strong pound sounds like a good thing on the face of it. But it usually creates problems for those UK companies that export a lot of what they manufacture. This is because, as the pound gets stronger (and the foreign currency correspondingly weaker), it costs the overseas buyer more in his home currency to buy the sterling-priced goods. It has not cost the UK company any more to make the goods in sterling terms but they cost the buyer more in US dollars, euros or any other home currency. The foreign buyer may well decide to buy from another supplier, in another country.

  Similarly, UK companies that import their raw materials from overseas will suffer if the pound is weak. When they sell sterling to buy the foreign currency they need to pay their overseas suppliers, they will get fewer units of the foreign currency per £1. So it will cost them more, in sterling, to buy their raw materials – which means that either they must raise their prices (which may make them uncompetitive in sterling terms) or they earn lower profits. In terms of the stock market, currency can have an impact. If the pound falls, the price of shares on the London Stock Exchange may be relatively cheap to foreign buyers, when translated into their home currencies – so there may be an increase in overseas buying.

2.2.2 Capital Risk

This is the risk that the investor's capital falls in value (or fails to grow at an acceptable rate). Some investments, such as equities, carry significant capital risk; others carry virtually none. An investor who cannot tolerate any loss of capital at all should opt for an investment in the latter class. An example, for a retail investor, might be one of the products offered by National Savings & Investments; for an institutional investor it would include UK gilts bought at or below par and held to maturity. In both cases this is because the issuer is the UK government, and the risk of the government defaulting on its debts is regarded as very low.

This capital security should, however, be weighed against the low returns to be obtained from such investments. In addition, inflation may still erode the real value of the investor's capital unless he has selected an index-linked option.

2.2.3 Income Risk

This is the risk that the income from an investment falls, or does not rise in line with inflation, or in some cases the investment ceases any payouts. Examples are:

- a fixed-income security defaulting on an interest payment; or
- a company suffering falling profits and paying lower or no dividends for a given year.

An investor requiring absolute certainty of income might be well advised to consider an investment such as:

- a bank deposit paying interest at frequent periods; and/or
- a gilt.

In both cases, however, they should consider the impact of inflation on their long-term returns.

2.2.4 Currency Risk

Currency risk arises from fluctuations in the value of currencies against one another. A UK resident who buys foreign stocks or bonds faces currency risk.

Suppose that a UK investor buys shares in a US company which does most of its trading in the US.

- The share price in US dollars fluctuates on the US stock market; this is market risk.
- Additionally, the value of sterling fluctuates against the US dollar; this is currency risk.

The sterling value of the investment will fluctuate in time as a result of two effects; the changing dollar share price, and the changing US dollar/sterling exchange rate.

Some companies **hedge** their foreign exchange earnings or their foreign raw materials costs, to give them greater certainty about future earnings and to reduce currency risks. The term hedging means undertaking transactions to protect against a certain event – in this case, an adverse currency movement. This may be done, for example, by entering into **forward currency contracts**, a type of agreement which fixes the value of future currency inflows at the time of transaction.

2.2.5 Inflation Risk

Rising prices can reduce the purchasing power of an amount of capital, or income. By investing money in assets which may not keep up with inflation, the investor may be risking loss in the purchasing power of their portfolio over the life of the investment.

Some economies suffer **deflation in prices**. Japan has done so for most of the last two decades. If prices are falling, buying goods today bears the 'risk' that those same goods could have been purchased for less later. There is then a strong incentive for people to save, since the purchasing power of cash, even if no interest is being earned, will increase over time. This is one reason why deflation can be an economic problem. If people have a strong incentive to save, demand for goods and services may suffer.

2.2.6 Interest Rate Risk

Interest rate risk means that interest rates move against the investor. For example:

- they invest in an asset with a fixed interest rate of 4% over three years. Meanwhile, interest rates move up to, say, 8% but they are still locked into their lower rate; or
- they invest in a bank deposit paying a variable rate of interest, and rates fall – so their income falls accordingly.

Interest rate risk can also affect an investor's capital, since the price of fixed-interest securities tends to vary inversely with the direction of interest rates.

Financial gearing is a term used to describe the relationship between the amount of debt (or long-term loans) taken out by a firm to finance its business activities, as a proportion of financing from its shareholders. Total financing is made up of debt plus shareholder funds and debt as a proportion of the total financing is a measure of a financial gearing ratio.

A highly-geared company usually has a sizeable amount of financing raised through long-term debt issuance. Regular interest has to be paid on debt taken out by the company and this payment takes precedence over dividends paid to shareholders. Financial risk increases as gearing rises because if a company's earnings are volatile, under difficult business conditions it may not be able to meet its obligations to its debt holders.

2.2.7 Issuer Risk

This is the risk that the issuer of a security **defaults** – cannot repay the capital, or (in the case of a fixed-interest security) the interest, as it falls due. A review of an issuer's credit rating can give some comfort as to the likelihood of this, but is not an absolute guarantee.

Financial crime is any kind of criminal conduct relating to money or to financial services or markets involving:

- fraud or dishonesty;
- bribery or corruption;
- false accounting;
- misconduct in, or misuse of information relating to, a financial market;
- money laundering/terrorist financing;

- handling the proceeds of crime;
- financial sanction breaches.

It arises from the risk that a company may fail to comply with financial crime legislation and industry laws on anti-money laundering, may suffer losses as a result of internal or external fraud, or may fail to ensure the security of personnel, physical premises and its assets. Fraud is one form of financial crime that can also be a significant threat to the earnings, capital and reputation of a company or organisation, particularly when associated with a failure to comply with a core regulatory requirement or expectation. In the UK, the Financial Services Authority (FSA) has a statutory objective to reduce the extent to which it is possible for a financial business to be used for a purpose connected with financial crime.

With financial crime having been on the rise in recent years, companies, especially those in the financial services sector, have established protocols that assess the implications of all emerging legal and regulatory requirements that impact them. They establish and operate risk control frameworks in respect of anti-money laundering, terrorist financing, sanctions and bribery and corruption crimes.

2.2.8   Non-Systematic Risk

Non-systematic risks can also be known as **specific risks** or **unique risks.**

Non-systematic risks are those which relate to a particular business, investment or share. They can usually be reduced through diversification. We will now look at some examples of non-systematic, or specific, risks.

- **Business risks** – these are risks which are associated with the nature of a company's profits and dividends – they include factors such as:
  - product design;
  - labour relations;
  - the costs of raw materials;
  - the strength of the company's balance sheet.

  We could think of these things as internal business risks.

- **Industry risks**. These include:
  - tariffs and barriers to trade;
  - industry-wide strikes;
  - changes in consumer taste;
  - seasonal factors.
- **Management risks** – these are risks that relate to the calibre of management of a company – are the managers good enough to plan and manage the company effectively, or are they out of their depth and unable to cope with challenges?
- **Financial risk** – any risk associated with the nature of the financing options selected by a firm. For example, a company's assets may be financed through a mixture of debt and equity. Thus it is directly related to its capital structure. A firm which is 100% equity-financed has no financial risk. Incorporation of debt financing in the capital structure brings with it financial obligations to repay the coupons and principal on the debt at various stages.

2.2.9 Counterparty Risk

Counterparty risk (also referred to as credit risk or default risk) is the risk that your counterparty in a transaction cannot honour its obligation to you. For example, you have bought a corporate bond from company XYZ, expecting to receive coupon payments and the nominal value of the bond at maturity. Under this transaction, you are exposed to the risk that XYZ cannot pay you the coupons and principal at the agreed point in time.

Another example is an equity put option bought on the OTC market. If markets plunge, as they have done in recent times, the mark-to market value of the put option increases sharply, introducing significant counterparty risk to the buyer of the put option. Similar risk exists in swaps, swaptions, and inflation-linked swaps.

2.2.10 Mitigating Risk by Diversification

Sectors

It is possible to mitigate the risk of investing into any one stock by buying shares in several companies. Ideally, they will not all be stocks in the same sector. This is diversifying across different sectors; for example, a well-diversified portfolio of shares might include holdings in the banking sector, the manufacturing sector, the retail sector and so on. Diversification can be thought of as 'not having all your eggs in one basket'.

Research shows that a portfolio of shares is well diversified if it has roughly equal amounts invested in 15–20 different holdings across different sectors. Very big portfolios (such as those operated by the big fund companies) often hold over a hundred different shares.

Markets

Just as it increases risk to be exposed to any one company or sector, so it may be risky to be exposed only to one market. For example, the UK stock market as a whole may suffer if there is an announcement of poor economic figures. The types of factors that can affect the market were examined in Chapter 1.

While different world markets are rather more closely correlated in their performance than was once the case, they do not usually move in tandem for long periods; one country's economy may be booming while that of another is struggling, and their markets will reflect the economic backdrops. So an investor with sufficient assets to do so may well wish to diversify his exposure by holding some investments in his home market and some in the other major (and perhaps also emerging) markets of the world.

Asset Classes

The factors that affect one asset class may affect another in quite a different way – or even not affect it at all. It may therefore also be important to diversify across asset classes, to ensure that a portfolio includes elements of:

- liquidity (cash);
- interest-bearing investments (eg, bonds); and
- equities.

This will reduce the risk associated with any one of these – ie, interest rate risk, inflation risk and stock market risk. This is asset class diversification.

2.2.11 Market Timing and Timescale

Timing and **timescale** are also important factors in investing. Ideally, in terms of timing, an investor would be able to put his money into the stock market just as it begins a strong rise (and would manage to take his money out just before it fell!); however, market timing is very difficult to predict, and sudden events can cause stock market falls. So, while over the long term it can be shown that shares generally deliver better returns than other, less risky asset classes, in the short term they can also go up and down (they are more 'volatile').

For this reason a sensible investor will accept the fact that stock markets are prone to rises and falls, and be prepared to tie their money up over the long term to 'ride out' the volatility.

Nonetheless, there are times when waiting to invest can pay off. It may be prudent to keep some available cash liquid, and invest it as and when opportunities arise.

2.3 RETURN

LEARNING OBJECTIVE

3.2.2   Understand the main risk and return measures, and how they are used within asset and portfolio evaluation, and their purposes: holding period return; total return and its components; standard deviation; volatility; covariance and correlation; risk-adjusted returns; benchmarking

2.3.1   Holding Period Return (HPR)

When comparing the returns on one investment with another, in the context of their relative degrees of risk (measured by standard deviation; see Section 2.3.3) we should remember to include all the total holding period returns. The total holding period return on an investment is made up of:

- the income earned on it (ie, any dividends or interest paid);
- any capital gain or loss over the period; and
- the current yield and the capital appreciation yield.

$$HPR = \frac{(P1 - P0 + I)}{(P0)}$$

where:

P1   =   the price at the end of the holding period

P0   =   the price at beginning of the holding period

I   =   the sum of all income received from the investment over the holding period.

2.3.2 Total Return

Total return is a measure of investment performance that includes the change in price of the asset plus any income (dividends and interest). It is assumed that all income is reinvested. The calculation of total return is expressed as a percentage of the purchase value.

There are three different methods used to measure portfolio performance:

- holding period yield – sometimes referred to as total return;
- money-weighted rate of return;
- time-weighted rate of return.

Money-Weighted Rate of Return

The money-weighted rate of return is used to measure the performance of a fund that has had deposits and withdrawals during the period of investment. It is also referred to as the **internal rate of return (IRR)** of the fund. The standard money-weighted return measurement used in the UK is the Modified Bank of America Institute (BAI) method. It is also called a linked internal rate of return method.

Essentially, the formula for calculating the return takes the beginning and the end values of the portfolio together with the timing and size of any interim cash flows.

We wish to determine the overall growth rate of the fund over its holding period, identified in the equation below with a letter 'r'.

The BAI equation takes the beginning value of the fund as V_0 and the ending value as V_1. Multiple cash flows made or received into the fund during this period (cash injections, withdrawals or even income) are C_k, where C is the cash flow and the subscript k (1, 2, 3, etc) denotes the timing in days from the initial investment.

All are connected through the following ending-value equation:

$$V_1 = V_0(1+r) + \sum C_k(1+r)^{Wk}$$

r is the rate we are trying to determine and it is the IRR that satisfies the above ending value expression.

Wk is the fraction of which a particular cashflow applies. More precisely: $Wk = (TD-D_k)/TD$.

where:

TD = the total number of calendar days in the period.

D_k = the number of days from the beginning of the period for the cashflow at k. Note k is related to each of the cashflows 1, 2, 3....k..

The objective is to determine r from this equation. However, this may not be a straightforward task and r has to be determined by 'trial and error'. A simple calculation can be set-up on an excel spreadsheet and to solve r using an iterative procedure.

EXAMPLE

Consider a simple case where the investment is worth £200 million at the beginning of a time period. At the end of the period the investment is £250 million, the whole time period between the start and end dates is 31 days and a cash inflow of £20 million is made ten days into the beginning of the holding period. Determine the return from this investment.

Note that r is the linked internal rate of return for the investment we have to determine. A simple equation is set-up using the expression given earlier.

$$W_1 = (31-10)/31 = 0.677$$

$$250 = 200(1+r) + 20(1+r)^{0.677}$$

By using trial and error method the return is 14.1% over this holding period.

Time-Weighted Rate of Return (TWRR)

The time-weighted rate of return removes the impact of cash flows on the rate of return calculation. The TWRR is established by breaking the investment period into a series of sub-periods. This could be monthly, quarterly or another time period. A sub-period is created whenever there is a movement of capital into or out of the fund. Immediately prior to this point, a portfolio valuation must be obtained to ensure that the rate of return is not distorted by the size and timing of the cash flow. The TWRR is calculated by compounding the rate of return for each of these individual sub-periods, applying an equal weight to each sub-period in the process.

For each sub-holding period, the rate of return is determined by using the following formula :

$$R_t = (V_t / V_{t-1}) - 1$$

where:

V_t = ending period value.

V_{t-1} = beginning period value.

The geometric return of all the holding period returns of sub-periods is determined. This is known as unitised fund performance. The formula for time-weighted rate of return is:

$$\text{TWRR} = [(1 + RSP1)(1 + RSP2)........(1 + RSP_n)] - 1$$

where:

SP_n = the percentage return during a sub-period.

This can be seen in the following example.

EXAMPLE

A portfolio is valued at £1,000 at the beginning of October and grows in value to £1,100 by 15 October. It receives a cash inflow of £215 on 16 October and at 31 October is valued at £1,500.

Using TWRR, a percentage return is calculated for each separate period as follows:

Period 1: r = 1,100/1,000 – 1 = 0.10

Period 2: r = 1,500//(1,100 + 215) – 1 = 0.141

TWRR = [(1 + 0.10)(1+0.141)] – 1 = 1.2551 – 1 = 25.51%

In many cases, the differences between the money-weighted rate of return and the time-weighted rate of return will be relatively small, but in certain circumstances wide variations can occur. As a result, the time-weighted rate of return is more widely used.

2.3.3 Standard Deviation

There are various ways in which risk can be measured. Usually, these measure risk in terms of the degree of fluctuation, or **volatility**, that an investment has shown historically. We can see the variability, or volatility, of different assets' investment values by looking at graphs of daily share prices or share indices over a period of time. The standard deviation is a square root of the variance of the dispersion.

The volatility in the value of an investment can be quantified statistically by calculating the **standard deviation** of the values. Standard deviation measures how widely the value of an investment is dispersed around its **mean** or **average**. The more volatile the value of an investment is, the greater its standard deviation.

- An investment with returns that do not vary much from its average return has a low standard deviation. **Low standard deviation** implies **lower risk**.
- An investment with returns that do vary greatly from its average return has a high standard deviation. **High standard deviation** implies **higher risk**.

The standard deviation is calculated on the basis of past data.

Knowing the standard deviation can help us to understand the range of returns we may expect from an investment.

For example, suppose that an investment has an average annual return of 9% and a standard deviation of returns of 4%. Then we can expect that, if we make the investment:

- there is a chance of 2/3 that the annual return will be between 5% and 13%;
- there is a chance of 1/3 that the annual return will be below 5% and above 13%.

The volatility of a share, or holding in a fund, can be compared with a **benchmark** – a standard against which its performance can be compared. This might be the volatility of the index which relates most closely to that share or fund (for example, a blue chip share's standard deviation might be benchmarked against that of the FTSE 100 index); or for a fund, against other funds in the same sector.

Investments with high volatility involve higher risk; there will be a greater variation in returns than for a lower-volatility investment. Rational investors should be particularly interested to hold investments that produce **higher than average returns** but with **low volatility**.

2.3.4 Correlation

In investment terms, correlation is the extent to which the values of different types of investments move in tandem with one another in response to changing economic and market conditions.

Correlation is measured on a scale of -1 to $+1$. Investments with a correlation of $+0.5$ or more tend to rise and fall in value at the same time. Investments with a negative correlation of -0.5 to -1 are more likely to gain or lose value in opposing cycles.

2.3.5 Covariance

Covariance is a statistical measure of the relationship between two variables such as share prices. Technically, it is a product of the movements of each of the two random variables from their means. The covariance is also related to another similar statistic called the correlation coefficient. The correlation coefficient is easier to understand because it is only ever found in a range from -1 to $+1$. A positive perfect correlation $(+1)$ suggests that two returns are perfectly correlated. If one security goes up, the other matches its move identically. The other extreme is a perfect negative correlation (-1). In this case the co-ordination between a pair of securities is still perfect but they are moving in unison in opposing directions. States of correlation in between show the less than perfect co-ordination of return between pairs.

The covariance between two shares (σ_{AB}) is calculated by multiplying the standard deviation of the first (σ_A) by the standard deviation of the second share (σ_B) and then by the correlation coefficient (ρ_{AB}).

$$\sigma_{AB} = \rho_{AB} \times \sigma_A \times \sigma_B$$

A positive covariance between the returns of A and B means they have mostly moved in the same direction, while a negative covariance means they have mostly moved inversely. The larger the covariance, the greater the historic joint movements of the two securities in the same direction. From these two equations, the following conclusions can be drawn:

1. Although it is perfectly possible for two combinations of two different securities to have the same correlation coefficient as one another, each may have a different covariance, owing to the differences in the individual standard deviations of the constituent securities.
2. A security with a high standard deviation in isolation does not necessarily have a high covariance with other shares. If it has a low correlation with the other shares in a portfolio then, despite its high standard deviation, its inclusion in the portfolio may reduce overall portfolio risk.
3. Portfolios designed to minimise risk should contain securities as negatively correlated with each other as possible and with low standard deviations to minimise the covariance.

2.4 RISK-ADJUSTED RETURNS

Having calculated how a portfolio has performed, the next stage is to compare its performance against the market as a whole or against other portfolios. This is the function of risk-adjusted performance measurements, of which there are four main methods in use:

- Sharpe ratio;
- Treynor ratio;
- Jensen measure;
- Information ratio.

2.4.1 Sharpe Ratio

The Sharpe ratio measures the return over and above the risk-free interest rate from an undiversified equity portfolio for each unit of risk assumed by the portfolio: risk being measured by the standard deviation of the portfolio's returns.

The ratio is expressed as follows:

$$\text{Sharpe ratio:} \quad \frac{(R_p - R_f)}{\sigma} \quad \text{or} \quad \frac{\text{(return on the portfolio} - \text{risk-free return)}}{\text{standard deviation of the portfolio}}$$

The higher the Sharpe ratio, the better the risk-adjusted performance of the portfolio and the greater the implied level of active management skill.

2.4.2 Treynor Ratio

The Treynor ratio takes a similar approach to the Sharpe ratio but is calculated for a well-diversified equity portfolio. As the portfolio's return would have been generated only by the systemic risk it had assumed, the Treynor ratio, therefore, divides the portfolio's return over and above the risk-free interest rate by its CAPM beta (see Section 3.3).

The ratio is expressed as follows:

$$\text{Treynor ratio:} \quad \frac{(R_p - R_f)}{\beta_p} \quad \text{or} \quad \frac{\text{(return on the portfolio} - \text{risk-free return)}}{\text{beta of the portfolio}}$$

Once again, the higher the ratio, the greater the implied level of active management skill.

2.4.3 Jensen Measure

The Jensen measure of risk-adjusted equity portfolio returns is employed to evaluate the performance of a well-diversified portfolio against a CAPM benchmark with the same level of systematic risk as that assumed by the portfolio. That is, the CAPM benchmark beta is the same as that of the portfolio.

The ratio is expressed as follows:

$$\text{Jensen measure} = R_p - R_{capm} \quad \text{or} \quad \text{return on the portfolio} - \text{return predicted by CAPM}$$

The Jensen measure establishes whether the portfolio has performed in line with its CAPM benchmark and, therefore, lies on the security market line (SML; see Section 3.3) or whether it has out- or under-performed the benchmark and is, therefore, positioned above or below the SML. The extent of any out- or underperformance is known as the portfolio's alpha.

2.4.4 Information Ratio

The information ratio compares the excess return achieved by a fund over a benchmark portfolio to the fund's tracking error. Its tracking error is calculated as the standard deviation of excess returns from the benchmark. The tracking error gives us an estimate of the risks that the fund manager takes in deviating from the benchmark.

The ratio is expressed as follows:

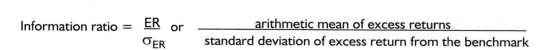

$$\text{Information ratio} = \frac{ER}{\sigma_{ER}} \quad \text{or} \quad \frac{\text{arithmetic mean of excess returns}}{\text{standard deviation of excess return from the benchmark}}$$

A fund's performance may deviate from the benchmark due to the investment manager's decisions concerning asset weighting. If the fund outperforms, the ratio will be positive, and if it underperforms it will be negative. A high information ratio is therefore a sign of a successful fund manager.

2.5 BENCHMARKING

If the performance of an investment fund or investment manager is to be assessed, then the first issue to address is how to measure that performance. Investment performance is usually monitored by comparing it to a relevant benchmark.

There are three main ways in which portfolio performance is assessed:

- Comparison with a relevant bond or stockmarket index.
  - An index comparison provides a clear indication of whether the portfolio's returns exceed that of the bond or stock market index that is being used as the benchmark return.
  - As well as the main stock market indices that are generally seen, many sub-indices have been created over the years which allow a precise comparison to be made.
- Comparison to similar funds or a relevant universe comparison.
  - Investment returns can also be measured against the performance of other fund managers or portfolios which have similar investment objectives and constraints.
  - A group of similar portfolios is referred to as an investment universe.
- Comparison to a custom benchmark.
  - Customised benchmarks are often developed for funds with unique investment objectives or constraints.
  - Where a portfolio spans several asset classes, then a composite index may need to be constructed by selecting several relevant indices and then multiplying each asset class weighting to arrive at a composite return.

2.5.1   Alternative Benchmarking Methods

Rather than use an established index to benchmark portfolio performance, a peer group average is often employed. **World Markets (WM)** company is a worldwide independent investment information services company which provides, among other services, performance measurement services to pension funds and other investing institutions. **Combined Actuarial Performance Services Ltd (CAPS)** is an independent investment performance measurement service for the UK, covering over 1,800 pension funds. CAPS was set up as a joint venture by firms of consulting actuaries.

Most pension funds adopt cautious investment policies, and the guidance and benchmarks they set for fund managers mean that most schemes keep their asset allocation close to the CAPS or WM averages. Both create universes which are an aggregation of funds or portfolios with similar investment briefs or types of owner and are used for peer group comparisons. There are many specialist sub-groups of universe groupings to cater for a wide range of fund structures and investment management styles to provide a relevant and accurate relative comparison.

Global Investment Performance Standards (GIPS) are not a way of benchmarking performance, but are global standards for calculating and presenting performance figures. As such, they represent a great leap forward for the performance measurement industry. Originally established in 1999 by the CFA Institute, GIPS were significantly enhanced in 2005 and have been voluntarily adopted by industry representative organisations in over 20 countries in order to help promote best standards.

2.5.2   Performance Attribution

Performance attribution analysis attempts to explain why a portfolio had a certain return. It does so by breaking down the performance and attributing the results based on the decisions made by the fund manager on asset allocation, sector choice and security selection.

3.   MODELS OF INVESTMENT THEORY

The study of how markets behave, in terms of sentiment, is known as the study of market psychology. In essence it is the study of the collective behaviour of all the investors – both buyers and sellers – making up a market.

3.1   THE EFFICIENT MARKET HYPOTHESIS (EMH)

LEARNING OBJECTIVE

3.3.1   Understand the main propositions and limitations of the efficient
           markets hypothesis (EMH): strong form; semi-strong form; weak form

One of the key theories used in the study of market psychology is the **efficient market hypothesis (EMH)**. This theory states that because information about companies is generally freely available and known to investors/potential investors, it will lead to their shares (or other securities) being correctly priced, providing that:

- the securities are freely traded (so that the pricing mechanism can work efficiently); and
- the markets themselves are operationally efficient (so that supply and demand will lead to the price reflecting investors' informed viewpoints).

There are three versions of the EMH, depending on how efficient you believe the market actually is. They are as follows:

- The **weak form** assumes that the market price of shares currently reflects all relevant information implied in historic share prices.
- The **semi-strong form** of the theory assumes that the market currently reflects all publicly available relevant information.
- The **strong form** assumes that the market price of a share currently takes into account all publicly and privately available relevant information.

Each version is similar, in that it assumes that because information is available it will have been used by investors in arriving at their decisions (and therefore be reflected in current share pricing).

The validity of the theory is hotly debated among market practitioners and theorists; those who argue against it point out that just because information on a share is available, that does not mean that it will have been discovered – or taken into account – by an investor. Further, it does not take account of the fact that some investors (particularly large institutions) have a long, drawn-out decision-making process – so the fact that they have information available to them and are using it does not mean that it has yet been reflected in a share's price, through their buying and selling decisions.

3.2 MODERN PORTFOLIO THEORY (MPT)

LEARNING OBJECTIVE

3.3.2 Understand the main principles of Modern Portfolio Theory, the capital asset pricing model (CAPM), its application and limitations: risk free rate of return; risk premium; cost of capital and return on capital; excess returns; correlation measures; systematic and unsystematic risk; risk and diversification; efficient frontier, portfolio optimisation and leverage; assumptions and shortcomings

You can find a trio of modern portfolio theory statistics on most fund company fact sheets. So what does this all mean, if anything? To start, you need to have a brief understanding of the basic assumptions of Harry Markowitz's Modern Portfolio Theory (MPT), which was thought to be at the forefront of portfolio analysis in the 1950s but has come under scrutiny more recently.

The underpinnings of the theory are twofold. First, it assumes that rational investors will demand a higher rate of return to invest in a riskier asset than they will to invest in a less risky asset. Second, the cornerstone of the theory is that diversifying your portfolio by adding securities (or funds) which do not behave in the same way reduces its overall risk, even if those securities individually are higher-risk.

Investors probably keep the above in mind while building their portfolios without always realising it. Your asset allocation is the direct result of your time horizon, risk tolerance and financial goal, and to achieve that goal in a timely way you take on a certain level of risk.

Furthermore, you may mix different investments that are weakly correlated in the aim of protecting the value of your portfolio under different market conditions. For example, stock and bond markets don't typically move in the same direction. For most investors, the risk from holding a stock is that the returns will be lower than expected.

Modern portfolio theory states that the risk for individual stocks consists of:

- **Systematic risk** – these are market risks that cannot be diversified away.
- **Unsystematic risk** – this is the risk associated with a specific stock and can be diversified away by increasing the number of stocks in a portfolio. So a well-diversified portfolio will reduce the risk that its actual returns will be lower than expected.

This then leads on to how to identify the best level of diversification. This is described by the **efficient frontier**.

CISI
CHARTERED INSTITUTE FOR
SECURITIES & INVESTMENT

The chart shows that it is possible for different portfolios to have different levels of risk and return. Each investor decides how much risk they can tolerate and diversifies their portfolio accordingly. The optimal risk portfolio is usually determined to be somewhere in the middle of the curve because, as you go up the curve, you take on proportionately higher risk for lower incremental returns. Equally, positioning a portfolio at the low end of the curve is pointless, as you can achieve a similar return by investing in risk-free assets.

Since its origins in the early 1950s, this basic portfolio selection model has been developed into more sophisticated models, such as the capital asset pricing model (CAPM) in the mid-1960s and arbitrage pricing theory (APT) in the late 1970s. However it remains the backbone of finance theory and practice.

CAPM and APT are considered in Sections 3.3 and 3.4.

3.3   CAPITAL ASSET PRICING MODEL (CAPM)

LEARNING OBJECTIVE

3.3.2   Understand the main principles of Modern Portfolio Theory, the capital asset pricing model (CAPM), its application and limitations: risk free rate of return; risk premium; cost of capital and return on capital; excess returns; correlation measures; systematic and unsystematic risk; risk and diversification; efficient frontier, portfolio optimisation and leverage; assumptions and shortcomings

The capital asset pricing model or CAPM says that the expected return on a security or portfolio equals the rate on a risk-free security plus a risk premium (see Section 2.1), and that, if the expected return does not meet or beat this required return, then the investment should not be undertaken.

CAPM has some built-in assumptions:

* All market participants borrow and lend at the same risk-free rate.
* All market participants are well-diversified investors and specific risk has been diversified away.
* There are no tax or transaction costs to consider.
* All investors want to achieve a maximum return for minimum risk.
* Market participants have the same expectations about the returns and standard deviations of all assets.

Using those assumptions, CAPM is used to predict the expected or required returns to a security by using its systematic risks, ie, its **beta**. Systematic risk is assessed by measuring beta, which is the sensitivity of a stock's returns to the return on a market portfolio, and so provides a measure of a stock's risk relative to the market as a whole.

Beta is calculated by constructing a scattergram of returns achieved by the stock against the market as a whole. By using regression analysis, a line of best fit is then drawn and the gradient of the line represents the stock's beta:

- If the stock's beta is 1, then the stock has a similar volatility to and moves in line with the market as a whole.
- If it has a beta of greater than 1, then the stock is more volatile than the market as a whole. If a stock has a beta of 1.5, then it has 50% greater volatility than the market portfolio.
- If it has a beta of less than 1, the stock is less volatile than the market as a whole, so a stock with a beta of 0.7 has 30% less volatility.

We can use a stock's beta in conjunction with rate of return on a risk-free asset and the expected return from the market to calculate the return we should expect from a stock. The CAPM formula is usually expressed as:

Required return: risk-free rate + (market rate – risk-free rate) x beta

By using the CAPM equation, it enables what is termed the **security market line** to be presented graphically. If a graph is plotted depicting the expected return from a security against its beta, then the relationship is revealed as a straight line.

The security market line shows that the higher the risk of an asset, the higher the expected return. The market risk premium is the return an investor would expect over and above the risk-free rate as a reward for taking on the additional market risk.

We can use the CAPM formula to calculate the return we should expect from a stock. For example, if the current risk-free rate is 5% and the expected return from the market is 10%, what return should we expect from a security that has a beta of 1.5?

The beta of the individual stock tells us that it carries more risk than the market as a whole, and the CAPM formula tells us that we should expect a return of:

$$\text{Expected return} = 5\% + (10\% - 5\%) \times 1.5 = 12.5\%$$

CAPM, by providing a precise prediction of the relationship between a security's risk and return, therefore, provides a benchmark rate of return for evaluating investments against their forecasted return.

3.4 ARBITRAGE PRICING THEORY (APT)

LEARNING OBJECTIVE

3.3.3   Understand the main principles behind arbitrage pricing theory (APT), its application and limitations: factor structure and analysis; macro-economic and market factors; arbitrage theory and mechanics; relationship with CAPM; assumptions and shortcomings

Arbitrage pricing theory was developed in the late 1970s in response to CAPM's main limitation that a single market beta is assumed to capture all factors that determine a security's risk and expected return. APT, rather than relying on a single beta, adopts a more complex multi-factor approach by:

- seeking to capture exactly what factors determine security price movements by conducting regression analysis;
- applying a separate risk premium to each identified factor;
- applying a separate beta to each of these risk premiums, depending on a security's sensitivity to each of these factors.

Examples of factors that are employed by advocates of the APT approach include both industry-related and more general macro-economic variables, such as anticipated changes in inflation, industrial production and the yield spread between investment grade and non-investment grade bonds. The underlying assumptions of APT include:

- Securities markets are price-efficient.
- Investors seek to maximise their wealth, though do not necessarily select portfolios on the basis of mean variance analysis.
- Investors can sell securities short. Short-selling is selling securities you don't own with the intention of buying them back at a lower price in order to settle and profit from the transaction.
- Identified factors are uncorrelated with each other.

APT is attractive in that it:

- explains security performance more accurately than CAPM by using more than one beta factor;
- uses fewer assumptions than CAPM;
- enables portfolios to be constructed that either eliminate or gear their exposure to a particular factor.

However, APT's shortcomings include a reliance on:

- identified factors being uncorrelated with each other;
- stable relationships being established between security returns and these identified factors.

3.5   BEHAVIOURAL FINANCE

LEARNING OBJECTIVE

3.3.4   Understand the principles of behavioural finance: loss aversion;
price reaction and price trends; barriers and biases – practical and
psychological; relationship with EMH; assumptions and shortcomings

Behavioural finance picks up where modern portfolio theory leaves off, completing the circle. It describes how investors actually behave, rather than how they should behave. It recognises that we sometimes act in our own best economic interests, and sometimes don't. Assuming that modern portfolio theory largely correctly describes the way markets operate, behavioural finance describes how we might best profit from that knowledge.

Behavioural finance is a field of study that has evolved which attempts to better understand and explain (through the use of psychology and other social sciences) how emotions and cognitive errors influence investors and the decision-making process.

The key observations from the study of behavioural finance are that:

- people often make decisions based on approximate rule of thumb, not strictly rational analysis;
- people do not appear to be consistent in how they treat economically equivalent choices if the choices are presented in significantly different contents, which is referred to as the **framing effect**;
- there are explanations for observed market outcomes that are contrary to national expectations and market efficiency, which include mispricing, non-rational decision-making and return anomalies.

From these observations it is clear that judgments can be systematically wrong in various ways. Systematic errors of judgment are called **biases**. Financial decisions are made in situations of high complexity and high uncertainty that preclude reliance on fixed rules and compel the decision-maker to rely on intuition.

3.5.1   Biases

Loss Aversion

Loss aversion refers to people's tendency to strongly prefer avoiding losses to making gains. Some studies suggest that losses are twice as powerful, psychologically, as gains. This leads to risk aversion when people evaluate a possible gain. Conversely, people strongly prefer risks that might possibly mitigate a loss (called risk-seeking behaviour). Loss aversion implies that a person who loses £100 will lose more satisfaction than another person will gain satisfaction from a £100 windfall.

Confirmation Bias

Confirmation bias suggests that an investor is more likely to look for information that supports their original idea about an investment rather than seek out information that contradicts it. As a result, this bias can often result in faulty decision-making, because one-sided information tends to skew an investor's frame of reference, leaving them with an incomplete picture of the situation.

Hindsight Bias

Hindsight bias tends to occur in situations where a person believes (after the fact) that the onset of some past event was predictable and completely obvious, whereas in fact the event could not reasonably have been predicted. Many events seem obvious in hindsight. Psychologists attribute hindsight bias to our innate need to find order in the world by creating explanations which allow us to believe that events are predictable. While this sense of curiosity is useful in many cases (in science, for example), finding erroneous links between the cause and effect of an event may result in incorrect oversimplifications.

Cognitive Biases

A cognitive bias is a pattern of deviation in judgement that occurs in particular situations, Many of these biases are studied for how they affect belief formation, business decisions, and scientific research.

- **Bandwagon effect** – the tendency to do (or believe) things because many other people do (or believe) the same. Related to groupthink and herd behaviour.
- **Base rate fallacy** – the tendency to ignore available statistical data in favour of particulars.
- **Bias blind spot** – the tendency not to compensate for one's own cognitive biases.
- **Choice-supportive bias** – the tendency to remember one's choices as better than they actually were.
- **Congruence bias** – the tendency to test hypotheses exclusively through direct testing, in contrast to tests of possible alternative hypotheses.
- **Contrast effect** – the enhancement or diminishing of a weight or other measurement when compared with a recently observed contrasting object.
- **Denomination effect** – the tendency to spend more money when it is denominated in small amounts (eg, coins) rather than large amounts (eg, bills).
- **Distinction bias** – the tendency to view two options as more dissimilar when evaluating them simultaneously than when evaluating them separately.
- **Endowment effect** – 'the fact that people often demand much more to give up an object than they would be willing to pay to acquire it'.
- **Experimenter's or expectation bias** – the tendency for experimenters to believe, certify and publish data that agree with their expectations for the outcome of an experiment, and to disbelieve, discard or downgrade the corresponding weightings for data that appear to conflict with those expectations.
- **Focusing effect** – the tendency to place too much importance on one aspect of an event; this causes error in accurately predicting the utility of a future outcome.
- **Framing** – using an approach or description of the situation or issue that is too narrow. Also **framing effect** – drawing different conclusions based on how data is presented.
- **Hyperbolic discounting** – the tendency for people to have a stronger preference for more immediate payoffs relative to later payoffs, where the tendency increases the closer to the present both payoffs are.
- **Illusion of control** – the tendency to believe that outcomes can be controlled, or at least influenced, when they clearly cannot.
- **Impact bias** – the tendency to overestimate the length or the intensity of the impact of future feeling states.
- **Information bias** – the tendency to seek information even when it cannot affect action.

- **Interloper effect** – the tendency to value third-party consultation as objective, confirming, and without motive. Also **consultation paradox**, the conclusion that solutions proposed by existing personnel within an organisation are less likely to receive support than from those recruited for that purpose.
- **Irrational escalation** – the tendency to make irrational decisions based upon rational decisions in the past or to justify actions already taken.
- **Just-world phenomenon** – the tendency to rationalise an inexplicable injustice by searching for things that the victim might have done to deserve it.
- **Mere exposure effect** – the tendency to express undue liking for things merely because one is familiar with them.
- **Money illusion** – the tendency to concentrate on the nominal (face value) of money rather than its value in terms of purchasing power.
- **Moral credential effect** – the tendency of a track record of non-prejudice to increase subsequent prejudice.
- **Need for closure** – the need to reach a verdict in important matters; to have an answer and to escape the feeling of doubt and uncertainty. The personal context (time or social pressure) might increase this bias.
- **Negativity bias** – the tendency to pay more attention and give more weight to negative than positive experiences or other kinds of information.
- **Neglect of probability** – the tendency to completely disregard probability when making a decision under uncertainty.
- **Normalcy bias** – the refusal to plan for, or react to, a disaster which has never happened before.
- **Not Invented Here** – the tendency to ignore that a product or solution already exists, because its source is seen as an 'enemy' or as 'inferior'.
- **Omission bias** – the tendency to judge harmful actions as worse, or less moral, than equally harmful omissions (inactions).
- **Outcome bias** – the tendency to judge a decision by its eventual outcome instead of basing the judgement on the quality of the decision at the time it was made.
- **Planning fallacy** – the tendency to underestimate task-completion times.
- **Post-purchase rationalisation** – the tendency to persuade oneself through rational argument that a purchase was good value.
- **Pseudocertainty effect** – the tendency to make risk-averse choices if the expected outcome is positive, but make risk-seeking choices to avoid negative outcomes.
- **Reactance** – the urge to do the opposite of what someone wants you to do out of a need to resist a perceived attempt to constrain your freedom of choice.
- **Restraint bias** – the tendency to overestimate one's ability to show restraint in the face of temptation.
- **Selective perception** – the tendency for expectations to affect perception.
- **Semmelweis reflex** – the tendency to reject new evidence that contradicts an established paradigm.
- **Status quo bias** – the tendency to like things to stay relatively the same (see also loss aversion, at the start of Section 3.5.1, and endowment effect, above).
- **Wishful thinking** – the formation of beliefs and the making of decisions according to what is pleasing to imagine instead of by appeal to evidence or rationality.
- **Zero-risk bias** – preference for reducing a small risk to zero over a greater reduction in a larger risk.

3.5.2 Behavioural Finance and the EMH

In finance, the efficient market hypothesis (EMH) asserts that financial markets are efficient and implies that investors cannot consistently achieve returns in excess of average market returns on a risk-adjusted basis. Investors and researchers dispute the efficient market hypothesis both empirically and theoretically. Behavioural economists attribute the imperfections in financial markets to a combination of cognitive biases such as overconfidence, overreaction, representative bias, information bias, and various other predictable human errors in reasoning and information processing.

3.5.3 Assumptions and Shortcomings of Behavioural Finance

If we assume that financial markets are efficient and investors are rational, then why there are so many studies about investors' psychology?

Investment managers seek to make money for themselves and their clients. That is the reason they care about the psychology factor of financial market as well as investors.

The behaviour of investors is not always rational, so investment managers do not forget how the psychology factor of a person plays a substantial role in the behaviour of financial markets.

But, modern finance theories have almost completely ignored the role of the complex motivational and cognitive factors that influence investor's decision-making.

3.5.4 Theories of Behavioural Finance

There are four theories of behavioural finance. They are as follows:

1. Prospect theory
2. Regret theory
3. Anchoring
4. Over- and under-reaction

Prospect Theory

This theory says people respond differently to equivalent situations depending on whether it is presented in the context of a loss or a gain. Most investors are risk-averse when chasing gains but become risk-lovers when trying to avoid a loss.

Regret Theory

Regret theory is about people's emotional reaction to having made an error of judgment. Investors may avoid selling stocks that have gone down in order to avoid the regret of having made a bad investment and the embarrassment of reporting the loss. They may also find it easier to follow the crowd and buy a popular stock. If it subsequently goes down, it can be rationalised as everyone else owned it.

Anchoring

Anchoring is a phenomenon in which, in the absence of better information, investors assume current prices are about right. People tend to give too much weight to recent experience, extrapolating recent trends that are often at odds with long-run averages and probabilities.

Over- and Under-Reaction

The consequences of investors putting too much weight on recent news at the expense of other data are market over- or under-reaction. People show overconfidence. They tend to become more optimistic when the market goes up and more pessimistic when the market goes down. Hence, prices fall too much on bad news and rise too much on good news. In certain circumstances, this can lead to extreme events.

3.5.5 Conclusion

The field of modern financial economics assumes that people behave with extreme rationality, but they do not. The two common mistakes investors make, ie, excessive trading and the tendency to disproportionately hold on to losing investments while selling winners, have their origins in human psychology. The tendency for human beings to be overconfident causes the first mistake and the human desire to avoid regret prompts the second. So, psychological research teaches us about the true form of preferences, allowing us to make finance more realistic within the rational choice framework.

Behavioural finance is subject to criticism. While all of us are subject to behavioural biases from time to time, traditional economic theorists argue that market forces will always act to bring prices back to rational levels, implying that the impact of irrational behaviour on financial market is generally negligible and therefore irrelevant.

3.6 MULTI-FACTOR MODELS, ASSUMPTIONS AND LIMITATIONS

LEARNING OBJECTIVE

3.3.5   Understand the types and uses of multi-factor models, their assumptions and limitations

A multi-factor model is a financial model that may be used in the analysis of securities when constructing an investment portfolio for a client. The model compares two or more factors in order to help illustrate the relationship between these variables and the level of returns achieved.

There are three broad categories of multi-factor models:

1. Macro-economic.
2. Fundamental.
3. Statistical.

Macro-economic models look to compare the returns achieved by a security against factors such as employment statistics, inflation and interest rates, whereas **fundamental models** compare the returns against underlying factors such as earnings, eg, company profits or dividend ratio, when assessing equities. **Statistical models** compare the performance of a range of different securities based on the statistics for each individual security.

The following model explains how these factors are compared:

$$Ri = ai + ßi(m) Rm + ßi(1)F1 + ßi(2)F2 +...+ ßi(N)FN + ei$$

where:

Ri	=	the returns of security i
Rm	=	the market return
F(1,2,3…N)	=	each of the factors used
ß	=	the beta with respect to each factor including the market (m)
e	=	the error term
a	=	the intercept

In general, multi-factor models are used to assist in the construction of portfolios with certain characteristics, such as a certain level of risk or those designed to track certain indexes. The models do have some limitations, however; for example, it can be difficult to decide exactly how many and which factors to include. The models also use historical information, which may be very different from current performance.

3.7 REDUCING PORTFOLIO RISK

LEARNING OBJECTIVE

3.3.6   Understand how to reduce portfolio risk through diversification and hedging: significance of alpha and beta; correlation and relative risk; principles of asset allocation; hedging and immunisation; active and passive strategies

The following paragraphs discuss methods of assessing and managing risk within a portfolio.

3.7.1   Alpha, Beta and R-Squared

MPT statistics provide a snapshot of the portfolio's returns versus the return of the benchmark index.

Beta is an expression of a fund's sensitivity to movements in the benchmark index. It is thus a measure of volatility, or risk, relative to the index. The beta of the benchmark is by definition 1 (because it is simply measuring the benchmark's volatility relative to itself). So, if beta is greater than 1 then that implies the fund has been more volatile – hence more risky – than the index; a beta of less than one indicates lower volatility.

Alpha measures the difference between a fund's actual returns and its expected performance, given its level of risk (as measured by beta). A positive alpha figure indicates the fund has performed better than its beta would predict. In contrast, a negative alpha indicates a fund has underperformed, given the expectations established by the fund's beta. Some investors see alpha as a measurement of the value added or subtracted by a fund's manager, and it is often cited as such in the media. An alpha that looks at a fund's returns over the risk-free rate, relative to the benchmark's returns over the risk-free rate, is commonly known as **Jensen's alpha**.

R-squared ranges from 0 to 100 and reflects the percentage of a fund's movements that are explained by movements in its benchmark index. An R-squared of 100 means that all movements of a fund are completely explained by movements in the index.

Thus, index funds that invest only in FTSE 100 stocks will have an R-squared very close to 100. Conversely, a low R-squared indicates that very few of the fund's movements are explained by movements in its benchmark index. An R-squared measure of 35, for example, means that only 35% of the fund's movements can be explained by movements in its benchmark index. Therefore, if you already own a fund with a very high R-squared with the FTSE All Share, you might avoid buying another that correlates too closely to that index.

Use with Care!

As we've seen, MPT statistics can help inform investors about their fund's risks, value-added, and ability to diversify their portfolio. However, one needs to be careful about placing too much faith in them.

First, they are based purely on past performance. Looking at funds with attractive alphas and betas does not imply they will behave the same way in the future. For example, a fund might have had a different manager or strategy during the period over which the statistics were calculated. Further, the market environment could change dramatically.

Also, whenever you use alpha or beta, you need to be aware of the index used and the fund's R-squared with the index. Without getting too technical, these figures all rely on taking a scatter-plot graph of a fund's returns (vertical axis) against the benchmark's returns (horizontal axis) and drawing a straight line through the middle of the scatter that represents the best fit to all the points. The beta is the slope of the line, and alpha marks where the line intercepts the vertical axis, ie, the fund's return when the benchmark's return is zero.

The weak link is the 'fit' of the line to the scatter-plot of returns, which is what R-squared measures. If R-squared is low, it means the points are widely scattered around the line and therefore that beta and alpha are not good estimates of actual fund behaviour. Thus, if you look at alpha and beta without checking R-squared, you may be misled by the results.

Look Beyond the Numbers

MPT statistics can be very useful, subject to the limitations described above. However, investors should remember to look beyond mere past performance when making investment decisions. There are many fundamental risks which may not be apparent from past performance. Credit risk is one notable example. In a strong credit environment, a bond fund laden with poorly rated credits may perform well for years, but if the credit environment changes sharply, as it has recently, the fund could find itself in difficulty.

3.7.2 Correlation

Correlation is the degree of co-movement between two variables determined through regression analysis and quantified by the correlation coefficient. Correlation does not prove that a cause-and-effect or, indeed, a steady relationship exists between two variables, as correlations can arise from pure chance.

3.7.3 Asset Allocation

Asset allocation is the result of top-down portfolio managers considering the big picture first, by assessing the prospects for each of the main asset classes within each of the world's major investment regions, against the backdrop of the world economic, political and social environment. Within larger portfolio management organisations, this is usually determined on a monthly basis by an asset allocation committee. The committee draws upon forecasts of risk and return for each asset class and correlations between these returns.

It is at this stage of the top-down process that quantitative models are often used, in conjunction with more conventional fundamental analysis, to assist in determining which geographical areas and asset classes are most likely to produce the most attractive risk-adjusted returns taking full account of the client's mandate.

Most asset allocation decisions, whether for institutional or retail portfolios, are made with reference to the peer group median asset allocation. This is known as asset allocation by consensus and is undertaken to minimise the risk of underperforming the peer group.

When deciding if and to what extent certain markets and asset classes should be over- or under-weighted, most portfolio managers set tracking error, or standard deviation of return, parameters against peer group median asset allocations, such as the CAPS median asset allocation in the case of institutional mandates. Remember (see Section 2.5.1) that CAPS is one of the performance measurement services that tracks the investment performance of institutional portfolios for comparison purposes.

The decision whether to hedge market and/or currency risks must be taken. Over the long term, recent academic studies conclude that asset allocation accounts for over 90% of the variation in pension fund returns.

3.7.4 Hedging

In finance, a **hedge** is a position established in one market in an attempt to offset exposure to price fluctuations in an opposite position in another market with the goal of minimising exposure to unwanted risk. There are many different ways to accomplish this, including insurance policies, forward contracts, swaps, options, many types of over-the-counter and derivative products, and, perhaps most popularly, futures contracts.

3.7.5 Immunisation

In finance, **interest rate immunisation** is a strategy that ensures that a change in interest rates will not affect the value of a portfolio. Similarly, immunisation can be used to ensure that the value of a pension fund's or a firm's assets will increase or decrease in exactly the opposite amount to their liabilities, thus leaving the value of the pension fund's surplus or firm's equity unchanged, regardless of changes in the interest rate.

Interest rate immunisation can be accomplished by several methods, including cash flow matching, duration matching, and volatility and convexity matching. It can also be accomplished by trading in bond forwards, futures, or options.

Other types of financial risks, such as foreign exchange risk or stock market risk, can be immunised using similar strategies. If the immunisation is incomplete, these strategies are usually called hedging. If the immunisation is complete, these strategies are usually called **arbitrage**.

3.8   BOND STRATEGIES

Just like equities, bonds can be managed along active or passive lines.

3.8.1   Active Bond Strategies

Generally speaking, active-based strategies are used by those portfolio managers who believe the bond market is not perfectly efficient and, therefore, is subject to mispricing. If a bond is considered mispriced, then active management strategies can be employed to capitalise upon this perceived pricing anomaly. Bond switching, or bond swapping, is used by those portfolio managers who believe they can outperform a buy-and-hold passive policy by actively exchanging bonds perceived to be overpriced for those perceived to be underpriced.

Bond switching takes three forms:

- **Anomaly Switching** – this involves moving between two bonds similar in all respects apart from the yield and price on which each trades. This pricing anomaly is exploited by switching away from the more to the less highly priced bond.
- **Policy Switching** – when an interest rate cut is expected but not implied by the yield curve, low-duration bonds are sold in favour of those with high durations. By pre-empting the rate cut, the holder can subsequently benefit from the greater price volatility of the latter bonds.
- **Intermarket Spread Switching** – when it is believed that the difference in the yield being offered between corporate bonds and comparable gilts, for example, is excessive given the perceived risk differential between these two markets, an intermarket spread switch will be undertaken from the gilt to the corporate bond market. Conversely, if an event that lowers the risk appetite of bond investors is expected to result in a flight to quality, gilts will be purchased in favour of corporate bonds.

Active management policies are also employed where it is believed the market's view on future interest rate movements, implied by the yield curve, are incorrect or have failed to be anticipated. This is known as **market timing**. **Riding the yield curve** is an active bond strategy that does not involve seeking out price anomalies but instead takes advantage of an upward-sloping yield curve.

EXAMPLE

If a portfolio manager has a two-year investment horizon, then a bond with a two-year maturity could be purchased and held until redemption. Alternatively, if the yield curve is upward-sloping, and the manager expects it to remain upward-sloping without any intervening or anticipated interest rate rises over the next two years, a five-year bond could be purchased and sold two years later when the bond has a remaining life of three years. This rate anticipation method may use horizon analysis to project a bond portfolio's expected returns over several time frames, or investment horizons, to arrive at a more realistic expectation of performance from different bond strategies.

Assuming that the yield curve remains static over this period, the manager will benefit from selling the bond at a higher price than that at which it was purchased as its gross redemption yield falls.

3.8.2 Passive Bond Strategies

Passive bond strategies are employed either when the market is believed to be efficient, in which case a buy-and-hold strategy is used, or when a bond portfolio is constructed around meeting a future liability fixed in nominal terms.

Immunisation is a passive management technique employed by those bond portfolio managers with a known future liability to meet. An immunised bond portfolio is one that is insulated from the effect of future interest rate changes. Immunisation can be performed by using either cash matching or duration-based immunisation. **Cash matching** involves constructing a bond portfolio whose coupon and redemption payment cash flows are synchronised to match those of the liabilities to be met. **Duration-based immunisation** involves constructing a bond portfolio with the same initial value as the present value of the liability it is designed to meet and the same duration as this liability. A portfolio that contains bonds that are closely aligned in this way is known as a **bullet portfolio**. Alternatively, a **barbell strategy** can be adopted. If a bullet portfolio holds bonds with durations as close as possible to ten years to match a liability with a ten-year duration, a barbell strategy may be to hold bonds with a durations of five and 15 years. Barbell portfolios necessarily require more frequent rebalancing than bullet portfolios.

Finally, a **ladder portfolio** is one constructed around equal amounts invested in bonds with different durations. So, for a liability with a ten-year duration, an appropriate ladder strategy may be to hold equal amounts in bonds with a one-year duration, and a two-year duration, right through to 20 years.

KEY CHAPTER POINTS

- Money has a 'time value'; having it now is better than having a promise of it in the future.
- Inflation erodes the value of money. The 'real rate of return' measures how much is being earned, over and above the rate of inflation.
- Compounding and discounting are key concepts in calculating returns through time.
- Investors face a variety of investment risks.
- In general, seeking a higher return involves taking higher risks. This means that, instead of the higher return hoped for, losses could be incurred instead. Investors in risky investments, such as equities, require a 'risk premium'. The risk premium is reflected in the amount by which the long-term higher average rate of return exceeds the risk-free rate of return on a very safe investment.
- Diversification involves choosing investments in different asset classes, and choosing different investments within a particular asset class.
- Overall risk can be measured from the variability or volatility of investment returns.
- Volatility arises from:
  - the 'systematic' fluctuations in the wider market, which cannot be diversified away; and
  - the 'non-systematic' investment-specific risks of the particular investment.
- Standard deviations of returns from an investment measure their variability.
- Beta factors measure how much returns from an investment vary relative to the market or a sector benchmark.
- Data on past performance has its uses in checking the track record of certain types of investment, but the future performance of risky investments may differ significantly from the past.
- A variety of factors relating to an investor's personal circumstances need to be considered when arriving at a financial plan for him.
- Attitudinal factors and the investor's past experiences may also be a factor.

CHAPTER FOUR

TAXATION OF INVESTORS AND INVESTMENTS

This syllabus area will provide approximately 16 of the 80 examination questions

1. PERSONAL TAXATION

LEARNING OBJECTIVE

4.1.1   Understand how a private individual's income tax liability is determined using: tax rates; tax rate bands; personal allowances

4.1.3   Understand the application of income tax in respect of: individuals; trusts; charities

The income tax position for a private individual is dependent on the source of income, ie, employment, investments, savings, dividends or a combination of each. The following tax rates, bands and allowances apply to income received in the current tax year (2011/12) as well as previous years..

1.1   INCOME TAX RATES AND TAXABLE BANDS

		2009/10	2010/11	2011/12
Starting rate for savings	10%	£0–£2,440	£0–£2,440	£0–£2,560
Basic rate	20%	£0–£37,400	£0–£37,400	£0–£35,000
Higher rate	40%	Over £37,400	Over £37,401–£150,000	£35,001–£150,000
Additional rate	50%	Not applicable	Over £150,000	Over £150,000

During 2008/09 a starting rate of 10% was introduced for savings income only. If non-savings income is above this limit, then the 10% starting rate does not apply.

The rates of tax applicable to dividends are 10% basic rate, 32.5% higher rate and 42.5% additional rate.

1.2   INCOME TAX ALLOWANCES

The personal allowance enables individuals to earn a certain amount of income each year without it falling within the income tax net. If an individual does not use up his personal allowance in earned income, then unearned (eg, investment income) may fall within this band.

	2008/09	2009/10	2010/11	2011/12
Personal allowance (1)	£6,035	£6,475	£6,475	£7,475
Income limit for personal allowance	Not applicable	Not applicable	£100,000	£100,000
Personal allowance for people aged 65–74 (1) (2)	£9,030	£9,490	£9,490	£9,490
Personal allowance for people aged 75 and over (1) (2)	£9,180	£9,640	£9,640	£10,090
Married couple's allowance (born before 6 April 1935 but aged under 75) (2) (3)	£6,535	Not applicable	Not applicable	Not applicable
Married couple's allowance aged 75 (2) (3)	£6,625	£6,965	£6,965	£7,295
Income limit for age-related allowances	£21,800	£22,900	£22,900	£24,000
Minimum amount of married couple's allowance	£2,540	£2,670	£2,670	£2,800
Blind person's allowance	£1,800	£1,890	£1,890	£1,980

1. With effect from 2010/11, the personal allowance is reduced by £1 for every £2 of income over the £100,000 limit and this reduction applies irrespective of age.
2. If total income exceeds the income limit then each of the allowances is reduced by £1 for every £2 of income over the limit. During 2008/09 and 2009/10 the allowances would not reduce below the basic personal allowance or minimum married couple's allowance. However, from 2010/11, the personal allowances for people aged 65 to 74 and aged 75 and over can be reduced below the personal allowance if income is above £100,000.
3. Tax relief for the married couple's allowance is given at a rate of 10%.

The following example illustrates how income tax payments are calculated for an employed individual with interest and dividends from savings and investments.

EXAMPLE

John is 35 years old and has employment income of £50,000 in the current tax year (2011/12). In addition, he also receives £500 in interest from cash savings held at the bank and £250 in dividends from his holding of shares in **XYZ** Ltd. His total personal income tax liability is calculated as follows:

Employment Income before Tax		**£50,000.00**
Basic Personal Allowance	**£7,475.00**	
Taxable Income	(£50,000–£7,475)	£42,525.00
Basic Rate Band	£35,000@20%	£7,000.00
Higher Rate Band	(£42,525–£35,000 = £7,525@40%)	£3,010.00
Interest Income	(£500@40%)	£200.00
Dividend Income	(£250@32.5%)	£81.25
Total income tax		**£10,291.25**

If John were 65 then he would be entitled to a higher personal allowance of £9,490 in the current tax year. This would have the effect of reducing the amount of income that is chargeable to tax.

However, his income would exceed the age-related income limit by £26,000 (£50,000–£24,000) and so the increased personal allowance would be progressively reduced by £1 for every £2 of income over the age related income limit, until it reaches the basic personal allowance of £7,475.

If income exceeds £100,000 per annum in 2011/12 then the personal allowance is progressively reduced below the basic amount of £7,475 until it is fully exhausted.

1.3   **TAXATION OF CHARITIES**

Registered UK charities qualify for a number of exemptions, reliefs, and allowances against income tax, capital gains tax (CGT), and tax on profits from certain activities. However, in order to qualify for these deductions, the charity must register with HMRC.

In general, most of the income and gains received by charities are exempt from tax as long as the income is used for charitable purposes. Charities can also claim tax relief on donations made by UK taxpayers under the Gift Aid Scheme. Furthermore, charities can register to have bank interest paid gross in the same way as non-taxpaying individuals. However, they are unable to reclaim the tax deducted at source on dividends received from UK companies.

Charities are exempt from paying stamp duty land tax on any property transactions and may be able to reclaim VAT on any goods or services they acquire in the pursuit of their charitable aims.

If charities trade in the provision of goods and services, they may be subject to tax on profits. Also, if the level of income from trading activities exceeds £70,000 in 2011/12, they will need to become VAT-registered and account for VAT in the usual way.

Charities are exempt from CGT as long as the proceeds from the disposal are used for charitable purposes.

2.   TAXATION OF TRUSTS

LEARNING OBJECTIVE

4.1.2   Understand how the income tax liability for a trust is determined based on: trust type; tax rates; tax rate bands

4.1.3   Understand the application of income tax in respect of: individuals; trusts; charities

A trust is a legal arrangement where one or more parties (the trustees) hold assets for the benefit of someone else (the **beneficiaries**). The person introducing the money or assets into the trust is known as the **settlor**. There are many different types of trust, which are outlined in Section 2.1.

The rules in respect of tax and trusts can be complex, and can merit a whole book in their own right, especially where offshore trusts are concerned.

However, candidates need to be aware of the fact that, because trusts are not separate legal entities (in the way that companies are), in many cases the trustees are assessed on the income and gains earned by the trust.

However, almost invariably they pay the tax liability from the trust's assets. Otherwise few people would be willing to act as trustees!

There are some exceptions to the rule that liability for capital gains tax (CGT) falls on the trustees – for example if:

- if the settlor, settlor's spouse or civil partner, minor child or step-child can benefit from the trust, then it is the settlor who is liable;
- if the trust is an offshore trust, any gains may fall to the settlor.

Gains of trustees are taxed at the tax rates applicable for trusts. The rate of CGT for trustees for 2011/12 is 28%.

The capital gains tax allowance in 2011/12 for most trusts is £5,300, ie, half the annual exemption of £10,600 available to individuals. An exception to this is a trust set up for a beneficiary who is disabled. In these circumstances the annual allowance is £10,600.

2.1   TYPES OF TRUST

There are four main types of trust:

- Trusts with an **interest in possession** – where one or more of the beneficiaries has, for the time being, a right to the trust income as it arises or to the use or enjoyment of the trust property.
- **Discretionary trusts** – where the trustees generally have wide powers over the application of both the trust income and the trust capital.

- **Accumulation and maintenance trusts** – where one or more of the beneficiaries must become entitled either to the trust income or to the trust capital absolutely by a specified age not exceeding 25. Until then the income must be accumulated or applied for the maintenance, education or benefit of the beneficiary.
- **Bare or absolute trusts** – where the beneficiary has an immediate and absolute right to both capital and income, which cannot be taken away.

2.2 TAXATION OF TRUSTS

2.2.1 Trusts with an Interest in Possession

The Trustees

The trustees are charged basic rate tax (20% for 2011/12) on income arising within the trust fund. Note that for UK equity and dividend income, the notional 10% tax credit satisfies the trustees' liability and no further charge arises.

The Beneficiaries

Beneficiaries entitled to trust income are personally liable to income tax on it, whether they draw the income or leave it in the trust fund. The beneficiaries receive a credit for tax paid by the trustees. In general, if the basic rate of tax is 20% and if the trust income for the year is £100 gross, the beneficiary will receive £80 net of basic rate tax. The beneficiary will then be taxed on the full £100 but will receive credit for the £20 paid by the trustees.

If the beneficiary is a basic rate taxpayer, they will have no further liability to tax on the money received. If, however, they are a 40% or 50% taxpayer, then they will be liable for additional tax. If the beneficiary is a non-taxpayer then they can reclaim the tax paid by the trustees. If the trust income is UK savings income, and the beneficiary is a starting rate taxpayer, they can reclaim £10 of the £20 tax credit. Where the trust income is UK dividends, the notional 10% tax credit is non-reclaimable even for non-taxpayers, although starting rate and basic rate taxpayers have no further liability. The higher rate tax on UK dividends is 32.5% of the gross dividend or 42.5% for additional rate taxpayers.

2.2.2 Discretionary Trusts and Accumulation and Maintenance Trusts

The Trustees

Trustees are responsible for declaring and paying income tax on income received by the trust.

In both discretionary trusts and accumulation and maintenance trusts, income is taxed at the special trust rates, apart from the first £1,000 of trust income, which is known as the 'standard rate band'. Income that falls within the standard rate band is taxed at lower rates, depending on the nature of the income. This is shown in more detail in the following tables.

If the settlor has more than one trust, the £1,000 standard rate band is divided by the number of trusts the settlor has. If the settlor has more than five trusts, the standard rate band is £200 for each trust.

Trust income below £1,000 per tax year:

Description of Income	Tax Rate (2011/12)
Rental income, savings interest	20%
UK dividend income	10%

Trust income above £1,000 per tax year:

Description of Income	Tax Rate (2011/12)
Rental income, savings interest, etc.	50%
UK dividend income	42.5%

The Beneficiaries

A beneficiary is taxable only on income paid to them by the trustees or applied by the trustees for their maintenance, education or benefit. Amounts received by the beneficiary are deemed to be net of the special trust rate and a corresponding credit is available. If a beneficiary receives £50, they will be taxable on £100 but a credit of £50 is available. Thus, if the beneficiary is a non- or basic rate taxpayer, some or all of the tax can be reclaimed. Where trust income is made up of dividends, then the 10% tax credit is not reclaimable.

If the settlor of a trust is also a beneficiary or potential beneficiary, then the trust income is regarded as theirs for income tax purposes. The trustees remain liable, but if the settlor is not a higher-rate taxpayer they may reclaim the balance of tax.

Trustees of a discretionary or an accumulation and maintenance trust have the power to make discretionary payments and therefore need to make sure that they have paid enough tax to cover the tax credit given to the beneficiary. They do this by using a 'tax pool', which keeps a record of all discretionary income payments made by the trustees, and the tax the trustees have paid.

2.2.3 Bare or Absolute Trusts

The tax treatment of these trusts reflects the substantive position. The trust is effectively ignored, with any income tax liability falling on the beneficiary at their own rates, subject to their own personal allowances. The exception to this principle is income arising from assets placed in trust by parents for their own minor children (see Section 2.2.4).

2.2.4 Parental Settlements

Minor children have their own personal allowances and starting/basic rate limits. However, if parents create a trust for the benefit of their own minor children, any income paid to the beneficiaries while they are minors and unmarried will be assessed to tax on the parents, unless the total income paid to the beneficiary in any tax year is £100 or less (2011/12 figures).

From 9 March 1999, income generated by bare trusts created by parents for the benefit of their own minor and unmarried children is assessed on the parents, whether or not the income is distributed (subject to the £100 limit).

2.2.5 Trusts for the Vulnerable

Special tax provisions have applied as from 6 April 2004 to any type of trust whose beneficiaries are disabled or relevant minors (such trusts being referred to collectively as trusts for the vulnerable).

- A disabled person is defined as one who is incapable of administering their own property or managing their affairs by reason of mental disorder, or who is in receipt of attendance allowance or disability living allowance.
- A relevant minor is one who is under the age of 18 and has been predeceased by at least one parent.

If a trust has a vulnerable beneficiary, the trustees are entitled to a deduction of tax against the amount they would otherwise pay. The trustees calculate what their trust income tax will be if there is no claim for special treatment, which will vary according to which type of trust it is. They then calculate what income tax the vulnerable person would pay if the income that the trust produced had been paid directly to them as an individual. This takes into account any other income, capital gains and allowances, but ignores any discretionary income payments to the beneficiary. The trustees can then claim the difference between these two figures as a deduction from their own income tax liability.

3. TAXATION OF INVESTMENT INCOME

3.1 THE INCOME TAX TREATMENT OF VARIOUS ASSET TYPES

LEARNING OBJECTIVE

4.2.1   Understand the tax treatment of investment income: savings income; dividend income

3.1.1 Savings Income

Normally, UK banks deduct basic rate income tax at source before crediting interest to a UK resident's account. However, those UK residents who are non-taxpayers – and overseas residents who are not liable for UK tax – are able to apply to HMRC to receive their interest gross on deposits with UK banks and building societies.

If a deposit-taker's interest rate is quoted as a net rate, this is the rate the investor will receive after deduction of basic rate tax. This means that the rate shows what the investor will receive, after the deposit-taker has deducted income tax at the savings rate of 20% on the amount of interest paid.

If the depositor is a starting rate or basic rate taxpayer, there will be no further tax to pay on the interest. If they are a higher-rate or additional rate taxpayer, then a further 20% or 30% tax will be payable to HMRC (to make up the taxpayer's total 40% or 50% liability to tax on income).

It is rare to see the net rate of income tax for higher-rate taxpayers quoted by a deposit-taker: usually, the rate is quoted net of basic rate tax, and higher-rate taxpayers have to do their own calculations to work out what they would get. However this isn't too hard to do.

To calculate a net rate from a gross rate:

- For a basic rate taxpayer, take the gross flat rate and multiply it by 0.8 (this has the effect of deducting 20% from it). So, a rate of 4% gross would translate to 3.2% net of basic rate tax.
- For a 40% rate taxpayer, take the gross flat rate and multiply it by 0.6 (this has the effect of deducting 40% from it). So, a rate of 4% gross would translate to 2.4% net of basic rate tax.
- For a 50% rate taxpayer, take the gross flat rate and multiply it by 0.5 (this has the effect of deducting 50% from it). So, a rate of 4% gross would translate to 2.0% net of basic rate tax.

3.1.2 Interest on Bonds

Interest on **corporate bonds** is usually received net of tax, with a 20% tax credit attached. Higher-rate and additional rate taxpayers will have to pay further tax on the interest they have received.

Eurobonds are a type of international bond, and no withholding tax or other taxes are deducted on interest at source.

Interest on **gilts** bought since 6 April 1998 is usually paid gross, but investors can apply to have it paid net of tax if this is easier for them than having to save some to pay the HMRC at a later stage. Gilts bought before 6 April 1998 usually pay interest net, but non-taxpayers can apply to have it paid gross.

3.1.3   Dividend Income

Two different income tax rates are applicable for UK dividend income. The one which is applicable will depend on what the investor's overall tax position is, taking account of his allowances, and whether he is a basic or higher-rate taxpayer.

Tax rate applied (after deduction of personal allowance/blind person's allowance).

Dividend income falling below the basic rate tax limit	10.0%
Dividend income over the basic rate tax limit and below £150,000	32.5%
Dividend income above £150,000	42.5%

On receipt of the dividend (whether by cheque or direct into his bank account), the investor should also receive a 'voucher' which sets out the sum he has received, and the **tax credit** associated with this. The tax credit reflects the fact that the company paying the dividend has done so out of profits on which it has, itself, already paid tax (or is due to). It allows the investor to offset this against his own income tax liabilities on his dividend income. Thus, in declaring their taxable income, investors should include both the dividend received and the tax credit to arrive at the total dividend income. So the dividend an investor receives, if it has a 10% tax credit, should be seen as 90% of his dividend income. The other 10% comprises the tax credit itself.

For investors who pay basic rate tax, or no tax, their liability will be 10% – and, as this has already been paid by the company, the tax credit is their evidence that it has been taken care of.

Higher-rate taxpayers are liable to pay a total of 32.5% on any dividend income falling above the basic rate tax limit. As the first 10% of this has already been covered by the tax credit, their outstanding liability is for 22.5%. Additional rate taxpayers are liable to pay a total of 42.5% on any dividend income. As the first 10% of this has already been covered by the tax credit, their outstanding liability is for 32.5%.

People who usually pay no tax cannot reclaim the 10% credit.

3.2   THE TAX TREATMENT OF COLLECTIVE INVESTMENTS

The tax treatment of distributions from collectives depends on the type of investments in which the scheme invests.

- Funds invested mainly in cash deposits and interest-bearing securities pay out distributions which are mostly made up of interest, and the distribution will be taxed at the applicable rate for savings income.
- Those investing mainly in companies make distributions which are mostly made up of dividends, and the distribution will be taxed at the rate for dividends.

UK funds pay distributions net of basic rate tax, and the investor should receive a tax voucher showing the tax credit for tax already paid. They return this with their income tax return. Lower and basic rate taxpayers have nothing more to pay; higher rate taxpayers will have to pay an additional sum. (See the appendix for an example of what a tax return form looks like.)

3.2.1 Open-Ended Investment Companies (OEICs), Unit Trusts and Exchange-Traded Funds (ETFs)

Noted below is the tax treatment of OEICs, unit trusts and ETFs. For simplicity, the text only mentions OEICs but you should be aware that it refers to the tax treatment of each.

Capital Gains Tax (CGT)

- Capital gains made within an OEIC are exempt from tax.
- Capital gains made by a taxpayer on any disposal of the OEIC may trigger a CGT liability depending on whether they have exceeded their annual CGT exemption. If they make a loss, this may be offset against realised gains made elsewhere. Such losses can be carried forward indefinitely if they have no gains to offset in the year they dispose of their OEIC holding.

Income Tax

HMRC taxes investors in OEICs on their dividends, based on what the OEIC is mainly invested in. So dividends from OEICs investing mainly in shares are taxed as dividend income; those from OEICs invested mainly in interest-bearing securities are taxed as interest distributions.

OEICs Investing Predominantly in Shares

Where such an OEIC pays a dividend, this will carry a 10% tax credit. So, for every 90p of OEIC dividend paid to an investor, there is a 10% tax credit attached making a gross dividend of 100p.

- A non-taxpayer, starting rate taxpayer and basic rate taxpayer need take no further action. The 10% tax credit fully covers the liability. Non-taxpayers, however, cannot reclaim the tax credit from HMRC.
- 40% or 50% rate taxpayers need to pay a further 22.5% or 32.5% of the net dividend – therefore, bringing the total liability to 32.5% or 42.5% of the gross dividend.

OEICs Investing Predominantly in Fixed-Interest Securities

Dividends from such funds are taxed differently from those distributing mainly equity income; they are paid net of 20% tax. For example:

Dividend paid by OEIC	£10.00
Less 20% tax	£2.00
Net interest distribution	£8.00

- Non-taxpayers can reclaim the £2.00 tax deducted.
- Taxpayers on lower incomes can reclaim half the tax (£1.00).
- Basic rate taxpayers have no further liability.
- 40% or 50% rate taxpayers are subject to a further 20% (£2.00) or 30% (£3.00) tax.

Equalisation Payments

When an investor first buys units or shares in a fund, they may receive an equalisation payment as part of the next distribution that the fund pays. This equalisation payment is treated differently for tax purposes.

When an investor buys units, the price that they have paid is based on the **net asset value** of the fund, that is, the value of the underlying portfolio plus any income that has been received but not yet paid out. When the next distribution is made, therefore, a part of the distribution that the investor will receive includes this income that they have paid for in the purchase price. It is effectively a return of part of the amount invested, and so is treated differently for tax purposes.

When the distribution is paid, the investor will receive a tax voucher that splits the payment into two parts: the normal distribution and the equalisation payment. As the equalisation payment is a return of the investor's money, it is not liable to income tax. Instead, as it is a return of the amount invested, the payment can be deducted from the cost of the holding when calculating any chargeable gain on an eventual disposal.

Accumulated Income

If a fund does not pay out the income it earns during the year (ie, is a 'roll-up' or 'accumulation' fund), but rolls it up in the fund's unit or share price, the investor has nonetheless earned that income and should receive a tax voucher from the fund manager.

They must enter the details on their tax return, and will be assessed on it. HMRC regards this as still being a receipt of income by the investor and will assess them for income tax on the amount accumulated.

3.2.2 Investment Trusts

Capital Gains Tax

- **Investment trusts**, providing that they comply with the relevant rules, do not pay CGT on internal gains.
- An **investor** in an investment trust may be liable to CGT on any gains they make on disposal of it. They make a loss which may be offset against gains made elsewhere or it may be carried forward to future years.

Income Tax

Investment trusts receiving income from the assets in which they invest pay tax as follows:

- UK dividends are received with a 10% tax credit and the investment trust has no further liability. This is franked income.
- Overseas dividends may be received net of foreign withholding tax. The investment trust is liable for corporation tax on the grossed-up income, but, depending on any double taxation agreements, some of the tax already withheld may be offset against this liability.
- The investment trust is liable for tax on other income at the corporation tax rate applicable.

An **investor** in an investment trust is taxed on dividends paid by it in the same way as he would be for any other share. That is, the dividends will be received with a tax credit of 10%.

- Non-taxpayers cannot reclaim this tax.
- Lower-rate and basic rate taxpayers have no further liability.
- 40% or 50% rate taxpayers are liable to a further 22.5% or 32.5% on the grossed-up dividend.

3.2.3 Real Estate Investment Trusts (REITs) and Direct Property Rental Income

LEARNING OBJECTIVE

4.2.2   Understand the tax treatment of rental income from property and property investment funds for both the fund and UK investors

Capital Gains Tax

- UK **REITs** are not subject to CGT on gains made on the disposal of property, provided they distribute at least 90% of their profits each year to shareholders as dividends.
- **Investors** disposing of a holding in a REIT may be liable to CGT on any gains made, as for any other shareholding. Losses may be offset or carried forward.

Income Tax

- **REITs** are required to pay away at least 90% of the property rental income they receive in a year.
- These dividends are taxed as property rental income in the hands of the investor (not as ordinary dividends). This tax is deducted at source.

So the main benefit of a REIT over a traditional property investment trust or property company is that investors in the latter suffer more tax overall. That is, the traditional property company pays both corporation tax and CGT on its property-related activities; plus, the investor pays income tax on his dividends. REITs, however, do not pay corporation taxes so long as they distribute 90% of their profits.

The investor does, however, as we can see, pay a bit more income tax on his dividend than they will for other sorts of share, because it is classed as rental income. Where they would normally pay 10% (basic rate taxpayers), 32.5% (higher-rate taxpayers) or 42.5% (additional rate taxpayers) on dividend income, they will pay 20%, 40% or 50% depending on his personal tax band.

Direct Property Rental Income Taxation

Rental income on **residential property** is taxed at normal income tax rates: if an individual rents out a residential property he will be treated as running a business, and should report the rental income on their tax return. (There is an exemption for people renting out a room in their own home, on the **rent-a-room** scheme, where someone can earn up to £4,250 pa tax-free). The tax payable will be based on the investor's net profit from the activity:

- total rental income;
- less total allowable expenses.

Allowable expenses include things like wear and tear on furnishings – usually calculated as a percentage of the rent, and renewals – items that have become unusable and have had to be replaced.

Rental profits from **commercial property** are taxed in the same way as any other rental income. As with residential property, an investor is entitled to a deduction against the rental income for the general costs of running the property (eg, repairs). There is, however, no annual wear and tear allowance as there is for residential rentals. Instead, the investor is entitled to various capital allowances, which vary depending on the nature of the capital item involved.

4. NATIONAL INSURANCE CONTRIBUTIONS

LEARNING OBJECTIVE

4.3.1 Understand the basis on which National insurance contributions (NICs) are levied: employers; employees; self-employed; voluntary

National insurance contributions build entitlement to certain social security benefits, including the state pension. The type and level of national insurance contributions paid depend on how much people earn and whether they are employed or self-employed. National insurance contributions cease in the year an individual reaches state pension age.

4.1 WHO PAYS NATIONAL INSURANCE?

National insurance contributions are paid by employees and the self-employed aged 16 and over, providing their earnings are above a certain threshold. National insurance contributions cease at state retirement age (currently age 65 for men and age 60 for women but this will gradually increase over the period 2010 to 2020 to age 65 for women).

4.1.1 Employers

Employers are responsible for calculating, deducting and paying **Class 1 primary NICs** (employees' contributions), to HM Revenue & Customs (HMRC) on behalf of all employees, including directors, earning above the earnings threshold. These must be deducted from their earnings.

Employers (or those treated as the employer if the actual employer is outside the UK) must also calculate and pay **Class 1 secondary NICs** (employers' contributions) for all employees earning above the earnings threshold.

Employers must keep adequate records showing how NICs were calculated and what payments have been made for each employee.

Rates and Allowances – National Insurance Contributions

National Insurance – Rates and Allowances			
£ per week	2009/10	2010/11	2011/12
Lower earnings limit, primary Class 1	£95	£97	£102
Upper earnings limit, primary Class 1	£844	£844	£817
Upper accruals point	£770	£770	£770
Primary threshold	£110	£110	£139
Secondary threshold	£110	£110	£136
Employees' primary Class 1 rate between primary threshold and upper earnings limit	11%	11%	12%
Employees' primary Class 1 rate above upper earnings limit	1%	1%	2%
Class 1A rate on employer-provided benefits (1)	12.8%	12.8%	13.8%
Employees' contracted-out rebate	1.6%	1.6%	1.6%
Married women's reduced rate between primary threshold and upper earnings limit	4.85%	4.85%	5.85%
Married women's rate above upper earnings limit	1%	1%	2%
Employers' secondary Class 1 rate above secondary threshold	12.8%	12.8%	13.8%
Employers' contracted-out rebate, salary-related schemes	3.7%	3.7%	3.7%
Employers' contracted-out rebate, money-purchase schemes	1.4%	1.4%	1.4%
Class 2 rate	£2.40	£2.40	£2.50
Class 2 small earnings exception	£5,075 per year	£5,075 per year	£5,315 per year
Special Class 2 rate for share fishermen	£3.05	£3.05	£3.15
Special Class 2 rate for volunteer development workers	£4.75	£4.85	£5.10
Class 3 rate	£12.05	£12.05	£12.60
Class 4 lower profits limit	£5,715 per year	£5,715 per year	£7,225 per year
Class 4 upper profits limit	£43,875 per year	£43,875 per year	£42,475 per year
Class 4 rate between lower profits limit and upper profits limit	8%	8%	9%
Class 4 rate above upper profits limit	1%	1%	2%
Additional primary Class 1 percentage rate on deferred employments	1%	1%	2%
Additional Class 4 percentage rate where deferment has been granted	1%	1%	2%

4.2   HOW MUCH CAN BE EARNED WITHOUT PAYING TAX AND NATIONAL INSURANCE?

4.2.1   Income Tax

Everyone can earn a certain amount each year without paying any income tax. This is called the personal allowance, and in 2011/12 the personal allowance is £7,475. Some people can earn a bit more before they start paying tax – if they're over 65, for example.

There are a number of other allowances and reliefs available which can reduce the total tax bill, and in some cases mean there is no tax to pay.

4.2.2   National Insurance

It is possible to earn up to £139 a week (2011/12) before paying any National Insurance contributions. This is known as the **primary threshold**. However, as long as earnings are greater than £102 a week (2011/12) it is still possible to build an entitlement to state pension and certain other benefits. This is known as the **lower earnings limit**.

4.3   HOW MUCH NATIONAL INSURANCE IS PAYABLE?

The amount and type of national insurance contributions that are payable depend on whether the individual is employed or self-employed and how much they earn. The rates shown below are for the 2011/12 tax year.

4.3.1   Employed

Employees pay Class 1 national insurance contributions and the rates are:

*   Employees pay 12% of earnings between £139 a week and up to £817 a week.
*   They also pay a further 2% on all earnings in excess of £817 per week.

You pay a lower rate if you are a member of your employer's contracted-out pension scheme. Contributions are deducted from wages by employers.

4.3.2   Self-Employed

The self-employed pay Class 2 and Class 4 National Insurance contributions.

The rates are as follows:

*   Class 2 national insurance contributions are paid at a flat rate of £2.50 a week
*   Class 4 national insurance contributions paid as a percentage of annual taxable profits, ie, 9% on profits between £7,225 and £42,475 and a further 2% on profits over that amount

If profits are expected to be less than £5,315, Class 2 national insurance contributions may not have to be paid.

Class 2 National Insurance Contributions

Class 2 national insurance contributions are paid at a flat rate of £2.50 a week if earnings are above £5,315 per year (2011/12).

Class 2 contributions count towards certain benefits, like the basic state pension, maternity leave and bereavement benefit. But they do not count towards the additional state pension, statutory sick pay or jobseeker's allowance.

Exceptions to Paying Class 2 National Insurance Contributions

If earnings are less than £5,315 per year, a certificate of small earnings exception can be applied for which means Class 2 national insurance contributions will not have to be paid. However, it is possible to carry on paying voluntarily to retain entitlement to state pension and other benefits.

Class 4 National Insurance Contributions

The amount of Class 4 national insurance contributions to be paid in any tax year is based on the profits for that year. 8% is payable on annual profits between £7,225 and £42,475 (2011/12) and 2% on any profit over that amount.

Class 4 national insurance contributions do not count towards benefit entitlements.

4.4   VOLUNTARY CONTRIBUTIONS

Any individuals whose work or personal situation means that they do not currently have to pay national insurance contributions, or are not entitled to receive national insurance credits, may still be able to make voluntary contributions to fill in any gaps in their national insurance record. Voluntary contributions count towards some state benefits and can also increase the amount of benefit they receive.

Voluntary national insurance contributions are normally Class 3 contributions, but if individuals are self-employed or living abroad they may be able to pay Class 2 contributions voluntarily instead.

4.4.1   Circumstances Where Voluntary Contributions May Be Payable

Any individual may choose to pay national insurance contributions voluntarily if they are:

- unemployed and not claiming benefits;
- employed but don't earn enough to pay national insurance contributions and don't get national insurance credits;
- self-employed and have a certificate of small earnings exception that means that they do not have to pay Class 2 national insurance contributions;
- a married woman or widow who cancels her reduced rate election part-way through a tax year;
- living abroad.

4.4.2   How Much Do Voluntary Contributions Cost?

If someone wants to pay voluntary national insurance contributions for the 2011/12 tax year they will pay:

- £12.60 a week for Class 3 voluntary contributions;
- £2.50 a week for Class 2 contributions.

If they are self-employed there are some circumstances when they won't be able to pay Class 2 contributions voluntarily. See Section 4.4.3.

4.4.3   Voluntary Contributions Choices for the Self-Employed

The self-employed can choose to pay Class 2 voluntary national insurance contributions even if they do not have to pay them. It's normally better to pay Class 2 contributions voluntarily than to pay Class 3 voluntary contributions. It will cost less and they will receive a wider range of state benefits.

The self-employed may choose to pay Class 2 contributions voluntarily when earnings are low or because they are working outside the UK. However, there are conditions they will need to meet in order to pay Class 2 contributions voluntarily if they are working outside the UK.

5.   CAPITAL GAINS TAX (CGT)

LEARNING OBJECTIVE

4.4.1   Understand the application of capital gains tax in respect of: individuals; trusts; charities

4.4.2   Understand the application of capital gains tax to the sale of assets, such as: shares; government bonds; corporate bonds; real estate; chattels

Capital gains tax (CGT) is a tax on capital gains made when an asset is disposed of.

A chargeable gain (or an allowable loss) is generally calculated as follows:

	£
Disposal consideration	X
Less incidental costs of disposal	X
Net proceeds	X
Less allowable costs	X

The **incidental costs of disposal** referred to above may include:

- valuation fees (but this would not include the costs of any appeal against HMRC's valuation);
- estate agency and legal fees;

- advertising costs.

These costs should be deducted separately from any other allowable costs.

Allowable costs include:

- the original cost of acquiring the asset;
- any incidental costs of acquiring the asset;
- capital expenditure incurred in enhancing the asset.

5.1   THE APPLICATION OF CGT TO DIFFERENT PARTIES

5.1.1   Individuals

When an individual buys an asset and disposes of it at a profit, the difference between its acquisition cost and disposal value is taxed as a capital gain.

Individuals pay CGT on their net chargeable gains – that is, the gains they have made less any losses realised – in a relevant tax year, less unrelieved losses brought forward from previous years and the annual exemption.

Individuals are liable to CGT on their disposal of assets situated anywhere in the world if, for any part of the tax year of disposal, those individuals are either resident, or ordinarily resident, in the UK. Their liability may be affected by any international double taxation agreements.

There is an **annual exemption** for each tax year and for 2011/12 it is £10,600.

The rate of CGT is currently 18% or 28% depending on the personal income level. Trustees and their representatives are liable for tax on gains at a rate of 28%. Entrepreneurs' relief is also available on lifetime gains of up to £10 million at an effective rate of 10%, which came in to effect on 6 April 2011.

5.1.2   Charities

A charity is exempt from CGT on any gains where the proceeds of the disposal are applied for, or to be applied for, charitable purposes.

5.1.3   Trusts

There are some exceptions to the rule that liability for CGT falls on the trustees – for example:

- if the settlor, settlor's spouse or civil partner, minor child or step-child can benefit from the trust, then it is the settlor who is liable;
- if the trust is an offshore trust, any gains may fall to the settlor.

Gains of trustees are taxed at the tax rates applicable for trusts, which was changed in April 2011 to 28%.

Trusts have an annual CGT exemption which depends on the type of trust in question. For personal representatives of deceased persons and trustees of certain settlements for the disabled it is £10,600. For most others it is £5,300 – half the level for individuals of £10,600.

5.2 CHARGEABLE ASSETS

Individuals that are resident and ordinarily resident in the UK are known as chargeable persons for CGT purposes. Chargeable persons are potentially liable to CGT on capital gains made on the disposal of chargeable assets regardless of where in the world the capital gain arose.

Most assets are chargeable to CGT including:

*   shares in a company;
*   units in a unit trust;
*   land and buildings;
*   higher-value jewellery, paintings, antiques and other personal effects;
*   assets used in a business, such as goodwill.

There are some exceptions to this, and the following assets are exempt:

*   an individual's nominated main or principal private residence (PPR);
*   gilts and qualifying corporate bonds;
*   jewellery, paintings, antiques and other personal effects that are individually worth £6,000 or less;
*   savings certificates and premium bonds;
*   assets held in an ISA;
*   EIS and VCT investments subject to being held for a qualifying period;
*   betting, lottery or pools winnings;
*   personal injury compensation.
*   assets held in a self-invested pension plan (SIPP).

CGT arises when a chargeable asset is disposed of. A disposal arises as a result of a transfer of ownership, the making of a gift, the receipt of a capital sum from an asset and even the destruction of an asset. However, a disposal is not potentially chargeable to CGT, or allowable as a capital loss, if made between spouses, made upon death or if the asset is exempt.

5.3 CGT CALCULATION

The following example illustrates how CGT is calculated on disposal of a chargeable asset for a basic rate taxpayer.

Cost	£10,000	
Proceeds	£25,000	
Gain	£15,000	
Allowance	£10,600	
Taxable gain	£ 4,400	(£15,000 – £10,600)
Tax	£792	(£4,400 x 18%)
Proceeds net of tax		**£24,208**

If the owner also has capital losses carried forward from previous tax years, these are also used to reduce the taxable gain as follows:

Cost	£10,000	
Proceeds	£25,000	
Gain	£15,000	
Losses carried forward	£4,000	
Allowance	£10,600	
Taxable gain	£400	(£15,000 – (£4,000 + £10,600))
Tax	£72	(£400 x 18%)
Proceeds net of tax		**£24,928**

6. INHERITANCE TAX

LEARNING OBJECTIVE

4.5.1   Understand the application of inheritance tax: chargeable transfers; potential exempt transfers; transfers on death; nil rate band; exemptions and reliefs; gifts with reservation; valuation of assets; deed of variation

4.5.3   Understand the application of IHT to: transfers into trusts; assets held in trusts; transfers out of trusts

6.1   THE APPLICATION OF INHERITANCE TAX

Inheritance tax (IHT) is often thought of as a tax which is levied when someone dies; but in fact this is something of a misnomer, as IHT can, in fact, apply when assets are transferred in a variety of ways, for example on death and by gifts. If this were not the case, people would avoid it simply by giving away their assets to their children before they died.

Inheritance tax (IHT) is primarily a tax on **wealth**. Usually this means wealth that is left to someone else on its owner's death, but it also applies to **gifts up to seven years before death** and to certain **lifetime transfers of wealth**.

IHT is different from income tax and CGT.

- For income tax and CGT, the key question is: how much money has the taxpayer made?
- With IHT, the question is: how much have they given away?

It is the amount which the taxpayer has transferred that is taxed. You can also see this as the amount by which he is worse off. Thus if a taxpayer has to pay IHT on a **lifetime gift**, they will be worse off by the amount of the gift plus the tax; this must be taken into account when calculating the cost of making this gift.

6.1.1   Chargeable Transfers

Inheritance tax (IHT) is a tax on gifts or transfers of value. There are two main chargeable occasions:

- Gifts made during the lifetime of the donor (lifetime transfers).
- Gifts or transfers on death, for example, when property is left to someone in a will (the death estate).

Inheritance tax cannot arise unless there is a **transfer of value**. A transfer of value means any gratuitous disposition made by someone which results in his being worse off – that is, he diminishes the total value of his estate.

The sale of an asset at its open market (arm's length) value will thus not give rise to an IHT charge. (It might, however, give rise to a CGT charge if the seller makes a gain on the asset.)

The measure of a gift is always the loss to the transferor (the reduction in value of their estate), not the amount gained by the transferee. In most cases these figures will be the same, but this may not always be so.

Inheritance tax arises on any **chargeable transfer**. A chargeable transfer is any transfer of value not covered by an **exemption**.

Individuals and trustees of settled property (trust property) are chargeable persons for IHT purposes – that is, they may be liable to IHT.

All transfers of assets (worldwide) made by people who are domiciled in the UK – essentially, people who regard the UK as their permanent home – whether during their lifetime or on death, are capable of being liable for IHT. For individuals not domiciled in the UK, only transfers of UK assets are caught within the IHT 'net'.

6.1.2   Potentially Exempt Transfers (PETs)

A lifetime transfer made by an individual to another individual is known as a potentially exempt transfer (PET). A PET is treated as being exempt from IHT when made – and will remain so providing that the transferor survives for at least seven years after the date on which he makes the gift. If the transferor dies within seven years of making the gift, it will become chargeable to IHT.

A lifetime transfer to a discretionary trust is a chargeable lifetime transfer (CLT).

6.1.3   Transfers on Death

When someone dies, the following steps are taken to establish the IHT due:

Step 1   Look back seven years from the date of death to see if any chargeable lifetime transfers have been made. If so, these transfers use up the nil rate band available for the death estate. Work out the value of any nil rate band still available after this exercise.

Step 2   Calculate the gross value of the death estate.

Step 3   Any part of the death estate covered by the nil rate band is not taxed. Any part of the death estate in excess of the nil rate band is charged at 40%. Deduct any relevant reliefs from the death tax.

Step 4   Where relevant, divide the tax due between personal representatives, the person in possession of a gift subject to a reservation and trustees (where applicable).

The Nil-Rate Tax Band

For 2011/12, the first £325,000 of transfers is taxed at 0% (the nil-rate band) and is, therefore, effectively IHT-free.

6.1.4   Exemptions and Reliefs

There are various exemptions available to eliminate or reduce the chargeable amount of a lifetime transfer or property passing on an individual's death:

- Some exemptions apply to both lifetime transfers and property passing on death.
- Other exemptions apply only to lifetime transfers (including PETs becoming chargeable on death within seven years).

Transfer of Unused Nil-Rate Band Between Spouses

The Chancellor of the Exchequer's Autumn Statement on 9 October 2007 announced that inheritance tax allowances (often referred to as the nil-rate band) were to be transferable between married couples and between civil partners. Thus, for the 2011/12 tax year, a married couple will in effect have an allowance of £650,000 against inheritance tax, whilst a single person's allowance remains at £325,000. The mechanism for this enhanced allowance is that, on the death of the second spouse, the nil-rate band for the second spouse is increased by the percentage of the nil-rate band which was not used on the death of the first spouse to die.

For example, if in 2011/12 the first married spouse (or civil partner) to die were to leave £130,000 to their children and the rest of their estate to their spouse, there would be no inheritance tax due at that time and £195,000 or 60% of the nil-rate band would be unused. Later, upon the second death, the nil-rate band would be increased by the remainder of the unused allowance from the first death, so that if the surviving spouse also died in 2011/12 the first £520,000 (£325,000 x 160%) of the surviving spouse's estate will be exempt from inheritance tax.

This measure was also extended to existing widows, widowers and bereaved civil partners on 9 October 2007, so if their late spouse or partner had not used all of their inheritance tax allowance at the time of their death, then the unused percentage of that allowance can now be added to the single person's allowance when the surviving spouse or partner dies. This applies however long ago the first spouse died, but there are special rules if the surviving spouse remarried.

In a judgement following an unsuccessful appeal to a 2006 decision by the European Court of Human Rights, it was held that the above does not apply to siblings living together. The crucial factor in such cases was determined to be the existence of a public undertaking, carrying with it a body of rights and obligations of a contractual nature, rather than the length or supportive nature of the relationship.

Prior to this legislative change, the most common means of ensuring that both nil-rate bands were used was called a nil band discretionary trust (now more properly known as NRB relevant property trust). This is an arrangement in both wills which says that whoever is the first to die leaves their nil band to a discretionary trust for the family, and not to the survivor. The survivor can still benefit from those assets if needed, but they are not part of that survivor's estate.

Exemptions Applying to Lifetime Transfers Only (including PETs)

Small gifts exemption – outright gifts to individuals totalling £250 or less per donee (the person receiving the gift) in any one tax year are exempt. If a gift totals more than £250, the whole of it is chargeable. A donor can give up to £250 each year to each of as many donees as he wishes. The small gifts exemption cannot apply to gifts into trusts.

Annual exemption – the first £3,000 of value transferred in a tax year is exempt from IHT (but you cannot use your £3,000 annual exemption and then your £250 small gifts exemption to give the same person a total of £3,250).

The annual exemption is used only after all other exemptions (such as for transfers to spouses/civil partners or to charities). If several gifts are made in a year, the £3,000 exemption is applied to earlier gifts before later gifts. Any unused portion of the annual exemption is carried forward for one year only.

Normal expenditure out of income – IHT is a tax on transfers of capital, not on dispositions of income. A transfer of value is exempt if:

* it is made as part of the normal expenditure of the transferor;
* taking one year with another, it was made out of income; and
* it leaves the transferor with sufficient income to maintain his usual standard of living.

As well as covering such things as regular presents, this exemption can cover regular payments out of income under deeds of covenant, and the payment of life assurance premiums on a policy for someone else.

Gifts in consideration of marriage or civil partnership are exempt up to:

* £5,000 if from a parent of a party to the marriage or civil partnership.
* £2,500 if from a grandparent or a remoter ancestor of one of the parties to the marriage or civil partnership.
* £1,000 if from any other person.

The limits apply to gifts from any one donor for any one marriage or civil partnership.

Exemptions Applying to Both Lifetime Transfers and Transfers on Death

Transfers of value **between spouses or civil partners** are exempt providing that the transferee (that is, the recipient) is domiciled in the UK at the time of transfer.

The exemption:

* applies whether or not the spouses or partners are living together;
* ceases to apply on divorce.

Transfers (whether outright or by settlement) **to charities** which are established in the UK are wholly exempt from inheritance tax.

Gifts to a qualifying political party are exempt. A political party qualifies if, at the general election preceding the transfer of value, either:

- at least two members were elected to the House of Commons; or
- one member was elected and the party polled at least 150,000 votes.

Gifts for national purposes are also exempt. Eligible recipients include museums, art galleries, the National Trust, universities, local authorities and government departments.

Gifts of land to housing associations are exempt.

Maintenance settlements can be made free of inheritance tax if they are for the upkeep of historic property.

6.1.5 Gifts with Reservation

There are rules to stop people from avoiding IHT by making **gifts with reservation** – that is, incomplete lifetime gifts where the donor continues to enjoy the 'gifted' asset. If there were not these rules, people would make incomplete gifts so as to escape the charge to IHT. Instead they would be making a PET; they would also be reducing their estate at death. The value of the assets could in theory thus escape tax entirely, despite the original owner deriving some benefit from them – possibly right up to his death.

An obvious example is a gift of a home to the donor's children – but with the donor continuing to live in it rent-free. Another example is a gift of income-producing assets to someone else, with the income continuing to be received by the donor.

Property given subject to a reservation is property where:

- such property is not enjoyed to virtually the entire exclusion of the donor; or
- possession and enjoyment of the property transferred is not bona fide assumed by the donee.

The term 'to virtually the entire exclusion' will, for example:

- include cases where a donor is allowed occasional brief stays in a house he has given away, without creating a reservation; but
- not include cases where he spent most weekends in the house. This would create a reservation.

Where a gift with reservation is made, it is treated in the same way as any other gift at the time it is made (as a PET or a chargeable lifetime transfer, as appropriate). However, special rules apply on the **death of the donor**:

a. If the reservation still exists at the date of the donor's death, the asset is included in the donor's estate at its value at that time (not its value at the date the gift was made). So any attempt to 'peg' the value of the assets for IHT purposes at an earlier – and therefore probably lower – value will fail.

b. If the reservation ceases within the seven years before death, then the gift is treated as a PET made at the time the reservation ceased. The charge is based on its value at that time. The annual exemption cannot be used in calculating the value of this PET.

A gift will **not** be treated as being with reservation if:

a. Full consideration (ie, payment) is given for any right of occupation or enjoyment retained or assumed by the donor, and the property is land or chattels. For example, an individual might give away his house and continue to live in it, but pay a full market rent for doing so.
b. The circumstances of the donor change in a way that was unforeseen at the time of the original gift and the benefit provided by the donee to the donor only represents reasonable provision for the care and maintenance of the donor, being an elderly or infirm relative. This exception only applies to interests in land.

Pre-owned Assets Tax (POAT)

From 6 April 2005 an income tax charge applies where an individual has the benefit of the free or low-cost use of an asset that they previously owned. The intention behind the charge is to counter schemes which avoid IHT on gifts with reservation. The charging provisions will apply to land (including buildings), chattels and gifts into settlements (trusts) of intangible assets.

The charge for land is based on the rental value. The charge for chattels is calculated by applying a statutory rate of interest to the value of the asset (reduced by any payments made for its use). The charge for intangible assets is calculated by applying a statutory rate of interest to its value, reduced by any capital gains tax payable. There is no charge if the value of the benefit is £5,000 per annum or less.

Transitional provisions will allow individuals to elect for the POAT charge not to apply, but this will have the effect that the property, chattel or intangible asset will be included in the individual's estate for IHT purposes.

6.1.6 Property Valuations

The value of any property for the purposes of IHT is the price which the property might reasonably be expected to fetch if sold in the open market at the time of the transfer.

Quoted Shares and Securities

The valuation of quoted shares and securities is relatively simple. The Stock Exchange's Daily Official List is a publication which gives the closing bid and offer prices of all quoted securities. Inheritance tax valuations are done on the basis of the '**quarter up rule**', taking the bid (lower) price plus a quarter of the difference between it and the offer price. Thus if the closing price for a particular day is 300–304p the inheritance tax valuation is $300 + (304 - 300)/4 = 301$p.

The other way of valuing securities is to use the **marked bargains** price. Each day, certain trades on the Stock Exchange will be marked, and the valuer may take the average of the highest and lowest marked bargains, ignoring bargains marked at special prices.

The rule for valuation of quoted securities is, therefore, to take the **lower of**:

*   the value on the quarter up basis; and

- the average of the highest and lowest marked bargains for the day, ignoring those marked at special prices.

Valuations for transfers on death must be **cum-dividend** or **cum-interest**, including the value of the right to the next dividend or interest payment.

Unit Trusts

Units in authorised unit trusts are valued at the managers' bid price (the lower of the two published prices).

Unquoted Company Shares

There is no easily identifiable open market value for shares in an unquoted company. The Shares Valuation Division of HMRC is the body with which the taxpayer must negotiate. If agreement cannot be reached, appeal lies to the Special Commissioners and then to the Courts.

6.1.7   Life Policies

If a person's estate includes a life policy which matures on his death, the proceeds payable to his personal representatives must be included in his estate for IHT purposes. But if a person's estate includes a life policy which matures on the death of someone else, the open market value must be included in his estate.

If an individual takes out a policy on his own life, pays some premiums and then decides to give the policy to someone else by assignment or by declaration of trust, he makes a PET.

The value transferred is the greater of the:

- premiums or other consideration paid before the transfer of the policy; and
- open market value of the policy at the date of transfer.

If an individual writes a policy in trust, or assigns a policy, or makes a subsequent declaration of trust, the policy proceeds will not be paid to his estate but to the assignee or to the trustees, for the trust beneficiaries. The proceeds will, therefore, not be included as part of his free estate at death.

It is common to write policies in trust for the benefit of dependants to avoid IHT. In many cases, these transfers will be exempted as normal expenditure out of income.

6.1.8   Deed of Variation

Sometimes, an individual will inherit under a will but want to change the terms – perhaps because to inherit directly will give him a tax problem, or perhaps because he wants someone else to benefit. In these circumstances, it may be possible for a deed of variation to be used. For a deed of variation to be valid, it must:

- relate to a valid will, to an intestate estate or to a trust;
- be signed by all the parties who would have benefited had the variation not been made (all of whom must be over 18 and must be of sound mind);
- be executed within two years of the death of the legator (the person who left the money);

- not be made for any consideration (ie, no one should have received money or value as encouragement for them to sign).

The deed must also contain a statement to the effect that it is intended that the inheritance tax effect of the variation will be the same as if the deceased had made that variation himself.

6.1.9   IHT on Transfers into and out of Trusts and IHT on Trust Assets

The IHT position on transfers of wealth into a trust depends on the nature of the trust itself. In general, transfers of wealth into trusts are treated as **Potentially Exempt Transfers (PETs)**, and are therefore excluded from the donor's estate for IHT purposes if they survive seven years from the date of making the transfer. However, a transfer of wealth into a discretionary trust is deemed to be a **chargeable lifetime transfer** and may be subject to an IHT charge if it causes the individual's IHT allowance to be exceeded at the date the transfer is made.

The position once the assets are in the trust depends on the individual's connection with the trust, ie, settlor or beneficiary. Again, in general terms, the assets do not form part of the estate of the beneficiary unless a distribution of trust capital or income is made to them.

If an asset that has been held within a trust is passed to a beneficiary then it becomes part of their own estate and may create an IHT charge on their own death if it causes the IHT allowance to be exceeded.

6.2   ESTATE ADMINISTRATION

The rules as to what happens to the assets and liabilities of an individual upon his death are governed by the laws of succession.

When someone dies, their assets and liabilities still exist and they need to be dealt with. The legal system with regard to succession provides a set of rules governing who will get the assets, and how they must be distributed. The 'who' is determined according to the rules relating to testate and intestate succession (see Section 6.3), and the 'how' by the rules relating to the administration of estates.

Administration of the estate of a deceased person is carried out by one or more **personal representatives**. These may be either:

- **executors** – in cases where the deceased left a valid will (died testate). The executors will obtain a **grant of probate**; or
- **administrators**, where the deceased left no valid will (died intestate). The administrators will obtain **letters of administration**.

Letters of administration *cum testamento annexo* (with the will annexed) are needed when a will is left, but, owing to some small defect in it, probate cannot be granted. Both executors and administrators are responsible for putting the deceased's affairs in order and distributing the estate to those entitled to it, either under the terms of the will or under the relevant laws of intestacy.

6.2.1 Personal Representatives – The Charge to Tax

The personal representatives of a deceased person are responsible for:

- settlement of any outstanding income tax liabilities of the deceased in respect of his or her income up to the date of death; and
- accounting for tax liabilities arising during the administration period running from the date of death until ascertainment of the residue of the estate.

At the end of the administration period, the residue may pass absolutely to a residuary beneficiary and/or be held in trust under the terms of the deceased's will.

Income during the Administration Period

The personal representatives are liable to income tax at a rate of 10% on UK dividend income and at the basic rate on any other income arising during the administration period. The income arising is classified in the same way as in accordance with the rules for individuals. Personal representatives are not, however, entitled to personal allowances or the starting rate tax band.

6.3 INTESTACY RULES

LEARNING OBJECTIVE

4.5.2   Understand how intestacy rules may apply in England and Wales, and the implications of these rules for estate planning

When a person dies without leaving a valid will, their property (the estate) must be shared out according to certain rules. These are called the 'rules of intestacy'. A person who dies without leaving a will is called an intestate person. Only married or civil partners and some other close relatives can inherit under the rules of intestacy. If someone makes a will but it is not legally valid, the rules of intestacy decide how the estate will be shared out, not the wishes expressed in the will.

Married Partners and Civil Partners

Married partners or civil partners inherit under the rules of intestacy only if they are actually married or in a civil partnership at the time of death. So, if you are divorced or if your civil partnership has been legally ended, you cannot inherit under the rules of intestacy. But partners who separated informally can still inherit under the rules of intestacy.

If there are surviving children, grandchildren or great-grandchildren of the person who died and the estate is valued at more than £250,000, the partner will inherit:

- all the personal property and belongings of the person who has died, and
- the first £250,000 of the estate; and
- a life interest in half of the remaining estate. This means that if you are entitled to the life interest, you cannot dispose of or spend that part of the estate. You can, however, have the benefit of it during your lifetime.

Children

What children of the intestate person will inherit depends on whether there is a surviving married or civil partner.

If there is no surviving partner, the children of a person who has died without leaving a will inherit the whole estate. This applies however much the estate is worth. If there are two or more children, the estate will be divided equally between them.

If there is a surviving partner, a child only inherits from the estate if the estate is valued at over £250,000. If there are two or more children, the children will inherit in equal shares:

- one half of the value of the estate above £250,000; and
- the other half of the value of the estate above £250,000 when the surviving partner dies.

All the children of the parent who has died intestate inherit equally from the estate. This also applies where a parent has children from different relationships. A child whose parents are not married or have not registered a civil partnership can inherit from the estate of a parent who dies intestate. These children can also inherit from grandparents or great-grandparents who have died intestate.

Adopted children (including step-children who have been adopted by their step-parent) have rights to inherit under the rules of intestacy. But otherwise you have to be a biological child to inherit.

Children under 18 do not receive their inheritance immediately. The inheritance is managed by trustees on the child's behalf until they reach the age of 18.

Grandchildren and Great-Grandchildren

A grandchild or great-grandchild cannot inherit from the estate of an intestate person unless their parent or grandparent has died before the intestate person. The grandchildren and great-grandchildren will inherit equal shares of the share to which their parent or grandparent would have been entitled.

Other Close Relatives

Parents, brothers and sisters and nieces and nephews of the intestate person may inherit under the rules of intestacy. This will depend on a number of circumstances:

- whether there is a surviving married or civil partner;
- whether there are children, grandchildren or great grandchildren;
- in the case of nephews and nieces, whether the parent directly related to the person who has died is also dead;
- the amount of the estate.

Other relatives may have a right to inherit if the person who died intestate had no surviving married partner or civil partner, children, grandchildren, great-grandchildren, parents, brothers, sisters, nephews or nieces. The order of priority amongst other relatives is as follows:

- grandparents;
- uncles and aunts;
- cousins.

Who Cannot Inherit?

The following people have no right to inherit where someone dies without leaving a will:

- unmarried partners;
- lesbian or gay partners not in a civil partnership;
- relations by marriage;
- close friends;
- carers.

No Surviving Relatives

If there are no surviving relatives who can inherit under the rules of intestacy, the estate passes to the Crown. This is known as *bona vacantia*. The Treasury Solicitor is then responsible for dealing with the estate. The Crown can make grants from the estate but does not have to agree to them.

6.3.1   Rearranging the Way the Estate is Shared Out

It is possible to rearrange the way property is shared out when someone dies without leaving a will, provided this is done within two years of the death. This is called **making a deed of family arrangement** or **variation**. All the people who would inherit under the rules of intestacy must agree.

If they agree, the property can be shared out in a different way so that people who do not inherit under the intestacy rules can still get some of the estate. Or they could agree that the amount that people get is different from the amount they would get under the rules of intestacy.

7.   RESIDENCY AND DOMICILE

7.1   RESIDENCE AND DOMICILE

LEARNING OBJECTIVE

4.6.1   Understand the impact of the rules on residency and domicile and the implications for income tax and CGT

The UK tax you pay may depend on whether you are **resident**, **ordinarily resident** or **domiciled** in the UK. You can be more than one of these – or none.

Resident

If you are in the UK for 183 days or more in a tax year, you are resident for that year for tax purposes. If you come to the UK to live here for two years or more, you are resident from the date of arrival. You are also likely to be UK resident if you come to the UK regularly each year and are in the UK for an average of 91 days or more in a tax year – usually worked out over a maximum of four consecutive tax years.

Ordinarily Resident

If you are resident in the UK year after year you will normally be ordinarily resident. You are ordinarily resident in the UK from the date you arrive if it's clear that you intend to stay for at least three years.

If you are resident in the UK, your ordinary residence position generally matters only if you earn income outside the UK. In exceptional circumstances you may be not resident but still ordinarily resident in the UK. This is very rare, but if applicable you will also pay UK tax on your capital gains. Ordinary residence is different from residence. It is not defined in tax law and is based on cases heard by the Courts. For example, if you are resident in the UK year after year, this would indicate that you normally live here and are therefore ordinarily resident here.

Domiciled

Domicile is a general legal concept; it refers to the country which is your permanent home. There are a range of factors that can affect where you are domiciled at any point in your life.

Your domicile status is usually acquired from your father, although you can change it when you become an adult. So if both you and your father were born in the UK, have lived in the UK for all or most of your lives, and do not have strong connections outside the UK then you will be domiciled in the UK. Your domicile is only usually relevant if you have income or capital gains outside the UK.

Non-resident

If you do not meet the requirements to be resident in the UK for income and capital gains tax purposes, you are non-resident. If you are not resident in the UK you might not have to pay UK tax on some of your income and gains. If your normal home is outside the UK and you are in the UK for fewer than 183 days in the tax year you may be non-resident. But you might still be resident even if you spend fewer than 183 days in a tax year in the UK. Being resident in the UK is not simply a question of the number of days you spend in the country.

Resident but Not Ordinarily Resident

You can be resident in the UK but not ordinarily resident here. When we talk about someone being not ordinarily resident in the UK we mean that, although they are resident in the UK for a particular tax year, they normally live somewhere else. For example, if you are resident in a tax year because you have been in the country for more than 183 days but you normally live outside the UK, it is likely that you are not ordinarily resident.

Ordinarily Resident but Not Resident

You can be ordinarily resident in the UK but not resident. An example is if you normally live in the UK but, during a tax year, you have gone abroad for a long holiday and you do not set foot in the UK in the tax year. This is very rare.

7.1.1   The Tax Implications of Residence and Domicile

If you are resident in the UK you are normally treated as being on the **arising basis** of taxation. This means that you will pay UK tax on all of your income as it arises and on your gains as they accrue, wherever income and gains are earned in the world. There are some exceptions to this, and these are also outlined in the following paragraphs.

It is possible to be resident in the UK, but not ordinarily resident, or to be resident but not domiciled here. If either of these circumstances applies, then you have a choice of whether to use the arising basis of taxation to account for your worldwide income and gains as they arise/accrue, or to use the remittance basis of taxation.

Broadly, this involves paying tax on income arising and gains accruing in the UK (as with the arising basis), but paying tax on foreign income and gains only as these are brought (remitted) to the UK. Using the remittance basis of taxation is not automatic and, depending on the foreign income and gains, you may have to make a claim if you want to use it by completing the relevant boxes of a self-assessment tax return.

When you are taxed on foreign income and/or gains on the arising basis you might find that your foreign income/gains have already been taxed in the country in which they are located. That does not mean that they are not taxable in the UK. You must still declare all of your foreign income and gains. In many cases, relief is given in the UK for foreign tax paid on foreign income and gains under the provisions of the relevant **double taxation agreements**. Even if no UK tax is payable because it is covered completely by the foreign tax you have paid, you must claim relief under a double taxation agreement by completing a self-assessment tax return.

Remittance Basis

The remittance basis is an alternative to the arising basis of taxation. You can only use the remittance basis of taxation if you are resident in the UK during a tax year and:

- not ordinarily resident in the UK; or
- not domiciled in the UK.

In addition, it applies only if you have foreign income and/or gains during a tax year in which you are resident in the UK. If you are neither of these, then the remittance basis is not applicable for that year.

When you use the remittance basis you will pay UK tax on your UK-source income and gains as they arise or accrue. But you may only have to account for UK tax on foreign income and/or gains when you actually bring (remit) them into the UK.

- If you are **resident but not domiciled** in the UK, you can use the remittance basis for **both foreign income and foreign capital gains**.
- If you are **resident and domiciled in the UK but are not ordinarily resident**, you can only use the remittance basis for foreign **income**; the remittance basis does not apply to foreign **capital gains**, which will be taxed on the arising basis.

Even if you are eligible to use the remittance basis, it does not have to be used. You might decide instead to pay UK tax on your worldwide income (and gains if you are not domiciled in the UK) on the arising basis and claim relief from UK tax for foreign tax that you have also had to pay. You might choose to do this rather than lose your personal allowances, as your tax bill could be higher on the remittance basis.

If you decide to use the remittance basis, the impact of these special rules will depend on personal circumstances – how much foreign income and/or gains that arise in a tax year you decide to leave outside the UK, whether or not you are aged 18 or over, and how long you have been resident in the UK. These factors will determine whether to use the remittance basis without having to make a formal claim or if you need to make a claim to use it. They will also determine whether you will need to pay the £30,000 remittance basis charge (RBC).

If you have less than £2,000 unremitted foreign income and/or gains which arise or accrue in the relevant tax year you can use the remittance basis without making a claim.

If you have £2,000 or more unremitted foreign income and/or gains arising/accruing in the relevant tax year and you want to use the remittance basis, you must make a claim for that year. Your claim must be made by completing the relevant boxes of a self-assessment tax return. When you make the claim you will lose your entitlement to UK personal tax allowances and the annual exempt amount for capital gains tax. Depending on how long you have been resident in the UK, you may also be required to pay the RBC.

If you choose to claim the remittance basis and, at any time in the year of the claim, you are aged 18 or over and have been resident in the UK for at least seven of the previous nine tax years, you will have to pay the RBC when you have £2,000 or more unremitted foreign income and/or gains arising/accruing in the tax year. The RBC is an annual charge of £30,000 and is tax on your unremitted foreign income and/or gains. There are rules on how you pay the charge, which is made through the self-assessment system.

If you pay the RBC you will still have to pay UK tax on:

- your UK income and gains (and foreign gains if you are domiciled in the UK but are not ordinarily resident);
- any foreign income and gains which you remit to the UK.

You will also lose your entitlement to UK personal tax allowances and reliefs for income tax and the annual exempt amount for capital gains tax. If you do not wish to pay the RBC, you can choose to pay tax on your worldwide income and gains on the arising basis.

7.2　THE USE OF DOUBLE TAX TREATIES

LEARNING OBJECTIVE

4.6.2　　Understand the use of double taxation treaties

Income tax is payable by UK residents. If someone spends a period of time working abroad, they will normally be taxed on their overseas earnings by the country where the income is earned. To prevent those earnings also being taxed in the UK, there exist a number of **double taxation agreements (DTAs)** with most countries of the world, generally stipulating that the earnings will be taxed only by the country in which they are earned.

Investment income from overseas will be taxed by the UK HMRC at the time the investor becomes entitled to it. If tax is deducted in the overseas country, it will – again depending on any double tax treaties between the UK and the other country – be allowed as a credit against UK tax.

7.3　HOW WITHHOLDING TAX IS APPLIED

LEARNING OBJECTIVE

4.6.3　　Understand how withholding tax is applied based on: residency; product; tax regime (at source or reclaimable); beneficiary; European Savings Directive; qualified intermediaries scheme

Withholding tax is a tax deducted by the government in one country, when income earned in that country is paid to someone overseas.

The country from which the payment is made taxes it before it leaves the country to be remitted to the overseas investor, by withholding a proportion of it. The amount withheld is usually somewhere between 10% and 30%.

If there is a double tax treaty in effect, it is often possible to reduce the tax withheld – or to reclaim some or all of the money that was withheld. Further, some recipient countries allow the investor to offset the tax withheld against their domestic tax liabilities.

7.3.1　Residence

An individual's tax residence will be important for determining what rates of withholding tax are deducted by the authorities in other countries. For example, the range of DTAs might mean that if they can show that they are UK resident, they will be liable at a lower rate of withholding tax than if they are resident in a country that does not have a DTA.

7.3.2　Product

Different rates of tax are levied on different forms of income. For example, one country might have a DTA with another, setting out that it will apply withholding tax of one rate of dividend income, another for interest income and yet another for royalties.

7.3.3 Tax Regime

Depending on the nature of the withholding taxes deducted in the country of source of any income, and the terms of any DTA, any reduction of withholding taxes may be effected by:

- relief at source (ie, on notification of the investor's status, the withholding tax is reduced or not applied); or
- reclaim – that is, the withholding tax is deducted, but the investor can submit the appropriate paperwork and reclaim some or all of the sum that was withheld.

7.3.4 Beneficiary

Complications can arise when the entity receiving the overseas income is not the true beneficiary of the investment. In this case, if there are reliefs to be obtained, any DTA should provide that the recipient has a mechanism for reporting to the overseas tax authority on the identity and status of the true beneficiary, and of the relationship between the recipient and the beneficiary, so that an appropriate reclaim/relief at source can be obtained. This could arise where, for example, a financial institution holds shares in overseas companies – registered in its client account name – for its customers' benefit. It could also arise where a trustee holds investments for beneficiaries.

7.3.5 European Savings Directive

An attraction of offshore banking could be the opportunity to receive gross interest, which may be tax-efficient, depending upon the tax rules in the country where the investor is resident.

However, if they live in an EU member state they are likely to be affected by the European Union Savings Directive (EUSD) which came into effect on 1 July 2005. The EUSD was introduced primarily to facilitate the exchange of tax information between member states. However, for a transitional period Austria, Belgium and Luxembourg will withhold tax from savings instead of exchanging information. Some other participating countries and territories may also decide to withhold tax initially rather than exchange information.

The tax withheld under this system will be in addition to any tax withheld under the territory's domestic legislation. Alternatively, they may continue to receive gross interest, but the bank will have to report details about them and the interest they have received to the tax authority in the EU member state where they are resident. It is important to note that the EUSD should only affect the investor if they are resident in an EU member state.

7.3.6 Qualified Intermediaries Regime

The US Qualified Intermediaries (QI) Regime is a regime whereby non-US financial intermediaries (including US branches of non-US entities) who generally hold US assets on behalf of investors are required to obtain documentation from the beneficial owners in order to apply the correct level of withholding tax on income (and in certain circumstances capital gains) generated by the assets.

At the end of the US tax year (1 January to 31 December), all income received by the beneficial owners must be reported to the Internal Revenue Service (IRS).

If the financial intermediary chooses to enter into a QI agreement with the IRS and become a QI, these reporting obligations become less onerous: only US persons are reported separately to the IRS (detailing each person's name, taxpayer identification number and income); non-US persons are collectively reported, meaning that person's individual details are not sent to the IRS. Non-US persons for these purposes include overseas corporations that are owned by US persons, and this has been identified as a potential limitation on the effectiveness of the QI regime.

The QI regime started in 2002 when about $2 billion of tax was withheld on US-sourced income moving offshore. In 2003, this figure increased to about $5 billion.

Reportable income broadly includes both dividends and interest income (unlike, for example, the European Union Savings Directive (EUSD) which only includes interest income) and includes corporates and individuals (unlike the EUSD which excludes corporates). In summary, an offshore (to the US) QI entity whose client is a US person is required to report annually to the IRS on the amount of income and, in certain circumstances capital, that the US person received during the past tax year which therefore enables the IRS to police their tax return.

Thus, through the constant obligations of documentation, withholding and reporting, the IRS uses overseas intermediaries to identify and report US persons back to it on an ongoing basis.

7.4 RESIDENCE, DOMICILE AND INHERITANCE TAX

LEARNING OBJECTIVE

4.6.4   Know the impact of residency and domicile on the liability to IHT

HMRC refer to the concept of **deemed domicile** when assessing an individual's liability to inheritance tax following a transfer of assets. Deemed Domicile means that HMRC will treat individuals as UK domiciled if, at the date of any transfer of assets, they were:

- domiciled in the UK during the three years before making the transfer; or
- were resident in the UK for at least 17 of the 20 previous income tax years of assessment ending in the year the transfer was made.

In general, individuals who are domiciled or deemed to be domiciled in the UK will be subject to inheritance tax on their assets irrespective of where those assets are situated. Individuals who are domiciled abroad will be subject to inheritance tax on their UK assets only. HMRC may also exclude certain assets which they refer to as 'excluded property' from their assessment.

An individual's 'residence' during the tax year has a bearing on their liability to UK income and capital gains taxes, whereas IHT is mostly concerned with the individual's domicile or the country they consider to be their permanent home.

8.   STAMP DUTY

8.1   STAMP DUTY AND STAMP DUTY RESERVE TAX ON SECURITIES

LEARNING OBJECTIVE

4.7.1   Understand the application of Stamp Duty and Stamp Duty Reserve Tax to the purchase of securities, including: company shares; share options; unit trusts and open-ended investment companies (OEICs); government bonds; corporate bonds; Exchange traded Funds (ETFs)

Stamp Duty and Stamp Duty Reserve Tax (SDRT) are taxes paid on the purchase of certain securities, issued by UK-incorporated companies (or by foreign companies which maintain a share register in the UK).

- Stamp duty is the tax payable when there is some paper-based transfer (eg, a stock transfer form).
- SDRT is payable when the transfer is effected electronically (eg, on CREST).

Note: Euroclear UK & Ireland is the central securities depository for the UK markets and Irish stocks. More specifically, Euroclear UK & Ireland operates an electronic settlement system, CREST, which was established in 1996 and is used to settle a vast number of international securities. The company can also physically hold stock certificates on the behalf of customers. By holding securities as well as maintaining an electronic clearing system, CREST can provide for same-day clearing of securities transactions if needed. Its overall ability to provide a fast transfer of title for the securities it handles is its most important advantage to investors.

8.1.1   Company Shares

Stamp duty is levied on purchases of shares where a stock transfer form is used. It is levied at 0.5% of the value of the trade (whether in cash or in the form of some other consideration), rounded up or down to the nearest £5.

Thus, someone buying shares for any amount up to £1,000 will pay stamp duty of £5. If the consideration is £1,050, the stamp duty will be £10, etc. Someone given shares for free will pay no stamp duty.

SDRT is payable on paperless purchases of UK shares (ie, no stock transfer form is used – for example, if the deal settles through CREST). It is levied at a flat rate of 0.5%, rounded up or down to the nearest penny and is based on what the buyer pays for the shares (not, for example, on what their true market value might be).

Thus, an individual buying shares for £1,000 in a paperless transaction will pay tax of £5 SDRT on the purchase, whatever the true value of the shares themselves. Someone acquiring the shares for a non-cash consideration will pay SDRT based on the value of the asset being given as consideration. Someone being given them for free will pay no SDRT.

8.1.2   Share Options

Stamp duty is also payable on share options in UK companies, and overseas issuers with a UK register.

8.1.3   Units in Unit Trusts

No stamp duty or SDRT is visibly charged to the buyer of units in a unit trust or shares in an OEIC. However the unit trust or OEIC pays SDRT on the underlying shares in which it invests, and takes this into account when setting the price at which units are sold (eg, with a dual-priced fund, this is allowed for in the spread).

8.1.4   Government Bonds

There is no stamp duty or SDRT on government bonds (gilts).

8.1.5   Corporate Bonds

Generally speaking, there is no stamp duty or SDRT on corporate bonds. However, there is stamp duty or SDRT (as applicable) on convertible loan stocks (that is, corporate bonds that can be converted into shares – whether that conversion right can be exercised either at the time of the purchase, or at a later date).

8.1.6   Exchange-Traded Funds (ETFs)

Stamp duty is not payable on the purchase of exchange-traded funds.

8.1.7   Property

There is no stamp duty or SDRT on the purchase of property (though there is, for example, on the purchase of shares in a property company). The tax due on purchase of a direct holding property is, instead, stamp duty land tax (SDLT).

8.2   STAMP DUTY LAND TAX ON PROPERTY

LEARNING OBJECTIVE

4.7.2   Understand the application of Stamp Duty Land Tax (SDLT), including the main reliefs and exemptions, to the purchase of property

Stamp Duty Land Tax (SDLT) is payable by the purchaser on purchases of land and property in the UK. For most residential property, it is calculated as follows:

Purchase Price, Lease Premium or Transfer Value	SDLT Rate	SDLT Rate for First-Time Buyers
Up to £125,000	0%	0%
£125,001 to £250,000	1%	0%
£250,001 to £500,000	3%	3%
£500,001 to £1,000,000	4%	4%
£1,000,000 and above	5%	5%

There are special rates for commercial property, and for properties in disadvantaged areas. If the property is in an area designated by the government as 'disadvantaged', a higher 0% threshold of £150,000 applies.

9. VALUE ADDED TAX

LEARNING OBJECTIVE

4.8.1   Understand how liability to Value Added Tax (VAT) arises and is charged

Value added tax (VAT) is a tax that is charged on most goods and services that VAT-registered businesses provide in the UK. It's also charged on goods and some services that are imported from countries outside the European Union (EU), and brought into the UK from other EU countries.

VAT is charged when a VAT-registered business sells to either another business or to a non-business customer. When a VAT-registered business buys goods or services, they can generally reclaim the VAT they have paid.

There are three rates of VAT, depending on the goods or services the business provides. The current rates are:

- standard – 20%;
- reduced – 5%;
- zero – 0%.

There are also some goods and services that are:

- exempt from VAT;
- outside the UK VAT system altogether.

9.1   WHAT IS VAT?

VAT is a tax that is charged on most business transactions in the UK. Businesses add VAT to the price they charge when they provide goods and services to:

- **business customers** – for example a clothing manufacturer adds VAT to the prices they charge a clothes shop;
- **non-business customers** – members of the public or consumers – for example a hairdressing salon includes VAT in the prices they charge members of the public.

If you are a VAT-registered business, in most cases you:

- charge VAT on the goods and services you provide;
- reclaim the VAT you pay when you buy goods and services for your business.

If you are not a VAT-registered business or organisation then you can't reclaim the VAT you pay when you purchase goods and services.

VAT-registered businesses add VAT to the sale price of most goods and services they provide.

9.2   REGISTERING FOR VAT

If you are a business and the goods or services you provide count as what is known as 'taxable supplies', you will have to register for VAT if either:

- your turnover for the previous 12 months has exceeded a specific limit – called the 'VAT threshold' (currently £73,000);
- you think your turnover will soon exceed this limit.

You can choose to register for VAT if you want, even if you don't have to.

9.3   EXEMPT ITEMS

Some items are exempt from VAT by law. Items that are exempt include the following:

- insurance;
- providing credit;
- education and training, if certain conditions are met;
- fundraising events by charities, if certain conditions are met;
- membership subscriptions, if certain conditions are met;
- most services provided by doctors and dentists.

Selling, leasing and letting commercial land and buildings are also exempt from VAT.

9.4   OUTSIDE THE SCOPE OF VAT

There are some things that are not in the UK VAT system at all – they are outside the scope of VAT. They are not taxable supplies and no VAT is charged on them.

Items that are outside the scope of VAT include:

- **non-business activities** like a hobby – for example, you might sell some stamps from your collection;

- fees that are fixed by law – known as '**statutory fees**' – for example the congestion charge and vehicle MOT tests.

9.5   THE DIFFERENCE BETWEEN EXEMPT AND ZERO-RATED

If you sell zero-rated goods or services they count as taxable supplies, but you do not add any VAT to your selling price because the VAT rate is 0%.

If you sell goods or services that are exempt, you don't charge any VAT and they're not taxable supplies. This means that you won't normally be able to reclaim any of the VAT on your expenses.

Generally you cannot register for VAT or reclaim the VAT on your purchases if you sell only exempt goods or services. If you sell some exempt goods or services you may not be able to reclaim the VAT on all of your purchases.

If you buy and sell only – or mainly – zero-rated goods or services, you can apply to HMRC to be exempt from registering for VAT. This could make sense if you pay little or no VAT on your purchases.

10. CORPORATION TAX

LEARNING OBJECTIVE

4.9.1   Understand how liability to Corporation Tax (CT) arises and is charged: companies and organisations: trading, non-trading; Taxable profits and accounting periods; Rates, allowances and reliefs; taxation of franked income

4.10.1   Understand how tax is accounted for and an adviser's duties regarding tax compliance, avoidance and evasion

10.1   HOW CORPORATION TAX IS CHARGED

Corporation tax is paid by limited companies, based on their profits. It is not paid by individuals in business as sole traders (the 'self-employed'), who are taxed on their earnings as income. HMRC lays down rules as to how profits must be calculated for this purpose.

10.2   DIFFERENT RATES OF CORPORATION TAX

There are two rates of corporation tax, the small profits rate and the standard or main rate. For financial years commencing on 1 April, the rates are as follows:

	2008	**2009**	**2010**	**2011**
Small Profits Rate	21%	21%	21%	20%
Small Profits Rate can be claimed by qualifying companies with profits at a rate not exceeding	£300,000	£300,000	£300,000	£300,000
Marginal Relief Lower Limit	£300,000	£300,000	£300,000	£300,000
Marginal Relief Upper Limit	£1,500,000	£1,500,000	£1,500,000	£1,500,000
Standard Fraction	7/400	7/400	7/400	3/200
Main Rate of Corporation Tax	28%	28%	28%	26%
Special rate for unit trusts and open ended investment companies	20%	20%	20%	20%

Marginal Relief Changes from 1 April 2010

From 1 April 2010 onwards, the terminology used to describe some corporation tax rates and reliefs changed. The table reflects the new terminology but for ease the changes are shown below:

- Small profits rate – previously small companies' rate.
- Marginal relief – previously marginal small companies' relief.
- Standard fraction – previously marginal small companies' relief fraction.
- Ring fence fraction – previously marginal small companies' relief fraction (ring fence profits) .

The main rate of corporation tax applies when profits (including ring fence profits) are at a rate exceeding £1,500,000, or where there is no claim to another rate, or where another rate does not apply.

Ring Fence Companies

For companies with ring fence profits (income and gains from oil extraction activities or oil rights in the UK and UK Continental Shelf), these rates differ. The small profits rate of tax on those profits is 19% and the ring fence fraction is 11/400 for financial years starting 1 April 2008, 2009 and 2010. The main rate is 30% for financial years starting on 1 April 2009, 2010 and 2011.

10.3 CAPITAL ALLOWANCES

Companies may be given capital allowances – a form of tax allowance on certain purchases or expenses. These enable the company to set such items off, up to a set percentage, against profits before calculating its tax liability – thus reducing the amount of tax it may have to pay. They may be available on such things as plant and machinery, buildings, and research and development. The rate permitted depends on what the item is.

10.4 THE TAXATION OF FRANKED INCOME

It is common for one company to hold shares in another, and therefore to receive dividends from that investee company.

Where this happens, tax will (in effect) already have been paid out on that dividend (because the investee company has paid it out of its post-tax profits).

For this reason, the dividend will be paid up to the investor company with a tax credit attached, reflecting the fact that the company which has paid the dividend has done so out of post-tax profits. This is called **franked income**. Franked income is free of further tax to the receiving company.

10.5 THE LEGAL REQUIREMENTS RELATING TO CONFIDENTIALITY AND DISCLOSURE

Financial advisers have a general professional duty to maintain the **confidentiality** of their clients' affairs, including in relation to tax matters; in addition, the **Data Protection Act** imposes obligations on advisers with regard to – among other things – the safekeeping of data on individuals and their affairs. Advisers may thus hold a good deal of sensitive information relating to clients' finances, which should not be disclosed to third parties without proper authority.

In spite of the professional reasons for maintaining confidentiality, there are circumstances in which **disclosure** of information of clients' affairs is required. The requirement concerns situations in which a financial adviser becomes aware that information held on a client indicates possible breaches of the law. The financial adviser could have disclosure obligations under various pieces of legislation, including the **Proceeds of Crime Act 2002 (POCA)**.

It is a criminal offence under POCA for anyone working in a regulated financial firm not to report any activity that they suspect, or ought to suspect, involves the proceeds of crime. This includes an act of tax evasion by an individual. The report should be made to the firm's **Money Laundering Reporting Officer (MLRO)**. The MLRO must report appropriate cases to the **Serious and Organised Crime Authority (SOCA)**.

11. TAX-PLANNING STRATEGIES

11.1 BASIC INVESTMENT TAX PLANNING

LEARNING OBJECTIVE

4.11.1   Apply the key principles of investment tax planning: use of personal allowances; spouses' personal allowances; children's tax position; pension contributions; use of tax wrappers; use of capital gains tax exemptions; tax deferral; use of life assurance bonds

Tax planning refers to the process of organising one's affairs so as to take best advantage of tax rules.

The practice of organising one's affairs so as to minimise tax liabilities, within the constraints of the law, is sometimes called '**tax avoidance**' or **tax mitigation**, and it is perfectly legal. To make changes to one's affairs in order to avoid tax that one might otherwise have to pay is a permissible activity, providing that no tax rule is being breached. However, caution is necessary with some of the more complex ways of taking advantage of tax rules; the HMRC may raise objections to schemes whose main objective is tax avoidance.

Tax evasion, on the other hand, is illegal. Tax evasion means failing to disclose one's affairs fully to the tax authorities, or breaching tax rules in other ways so as to evade the payment of tax. Penalties can be severe, and conviction for tax crimes could carry a prison sentence.

11.1.1 Use of Personal Allowance

The personal allowance enables individuals to earn a certain amount of income each year without it falling within the income tax net. If an individual does not use up his personal allowance in earned income, then unearned (eg, investment income) may fall within this band.

11.1.2 Spouse or Partner's Personal Allowance

A **husband and wife**, and those in same-sex **civil partnerships,** are taxed as separate people. Where spouses or civil partners jointly own income-generating property, it is assumed that they are entitled to equal shares of the income.

If, in fact, the couple are not entitled to equal shares in the income-generating property (other than shares in close companies) they may make a joint declaration to HMRC, specifying the proportion to which each is entitled. These proportions are used to tax each of them separately, in respect of income arising on or after the date of the declaration.

If one's spouse's or civil partner's **marginal rate of tax** (the rate on the highest part of their income) is higher than the other's marginal rate, they can choose to transfer income-yielding assets to the individual with the lower rate. If that spouse earns no other income, then the income from the transferred asset may thus be free (to the extent of the allowance) of tax altogether.

11.1.3 Children's Tax Position

The law prevents the parent of a minor child from transferring income to that child in order to make use of the child's personal allowance, and the child's starting and basic rate tax bands. Income which is directly transferred by the parent, or is derived from capital so transferred, remains income of the parent for tax purposes.

This applies only to parents, however, and tax savings are therefore possible through gifts from other relatives.

Even where a parent is involved, the child's income is not treated as the parent's if it does not exceed £100 a year.

This legislation is concerned with **gifts from a parent to a child**. It is possible to use the child's personal allowance and starting and basic rate bands if the child is employed in the parent's trade (but you should remember that there are rules on the hours which children are allowed to work).

11.1.4 Pension Contributions

Since **pensions simplification** (also known as 'A-Day', which took place on 6 April 2006), investors can now save up to certain limits into a pension scheme. The rules for claiming tax relief on their pension contributions are more flexible, though tax charges will apply if the investor contributes amounts in excess of certain **allowances**.

The investor will receive income tax relief on his pension contributions up to an equivalent of 100% of his earnings (salary and other earned income) each year, subject to an **annual allowance** above which tax will be charged at 40%, whether made by him and/or his employer. The annual allowance for the tax year 2011/12 is £50,000. Where an investor exceeds his annual allowance, he will need to declare the extra pension savings and pay an annual allowance charge through his income tax self-assessment.

There is also a **lifetime allowance**, above which a tax charge will apply. The value of any pensions savings above the lifetime allowance will be subject to a lifetime allowance charge; this will apply in addition to the usual income tax due on pension payments. The lifetime allowance limit for 2011/12 is set at £1,800,000 and will reduce to £1,500,000 from April 2012.

These limits notwithstanding, contributions to a pension fund can be tax-effective, particularly for the higher-rate taxpayer; and, again, contributions to a spouse's scheme can also be helpful where an investor is close to the limits on his own contributions.

An individual with no earnings may also contribute up to £3,600 per annum.

11.1.5 Use of Tax Wrappers

The use of **Individual Savings Accounts (ISAs)** as an investment wrapper is particularly important for individuals who wish to limit their capital gains tax liability.

Higher-rate taxpayers also benefit from the fact that they have no further tax to pay on dividends earned from shareholdings within an ISA.

Other wrappers include pensions, SIPPs, investment bonds, child trust funds (CTFs), etc. The individual tax benefits will vary depending on the wrapper used.

11.1.6 Use of CGT Exemptions

Each individual has an **annual CGT exemption**. An investor with significant investments (outside the tax-free wrapper of ISAs) may choose to plan disposals of investments that are subject to CGT so as to make use of the annual exemption, using the rules set out earlier in this chapter.

11.1.7 Tax Deferral

Various types of tax planning can be aimed at deferring tax, rather than avoiding it altogether. The benefits of a deferral strategy can be:

- cash flow – the money that would have been paid to HMRC stays with the investor for longer; and
- an eventual possibility of legitimate tax avoidance, if the tax becomes payable when the investor has moved to a lower income tax bracket (perhaps because he is no longer earning).

For example, if an investor invests through a collective investment scheme, then the gains made on underlying assets are sheltered within the fund at the point they are realised. The investor is only taxed on the aggregate gains made on the fund as a whole, if and when he eventually comes to realise his holding in it.

11.1.8 Use of Life Assurance Bonds

Life assurance bonds can provide the opportunity to combine an element of insurance protection, with an investment exposure and some tax efficiency. For example, an investor may be able to take up to 5% of the value of his policy out on an annual basis, spending it as income, while it is in fact treated as a return of his original capital and therefore is not taxed as income in his hands at the time he takes it.

11.2 CRITERIA FOR SELECTING A TAX-PLANNING STRATEGY

LEARNING OBJECTIVE

4.11.2   Analyse the criteria for selecting a tax-planning strategy

Any investment strategy should recognise that:

- the after-tax returns from different investments can be affected by tax rules;
- taxation should therefore be considered when choosing investments and how they are held.

Favourable tax planning should not, however, be the first priority, over and above the choice of investments appropriate to the individual's risk profile and objectives (that is, possible tax savings should not be used as a reason to choose inappropriate investments).

11.3 KEY PRINCIPLES OF IHT PLANNING

LEARNING OBJECTIVE

4.11.3   Apply the key principles of IHT planning: lifetime gifts; trusts; transferability of nil rate band

4.11.4   Apply common tax computations for: an individual's liability to income tax; age allowance; CGT liability on share disposals; IHT liability on lifetime transfers and at death

The key principles of IHT planning are as follows:

- Gifts during the client's lifetime.
- Use of trusts.
- Efficient use of the nil rate band.

11.3.1 Lifetime Gifts

It is possible to make gifts of capital during the course of a client's lifetime, which has the effect of reducing the value of the estate for inheritance tax purposes. Gifts may be made from income or capital and can include physical assets such as property. The type and circumstances of the gift will determine the tax position at the point the transfer is made, and on the subsequent death of the person making the transfer.

EXAMPLE

John is 70 years old, widowed, in good health and has two children, Mary and Paul. His estate is currently worth £600,000 and includes a property valued at £300,000. John has asked for advice on gifting assets to his family and wishes to mitigate any potential for inheritance tax on death.

The nil-rate band is currently £325,000 and means that £275,000 of John's estate could be subject to inheritance tax of 40% on his death, ie, a tax liability of 40% x £275,000 = £110,000.

As John has made no gifts previously, he is able to transfer £6,000 each to Mary and Paul in the current tax year, free of any immediate or future IHT liability. He should aim to use this allowance each year going forward. In addition, John has six grandchildren and is able to transfer £250 to each grandchild each year, thereby reducing his estate by a further £1,500 per tax year.

Taking these gifts into account, the amount of John's estate potentially subject to IHT is reduced to £96,500, ie,

2 x £3,000 gifts to Mary and Paul	£6,000
6 x £250 gifts to grandchildren	£1,500
Total	£7,500
Taxable estate before gifts	£275,000
Less total gifts	£7,500
Balance	£267,500

If John wishes, he could transfer the balance of his estate to his relatives now as a Potentially Exempt Transfer (PET). However, if he dies within seven years of making the transfer, then IHT will be levied on a sliding scale. However, in arriving at a decision over whether to make a PET and at what value, John also needs to consider his own current and future financial needs.

11.3.2 Use of Trusts

In addition to making transfers of wealth direct to relatives, John could also consider setting up a trust and transferring some or all of his wealth into the trust for future distribution to his family.

EXAMPLE

John decides to create a discretionary trust for the benefit of his family using £200,000 of his remaining capital.

The transfer of assets into a trust created during the settlor's lifetime is a 'chargeable transfer' for inheritance tax purposes. Inheritance tax is charged at a rate of 20% on the amount of the transfer that is in excess of the unused nil rate band.

As John has made no previous transfers of wealth, the full nil-rate band of £325,000 is available. As the gift of £200,000 is less than the available nil-rate band, John has no immediate charge to IHT.

11.3.3 Transferability of Nil-Rate Band

It is now possible for married couples to make use of both nil-rate bands and to transfer their allowance to one another. In effect, this means that £650,000 of joint assets may be transferred out of the estate on death without incurring a liability to inheritance tax

EXAMPLE

John is 65 and married to Mary who is 63. Their estate consists of a property worth £300,000 and additional assets in savings and investments worth a further £300,000.

Both John and Mary have the use of their own nil rate band of £325,000 and on this basis do not expect to suffer any charge to inheritance tax on death.

Value of estate on death	£600,000
Total nil rate bands	£650,000
Excess nil rate band available	£50,000

11.4   TAX PLANNING OF INVESTMENTS AND PENSIONS

LEARNING OBJECTIVE

4.11.5   Apply the above principles to basic recommendations relating to the taxation of investments and pensions

The following example highlights some of the issues typically encountered when discussing tax planning on investments.

EXAMPLE

Scenario

Michael is married to Sarah, and they have two children, James and Anne, who are aged eight and six. Michael and Sarah wish to invest a lump sum of £75,000 now in order to contribute towards the cost of their children's future university education. They do not require access to capital in the short term, and wish to invest the money in the most tax efficient way possible, as they are both 40% taxpayers. Michael and Sarah agree that they want to retain control over the capital.

Analysis

As Michael and Sarah wish to retain control, the investments should be made in their own names, either individually or jointly. As their objective is to provide a capital sum in the future, the investment strategy should focus on growth rather than income. As such, any tax liabilities arising from investment returns should be subject to capital gains rather than income tax. The benefit from this approach is that they will be subject to capital gains at the 28% rate rather than income tax at the 40% rate. Also, they will both have use of their annual CGT allowances of £10,600 (2011/12) to offset against the gains, whereas their personal allowances are already fully used.

Recommendation

Michael and Sarah should both invest their **ISA** allowances in the current tax year. The balance of the capital should be invested in a range of suitable collectives in joint names. At the start of each subsequent tax year, sufficient holdings should then be sold within the collective portfolio in order to fund future **ISA** allowances, whilst also using some or all of that year's **CGT** allowances.

Outcome

In this way, the entire capital amount will move to a tax efficient environment over time, whilst making effective use of both **ISA** and **CGT** allowances. The capital remains accessible within the **ISA** and collective wrappers, and can be used to fund the education costs in the future.

The following example highlights some of the issues typically encountered when discussing tax planning using pensions.

EXAMPLE

Scenario

Peter is 42 years old and self employed. Following successful completion of a recent contract, he received a payment of £150,000, and would like advice on the most tax efficient method of investing this for the future. He has an existing portfolio of ISAs and a **SIPP**, which was used to consolidate various pension arrangements in 2007. He tells you that he has no requirement for access to this capital before retirement, and has made no pension contributions since 2007/08.

Analysis

As Peter is self employed, he will be required to declare this payment on his next tax return, and should make provision now for the tax liability. However, if he invests this amount in his **SIPP** instead, then no tax will be payable as he will be entitled to tax relief on the whole amount. The maximum contribution that Peter can make to pension arrangements during 2011/12 is £50,000 gross. However, new rules introduced in 2011 enable him to carry forward his unused allowances for the previous three tax years (2008/09, 2009/10 and 2010/11).

Recommendation

You therefore recommend that Peter make a gross contribution to his **SIPP** in the current tax year using the entire £150,000 and continue to fund ISAs going forward wherever possible.

Outcome

This approach benefits Peter as he recovers unused pension contribution allowances from previous years, and avoids paying income tax on the £150,000. As he has no immediate need for the money, it is now invested in his **SIPP** and will grow free of tax until he retires. In retirement, Peter may be able to supplement the income he receives from his **SIPP** using capital withdrawals from his **ISA** portfolio, and position himself so that his taxable income each year is kept as low as possible.

KEY CHAPTER POINTS

- Employed and self-employed individuals are liable to pay income tax. Some income is received in full with no tax deducted, while some income has tax deducted at source.
- Various sources of income are aggregated in a personal tax computation. Some income is exempt from income tax and not included in the personal tax computation.
- An individual pays CGT on his net taxable gains in a tax year. There is an annual exemption for each tax year.
- There need to be three things for a capital gain to arise: chargeable person, chargeable disposal, chargeable asset. Disposals between spouses or civil partners are on a no gain/no loss basis.
- Capital losses are deducted against gains in the same tax year. Excess losses are carried forward. Brought-forward losses cannot reduce taxable gains below the annual exempt amount.
- Gilts and qualifying corporate bonds held by individuals are exempt from CGT.
- Inheritance tax (IHT) is a tax on gifts or 'transfers of value'.
- IHT is charged on the decrease in a donor's wealth.
- There are rules to prevent someone making a gift 'with reservation' to avoid IHT.
- Stamp duty or SDRT are payable at 0.5% on the purchase of UK shares.
- A range of planning vehicles allow for legitimate tax avoidance or deferral.
- There are various tax planning opportunities when an individual's investment strategy is being planned, but the tax tail should not wag the investment dog. In other words, tax considerations should not outweigh proper investment planning.

CHAPTER FIVE

INVESTMENT PRODUCTS

This syllabus area will provide approximately 17 of the 80 examination questions

1. TYPES AND PURPOSES OF COLLECTIVE INVESTMENT

LEARNING OBJECTIVE

5.1.1   Understand the main types, purposes, common investment
characteristics and behaviours of funds, collectives and other products

1.1   OPEN-ENDED AND CLOSED-ENDED FUNDS

Mutual funds are financial intermediaries that combine and pool more efficiently the financial resources of individuals and companies to create a larger diversified portfolio of assets. In addition to the benefits of pooling enjoyed by a large fund, there are economies of scale such as lower transaction costs and commissions. Inexperienced investors or busy professionals gain from the professional delivery of services in a managed fund by individuals who have expertise in money management to deliver the superior skills sought by investors.

Nowadays, a majority of mutual funds are **open-ended funds**. The investment company that creates and manages the fund issues shares created out of the large fund. The open-ended fund shares are sold to investors at the **net asset value (NAV) per share**. The total size of fund managed by the fund manager will vary depending on:

- the amount of money invested by all investors at the inception of the fund;
- any further investments or net redemptions of shares made by investors whilst the fund is operational.

The other type of mutual fund is a closed-end fund, which is so-called because it does not accept any new money or redemptions whilst the fund is being managed.

The growth in the mutual fund industry has been partly explained by the distinct advantages provided by open-ended funds. There are at least five benefits identified for investment made in an open-ended fund:

1. Liquidity – there are no penalties for early redemptions. Investors can convert their funds into cash quickly because open-ended funds can be sold at any time and in any amount.
2. Access to large denomination securities – small investors gain access to large securities with a small amount of money. For example, if an investor wanted to buy a money market security in the US, the denominations of such instruments are in $100,000. The small investor can easily invest in this type of security and many others because their funds have been pooled with other investors who have invested in the fund.
3. Diversification benefits – risk is lowered depending on how diversified a portfolio of securities is invested.
4. Cost benefits – since the fund will buy large blocks of stock, lower transaction costs will reduce the overall cost.

5. Managerial expertise – professional money managers have access to a wealth of information and research that ordinary investors do not have. The scope and breadth of the investment company's operations on an international scale offers significant advantages in terms of local knowledge about markets and the selection of international securities. The investor is delegating the portfolio revision responsibility to an expert who is monitoring the fund round the clock.

The money management industry has two sectors: short-term funds and long-term funds. Short-term funds invest in money market instruments and construct a portfolio that delivers pre-determined objectives of the fund. Long-term funds are made up of equity funds, bond funds or hybrid funds with a balance of bond and equity securities. A number of index funds have also been introduced in recent years. The fund may be designed to deliver income, capital appreciation or a balance of income and growth.

The value of each managed fund will depend on the performance of the underlying securities in the fund. As a result, each investor has a direct investment in the fund; however, the investor is not a direct holder of the underlying securities in the fund.

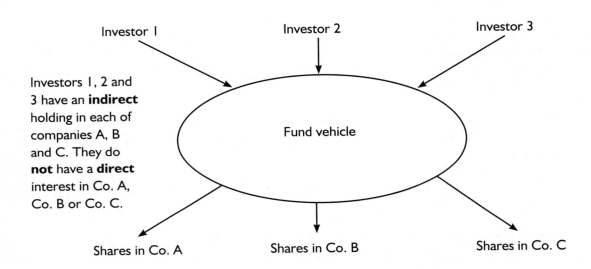

The nature of an open-ended fund allows new investors to buy into the underlying investment scheme without the need to find a matching seller.

As the fund grows, new shares are issued by the manager. The definition of 'net asset value (NAV) per share' is:

> **Net asset value** – the total value of a fund's assets, less liabilities.
>
> **Net asset value per share/unit** – the total NAV of the fund, divided by the number of shares in issue.

Now, we are in a position to consider whether new investments into open-ended funds affect existing investors to any significant degree.

EXAMPLE

Fund ABC has a portfolio valued at £1 million.

It is made up of 1,000,000 shares.

Therefore, the net asset value per share is:

£ 1,000,000/1,000,000 = £1 per share.

New investor Stephen Turner has £100,000 to invest.

How many shares will this buy him?

Shares are priced at £1 each so it will buy him 100,000 shares.

Two things happen to the fund:

- **It gains £100,000 in assets.**

- **100,000 more shares are created to give Stephen his holding.**

The number of shares in the fund is therefore:

- **The original 1,000,000 plus 100,000 new shares issued = 1,100,000.**

The assets of the fund are:

> **£1,000,000 (the original portfolio)**

> **£100,000 (new cash paid by Stephen for his shares)**

= £1,100,000

The NAV per share is therefore £1,100,000/1,100,000 = £1 per share – ie, unchanged by the introduction of a new investor.

There are different names given to open-ended funds – unit trusts, open-ended investment companies (OEICs) and mutual funds. In some countries, open-ended funds can also be set up as partnerships, or as purely contractual arrangements. In this chapter we will be focusing on unit trusts and OEICs.

Also we will contrast the features of **open-ended fund vehicles** with **closed-ended funds**. Closed-ended vehicles are limited companies often known as investment trusts. Closed-ended funds have fixed capital and are bought and sold on the stock market just like a stock such as Tesco. Like other shares, the price will move in response to supply and demand.

In summary, candidates need to be aware of the following capital structures:

- open-ended funds, unit trusts and OEICs; and
- closed-ended vehicles such as investment trusts.

1.2   MULTI-MANAGER AND MULTI-ASSET FUNDS

LEARNING OBJECTIVE

5.1.2   Understand the structure of multi-manager and multi-asset funds

The idea behind **multi-manager funds** is the recognition that no one fund manager or investment house has expertise in all asset classes, geographic regions and investment styles. Hence by selecting multiple managers a degree of diversification is obtained and the best managers are selected. They are currently the fastest-growing investment product in the UK. However, the fees associated with these products tend to be higher due to the additional layer of management.

The main types of multi-manager fund categories are: fund of funds and manager of managers.

A **fund of funds** has one overall manager. It invests in a portfolio of other existing investment funds and seeks to harness the best investment manager talent available within a diversified portfolio. Most funds of funds are managed on an **unfettered** basis, in that the component funds are run by a number of managers external to the fund management group marketing the fund of funds.

However, some are managed as a **fettered** product and are obligated to invest solely in funds run by the same management group as the fund.

By contrast a **manager of managers** fund does not invest in other investment schemes. Instead the fund arranges segregated mandates and appoints fund managers who they believe are the best in their sector to manage each pool. One disadvantage is that the initial investment required is usually substantially higher than that required for a fund of funds or other collective investment scheme.

The term **multi-asset funds** refers to funds which invest in several asset classes. This includes anything from traditional managed funds which may invest in equities (shares), bonds, property and cash, to the new breed of managed funds which invest in a greater variety of assets such as commodities.

Multi-asset funds invest in assets which tend to have different performance characteristics. This increases the diversification of the fund, reducing exposure to the market gains and losses of just one asset class. Multi-asset managers are creating the potential for capital growth and the conditions in which the better performers may offset the poorer performers.

2.   OPEN-ENDED FUNDS

LEARNING OBJECTIVE

5.1.1   Understand the main types, purposes, common investment
         characteristics and behaviours of funds, collectives and other products

2.1   UNIT TRUSTS

Unit trusts are, as the name suggests, constituted as **trusts**: that is, they have a **trust deed** and the fund's assets are held by a **trustee** on behalf of the **beneficiaries** (investors). Each unit trust will have a **manager** who makes the investment decisions. The way in which the fund operates is set out in a **trust deed**.

Unit trusts that are **authorised** by the FSA, can be marketed direct to the public in the UK; to obtain authorisation, they have to meet certain criteria, both in their set-up and day-to-day management.

These rules include:

- how the unit trust is set up and the contents of its **constitutional documents** (in this case, the trust deed);
- the types of investment a unit trust can hold;
- the fact that these investments must meet certain rules in terms of their liquidity and ease of valuation/trading (eg, the types of markets on which they must be listed and the maximum that may be invested in unlisted investments);
- the maximum amount that can be held in the securities issued by any one issuer (thus ensuring that the fund limits its exposure to a single issuer).

The rules are intended to protect investors in unit trusts to improve their safety relative to less diversified and liquid investments.

UK unit trusts are subject to proper regulation and are often regarded as a comparatively safe investment from the point of view of governance and investor protection.

Some points to remember are:

- Unit trusts are a common form of collective investment scheme, both in the UK and in many offshore centres.
- Like other types of fund, individual investors' assets are pooled together in a centrally managed fund which is then invested on a collective basis.
- The assets are valued on a NAV basis, and investors buy and sell units at a price determined by the NAV per unit.
- Each unit is equal, representing a fraction of a large portfolio.
- Unit trusts pay distributions periodically – equivalent to paying a dividend to shareholders in a company.
- Because unit trusts have an **open-ended** capital structure, new units can be created when new investments are made and redeemend when investors dispose of their holdings.

- Unit trusts have a manager, who is responsible for the management of the fund itself, and a trustee, who holds and is responsible for the oversight of the fund.

2.2 OPEN-ENDED INVESTMENT COMPANIES (OEICs)

OEICs are also described as Investment Companies with Variable Capital (ICVCs).

In the UK until 1997, only open-ended collective investment schemes structured as unit trusts were **authorised** by the regulator to be offered for sale to the general public. There were no alternative open-ended collective investment schemes which could be authorised. However, since the introduction of new laws permitting companies set up as regulated collective investment schemes to also have open-ended structures, OEICs have been competing with UTs for popularity as an investment vehicle. Legislation permitting funds with OEIC structures to be authorised in the UK was only introduced in January 1997 by introduction of the Open-Ended Investment Companies (Investment Companies with Variable Capital) Regulations 1996 (**the ECA Regulations**).

An OEIC has many features in common with a unit trust. However, the legal structure is that of a **company**, not a trust. The OEIC is constituted by an **instrument of incorporation** (instead of a trust deed), and the OEIC has shareholders and a board of directors.

For UK-authorised OEICs, the management of the fund is carried out by the **Authorised Corporate Director (ACD)** instead of a manager (in most offshore jurisdictions, however, this function is still carried out by a manager). In addition, the role of the trustee is replaced by a **custodian** – but the custodian carries out much the same activities, holding and safeguarding the assets and checking that the fund is being run in accordance with the rules.

Again, the assets of the OEIC are managed with the aim of maximising investment returns. Some points to remember are:

- As with a unit trust, individual investors' assets are pooled together in a centrally managed fund, which is then invested on a collective basis. The assets are valued on a NAV basis and the price of the shares will be related to that NAV.
- Similar investor protection rules apply in terms of the types of assets that the OEIC can hold, to those applicable to authorised unit trusts (AUTs).
- The investors' interests are represented by shares in the fund company, instead of – but operating in quite a similar way to – units in a unit trust.
- OEICs pay **dividends** (not distributions), because they are established as companies, not trusts.
- The capital of the company is open-ended, so, as with a unit trust, net sales and repurchases by investors are met by corresponding increases and decreases in the company's share capital and assets. Shares are created and redeemed to meet demand.
- Shares in an OEIC are bought and sold (and created and redeemed) by the ACD.
- OEICs are common in many offshore jurisdictions; Jersey, Guernsey and the Isle of Man have had OEICs for many years, although they differ in some ways from the OEICs regime in the UK.

2.3   UCITS FUNDS, INCLUDING UCITS III

'UCITS' stands for Undertakings in Collective Investments in Transferable Securities. The name refers to an EU directive which lays down common rules applied in EU states to retail schemes, with the aim of enabling them to be sold across EU borders. The idea is that the standards applied in (say) France should be so similar to those in (say) the UK, that an investor will be equally well protected, whether he buys a fund in one country or the other. Eventually this should improve cross-border competition and give consumers greater investment choice.

There have been three UCITS directives, progressively building a framework for retail funds within the EU. The UCITS I directive introduced a so-called European passport for UCITs which met various criteria, including that investments were made only in **transferable securities**.

This allowed a collective investment scheme established in one EU state, and meeting all the requirements in terms of permitted investments, to be registered for sale in other EU member states after a simple notification process.

Two new directives have since been introduced modifying UCITS I; collectively, they are known as UCITS III. They are also known separately as the Management Directive and the Products Directive.

Under UCITS III the concept of the European passport is maintained, but the range of investments in which a fund may invest, while qualifying as a UCITS, is extended. Under UCITS I, funds were restricted to investing primarily in listed securities (ie, mostly listed shares and bonds); the Products Directive extends this to include:

* liquid transferable securities;
* cash;
* money market instruments;
* their funds (both UCITS and non-UCITS);
* derivatives.

It also allows for **tracker** or **index** funds to qualify as UCITS funds.

As well as expanding the range of assets in which UCITS can invest, the Products Directive also extends the restrictions on concentration of investment applied to transferable securities to money market instruments as well. It introduces an **issuer restriction** so that a UCITS can now invest up to a maximum of 10% of its NAV in the securities of any one issuer, which now includes investment trust companies (with some exceptions).

It also introduces the concept of the **group**. The impact of this is that a UCITS must not only comply with the various restrictions set out; it must also ensure that the aggregate of its exposures to transferable securities, deposits and money market instruments issued by members of any one corporate grouping, and of OTC derivatives where a member of that corporate grouping is a counterparty, does not exceed 20% of the fund's NAV.

Some other notable amendments relating to specific types of fund are:

- **UCITS Funds-of-Funds** – under UCITS I, only 5% of a UCITS could be invested in other funds; under UCITS III this limit has been lifted completely, enabling funds-of-funds to be established. However, the funds must themselves be UCITS, or subject to similar regulation.
- **UCITS Tracker Funds** – the Products Directive makes tracker funds more possible than they were under UCITS I. Under UCITS I, there were difficulties where one of the shares which a tracker fund needed to buy accounted for a sizeable proportion of the index; the fund could only invest in the securities of any one issuer to a maximum of 10% of its net asset value, but occasions would arise when a share accounted for more than 10% of the index of which it was a constituent. Under the Products Directive, this limit has been raised to 20% of the securities of any one issuer for a tracker UCITS (and in some cases 35%).
- **UCITS investing in derivatives** – under UCITS III, funds may now have a stated investment policy on derivatives – providing that they abide by specified rules to limit the risk to investors.
- **Money Market UCITS** – UCITS funds can now invest in money market instruments (these include instruments such as certificates of deposit and Treasury bills).
- **UCITS investing in cash deposits** – under UCITS III a fund may now invest directly in cash deposits. Prior to UCITS III, cash could only be held for **ancillary purposes** – eg, the maintenance of 5% or so of the fund's NAV to meet investor redemptions. The UCITS fund may invest no more than 20% of its assets in the deposits of any one institution, or with institutions which are subsidiaries of the same group.

2.4 EXCHANGE-TRADED FUNDS (ETFs)

Exchange-traded funds (ETFs) are a relatively new type of open-ended fund. They have proved popular in the US, and are increasing in popularity in the UK. Like tracker funds, they follow the performance of an index closely (though some divergence – a percentage or so – can arise).

An increasing range of ETFs is available, tracking a variety of indices – for example, general share price indices (eg, the FTSE 100 Index in the UK, or the S&P 500 Index in the US) or indices for sub-sectors of the market (eg, pharmaceuticals, or energy stocks).

The fact that ETFs have prices quoted in **real time** – ie, throughout trading hours, and not a single price based on the previous day's market performance – sets them apart from other types of index-tracking fund. In addition, they have relatively low charges and are not subject to stamp duty. Shares in ETFs can be bought and sold throughout the trading day, enabling investors to speculate on movements in the index within a given day.

2.5 SICAVs and FCPs

Société d'Investissement Capital à Variables (SICAVs) are commonly used in many European countries, such as Luxembourg and France – but UK investors may come across them as the institutions that sell them may be permitted to market them in the UK, since they can be established to comply with UCITS requirements. A SICAV is an open-ended scheme – rather like an AUT or an OEIC – and is established as a company.

Fonds Commun de Placement (FCPs) are, like SICAVs, commonly established open-ended collective investment vehicles in Europe (typically France and Luxembourg).

FCPs are established by way of contract rather than as a trust or a company. In other respects, they are very similar to the UK's unit trust or open-ended investment company vehicles.

3. CLOSED-ENDED FUNDS

LEARNING OBJECTIVE

5.1.1 Understand the main types, purposes, common investment characteristics and behaviours of funds, collectives and other products

5.3.1 Understand the main types, purposes, common investment characteristics and behaviours of: onshore closed-ended funds and investment companies; offshore closed-ended funds and investment companies

5.3.2 Analyse the relative merits and limitations of investing in closed-ended funds and investment companies compared with other forms of direct and indirect investment, in terms of: risk; return; tax treatment; turnover, liquidity and access; expenses – transaction and administration; management and administration

3.1 INVESTMENT TRUSTS

Investment trusts are amongst the oldest form of collective investment; the first UK-based trust was created in the 1860s. The name is misleading as it is a public **company** not a trust, and is listed on the London Stock Exchange (though many offshore investment trusts are listed on other exchanges, such as the Channel Islands Stock Exchange or in Dublin). Some points to remember are:

- An investment trust has a capital structure like a company; this means that it has a **fixed number of shares** in issue at any one time.
- Its principal activity is to **invest** the funds it controls, according to its stated investment objectives.
- Investment trusts are also subject to some rules on the type of investments they can hold, and the concentration in the securities of any one issuer – but these **rules are more relaxed** than those for open-ended schemes (unit trusts and OEICs).
- As they are traded on a stock exchange, the price of the investment trust's shares fluctuates according to **supply and demand**.
- As with unit trusts and OEICs, a **net asset value** is calculated for investment trusts – but this **is not used for the share price**.
- Shares are generally bought and sold through a **broker**, not from the fund's manager.
- Like unit trusts or OEICs, investment trusts can be a suitable investment for **small investors**.
- An investment trust is run by its **board of directors**; the directors may undertake the investment management of the investment trust themselves (in which case it is called a **self-managed** investment trust). In practice, however, the board will commonly employ a **fund manager** to manage the investments and to provide other services, such as administration, registration and accountancy.

3.1.1 Share Classes

Investment trusts offer different **classes** of shares, each offering different rights and benefits. These investment trusts are known as **split capital** investment trusts or **splits**. We will look briefly at some of the different types of share class typically issued.

Split capital investment trusts usually have a limited lifespan and their various share classes are intended to appeal to different types of investor.

- Some classes are made up of shares which provide pure capital growth, in forms that range from the safe to the very risky.
- Some classes may provide relatively high levels of income.

On an agreed date, the split investment trusts may be wound up and the assets divided according to a set formula. With some split investment trusts, there is a provision for the shareholders to vote on whether or not to wind up the investment trust. A typical example is a split investment trust set up for an initial life of ten years, but with the provision to extend it by three years at a time.

Basic structure – with an **ordinary** (non-split capital) investment trust, the ordinary shares are normally entitled to all the income and capital of the investment trust (after any borrowings have been repaid). However, a simple form of split capital investment trust, of the kind which originated in the 1960s, is made up of two classes of shares:

- **Income shares**, which pay out broadly all the income received by the investment trust. The shareholders of this class will receive the nominal capital value when the trust is wound up.
- **Capital shares**, which pay no income at all. The shareholders of this class benefit from the bulk of the assets on wind-up of the investment trust, after prior-ranking shares have been paid.

Normally, the income shares are purchased by investors who find income convenient and tax-efficient; the capital shares are bought by investors who find capital gains more tax-efficient and who do not require a regular income stream to live on.

Since their origins in the 1960s, splits have become significantly more sophisticated and offer a wide range of different types of shares. We will now take look at a few different types of share class:

- **Income shares** – there are, in fact, several different types of income shares, with significant differences in capital entitlement. It is important to distinguish between these, because certain shares can give rise to substantial capital losses at redemption – so investors considering buying them should ensure that they understand the terms of investment or take advice before investing.
  - Traditional income shares give a right to the income earned by the investment trust (paid out in the form of regular dividends). They have a fixed redemption price, subject to there being sufficient assets left in the investment trust at the date of its winding-up after repayment of any debts, and other preferred classes of shares.
  - Many of the more recent split capital issues have included income shares which are rather closer to an annuity; an annuity is a product which pays a set, or contractually agreed, regular level of income. Such shares may pay a high level of income, but only a nominal redemption amount (eg, 1p for every 100p share).
  - Some income shares issues sit halfway between the above two examples, combining an element of fixed redemption price with a certain share of any remaining capital at redemption.

- **Capital shares** – these are the counterpart of the income shares, and they act as a kind of mirror image. In most cases they pay no income whatsoever.
  - ○ Investors receive the bulk of the assets of the IT when it is finally wound up;
  - ○ these shares are highly geared and tend to be very volatile (ie, their price can go up and down dramatically).

Some less common share types which may be encountered are:

- **'A' shares** are ordinary shares, but they carry no voting rights; they will often have dividend rights over and above those of ordinary shares.
- **Zero-dividend preference shares** or **zeros** – zero dividend preference shares pay no income but offer a predetermined rate of return when the investment trust is finally wound up.
  - ○ Zero holders have first call on the investment trust's assets when it is wound up after any bank loans are repaid.
  - ○ The return on zeros is not guaranteed (there may be insufficient assets left at wind up, after all) but there is a very strong likelihood that the return will be paid because of their prior claim on the investment trust's assets. Other classes of shares receive nothing until the zeros have been paid.
  - ○ The final redemption value of the zero at the liquidation date is predetermined, subject to the investment trust actually having enough assets to cover this at that date. Zeros are, therefore, issued at a price which usually rises by a compound growth rate to the final value.
  - ○ The returns on zeros are taxed as capital growth rather than income, and they are particularly attractive to investors who are not subject to capital gains tax – or to those who are able to use their CGT exemption.
- **Stepped preference shares** – these have an income entitlement which grows at a predetermined rate; they also carry a predetermined maturity value. They are not particularly common, but can appeal to investors who need certainty of future income and capital returns.
- **Income and residual capital shares** – income and residual capital shares were formerly called **highly geared ordinary shares** and are designed to give a highly geared return in terms of both capital and income. They are more volatile because the investment trust has significant levels of borrowings, which must be serviced before these shareholders can receive their benefits. These are also sometimes known as ordinary income shares or highly geared shares.
- **Packaged units** – some of the more recent investment trust issues have bundled together **packages** of capital, income and zero preference shares to create what is almost the equivalent of an ordinary share. The aim of the units is to reduce or eliminate the discount which may apply to the ordinary share alone.

- **'C' shares** were created in the 1990s, as a way of allowing an investment trust to increase its capital base without some of the apparent drawbacks of a traditional rights issue – these drawbacks being that:
  - existing holders may not choose to take up the rights and may feel their investment is being diluted by the new inflow of money;
  - the existing shareholders have to bear the costs of the rights issue;
  - the investment trust may wish to bring in new shareholders for strategic reasons.

  C shares allow the investment trust to raise new capital in the following way. Money received from a new issue is initially allocated to a temporary class of C shares. These are then converted in due course, and at a price determined by their net asset value, into the existing class of shares, once the new capital has been invested. The two portfolios are merged, and so are the share classes. This approach avoids flooding the existing portfolio with cash, which could unfairly dilute the short-term performance of the existing shares – to the disadvantage of the existing shareholders.

- **'S' shares** – these are a means of launching a new investment trust with a strategy which is close to, but not quite the same as, that of an investment trust already in existence:
  - The shares form a distinct and different portfolio which remains separate throughout the life of the investment trust.
  - They have separate price quotes and net asset values.
  - Speed and cost are the main advantages of launching S shares over launching a new investment trust. Shares have been described as **perpetual C shares**, because they aren't eventually merged into the original share class.

- **Convertibles in investment trusts** – like other companies, investment trusts can issue **convertible loan stocks**. Some points to remember are:
  - Convertibles offer investors the right to convert their fixed interest loan stock in the investment trust into a set number of the issuing company's ordinary shares.
  - One attraction for investors is that convertibles usually offer a higher running yield than the ordinary shares of the issuing company.
  - In rising markets, convertibles tend to be valued on a basis that takes into account the value of the ordinary shares into which they can be converted. But if the stock market falls below the conversion price, the stock is still valued as a fixed-interest security on the basis of its yield and chances of redemption.
  - Investors must make sure that they convert before the final conversion date, where appropriate, since after that date the stock generally falls in value and is valued simply as a fixed-interest security.

3.2 REAL ESTATE INVESTMENT TRUSTS (REITs)

REITs are another fund innovation with their roots in the US; they were introduced in early 2007 in the UK, as a way of enabling investors to gain exposure to the property market. Investors have – for a long time – been able to do this via property unit trusts, and property investment trusts, but REITs offer a potentially more tax-efficient way to do so. Indeed, a number of property-based investment trusts have already converted to REIT status, or announced their intention to do so.

Shares in REITs are bought and sold in the same way as for any listed share (ie, the investor bears stockbroking commissions and the usual dealing costs, but not the initial fees associated with some open-ended funds).

3.3 GEARING

5.1.3   Understand when and why borrowing/gearing is used by funds, and the benefits and risks associated with it

An important distinction between open-ended and closed-ended funds (ie, investment trusts) is that the latter has the power to borrow against the fund's assets. Authorised open-ended funds can generally only borrow in certain, limited circumstances. Investment trusts (ie, closed-ended vehicles) have much wider borrowing powers.

Any restrictions on a fund's power to borrow for investment purposes is generally controlled by its internal rules and offering documents. For closed-ended funds there are rarely any regulatory limitations. This means that they have the ability to **gear** portfolios. Only certain categories of open-ended fund can gear.

The benefits and risks are as follows. A fund which borrows, say, 50% of the value of its portfolio and invests this additional borrowed capital in the market has the following possibilities:

* If it invests well and the new investments gain in value, it stands to make greater gains than a fund which did not borrow; it has **geared up** its performance. The additional gains made on the extra investment will boost performance, even after it has repaid the capital of the loan and paid the interest due on it.
* If, on the other hand, the portfolio falls in value, the fund must be able to repay the loan when it falls due – and the interest on an ongoing basis. Thus, as well as falling due to the poorly performing investments, the portfolio is suffering from outflows to service the borrowings. The fund will do worse than a similar fund without gearing.

This ability to gear means that investment trusts have both the potential for greater gains than their open-ended peers – and the potential for greater losses. For this reason, investment trusts with borrowing powers should be seen as potentially higher-risk (but also potentially higher-reward) than unit trusts and OEICs.

4. THE TAX TREATMENT OF COLLECTIVE INVESTMENTS

LEARNING OBJECTIVE

5.1.4   Understand the tax treatment within the fund and for UK investors of income arising from collective investments: open-ended investment companies (OEICs); investment companies with variable capital; unit trusts; investment trusts; exchange-traded funds; real estate investment trusts (REITs)

The tax treatment of distributions from collectives depends on the type of investments in which the scheme invests:

- Funds invested mainly in **cash deposits** and **interest-bearing securities** pay out **distributions** which are mostly made up of interest, and the distribution will be taxed at the applicable rate for savings income.
- Those investing mainly in **companies** make distributions which are mostly made up of **dividends**, and the distribution will be taxed at the rate for dividends.

UK funds pay distributions net of basic rate tax, and the investor should receive a tax voucher showing the tax credit for tax already paid. He returns this with his income tax return. Lower and basic rate taxpayers have nothing more to pay; higher rate taxpayers will have to pay an additional sum.

4.1   OEICs, UNIT TRUSTS AND ETFs

Noted below is the tax treatment of OEICs, unit trusts and ETFs. For simplicity, the text only mentions OEICs, but you should be aware that it refers to the tax treatment of each.

4.1.1   Capital Gains Tax (CGT)

- Capital gains made within an OEIC are exempt from tax.
- Capital gains made by a taxpayer on any disposal of the OEIC may trigger a CGT liability depending on whether they have exceeded their annual CGT exemption. If they make a loss, this may be offset against realised gains made elsewhere. Such losses can be carried forward indefinitely if they have no gains to offset in the year they dispose of their OEIC holding.

4.1.2   Income Tax

HMRC taxes investors in OEICs on their dividends, based on what the OEIC is mainly invested in. So dividends from OEICs investing mainly in shares are taxed as dividend income; those from OEICs invested mainly in interest-bearing securities are taxed as interest distributions. It works as follows:

OEICs Investing Predominantly in Shares

Where such an OEIC pays a dividend, this will carry a 10% tax credit. So, for every 90p of OEIC dividend paid to an investor, there is a 10% tax credit attached making a gross dividend of 100p.

- A non-taxpayer, starting rate taxpayer and basic rate taxpayer needs to take no further action. The 10% tax credit fully covers the liability. Non-taxpayers, however, cannot reclaim the tax credit from HMRC.
- A higher rate taxpayer needs to pay a further 22.5% of the gross dividend – therefore, bringing the total liability to 32.5% of the gross dividend.
- An additional rate taxpayer needs to pay a further 32.5% of the gross dividend – therefore, bringing the total liability to 42.5% of the gross dividend.

OEICs Investing Predominantly in Fixed-Interest Securities

Dividends from such funds are taxed differently to those distributing mainly equity income; they are paid net of 20% tax. For example:

Dividend paid by OEIC	£10.00
Less 20% tax	£2.00
Net interest distribution	£8.00

- Non-taxpayers can reclaim the £2.00 tax deducted.
- Taxpayers on lower incomes can reclaim half the tax (£1.00).
- Basic rate taxpayers have no further liability.
- Higher-rate taxpayers are subject to a further 20% (£2.00) tax.
- Additional rate taxpayers are subject to a further 30% (£3.00) tax.

4.1.3 Equalisation Payments

When an investor first buys units or shares in a fund, they may receive an equalisation payment as part of the next distribution that the fund pays. This equalisation payment is treated differently for tax purposes.

When an investor buys units, the price that he has paid is based on the net asset value of the fund; that is, the value of the underlying portfolio plus any income that has been received but not yet paid out. When the next distribution is made, therefore, a part of the distribution that the investor will receive includes this income that he has paid for in the purchase price. It is effectively a return of part of the amount invested and so is treated differently for tax purposes.

When the distribution is paid, the investor will receive a tax voucher that splits the payment into two parts, the normal distribution and the equalisation payment. As the equalisation payment is a return of the investor's money, it is not liable to income tax. Instead, as it is a return of the amount invested, the payment should be deducted from the cost of the holding when calculating any chargeable gain on an eventual disposal.

4.1.4 Accumulated Income

If a fund does not pay out the income it earns during the year (ie, it is a **roll-up** or **accumulation** fund), but rolls it up in the fund's unit or share price, the investor has nonetheless earned that income and should receive a tax voucher from the fund manager.

He must enter the details on his tax return, and will be assessed on it. HMRC regards this as still being a receipt of income by the investor and will assess him for income tax on the amount accumulated.

4.2   INVESTMENT TRUSTS

4.2.1   Capital Gains Tax

- Investment trusts, provided they comply with the relevant rules, do not pay CGT on internal gains.
- An investor in an investment trust may be liable to CGT on any gains he makes on disposal of it; if he makes a loss, this may be offset against gains made elsewhere or it may be carried forward to future years.

4.2.2   Income Tax

Investment trusts receiving income from the assets in which they invest pay tax as follows:

- UK dividends are received with a 10% tax credit and the investment trust has no further liability. This is **franked income** (see Chapter 4, Section 10.4).
- Overseas dividends may be received net of foreign withholding tax (see Chapter 4, Section 7.3). The investment trust is liable for corporation tax on the grossed-up income, but depending on any **double taxation agreements** (see Chapter 4, Section 7.2) some of the tax already withheld may be offsettable against this liability.
- The investment trust is liable for tax on other income at the corporation tax rate applicable.

An investor in an investment trust is taxed on dividends paid by it in the same way as he would be for any other share. That is, the dividends will be received with a tax credit of 10%.

- Non-taxpayers cannot reclaim this tax.
- Lower-rate and basic rate taxpayers have no further liability.
- Higher-rate taxpayers are liable to a further 22.5% on the grossed-up dividend.
- Additional rate taxpayers are liable to a further 32.5% on the grossed-up dividend.

4.3   REAL ESTATE INVESTMENT TRUSTS (REITs)

4.3.1   Capital Gains Tax

- UK REITs are not subject to CGT on gains made on the disposal of property, provided they distribute at least 90% of their profits each year to shareholders as dividends.
- Investors disposing of a holding in a REIT may be liable to CGT on any gains made, as for any other shareholding. Losses may be offset or carried forward.

4.3.2   Income Tax

- REITs are required to pay away at least 90% of the property rental income they receive in a year.
- These dividends are taxed as property rental income in the hands of the investor (not as ordinary dividends). This tax is deducted at source.

So the main benefit of a REIT over a traditional property investment trust or property company is that investors in the latter suffer more tax overall. That is, the traditional property company pays both corporation tax and CGT on its property-related activities; plus, the investor pays income tax on his dividends. REITs, however, do not pay corporation taxes so long as they distribute 90% of their profits. Property investment trust companies hold shares in property companies, not the direct asset itself.

The investor does, however, as we can see, pay a bit more income tax on their dividend than they would for other sorts of share – because it is classed as rental income. Where they would normally pay 10% (basic rate taxpayers) or 32.5% (higher rate taxpayers) on dividend income, they will pay 20%, 40% or 50% depending on their personal tax band.

5. COMMON INVESTMENT CHARACTERISTICS OF A FUND

LEARNING OBJECTIVE

5.1.5   Analyse the common differences, merits and limitations of direct investment in securities and assets compared with indirect investment through collectives and other products, in terms of: risk; return; tax treatment; turnover, liquidity and access; expenses – transaction and ongoing; management and administration

5.1.6   Understand the main types, purposes, common investment characteristics and behaviours of: onshore collective investment funds; offshore collective investment funds

Collective investment schemes can provide a useful alternative to direct investment, for those investors without:

- the time to manage their own investments;
- the large sums of money required to get adequate diversification;
- the expertise to assess investments;
- sufficient money to interest investment managers running **segregated portfolios**.

The **advantages** of investing via a fund include:

- Economies of scale (transaction sizes that ensure commissions and other costs may be set at competitive levels).
- A greater degree of diversification (spread of risk) than the investor might be able to achieve investing a relatively small amount of money directly.
- Access to specialist investment expertise.
- Eliminating administrative burdens.
- Many funds are regulated, which can be a big comfort to some investors.
- The investor may gain access to foreign/specialist markets not always open to private individuals, but only to institutional investors.
- In some cases, offshore funds can act as a tax shelter – since the investor does not pay capital gains tax on gains made on the underlying investments as they arise. Instead, CGT will be paid on the sale of the fund-holding, and this may be at a time when the investor falls into a lower tax bracket.

The **disadvantages** of investing via a fund include:

- Costs; there is usually an initial charge and on-going management costs and fees.

- No guarantee of performance. Specialist investment expertise is not a guaranteed good performance.
- The investor has no choice in the investments – a fund will not suit an investor who likes to make their own investment decisions.
- Tax (again). Some offshore funds are not ideal for UK investors from a tax perspective, because of their unfavourable treatment by the UK taxman. Also, some funds may be liable to withholding taxes on underlying investments which cannot be reclaimed. Investment managers should seek to minimise the impact of such taxes.

5.1 OFFSHORE FUNDS

LEARNING OBJECTIVE

5.1.7   Understand the tax treatment of UK investors investing in offshore funds, including: differences between distributor and non-distributor offshore funds and reporting funds; taxation of offshore funds

Funds which are established and run outside the UK jurisdiction, usually in low tax areas, are generally referred to as **offshore funds**. Jurisdictions where they are commonly found include the Channel Islands, the Isle of Man, the Cayman Islands, Hong Kong and Bermuda. In recent years, Luxembourg and Dublin have also become important tax havens within the European Union.

Many offshore funds are run by companies associated with large UK unit trust groups, and most of the countries involved now have their own regulatory framework. Certain offshore funds receive recognition under sections 264, 270 and 272 of the Financial Services and Markets Act 2000 (FSMA 2000).

Since 1979, when UK exchange controls were abolished, it has become relatively easy for the UK resident to invest money abroad in equities, bonds or pooled investments such as bonds, UCITS and OEICs.

There may be income and capital gains tax advantages for UK expatriates who are non-UK resident.

In general terms there will be no tax paid by an offshore fund. However, there may be withholding tax, which may not be reclaimable by the fund. In addition, a fund may be subject to a small amount of local tax. Jersey funds are subject to a flat yearly corporation tax and Luxembourg funds to a tax on the asset value each year. The expenses of an offshore fund cannot be offset against its income.

However, investment in offshore funds may be not be as advantageous for UK residents as they think, particularly from a tax point of view. In most cases, the tax benefit is limited to a possible deferral of tax payments resulting from income being paid gross. There can even be tax disadvantages, particularly if the offshore fund invests in UK shares.

The Financial Services Authority recognises the following offshore pooled investments:

- Funds categorised as UCITS are constituted in other European Economic Area member states. These funds are automatically recognised by the Financial Services Authority and can be marketed freely in the UK.

- Funds authorised in designated territories, that is, non-EU territories such as the Channel Islands, Bermuda and the Isle of Man, may not be automatically recognised by the FSA. However, the FSA recognises that certain countries in which investments are based offer a similar regulatory authority and investor protection to that afforded to the UK investor onshore. These regulatory authorities are as follows.
  - Bermuda Monetary Authority;
  - Guernsey Financial Services Commission;
  - Isle of Man Financial Supervision Commission;
  - Jersey Financial Services Department.

The FSA also provides for the recognition of overseas schemes on an individual basis.

Non-regulated and non-recognised funds are subject to severe marketing restrictions in the UK. Prospectuses and details can only be forwarded to investment professionals such as stockbrokers and Independent Financial Advisers (IFAs).

5.1.1 Taxation of Offshore Funds

Offshore funds assume one of two structures. The taxation of the individual investor who has an interest or stake-holding in an offshore fund will depend upon the status of the fund, ie, whether it has distributor or non-distributor status, otherwise known as **reporting** and **non-reporting** funds respectively.

Offshore investment fund companies mainly market open-ended equity, fixed-interest, money market and currency funds. The main European offshore centres are Luxembourg, Dublin, the Channel Islands and the Isle of Man.

Offshore funds assume one of two structures:

- **Distributor Funds (Reporting)** – are funds recognised by HMRC and which distribute at least 85% of their net investment income. Funds with distributor status are treated the same as UK-based funds for tax purposes.
- **Non-Distributor Funds (Non-Reporting)** – typically roll up their capital gains and income. The tax treatment for UK-resident investors is different. Gains are subject to income tax rather than capital gains tax. When UK tax residents make withdrawals from non-distributor funds, all proceeds are subject to income tax. Investors are unable to use their capital gains tax allowance to mitigate any tax liabilities.

The Uses and Tax Benefits of Offshore Funds

Offshore pooled investments may be useful for those who require a wider choice of funds than is available onshore. Offshore funds are particularly attractive to investors who wish to use currency funds or hedge funds.

A fixed interest fund with distributor status may be useful for a non-taxpayer. Earnings will be invested in a fixed interest fund which is rolling up tax-free and the investor will receive a gross dividend. In the case of a non-distributor fund, the taxpayer will pay no tax while the income is rolling up.

If a higher-rate taxpayer can take encashment when his or her status will have fallen to basic rate status, the postponement of the encashment will provide a clear tax advantage.

The non-distributor fund may be useful for a UK resident who is anticipating retiring abroad. The investor can 'roll up' the investment tax-free and then encash it when no longer a UK resident and subject to UK tax. The tax treatment of the encashment then needs to be examined in relation to the tax code operating in the country in which residence is then established.

6. CHARGES AND PRICING OF COLLECTIVE INVESTMENT SCHEMES

LEARNING OBJECTIVE

5.1.8   Analyse the charges and pricing of collective investments: Initial, annual, exit and performance fee charging structures; single pricing; bid/offer pricing; dilution levies; forward pricing; premiums; discounts

5.1.9   Analyse the relative merits and limitations of investing in a collective investment fund compared with other forms of direct and indirect investment, in terms of: risk; return; tax treatment; turnover, liquidity and access; expenses – transaction and ongoing; management and administration

6.1   INITIAL, ANNUAL, EXIT AND PERFORMANCE FEE CHARGING STRUCTURES (OPEN-ENDED FUNDS)

All of the parties involved in the operation of a fund will seek payment for their services. Payment may be on the basis of a percentage of the size of the fund, per transaction, a fixed fee per annum or on the basis of expenditure claimed for specific work undertaken.

Before moving on to how a fund is priced, we will briefly look at those fees charged by the manager (unit trust) or ACD (OEIC) of an open-ended fund. Remember that other parties – custodians, advisers and the like – will also be levying fees.

The **manager/ACD** is entitled to:

- The **initial charge** (also sometimes known as the **front-end load**, or **preliminary charge**) – this is applied to subscriptions for shares or units by investors; a typical initial charge might be between 3% and 5% of the value of the subscription. This may be added to the NAV per share or included in the unit subscription price. Commissions to sales agents and IFAs are usually paid from this charge. In some cases, the manager/ACD may offer investors a discount on the initial charge (for example, where the subscription is very big, or where the fund has a **special offer** period on to try and increase subscriptions).
- The **exit charge** – taken from investors when they sell their units or shares. This may also be called a **back-end load**. This charge is generally levied instead of an initial charge. It is used as an incentive to encourage investors to stay in the fund. Exit charges are deducted from the bid price of the shares/units, and paid by the investor at sale. Exit charges are usually staggered – eg, 5% if the investor sells in the first year, 4% for the second year, and so on.

- The **annual management charge** or **management fee** – deducted periodically from the value of the fund and usually a fixed percent of its net asset value. A typical figure might be between 0.5% and 1.5% per annum of the value of the fund. For example, if a fund is valued at £25 million the quarterly management fee will be:

$$£25m \times 1\% \times 13/52 = £62,300.00$$

In addition, **agents**, such as tied sales people or IFAs selling the fund, often get paid a **commission** from the fund for introducing business. Up to 3% may typically be paid out of the initial charge. The agent has the option of waiving all or part of his fee to give a discount to the client.

An example of how this might work is as follows.

EXAMPLE

Initial charge on the deal	5% (levied by the manager)
of which:	
Manager retains	2%
Agent (eg, IFA) receives	2%
Discount to client (agreed by agent)	1%

Nowadays, repeat or **trail** commission is becoming increasingly commonplace. This allows agents to be rewarded for giving their clients ongoing investment advice and, potentially, **keeping** them invested in a management group's funds, rather than their simply receiving introductory commissions when monies are introduced. The manager will pay this to the introducing agent out of his annual management fee.

Trail commission and initial fees are due to be phased out in time for the implementation of the Retail Distribution Review (RDR) in January 2013 and are to be replaced by ordinary fees.

In addition, certain types of fund – typically those aimed at the more sophisticated and/or wealthy investor – may carry additional **performance fees**. These reward the manager or adviser with an additional percentage-based fee, if they outperform a specified benchmark. Performance fee structures can be complicated and there is a variety of ways of calculating them – each **fairer** to the investor in certain circumstances. In addition, they are usually stated to be payable only on **net new highs** – that is, the manager will not be rewarded if the fund falls in value and his 'outperformance' consists simply in regaining ground that was lost!

6.2   PRICING

6.2.1   Single Pricing (Open-Ended Funds)

Open-ended funds may be **single-priced** or **dual-priced**.

For single-priced funds, the manager/ACD will calculate a single price for the shares/units, which will apply to all transactions in that dealing period. The FSA lays down rules as to how this should be carried out, and the manager/ACD must abide by these rules and any additional rules that it sets out in the fund's offering documents.

It does this by valuing the fund net of liabilities and dividing this figure by the number of shares in issue to give the NAV per share.

For many single-priced funds, the manager may apply an initial charge to compensate for the costs of administration.

6.2.2   Dual Pricing (Bid/Offer Prices) (Open-Ended Funds)

As an alternative to single pricing, open-ended funds may be dual-priced – that is, the manager shows a bid and an offer price for shares/units in the fund. Again, the FSA lays down rules for authorised funds on how this must be done.

The **bid price** is the price which investors will receive if they sell their units/shares back to the fund. It is based on the NAV of the fund.

The **offer price** is the price investors will have to pay if they buy units/shares. It is also based on the NAV of the fund.

The difference between the bid and the offer price is known as the **bid-offer spread**.

6.2.3   Dilution Levies (Open-Ended Funds)

The **dilution levy** is also known as the **dealing charge**. It is a charge which may be imposed by the manager to cover dealing costs. **Dilution** describes the reduction in the capital of a fund due to dealing costs, including market spread of the underlying investments. Dilution only affects single-priced funds since the dual-price system includes dealing costs and spreads in the calculation of the bid and offer prices.

The dilution levy might be better known as an **anti-dilution levy**; it represents an amount that the fund manager may decide to charge on the purchase or disposal of shares. It is designed to ensure that existing investors do not suffer costs associated with inflows/outflows resulting from other investors subscribing for or redeeming shares. The manager will assess the costs and will estimate what, if any, levy is applicable. They are not obliged to apply a dilution levy, but the policy must be stated in the fund documentation so that investors know what to expect.

The important factor is consistency – application to all deals, those above a certain value or portion of the portfolio. Typical levies are of the order of 0.2%.

6.2.4 Forward and Historic Pricing (Open-Ended Funds)

Open-ended funds are dealt in at prices based on their NAV – but the NAV as calculated at what point, exactly? This can matter a great deal, since the prices of the underlying investments of the fund may themselves be very volatile. This could mean that the price of units/shares in a fund is very different at the start of the day and at the close of business.

Consequently, fund managers may have a policy to value funds on a **forward pricing** basis – and a policy on the cut-off time – or on a **historic pricing** basis (and again what the relevant cut-off times are).

Forward pricing – a forward basis means that orders are taken from investors, and the prices at which they deal are determined at the next valuation point. This may mean that the investor is dealing **blind** as they do not know the actual price at which they are dealing.

Historic pricing – here the managers will deal the last valuation price. The main benefit is that investors know the price they are dealing at. There are, however, circumstances in which the unit trust managers who normally deal on an historic basis may choose to deal on a forward basis. These are:

- the managers believe that the fund value has moved by more than 2% in either direction;
- the investor requests a forward price;
- the managers may choose to deal on a forward basis on large deals.

6.2.5 Premiums and Discounts (Investment Trusts Only)

Remember, shares in investment trusts are not priced directly in relation to the fund's NAV; rather, because they are traded on the stock market, they are priced in accordance with investor demand.

NAV is calculated as an open-ended fund but an investment trust will trade at either a premium (above NAV) or a discount (below NAV) depending on the performance of the share price. This is shown in newspapers alongside the share price to give investors full disclosure.

The discount or premium is calculated as a percentage so the investor can see how much the investment trust's current share price is as a percentage of the investment trust's actual NAV per share.

7. EXCHANGE-TRADED FUNDS (ETFs) AND EXCHANGE-TRADED COMMODITIES (ETCs)

LEARNING OBJECTIVE

5.2.1   Understand the main types, purposes, common investment characteristics and behaviours of: exchange-traded funds (ETFs); exchange-traded commodities (ETCs)

5.2.2   Analyse the relative merits and limitations of investing in exchange-traded funds (ETFs) or exchange-traded commodities (ETCs) compared with other forms of direct and indirect investment, in terms of: risk; return; tax treatment; turnover, liquidity and access; expenses – transaction and ongoing; management and administration

7.1   EXCHANGE-TRADED FUNDS (ETFs)

Exchange-traded funds (ETFs) are a relatively new type of open-ended fund. They have proved popular in the US, and are increasing in popularity in the UK. Like tracker funds, they follow the performance of an index closely (though some tracking error may occur). An increasing range of ETFs is available, tracking a variety of indices. For example, they may track a general share price index (eg, the FTSE 100 Index in the UK, or the S&P 500 index in the US) or sub-sectors of the market (eg, pharmaceuticals, or energy stocks).

ETFs are quoted in **real time** – ie, traded throughout the day in line with the underlying index. This sets them apart from other types of index-tracking fund. In addition, they have relatively low charges and are not subject to stamp duty.

ETFs are equally available to all investors, smaller individual investors and large institutions alike. There is not usually any leverage within an ETF. This means that the fund cannot borrow to increase its exposure to the marketplace. Accordingly, £100 invested will typically represent £100 value of equity exposure.

The liquidity of an ETF relates to the liquidity of the underlying basket of shares. Large orders will usually often be transacted within the visible market price even when volume is low.

The exchange traded-fund trades at a price that is very close to the exact value of the underlying stocks. The mechanism for creating new shares and redeeming old shares will prevent sustained premiums and discounts from occurring. Unlike other collective investment schemes, exchange-traded funds do not include charges within their secondary market pricing mechanism. The share price will reflect the underlying value of stocks and market movement.

Furthermore, since most funds are registered offshore, an investor will not be liable to pay stamp duty under current regulations. The costs involved within an ETF are exceptionally low. The costs of passive management are small and the administration/custodial charges are available to large funds at very competitive rates. Much of the expense of the investment process is external to the fund – ie, broker commission and savings plan costs.

	Price	**Dealing**
Unit Trusts	Advantage Subscribers buy units of scheme assets at around the net asset value	Disadvantage Historic pricing/paper processing/ administration in hands of single counterparty/slow settlement
Investment Trusts	Advantage Dealing and settlement are transparent, electronic and customer-friendly – effectively they trade like stocks	Disadvantage Investors do not buy in or sell out at prices that directly reflect the value of the scheme assets due to premiums and discounts
ETFs	Advantage Easy to deal just like a stock except no stamp duty	Disadvantage Narrow range of investments compared to mutual funds

7.1.1 Primary versus Secondary Market

The exchange-traded fund structure enables authorised participants in the ETF to create new units in the fund at NAV whenever necessary. This is done in large size, typically worth more than £1 million, with a creation basket usually to satisfy demand. The equities within this basket are in the precise proportions of their existing weight in the index. New ETF units are thereby created and available to investors within the secondary market. ETFs generally trade at a price very close to their NAV, eliminating opportunities for arbitrage.

7.2 EXCHANGE-TRADED COMMODITIES (ETCS)

An exchange-traded commodity (ETC) is like an ETF except that it tracks the performance of an underlying commodity or basket of commodities.

ETCs work on exactly the same principle as ETFs – with the ETC tracking the performance of a single underlying commodity or a basket of commodities.

ETCs offer investors a number of advantages over both shares and futures – without the associated vagaries of trading an individual stock or the dramatic risk inherent in futures trading. Benefits include:

- **Direct exposure to the commodities markets** – where the value of the investment will rise and fall in direct proportion to the price of the underlying commodity.
- **Liquidity** – ETCs are 'open-ended' securities, which are created and redeemed on-demand. This means that the supply of ETCs is unlimited and that price changes will accurately mirror developments in the price of the underlying commodity.
- **Stamp duty and CGT** – ETCs are generally registered offshore, so trades are exempt from stamp duty. Furthermore, ETCs can be traded within ISA accounts, allowing investors to shelter profit from capital gains tax. They are generally considered as having 'distributor' status coming under CGT rules.
- **Low dealing costs** – ETCs are traded on the regular stock exchange, making them both accessible and affordable.
- **Portfolio diversification** – ETCs give broad representation across individual or collective commodity types.

8. TAX-EFFICIENT SAVINGS

LEARNING OBJECTIVE

5.4.1   Analyse the key features, restrictions and tax treatment of ISAs and
Child Trust Funds (CTFs): eligibility; eligible investments; subscriptions;
transfers; withdrawals; use in investment and tax planning

8.1   INDIVIDUAL SAVINGS ACCOUNTS (ISAs)

ISAs are tax-assisted savings vehicles. They are not strictly investments in their own right. Providing
that the rules are complied with, all returns generated within an ISA are free of capital gains and income
taxes. This means that gains generated within the ISA roll up at a faster rate than they would for a
similar investment not held within an ISA.

There are two types of ISA:

- cash ISA; and
- stocks and shares ISA.

A **cash ISA** can contain:

- UK and European bank deposits;
- building society deposits;
- cash unit trusts.

A **stocks and shares ISA** can contain investments such as:

- unit trusts (other than cash unit trusts);
- shares in investment trusts;
- shares listed on a recognised stock exchange;
- bonds and gilts.

The annual ISA investment allowance for the 2011/12 tax year is £10,680 – of which up to £5,340
may be saved in cash with one provider. The remainder of the £10,680 can be invested in stocks and
shares with either the same or another provider. ISA savers can thus invest in two separate ISAs in
each tax year – one cash ISA, and one stocks and shares ISA. They may also decide to invest the whole
allowance in a stocks and shares ISA.

ISAs are only available to people who are UK-resident and ordinarily resident (see Chapter 4). In order
to subscribe, the investor must be:

- aged 18 years or over (stocks and shares ISA);
- aged 16 years or over (cash ISA).

ISAs, once established, can usually be transferred from one provider to another; however, there are generally charges involved. In addition, not all providers cater to all the classes of underlying investment, so the investor should check that they will be able to maintain their investments before initiating a transfer.

8.2   CHILD TRUST FUNDS (CTFs)

The Child Trust Fund (CTF) was introduced by the government to help and encourage parents to save for their child's future. The government's intention was that when the child reached 18, they would have some money to give them a start to life as an adult. At 18, they could carry on saving or use the money for other things – such as driving lessons or training courses.

The coalition government, however, announced on 24 May 2010 its plans to reduce and then stop government payments to CTF accounts. The changes required legislation to be passed by Parliament, which was introduced in September, and from 1 January 2011 no further government contributions were made.

No new accounts can be opened; however, existing accounts can continue. This means that further contributions can be made by parents, family and friends into the account subject to a maximum limit of £1,200 per annum per account.

The main characteristics of the CTF are as follows:

- It is a long-term savings and investment account that is available to children born on or after 1 September 2002.
- Money invested in a CTF belongs to the child and cannot be withdrawn until the child turns 18.
- There will be no tax on any interest or gains made on the money in the CTF.
- At 16, the child will be able to manage their CTF account, for example by deciding to change provider or type of account.
- At 18, young people with CTF accounts will be able to decide for themselves how best to use the money.
- CTFs are treated in the same way as ISAs in respect of tax benefits.

Providers offer up to three forms of CTF account: a savings account, an account that invests in shares or a stakeholder account. The **savings account** is a deposit account and offers a secure type of investment but one whose value will be affected by inflation. The **accounts that invest in shares** offer the potential for growth, but the risk of falling in value. The **stakeholder accounts** invest in shares but the government has set certain rules to reduce risk – in particular, when the child reaches the age of 13, the money starts to be moved from shares into safer investments.

Other types of account are also available, such as **Sharia'a accounts** and **ethical accounts**.

The first CTF accounts will mature in 2020, and if the child does not take the money out it will automatically roll over into an ISA on maturity. The aim is to encourage young people to maintain a savings habit into adulthood.

8.3   INVESTMENT BONDS

The range of investment options to which investment bonds can be linked is as broad as what the insurance company is willing to offer. For the types of bonds available, see Section 9.

Investment bonds are not a type of tax wrapper in the way that ISAs are; they are a product in their own right, being an insurance product with investment benefits, which happens to have tax benefits owing to the way insurance policies are treated.

Gains on these policies are subject to income tax at the policy owner's marginal rate and are calculated at the point of what is deemed to be a '**chargeable event**', ie, full and partial surrenders, the death of the assured, or the maturity of the policy.

The insurance fund in which the premiums are invested is subject to tax – levied on the life company, currently at a rate of 20%. In this way, the taxation of the product differs from that of many other investments; since the life company has already paid tax, there is no personal liability for basic rate taxpayers to income tax or CGT on any gains arising from investment in the policy.

Policyholders can withdraw up to 5% of their original premium annually (and this is cumulative – ie, if it is not used one year it can be carried forward to later years) for the first 20 years – that is, until 100% of the premium invested has been returned to the policyholder. This is treated as a return of capital.

For higher-rate taxpayers, there may be a liability to tax on withdrawals or encashment. This liability is calculated by reference to the **chargeable gain** on the policy. Chargeable gains are calculated as follows:

- If partial withdrawals have been made from the policy, then the chargeable gain is calculated as at the end of the relevant policy year, at the point when they can be totalled. The chargeable gain is the sum by which the total withdrawals in the period exceed the allowance available (ie, 5% for the current year plus any unused allowances from previous years, carried forward).
- When the policy is finally encashed, the total value at that point is added to the total of any withdrawals made previously. From this sum the initial premium invested is deducted, plus any previous chargeable gain. The net result is the final chargeable gain.

This sum is taxable as if it were an addition to the policyholder's income. However, since the life company has already paid income tax on the life fund, it is given a tax credit as though basic rate tax had already been withheld. Thus, it is only higher- or additional rate taxpayers (or basic rate taxpayers whose income is taken into the higher-rate bracket by the chargeable gain) who have any further liability.

If the latter happens, and the addition of a chargeable gain to a policyholder's income takes them over the threshold into the higher-rate band, then a principle known as **top slicing** can be used to mitigate the ensuing tax liability. With top slicing, the chargeable gain is divided by the number of relevant years, to produce an average gain. This is treated as the **top slice** of income in the tax year in which the gain actually arises. If any tax is payable on that top slice, it is then multiplied by the number of relevant years, and the result is the total arising income tax liability.

8.4 NATIONAL SAVINGS & INVESTMENTS

LEARNING OBJECTIVE

5.5.1 Analyse the key features, restrictions and tax treatment of National Savings & Investments: eligibility; eligible investments; subscriptions; transfers; withdrawals; premium bonds; use in investment and tax planning

National Savings & Investments (NS&I) was formerly called National Savings. NS&I products are offered by the government and, as such, are regarded as **risk-free** investments. Some NS&I products are available through post offices.

NS&I is an executive agency of the Chancellor of the Exchequer, and is accountable to the Treasury. It provides deposit and savings products to the investing public, and in doing so raises funds on behalf of the UK government. An investor holding an NS&I product is in essence lending to the government.

NS&I offers a wide range of products, from easy-access savings accounts to longer-term investments and, of course, premium bonds. As the products are **underwritten** by the government, they are regarded as effectively free from the risk of default. None of NS&I's products is subject to capital gains tax, but some products are subject to income tax. The following are a few of its key products:

Savings Accounts

NS&I offers a range of products aimed at savers, including:

- **Investment account** – this is in effect a 'passbook'-style savings account. Savers can operate it over the counter at their post office, by mail or by standing order. It pays variable rates, tiered interest rates and has no set term. The minimum deposit is £20 and the maximum £1 million. Interest is taxable and paid gross.
- **Easy-access savings account** – this account also has no set term. It earns variable interest, at tiered rates, and the minimum and maximum deposits are £100 and £2 million. Interest is taxable and paid gross.

Income-Providing Products

NS&I's products aimed at the investor who is seeking interest income include:

- **Guaranteed income bonds** – these provide a guaranteed monthly income. The minimum holding is £500 and the maximum total holding £1 million. The bonds are available for one-, three- and five-year terms. Interest is taxable and paid net.
- **Income bonds** – These pay monthly income, and have no set term: the holder can withdraw his money without notice. Interest is variable, tiered, taxable and paid gross. The minimum holding is £500, and the maximum £1 million.

Growth Products

NS&I's growth schemes include:

- **Index-Linked Savings Certificates** – these pay a guaranteed return linked to the inflation rate as measured by RPI. The minimum holding is £100, and the maximum £15,000 per issue. Certificates can be bought for terms of either three or five years. Returns are tax-free.
- **Fixed-Rate Savings Certificates** – these pay a fixed rate of return over a period of time, such as two and five years currently. The returns are guaranteed for the term and tax free on maturity. The minimum holding is £100 and maximum £15,000 per issue.
- **Guaranteed Growth Bonds** – these provide a guaranteed return on your investment. The minimum holding is £500 and maximum £1,000,000. There is a choice of terms of one, three and five years, with access available before maturity subject to a loss of 90 days' interest. Interest is taxable and paid net.
- **Guaranteed Equity Bonds** – these also provide a guaranteed return on your investment, linked to the performance of the FTSE 100 index over a set term. If the FTSE 100 index grows over the term, the investor will benefit from that growth. And if it falls, he will still get back 100% of their original investment. As the FTSE 100 index measures share prices only, the investor will not receive dividends. This may mean the investment may not achieve as high a return as a direct stock market investment. The returns on guaranteed equity bonds are subject to averaging and are liable to UK income tax on maturity. Although the capital is fully guaranteed, inflation may erode the real value of funds invested.

Tax-Free Products

Certain of NS&I's products provide returns free of tax. However the returns on these products are not generally high, reflecting also the fact that they are regarded as very safe. They include:

- **Premium bonds** – which carry no capital risk (the holder can withdraw his capital in full when he wishes). Instead of earning interest, bonds are entered into a monthly draw in which they could win their holder up to £1 million (or one of many smaller amounts). The minimum holding is £100 and the maximum £30,000.
- **Direct ISA** – investors can pay a maximum of £5,340 in the 2011/12 tax year into NS&I's Direct ISA, earning variable-rate interest on this free of income tax. There are no withdrawal restrictions.
- **Savings Certificates** – NS&I offers a range of savings certificates, some paying fixed interest and others variable-rate.
- **Children's Bonus Bonds** – these run for a period of five years and offer a guaranteed rate of interest (paid daily) from the outset. Returns are tax-free with no tax liability to the parents. The minimum investment per issue is £25 and maximum £3,000. A bonus payment is made on the fifth anniversary. Access is allowed during the term subject to loss of the bonus payment, and no interest is credited if the bond is cashed in during the first year.

9. UK ONSHORE AND OFFSHORE LIFE ASSURANCE COMPANY PRODUCTS

LEARNING OBJECTIVE

5.6.1   Analyse the key features, relative merits and limitations of investing in onshore and offshore life assurance-based investments compared with other forms of direct and indirect investment: risk; return; tax treatment; turnover, liquidity and access; expenses – transaction and ongoing; management and administration

It might seem odd to include financial products such as insurance policies and pensions in a chapter addressing investments. A professional investment manager would not generally use insurance and pensions products in a client's portfolio.

However, certain insurance and pensions products are regarded as investments, for technical and regulatory purposes. Further, if we are to consider investment planning for the private individual, we should certainly take account of the different investment risks of such products. For information on the tax treatment of investment bonds, see Section 8.3.

We will consider those insurance policies and pensions which fall into the domain of investments.

9.1   THE MAIN TYPES OF ONSHORE INVESTMENT BONDS

9.1.1   Single Premium/Regular Premium Bonds

Life companies offer a wide range of products which can be used to provide protection benefits (ie, a payout if one or more particular individuals, the life assured, dies). These are life assurance products, or life policies. Many of their products also fulfil other financial needs (providing a payout on the death of a policyholder). They may provide this return:

*   at a set date (or earlier, if the life assured dies before this date); or
*   they may simply run until either the individual dies or the policyholder redeems his policy.

Such policies may be single premium, or regular premium. With a single premium policy the policyholder (the investor) pays a one-off premium to the life company. Top-ups may be allowed depending on the terms of the policy.

Regular premium policies are paid for with a series of periodic premiums. These may be monthly, quarterly or annual. They may be the same sum or revised from time to time, again depending on the terms of the policy.

When applying for the policy, the policyholder will – if he is also the life assured – have to provide the life company with information about themselves, their lifestyle and health. (If someone else is to be the life assured, then their details will also be required.) This enables the life company to assess the risk of the life assured. It can then decide on what terms to issue the policy, what premium to ask for and indeed whether to proceed at all. This process of assessing the risk is called underwriting.

The benefits paid out on the death of the life assured, or maturity of the bond, or on encashment at the policyholder's request, will depend on the value of the policy at that time. Some policies pay out a guaranteed death benefit, but the maturity proceeds or early encashment value will depend on the value of the investments within the policy. It is therefore very important that the policyholder understands what sort of policy they have purchased. In this section you will see the word **bond** used; it does not have the same meaning as debt securities. It is, however, a promise to pay, on the part of the life company.

9.1.2 Unit-Linked Bonds

Here the premiums paid by the policyholder buy units in a fund run by the life company, or by an external institution with whom the life company has an arrangement (eg, a unit trust or OEIC). The value of the policy is measured in terms of the total number of units allocated to it, and the value of these units depends on the performance of the underlying investments.

The value of the bond generally fluctuates in line with the underlying investments. Generally, life companies offer a range of unit-linked options, with different risk profiles. These may include gilt or fixed-interest funds, UK equity funds, an international equity fund and other variants. In many cases the policy has no minimum maturity value; rather, its value is linked directly to the underlying funds.

In some cases the investor will need a **minimum sum assured** – for example, if the policy is being used as the repayment vehicle for an interest-only mortgage, then a lender will require that the borrower will cover the principal of the loan. This can be arranged through the purchase of appropriate life cover as a part of the policy. Unit-linked policies thus have no inherent basic sum assured; life cover is generally a built-in **add on** to the policy.

In practice how this works is that the policyholder pays a monthly premium to the life company. The life company uses this to purchase units in the relevant underlying fund(s); and will also, on a monthly basis, cancel sufficient units to pay for any life cover needed. Life companies do not pay bonuses on unit-linked policies (as they do on with-profits policies); the maturity value is linked solely to the value of units, which may fall as well as rise in value. There can thus be the risk that the policy does not pay out as much as was hoped; for example, it may not repay any associated mortgage loan at the end of its term. If this looks likely, the policyholder can increase his monthly premiums, or perhaps switch to a more appropriate linked fund.

9.1.3 With-Profits Bonds

With-profits endowments also offer a benefit payable at some future maturity date, or on the earlier death of the policyholder, or on encashment by the policyholder. The policyholder pays single or regular (usually monthly) premiums to the life company, which invests them in the markets with the aim of generating sufficient capital to pay the death/maturity benefits.

To achieve a return, the life office invests the premiums received from its many with-profits policyholders in the mix of investments it thinks is most appropriate. These include equities, debt securities, property and cash: in some cases it can also include other assets, such as holdings in hedge funds, foreign currencies and other alternative investments. The portfolio is generally constructed so as to avoid too high a degree of risk. However, since with-profits bonds are aimed at the retail investor.

The policyholder receives a **basic sum assured** plus a share in any investment profits made by the life company. These profits are shared by way of bonuses: **reversionary bonuses**, which are added each year and which, once paid, cannot be withdrawn, and **terminal bonuses**, which are awarded on maturity or earlier death. The policy provides built-in **life cover** (which can be used to assure repayment of a mortgage in the case that the policyholder dies).

The return (by way of bonus) on a with-profits bond is '**smoothed**' by the life company. That is, in years when the underlying portfolio performs well, the company will hold back some of the gains, and will allocate them to policyholders to boost their returns in years when performance is poor. Policyholders should experience lower volatility than with a regular investment.

With-profits policies may be **unitised**. Unitisation simplifies the life office's communication of performance, since a unit price can be published, so policyholders can monitor the growth in their investment. In addition, bonuses can be added by adding new units to a policyholder's account.

9.1.4 Distribution Bonds

Unit-linked bond funds generally do not treat income and capital separately. Returns from invested income are added to the price of units. If income is required, this can be provided by the regular encashment of units. However, distribution bonds do separate income and capital. In order to produce income, a distribution bond will invest in a mixture of gilts, fixed-interest securities, convertibles and high-yielding equities.

The difference between a distribution bond and an ordinary bond is that a distribution bond has a separate fund into which the income from the main fund is placed. The income in the separate fund can be **distributed** regularly, eg, quarterly or half-yearly. The advantage of this is that it allows investors to encash units representing just the income portion of the bond. All encashments, whether from income units or the main fund, are deemed by HMRC to be a return of the policyholder's original capital.

9.2 THE MAIN TYPES OF OFFSHORE INVESTMENT BONDS

The following assets may be held within an offshore bond wrapper:

- cash deposits and money market funds;
- equity, fixed interest or bond funds, but not direct equities;
- capital guaranteed investments, or alternative investments such as hedge funds.

The main benefits of an offshore bond are:

- Income and growth accumulate within the bond free of income and capital gains tax.
- Withdrawals of up to 5% per annum may be made without incurring an immediate tax liability.

- The 5% allowance is cumulative and, if unused, may be carried forward to future years (and, therefore, may be taxable on redemption).
- Bonds may be gifted without crystallising a tax charge.
- Upon encashment of the bond, gains are subject to income tax only.
- Income tax is levied only at the investor's marginal tax rate in the year of encashment, potentially lowering the tax liability.
- Suitable for an individual with a long-term investment horizon and a possible need for regular distributions.

Offshore bonds are offered in locations such as the Isle of Man, Dublin and Luxembourg. Offshore life companies may offer some variants such as the following:

9.2.1   Portfolio Bonds

These products are usually offered to wealthier investors. A personal portfolio bond allows a policyholder to select their own underlying investments, or perhaps to choose a particular fund manager to run the portfolio rather than buying units in the insurance company's various funds. In some cases, he may be able to use an existing portfolio of shares as the premium for the bond, although this may give rise to a charge to capital gains tax.

The personal portfolio bond operates in all other respects exactly like a normal bond. However the benefits paid on maturity, death or encashment depend on the value of the portfolio, rather than the value of units in which the bond is invested. Portfolio bonds are now rarely used by UK investors, as they are no longer tax-efficient. However they are still available and used by investors resident overseas.

9.2.2   Capital Redemption Bonds

Capital redemption bonds are life company products without an insurance element – ie, there is no life assured. Instead they are used purely for investment purposes, and so they only pay out on the expiry of the bond or an early encashment by the policyholder.

9.3   POLICYHOLDER PROTECTION ACTS

LEARNING OBJECTIVE

5.6.2   Understand the impact of the Policy-Holder Protection Act 1997

Policyholder protection was originally introduced in the Policyholder Protection Act 1975 (PPA 75) where the Policyholder Protection Board (PPB) acted as an industry-funded safety net when a UK insurer became insolvent. This responsibility was eventually taken on by the newly formed Financial Services Compensation Scheme in December 2001.

The PPA 75 applied in circumstances where policyholders were affected by the failure of an authorised insurance company in the UK, and in instances where it was unable to meet liabilities under policies issued or securities given by them. The Act was subsequently amended in 1997 (PPA97) and extended to include pensions and purchased life annuities. Claims by policyholders were met from funds provided by a levy on the industry.

In 2001, the Financial Services Authority (FSA) created the **Financial Services Compensation Scheme (FSCS)**, which replaced eight existing arrangements that provided compensation if a firm collapsed owing money to investors, depositors or policyholders. The compensation scheme is a final **safety net** for consumers when financial services firms go out of business and represents a key part of the FSA framework to ensure appropriate levels of protection for consumers.

The scope of the FSCS, along with the compensation and protection frameworks, continues to be amended and updated, while the Policyholder Protection Acts (PPA75 & PPA97) are still cited from time to time, eg, in the case of Equitable Life.

10. PRIVATE EQUITY

LEARNING OBJECTIVE

5.7.1   Understand the main types, purposes, structures, tax treatment and investment characteristics of private equity funds

Private equity funds typically invest in companies which are not listed on a stock exchange. Investors are typically more sophisticated and/or wealthy and can accept the additional risks of this type of investment.

Typically, private equity fund managers take an active role in the management of the companies they invest in – perhaps having a majority shareholding and/or a seat on the board. They look to add value for their investors by transforming the way the investee company is managed, and may aim to make their money by floating the company on the stock market again after a few years, once the company's performance has been improved.

The basic types of private equity and venture funds include:

*   bootstrap funding;
*   venture capital;
*   leveraged buyouts (LBOs);
*   mezzanine finance;
*   growth;
*   secondaries;
*   equity co-investment.

Financial bootstrapping is a term used to cover different methods for avoiding using the financial resources of external investors. Bootstrapping can be defined as a means to minimise the amount of outside debt and equity financing needed from banks and investors. The use of private credit card debt is the most known form of bootstrapping, but a wide variety of methods are available for entrepreneurs. While bootstrapping involves a risk for the founders, the absence of any other stakeholder gives the founders more freedom to develop the company

Venture capital (also known as VC or venture) is typically provided to early-stage, high-potential, growth companies in the interest of generating a return through an eventual realisation event such as an IPO or trade sale of the company. Venture capital investments are generally made as cash in exchange for shares in the invested company. Venture capital typically comes from institutional investors and high net worth individuals and is pooled together by dedicated investment firms.

A venture capitalist is a person or investment firm that makes venture investments. These venture capitalists are expected to bring managerial and technical expertise as well as capital to their investments. A **venture capital fund** refers to a pooled investment vehicle (often a limited partnership or limited liability company) that primarily invests the financial capital of third-party investors in enterprises that are too risky for the standard capital markets or bank loans.

Venture capital is most attractive for new companies with limited operating history that are too small to raise capital in the public markets and are too immature to secure a bank loan or complete a debt offering. In exchange for the high risk that venture capitalists assume by investing in smaller and less mature companies, venture capitalists usually have significant control over company decisions, in addition to a significant portion of the company's ownership (and consequently value).

Leveraged buyouts involve financial sponsors or private equity firms making large acquisitions without committing all the capital required for the acquisition. To do this, a financial sponsor will raise acquisition debt which is ultimately secured upon the acquisition target and also looks to the cash flows of the acquisition target to make interest and principal payments. Acquisition debt in an LBO is therefore usually non-recourse to the financial sponsor and to the equity fund that the financial sponsor manages. Furthermore, unlike in a hedge fund, where debt raised to purchase certain securities is also collateralised by the fund's other securities, the acquisition debt in an LBO has recourse only to the company purchased in a particular LBO transaction.

Therefore, an LBO transaction's financial structure is particularly attractive to a fund's limited partners, allowing them the benefits of leverage but greatly limiting the degree of recourse of that leverage. This kind of acquisition brings leverage benefits to an LBO's financial sponsor in two ways: the investor itself only needs to provide a fraction of the capital for the acquisition, and, assuming the economic internal rate of return on the investment (taking into account expected exit proceeds) exceeds the weighted average interest rate on the acquisition debt, returns to the financial sponsor will be significantly enhanced.

Mezzanine capital, in finance, refers to a subordinated debt or preferred equity instrument that represents a claim on company's assets that is senior only to that of the common shares. Mezzanine financings can be structured either as debt (typically an unsecured and subordinated note) or preferred stock. Mezzanine capital often is a more expensive financing source for a company than secured debt or senior debt. The higher cost of mezzanine capital is the result of its place as an unsecured, subordinated (or junior) obligation in a company's capital structure (ie, in the event of default, the mezzanine financing is less likely to be repaid in full after all senior obligations have been satisfied).

Additionally, mezzanine financing, which is usually a private placement, is often used by smaller companies and may also involve greater overall leverage levels than issuers in the high-yield market and involve additional risk. In compensation for the increased risk, mezzanine debt holder will require a higher return for their investment than secured or other more senior lenders.

Growth capital (also 'expansion capital' and 'growth equity') is a type of private equity investment, most often a minority investment, in relatively mature companies that are looking for capital to expand or restructure operations, enter new markets or finance a significant acquisition without a change of control of the business.

Companies that seek growth capital often do so to finance a transformational event in their life cycle. These companies are likely to be more mature than venture capital-funded companies, able to generate revenue and operating profits but unable to generate sufficient cash to fund major expansions, acquisitions or other investments. Growth capital can also be used to effect a restructuring of a company's balance sheet, particularly to reduce the amount of leverage (or debt) the company has on its balance sheet.

Growth capital is often structured as either common equity or preferred equity, although certain investors will use various hybrid securities that include a contractual return (ie, interest payments) in addition to an ownership interest in the company. Often, companies that seek growth capital investments are not good candidates for additional borowing, either because of the stability of the company's earnings or because of its existing debt levels.

In finance, the private equity **secondary market** (also often called **private equity secondaries** or **secondaries**) refers to the buying and selling of pre-existing investor commitments to private equity and other alternative investment funds. Sellers of private equity investments sell not only the investments in the fund but also their remaining unfunded commitments to the funds. By its nature, the private equity asset class is **illiquid**, intended to be a long-term investment for buy-and-hold investors. For the vast majority of private equity investments, there is no listed public market; however there is a robust and maturing secondary market available to sellers of private equity assets.

Driven by strong demand for private equity exposure, a significant amount of capital has been committed to dedicated secondary market funds from investors looking to increase and diversify their private equity exposure.

An **equity co-investment** (or co-investment) is a minority investment, made directly into an operating company, alongside a financial sponsor or other private equity investor, in a leveraged buyout, recapitalisation or growth capital transaction. In certain circumstances, venture capital firms may also seek co-investors. Private equity firms seek co-investors for several reasons. Most important of these is that co-investments allow a manager to make larger investments without either dedicating too much of the fund's capital to a single transaction (ie, exposure issues) or sharing the deal with competing private equity firms. Co-investors bring a friendly source of capital.

Typically, co-investors are existing limited partners in an investment fund managed by the lead financial sponsor in a transaction. Unlike the investment fund however, co-investments are made outside of the existing fund and, as such, co-investors rarely pay management fees or carried interest on an individual investment. Co-investments are a typically passive, non-controlling investment, as the private equity firm or firms involved will exercise control and perform monitoring functions.

For large private equity fund of funds and other investors, co-investments are a means of increasing exposure to attractive transactions and making investments that have a higher return potential because of the lower economics paid to the general partner. As a result, many private equity firms offer co-investments to their largest and most important investors as an incentive to invest in future funds.

11. ENTERPRISE INVESTMENT SCHEMES (EISs) AND VENTURE CAPITAL TRUSTS (VCTs)

5.8.1   Analyse the key features, relative merits and limitations of investing in venture capital trusts (VCTs) and enterprise investment schemes (EISs) compared with other forms of direct and indirect investment: partners/investors; investment management; tax characteristics; past performance in terms of risk and returns; discounts; premiums; secondary market liquidity

11.1   THE ENTERPRISE INVESTMENT SCHEME (EIS)

The enterprise investment scheme (EIS) is designed to help smaller, higher-risk trading companies to raise finance by offering a range of tax reliefs to investors who purchase new shares in those companies. Companies who wish to issue shares under the scheme have to meet a certain number of rules regarding the kind of company it is, the amount of money it can raise, how and when that money must be employed for the purposes of the trade, and the trading activities carried on.

An investor receives tax advantages when investing in EIS companies providing that they invest in fully paid ordinary shares that carry the full risk of ordinary shares and carry no preferential rights that protect the investor from the normal risks of investing in shares.

Income tax relief is given on investments in an EIS-qualifying company subject to a minimum of £500 and a maximum of £500,000. The relief is 30% of the cost of the shares which can be set against the individual's income tax liability for the year in which the investment was made. The shares must then be held for a minimum period of three years, otherwise the income tax relief is withdrawn. An investor may carry back part or all of the amount invested and claim tax relief for the previous year subject to the limits for relief for that year.

EIS shares can also qualify for **relief from capital gains tax** providing that they have qualified for income tax relief and that has not been withdrawn. If they have qualified for relief, then any disposals after the minimum three-year period are free from capital gains tax. If a gain is made, the payment of tax can be deferred if the gain is invested in shares of another EIS-qualifying company within a period of one year before or three years after the gain arose. If a loss is made instead, then the amount of the loss less any income tax relief can be set against income of the year in which they were disposed of or the previous year, instead of being set off against any capital gains.

EISs are only available to **individuals** who invest in shares in an EIS-qualifying company (though they can invest via a nominee). The individual must invest at least £500 in the shares of the EIS company in any one tax year. There are various reliefs available under the scheme:

- **Income tax reliefs** – as of April 2011, the investor is eligible for relief of 30% of the cost of the shares, to be set against his income tax liability for the tax year in which the investment was made. Relief can be claimed up to a maximum of £500,000 invested in such shares, which means a maximum tax reduction in any one year of £150,000 (assuming the individual had a big enough income tax liability to cover this). The relief cannot be set off against dividend income, as the tax credit attached to a dividend is not recoverable.

  Investors can also carry back up to £500,000 of their investment to the previous tax year for the purposes of income tax relief. This does not affect an individual's current tax year entitlement, thereby enabling a maximum investment of £1 million per individual in any tax year. Relief cannot be carried forward to a later year.

  The shares must be held for a certain period or income tax relief will be withdrawn. Generally, this is three years from the date the shares were issued.

  Income tax relief can only be claimed by individuals who are not connected with the company.

- **Capital gains tax relief** – if an investor has received income tax relief on the cost of the shares, and the shares are disposed of after they have been held for a set period, any gain is free from CGT.

- **Loss relief** – if the shares are disposed of at a loss, the investor can offset the loss, less any income tax relief given, against income for the year in which they were disposed of, or for the previous year, instead of being set off against any capital gains.

- **CGT deferral relief** – this is available to individuals and trustees of certain trusts. The CGT on a capital gain can be deferred if the gain is invested in shares of an EIS qualifying company. The gain can arise from the disposal of any kind of asset, but the investment must be made within the period one year before, or three years after, it arose. There are no minimum or maximum amounts for deferral, and in this case it does not matter whether the investor is connected with the company or not. Unconnected investors may claim both income tax and CGT deferral relief. There is no minimum period for which the shares must be held; the deferred capital gain is brought back into charge whenever the shares are disposed of.

EIS qualifying companies must be **unquoted** when the relevant shares are issued. They can, later, become quoted without the investors losing relief – but only if there were no arrangements for them to become quoted in existence when the shares were issued.

The company must not be controlled by another company, nor must there be any arrangements in existence for this to happen, at the time the shares are issued.

Any subsidiaries must all be **qualifying subsidiaries** – ie, the company has more than 50% of the ordinary share capital of the subsidiary, and it is not controlled by another company. If the EIS company has a property management subsidiary that must be at least a 90% subsidiary.

The EIS company must be a **small company**, in terms of the **gross assets test**. The gross assets of the company – or of the whole group if it is the parent of a group – cannot exceed £7 million immediately before any share issue and £8 million immediately after that issue. It must either carry on a qualifying trade, or be the parent company of a qualifying trading group.

The rules about not being controlled by another company, qualifying subsidiaries and the company carrying on the trade must be met for a stated period. Otherwise the investors will lose their reliefs.

It was proposed in the March 2011 budget that the following changes would take place to Enterprise Investment Schemes with effect from April 2012:

- The maximum annual EIS investment limit for individual investors to increase from £500,000 to £1 million.
- The qualifying company limits for both EIS and VCT to change from 50 employees with gross assets of £7 million to 250 employees with gross assets of £15 million.
- The maximum investment a company can accept from EISs and VCTs to increase from £2 million to £10 million.

11.2   VENTURE CAPITAL TRUSTS (VCTs)

Venture capital trusts (VCTs) are companies listed on the London Stock Exchange and are similar to investment trusts. They are designed to enable individuals to invest indirectly in a range of small higher-risk trading companies whose shares and securities are not listed on a recognised stock exchange, by investing through VCTs.

Investment in VCTs attracts special tax advantages and so the companies need to gain HMRC approval to be treated as such. Once approved, VCTs are exempt from corporation tax on any gains arising on the disposal of their investments. Investors may also be entitled to various income tax and capital gains tax reliefs.

As noted, venture capital trusts are structured so as to provide investors with preferential tax treatment in a number of ways; this is intended to encourage individuals to provide capital to smaller, start-up companies which might otherwise be unable to find the funding to grow – and to do so through a vehicle which provides the investor with:

- some incentives (the tax relief); and
- a measure of protection (the diversification of a collective investment).

The tax reliefs are only available to individuals aged 18 years or over, and cannot be claimed by trustees or companies (although there is nothing to stop such investors from holding shares in a VCT).

In terms of **income tax**, investors benefit from the following:

- Exemption from income tax on dividends from ordinary shares in VCTs (**dividend relief**);
- **Income tax relief** at the rate of 30% of the amount subscribed for shares issued from the tax year 2006/07 or later. For earlier issues, the rate is 40%. The shares issued must have been **new** ordinary shares, and must not carry any preferential rights. They must be held for at least five years (three years if they were issued before April 2006).
- The relief for dividend income and gains applies whether the shares were acquired at issue or subsequently via a stock exchange trade. The income tax relief is only available for initial subscriptions.

This tax relief can be set against any income tax liability that is due, whether at the lower, basic or higher rate.

There are two capital gains tax reliefs from which investors can benefit:

*   No capital gains tax on any gain made when the investor disposes of his VCT shares.
*   For investors having bought shares issued before 6 April 2004, gains on disposals may in some cases be postponed to a later year. Which may suit the investor better, for example if his circumstances change so that he is now in a lower tax bracket. This is called **deferral relief**.

Deferral relief is not available in respect of investments in shares issued after 5 April 2004. **Dividend relief** and **disposal relief** are available on both newly issued shares and second-hand shares (ie, those bought on the Stock Exchange – the secondary market). **Income tax relief** (and, for shares issued before 6 April 2004) **deferral relief**, can be claimed only for purchases of new shares. Conditions have to be met, and the reliefs can be lost or withdrawn if they are not.

11.2.1 Performance Characteristics (Risk versus Reward)

VCTs can provide very rewarding opportunities for investors – in part because start-up and developmental/growth companies can, in the right conditions, produce significant growth, and in part because the gains and income are not subject to the same **tax drag** as less favourably treated investments.

However, because of their nature they also involve a high level of risk. For example:

*   The companies in which VCTs invest are not listed and so it may be difficult for the VCT to sell them, in order to take advantage of better opportunities. There is a liquidity risk.
*   These smaller companies may be more vulnerable to downturns in the markets or the economy. Their share prices may be disproportionately affected by market sentiment. They may also (especially if they have high levels of borrowing) be very sensitive to changes in interest rates.
*   In some, but not all, cases they may have relatively young and inexperienced management teams and their lack of track record may mean that the best decisions are not always taken.

11.2.2 Discounts and Premiums

As with ordinary investment trusts, shares in VCTs are traded on the stock market and their prices are thus determined by supply and demand. Their prices will therefore trade at a discount or premium to the VCT's net asset value, as based on a valuation of the holdings in its underlying portfolio.

12. DISTRIBUTOR INFLUENCED FUNDS (DIFs) AND BROKER FUNDS

LEARNING OBJECTIVE

5.9.1 Understand the main types, purposes, structure and arrangement, tax treatment and investment characteristics of: broker funds; distributor influenced funds

5.9.2 Analyse the key features, relative merits and limitations of investing in a broker- or distributor-influenced fund compared with other forms of direct and indirect investment: roles and responsibilities of underlying parties; fee structure; expenses and commissions; tax characteristics; investment performance and risk; other risks – distributor power and expertise, conflicts of interest, suitability; secondary market liquidity

12.1 DISTRIBUTOR-INFLUENCED FUNDS (DIFs)

Distributor-influenced funds are becoming an increasingly common feature of the retail investment landscape and are created for the clients of a particular distributor – typically an adviser firm. Put simply, these are funds that can be created by an adviser firm for its client base and in which the firm has a role in fund governance but where fund management and administration are outsourced to third parties. They could be designed on a bespoke basis for the distributor or they could be set up using an existing fund that is tailored for the distributor. Fund administration and management is outsourced to other firms but the distributor may have a degree of influence over the fund (short of day-to-day asset selection). It may be, for example, that the distributor is able to:

- influence the hiring (or removal) of the delegated investment manager;
- create accountability of the investment adviser by attending investment committees; or
- appoint (or remove) the authorised corporate director.

They are commonly arranged as OEICs (where they may be known as broker OEICs or distributor-owned funds) and are often multi-manager funds, but they may also take other structures (like insurance funds). We have chosen to refer to them as distributor-influenced funds in this workbook, as this term covers the full range of possible structures.

They come somewhere in the fund spectrum between broker funds and independent, third-party funds.

12.2 BROKER FUNDS

Broker funds are set up by firms of independent financial advisers (IFAs) and managed by life insurance companies or unit trust managers. The fund management company provides the IFA with its **own** fund, the broker fund, which can even be in that IFA's name. It holds the assets but the IFA tells the company how the cash should be invested.

The IFA will typically receive a fee for placing the money in a broker fund. The management company may then charge up to 1.5% a year for managing the money.

13. DERIVATIVES

LEARNING OBJECTIVE

5.10.1   Understand the purposes, structure and risk/reward characteristics of the main types of financial derivatives pertaining to each main asset class: futures; forward contracts; options; warrants; contracts for differences

5.10.2   Understand the effects of implementing simple derivatives strategies for the purposes of hedging or speculation in terms of: risk transfer and risk/reward payoff; transaction costs and margin; ease of implementation and unwinding

Derivatives include such instruments as options, futures and contracts for differences. They can be used in a variety of ways – both to mitigate risk within an investment portfolio (hedging), and to increase risk by speculating on the direction of the market. Consequently derivatives should be regarded as specialist investments to be used only by experienced clients, where the risks of using them are fully understood and accepted.

Derivatives have a major role to play in the investment management of many large portfolios and investment funds, and are used for hedging, anticipating future cash flows, asset allocation change and arbitrage. Hedging is a technique employed by portfolio managers to reduce the impact of adverse price movements. For example, if a portfolio manager expects to receive a large inflow of cash to be invested in a particular asset, then futures can be used to fix the price at which it will be bought and offset the risk that prices will have risen by the time the cash flow is received. Changes to the asset allocation of a fund, whether to take advantage of anticipated short-term directional market movements or to implement a change in strategy, can be made more swiftly and economically using futures than by adjusting the underlying portfolio.

Arbitrage is the process of deriving a risk-free profit from simultaneously buying and selling the same asset in two different markets, where a price difference between the two exists. If the price of a derivative and its underlying asset are mismatched, then the portfolio manager may be able to profit from this pricing anomaly.

Derivatives are also used for speculation. Since only initial margin, and not the full notional value of the contract, is payable by the counterparties at the point of opening their respective positions, futures provide an ideal means by which to speculate on both rising and falling asset prices in a range of markets.

13.1   FUTURES

Derivatives are not a new concept – they have been around for hundreds of years. Their origins can be traced back to agricultural markets where farmers needed a mechanism to guard against price fluctuations caused by gluts of produce and drought. So, in order to fix the price of agricultural produce in advance of harvest time, farmers and merchants entered into **forward contracts**.

These set the price at which a stated amount of a commodity will be delivered between a farmer and a merchant (termed the **counterparties**) at a pre-specified future time.

These early derivative contracts introduced an element of certainty into commerce and gained immense popularity. They led to the opening of the world's first derivatives exchange in 1848, the Chicago Board of Trade (CBOT).

The exchange soon developed a **futures contract** that enabled **standardised** qualities and quantities of grain to be traded for a fixed future price on a stated delivery date. Unlike the forward contracts that preceded it, the futures contract could itself be traded. These futures contracts were subsequently extended to a wide variety of commodities and offered by an ever-increasing number of derivatives exchanges.

It was not until 1975 that CBOT introduced the world's first **financial futures** contract. This set the scene for the exponential growth in product innovation and the volume of futures trading that soon followed.

13.1.1 Characteristics of Futures

A future is an agreement between a buyer and a seller. The buyer agrees to pay a pre-specified amount for the delivery of a particular quantity of an asset at a future date. The seller agrees to deliver the asset at the future date, in exchange for the pre-specified amount of money. A futures contract is, therefore, a legally binding obligation between two parties for one to buy and the other to sell a pre-specified amount of an asset at a pre-specified price on a pre-specified future date.

EXAMPLE

A buyer might agree with a seller to pay US$75 per barrel for 1,000 barrels of crude oil in three months.

The buyer might be an electricity-generating company wanting to fix the price it will have to pay for the oil to use in its oil-fired power stations, and the seller might be an oil company wanting to fix the sales price of some of its future oil production.

In the example, the oil quality will be based on the oil field from which it originates (eg, Brent Crude, from the Brent oil field in the North Sea). The quantity is 1,000 barrels, the date is three months ahead and the location might be the port of Rotterdam.

Not all futures contracts require **physical delivery** of the underlying asset. Most commodity contracts are settled physically, while financial futures are instead settled between the counterparties by cash on the monetary gain or loss to date. These are known as **contracts for differences (CFDs)**.

The terms and conditions of a futures contract are standardised so that they can be traded on a derivatives exchange. Standardising the terms allows one investor to sell their future to another and so provide liquidity to the market. These standardised terms are known as **contract specifications**.

A futures contract, in summary, has two distinct features:

*   It is **exchange-traded** – for example on the derivatives exchanges like Liffe or the International Petroleum Exchange (IPE).
*   It is dealt on **standardised terms** – the exchange specifies the quality of the underlying asset, the quantity underlying each contract, the future date and the delivery location. Only the price is open to negotiation.

Derivatives markets have specialised terminology that it is important to understand.

*   **Long** – the alternative way to describe the buyer of the future. The long is committed to buying the underlying asset at the pre-agreed price on the specified future date.
*   **Short** – the alternative way to describe the seller of the future. The short is committed to delivering the underlying asset in exchange for the pre-agreed price on the specified future date.
*   **Open** – the initial trade. A market participant opens a trade when they first enter into a future. They could be buying a future – opening a long position, or selling a future – opening a short position.
*   **Underlying** – the underlying asset drives the value of the future and is usually referred to as the underlying security or cash asset.
*   **Basis** – basis quantifies the difference between the cash price of the underlying asset and the futures price.
*   **Delivery Date** – this is the date on which the agreed future transaction takes place and so represents the end of the future's life.
*   **Close** – the buyer of a future can either hold the future to expiry and take delivery of the underlying asset or sell the future before the expiry date. The latter is known as closing out the position.

Staying with the example above, the buyer of the contract to purchase 1,000 barrels of crude oil at US$75 per barrel for delivery in three months is said to go **long** of the contract, whilst the seller is described as going **short**. Entering into the transaction is known as **opening the trade** and the eventual delivery of the crude oil will **close out** the trade.

Most futures that are opened do not end up being delivered; they are closed out instead.

An opening buyer will avoid delivery by making a closing sale before the delivery date. If the buyer does not close out, he will pay over the agreed sum and receive the underlying asset. This may be something the buyer is keen to avoid, for example, because the buyer is actually a financial institution simply speculating on the price of the underlying asset using futures.

13.1.2 The Risk/Reward Profile of Futures

As we saw above, the **buyer** of the future is described as **going long**. In other words, the buyer is agreeing to take delivery of the underlying asset and hopes that the price of the underlying asset will rise.

As the diagram below shows, the long futures position makes money in a rising market and loses money in a falling market.

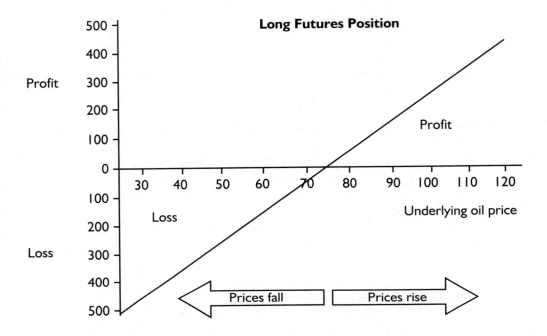

The **seller** of the future on the other hand is taking a short position. In other words, the seller is undertaking to make delivery of the underlying asset and hopes that the price of the underlying asset will fall. As the diagram on the next page shows, the short futures position hopes to make money in a falling market and loses money in a rising market.

As you can see, the long and short positions are mirror images of each other, so that if the long position gains then the short position loses. For this reason, futures contracts are often referred to as a zero sum game.

Given that futures are highly geared instruments, if the market moves against the speculator, then losses can mount up very quickly. Indeed, following several high-profile disasters involving derivatives, most non-practitioners tend to think of futures solely as speculative instruments, used in the pursuit of making quick profits, despite evidence to the contrary.

Whatever the perception, speculation *per se* should not be discouraged as, apart from adding to market liquidity, or brisk two-way trade, in futures contracts, without speculators, those wishing to use futures to hedge risk would be unable to do so.

13.2 OPTIONS

The growth of options can be traced to the work of two US academics – Fischer Black and Myron Scholes – who produced the Black-Scholes option-pricing model in 1973.

Until then, options contracts could not easily be priced, which prevented them from being traded. This model, however, paved the way for the creation of standardised options contracts and the opening of the Chicago Board Options Exchange (CBOE) in the same year.

This in turn led to an explosion in product innovation and the creation of other options exchanges, such as LIFFE. Options can still be traded off-exchange, or over-the-counter (OTC), in much the same way as forward contracts, where the contract specification determined by the parties is bespoke.

13.2.1 Characteristics of Options

An option gives a buyer the **right, but not the obligation**, to buy or sell a specified quantity of an underlying asset at a pre-agreed exercise price, on or before a pre-specified future date or between two specified dates. The seller, in exchange for the payment of a **premium**, grants the option to the buyer.

As with futures, options have their own terminology that it is important to understand:

- **Call option** – an option that gives the buyer the right, but not the obligation, to buy an underlying asset.
- **Put option** – an option that gives the buyer the right, but not the obligation, to sell an underlying asset.
- **Holder** – the term used to describe the buyer of the option, ie, the person who has bought it. It is also referred to as the long position.
- **Writer** – the term used to describe the seller of an option. It is also referred to as the short position.
- **Premium** – the term used to describe the price paid for an option.
- **Strike price** – the price at which the underlying asset may be bought or sold. Also referred to as the **exercise price**.
- **At-the-money** – a call option whose strike price is the same as the current price of the underlying asset.
- **In-the-money** – a call option whose strike price is below the current price of the underlying asset and which could therefore be exercised for a profit.
- **Out-of-the-money** – a call option whose strike price is above the current price of the underlying asset and so, if exercised, will result in a loss.
- **Expiry date** – the last day of the option's life.
- **European style** – an option that may be exercised on its expiry date only.
- **American style** – an option that may be exercised at any time during its life up to and including the expiry date.

The two parties to an options contract are the holder and the writer. The writer confers the right, rather than the obligation, to the holder to either buy or sell an asset at a pre-specified price in exchange for the holder paying a premium for this right. This premium represents a fraction of the cost of the asset or the notional value of the contract. Options, therefore, differ from futures in that a right is conferred in exchange for the payment of a premium.

As the holder is in possession of a right, rather than an obligation, the holder does not have to exercise this right if the transaction ultimately proves not to work in their favour. The option can simply be abandoned with the loss of the premium paid. The writer, however, is obliged to satisfy this right if taken up, or exercised, against them by the holder. Potentially the writer has an obligation to deliver the asset to the holder of a call option at the exercise price if the option is exercised. Alternatively, the writer could be required to take delivery from the holder of a put option if exercised.

All the holder can lose is the premium paid. As a result, only the writer is required to make initial and variation margin payments to the clearing house.

Most exchange-traded financial options are cash-settled rather than physically settled. Therefore, if exercised, the cash difference between the exercise price of the option and that of the underlying asset, rather than the asset itself, passes from the writer to the holder.

13.2.2 At-the-Money, In-the-Money and Out-of the-Money

The definition of the above terms was considered in Section 13.2.1. We will expand on this by looking at how this relates to a call and a put option.

Call Option

Assume an investor buys a call option on ABC shares at a premium of 10p and an exercise price of 100p.

The diagram shows:

1. **Out-of-the-money** – if the underlying share price is below 100p, the holder will abandon the option and lose the 10p premium.
2. **In-the-money** – if the underlying share price is above 100p, the holder will exercise the option.
3. **At-the-money** – the underlying share price is the same as the exercise price.
4. **Break even** – if at expiry the underlying share price is 110p, the holder will break even as it costs 100p to buy shares plus the premium of 10p.

Put Option

Assume an investor buys a put option on ABC shares for a premium of 60 which can be exercised at 200. The position will instead look as follows:

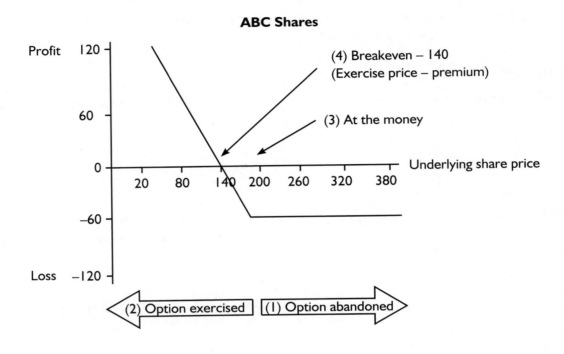

ABC Shares

1. **Out-of-the-money** – if the underlying share price is above 200p, then the holder will abandon the option.
2. **In-the-money** – if the underlying share price is less than 140p, the holder can exercise their option to sell at 200p.
3. **At-the-money** – the underlying share price is the same as the exercise price.
4. **Break even** – if, at expiry, the underlying share price is 140p, the holder can buy the shares in the open market and exercise the option to sell at 200p. Profit of 60p is offset by premium of 60p.

13.2.3 Option Strategies

In this section, we will consider four basic option strategies by looking at a call and put option from the perspective of the holder and the writer (seller).

Call Options

Buyers of a call option take a long call position, while the writer of the same option takes the opposite short call position. Using the same example as before, the buyer of a call pays a premium of 10p for the right to buy the underlying shares at expiry.

ABC Shares

The higher the price of the underlying shares, the more profit the buyer will make and vice versa. The potential risks and rewards for the **long call position** are:

- The maximum profit is unlimited.
- The maximum loss for the buyer is limited to the premium paid, as they can simply abandon the option.

The writer of the option clearly has a different perspective on the transaction. In return for writing the option, the seller of the option receives the premium and is hoping that the underlying share price will not rise and so the holder will not exercise the option but instead abandon it, leaving the writer with the premium.

The higher the price of the underlying asset, the more loss the writer of the option will make. As a result, potential risks and rewards for the **short call position** are:

- The maximum profit is the premium.
- The maximum loss for the writer is unlimited.

Put Options

Buyers of a put option take a long put position, while the writer of the same option takes the opposite short put position. With a put option, the buyer pays a premium for the right to sell the underlying asset on expiry if they wish. The more the price of the underlying asset falls, the more profit the buyer will make.

The potential risks and rewards for the **long put position** are:

- The maximum profit is the strike price less the premium paid.
- The maximum loss for the buyer is limited to the premium paid as they can simply abandon the option.

The seller of the put option will receive the premium but takes on the obligation to buy the underlying asset at expiry. From the perspective of the writer, therefore, they are hoping that the share price will not fall as expected and so the buyer will abandon the option, leaving them with the premium. As a result, potential risks and rewards for the **short put position** are:

- The maximum profit is the premium.
- The maximum loss for the writer is the strike price less the premium.

13.2.4 Option Premiums

The premium for an option is made up of its intrinsic value and its time value.

- **Intrinsic value** – this is the difference between the exercise price and the current share price.
- **Time value** – an option with a long time to expiry will have a greater amount of time value incorporated into its price, so that the longer the period, the greater will be the time value.
- **American-style** options can be exercised at any time before the contract expires while **European-style** options can only be exercised after the contract expires. As a result of this flexibility in exercise awarded, American-style options are more expensive than European options.

We can consider this by looking at a simple example.

EXAMPLE

A call option with the right to buy at 90 is trading at 30 when the underlying is trading at 100. The intrinsic value is 10 and the time value is the remaining 20.

In practice, the option premium will be affected by many factors including:

- **The underlying asset price** – the higher the asset price, the more valuable are call options and the less valuable are put options.
- **The exercise price** – the higher the exercise price, the less valuable are call options and the more valuable are put options.
- **Time to maturity** – the longer the term of the option, then generally the greater the chance of the option expiring in-the-money; therefore, the higher the time value and the higher the premium.
- **Volatility of the underlying asset price** – the more volatile the price of the underlying asset, the greater the chance of the option expiring in-the-money; therefore, the higher the premium.

There are two other factors that will affect the option premium: the income yield on the underlying asset, and short-term interest rates. It should be noted that their effects on option prices are fairly minor in relation to the other factors.

- **Income yield of the underlying asset** – the greater the income yield of the underlying asset, the greater the sacrifice being made by the call option holder by not holding this asset, but the greater the benefit to the put option holder. Therefore, the higher the income yield, the more valuable the put option and the less valuable the call option.
- **Short-term interest rates** – the higher the short-term rate of interest, the greater the interest income received by the call option holder on the cash not committed to buying the underlying asset. This makes call options more valuable. However, the outlay on a put option not earning this higher rate of interest makes put options less valuable.

13.3　WARRANTS

13.3.1 Characteristics of Warrants

Warrants are negotiable securities issued by companies which confer a right on the holder to buy a certain number of the company's ordinary shares at a preset price on or before a predetermined date.

Warrants are issued on a stand-alone basis and so, unlike convertible loan stock or preference shares, the conversion right contained within the warrant is traded separately.

Although these are essentially long-dated call options, they are traded on the London Stock Exchange (LSE) and if exercised result in the company issuing additional equity shares. The warrants market is relatively small.

Given the terms of the warrant issue, the conversion premium or discount can be calculated. The basis for calculating the conversion premium follows the same principles as we considered in Chapter 1 for convertible preference shares and convertible bonds.

13.3.2 Covered Warrants

Covered warrants are warrants in a company's shares issued by an organisation other than the company itself – they are also called securitised derivatives. Issuers cover their issues by either shares in the company or warrants issued by the company. Investment banks usually issue covered warrants in a different denomination or a different currency from the underlying share.

When the holder of a covered warrant exercises their right to buy the shares, they are exercising it against the issuer of the covered warrant rather than the company itself. Covered warrants are well established in most international markets but have only been available in the UK since 2002 and are traded on the London Stock Exchange.

A covered warrant gets its name from the fact that when issued, the issuer will usually buy the underlying asset in the market (ie, they are **covered** if they should need to deliver the underlying shares, and not exposed to the risk of having to buy them in the market at a higher price.

Covered warrants are issued by a number of leading investment banks and can be based on individual stocks, indices, currencies or commodities. They can be either leveraged, as with individual stock options, or unleveraged, as with commodities.

As with an option, a covered warrant gives the holder the right to buy or sell an underlying asset at a specified price, on or before a predetermined date. There are both call and put warrants available.

A covered warrant does not carry an obligation to buy or sell, so that an investor's maximum loss is restricted to their initial investment. Investors can buy and sell either call or put warrants daily on the LSE.

13.4   CONTRACTS FOR DIFFERENCE

As mentioned earlier, not all futures contracts require physical delivery of the underlying asset. Most commodity contracts are settled physically, while financial futures are instead settled between the counterparties by cash on the monetary gain or loss to date. These are known as contracts for differences (CFDs).

14. HEDGE FUNDS

LEARNING OBJECTIVE

5.11.1   Analyse the key features, relative merits and limitations of investing in hedge funds compared with other forms of direct and indirect investment: main types of hedge fund; regulatory environment; investment risk; use of short and long positions; custody and safe keeping practices; limitations in respect of voting capital; funds of hedge funds (FOHFs)

The term **hedge fund** is a very wide one, with no precise legal definition. In general it is taken to mean a type of fund which can engage in a wide range of investment strategies, many of them outside the strategies permitted for authorised schemes.

Hedge funds are often unregulated, although their operators (eg, the fund manager) will be authorised by the FSA if they are in the UK. Within the hedge fund **universe**, there are a variety of recognised strategies – for example, **absolute return funds** see Section 14.1) are those which aim to provide a positive return, regardless of the direction of the markets (it is quite common for such a fund to have the objective of outperforming one of the risk-free assets we looked at earlier. For example, a fund might have the objective of outperforming the return on three-month Treasury bills by a set percentage).

Hedge funds can have a higher level of risk than traditional assets, but they also have the potential for higher returns. Their performance can often be uncorrelated to other asset classes for long periods of time. However, when a major event or shock occurs in the financial markets the correlation returns to other asset classes and can increase markedly, which was the case during the recent financial crisis.

Many hedge funds have high initial investment sizes so access is effectively restricted to wealthy individuals and institutions. However, investors can also gain access to hedge funds through funds of hedge funds.

14.1   HEDGE FUND CHARACTERISTICS

The common aspects of hedge funds are:

- **Structure** – most hedge funds are established as unauthorised or unregulated collective investment schemes. They cannot be generally marketed to private individuals because they are considered too risky for the less financially sophisticated investor.
- **High minimum investment** – most hedge funds require minimum investments in excess of £50,000; some exceed £1 million.
- **Investment flexibility** – because of the lack of regulation, hedge funds are able to invest in a wider range of assets (subject to compliance with the restrictions in their constitutional documents and prospectus). In addition to being able to take long and short positions in securities, some take positions in commodities and currencies. Their investment style is generally aimed at producing **absolute** returns.
- **Gearing** – many hedge funds use leverage and derivatives with the aim of enhancing their returns.

- **Liquidity** – to maximise the hedge fund manager's investment freedom, hedge funds usually impose an initial **lock-in** period of between one and three years before investors can sell their investments.
- **Cost** – hedge funds typically levy performance-related fees which the investor pays if certain performance levels are achieved, otherwise charging a fee comparable to that charged by other growth funds. Performance fees can be substantial, with 20% or more of the **net new highs** being common.
- **Low correlation to world securities markets** – despite the greater concentration of their portfolio holdings, hedge funds, when combined with conventional portfolios, may provide additional diversification owing to their lower correlation with world equity and bond markets.
- **Performance-related fees** – hedge funds typically levy an annual management fee of 2% in addition to a performance-related fee of about 20% if an absolute performance target in excess of the risk-free rate of return is met or exceeded and previous losses have been recovered.
- **Manager investment** – hedge fund managers generally invest some of their own wealth into their funds. This can reinforce the alignment of manager and investor interests.
- **Dealing** – many hedge funds impose an initial lock-in period of between one and three years before investors may deal in the hedge fund's shares. Any dealing that subsequently takes place is then usually only permitted at the end of each month or quarter.
- **Regulation** – hedge funds are usually domiciled in an offshore financial centre such as the Cayman Islands or Dublin, and usually subject to a lighter regulatory regime.

14.2 HEDGE FUND STRATEGIES

Each hedge fund strategy aims to take advantage of a particular investment opportunity. Hedge fund strategies are often characterised by an investment style. A brief outline of styles is given below.

- **Equity market neutral** – takes both long and short positions in equities (undervalued and overvalued securities) and thus neutralises the exposure to market risk.
- **Convertible arbitrage** – exploits price anomalies in convertible securities (convertible bonds, warrants and convertible preferred stock). Mispriced securities are identified and then bought or sold. Simultaneously the associated risks are hedged with an offsetting purchase/sale of the underlying stock.
- **Fixed income arbitrage** – a portfolio of fixed income securities is created from mispriced securities (overvalued and undervalued). Since both long and short positions are created in the fund, the net market direction is then neutralised.
- **Distressed securities** – invest in companies that are close to bankruptcy on the view that the companies will be turned around.
- **Merger arbitrage** – in a deal arbitrage play, after an announcement, the fund manager will create a position that seeks to extract more of a deal premium from a merger and acquisition situation. One common trade is to purchase the target company stock while selling the bidder company.
- **Hedged equity** – also termed long-short funds. Long or net short bets are taken on equities. The long or short exposures are based on the managers' identification of overvalued and undervalued securities. Portfolios are not structured to be direction-neutral as with equity-market-neutral funds. However, based on the positions existing within the portfolio, the net exposure may have a long or short bias.
- **Global Macro** – takes views on global macro-trends and concentrate on major market trends. The hedge fund uses derivatives to gain exposure to the trends identified. Managed futures funds are often classified as global macro funds.

- **Emerging markets** – seeks out profitable investment opportunities in emerging or less developed markets. Often the absence of derivatives products and short-selling restrictions mean that the funds in this category are long in the underlying securities.
- **Fund-of-Funds (FOFs)** – the fund invests in a portfolio of hedge funds. The FOF provides some interesting and unique benefits that are not found with other strategies. FOFs were created to allow easier access to smaller investors:
    - **Economies of scale** – a single investment in a hedge fund could cost an investor several hundred thousand pounds. With the same amount of money, indirect investment into multiple hedge funds is possible in a FOF. Further, a hedge fund company may provide their client with access to other hedge funds in their portfolio that are closed to new clients.
    - **Diversification** – since many hedge fund returns are uncorrelated, the investment in a FOF may provide a larger diversified portfolio.
    - **Expertise** – the hedge fund industry is less regulated than the mutual fund industry. Hedge fund managers working in this industry will have specialist skills, expertise and access to vital proprietary information that even professional money managers in traditional mutual fund sectors may not have.
    - **Transparency** – the hedge fund industry is secretive, and for an institutional investor carrying out due diligence in a hedge fund, this process may use up significant resources. Investing in a FOF could overcome this problem as the FOF manager will perform due diligence on each of the hedge funds in its portfolio.

14.3   HEDGE FUND RISKS

Specific risks of hedge funds include:

- gearing is used widely;
- settlement is OTC;
- currency risk;
- dealing delays;
- illiquid investments;
- lack of transparency;
- fraud;
- lack of independent trustee boards.

As shown, hedge funds are reputed to be high-risk. However, in many cases, this perception stands at odds with reality. In their original incarnation, hedge funds sought to reduce market risk. That said, there are now many different styles of hedge fund – some risk-averse, and some employing highly risky strategies. It is, therefore, not wise to generalise about them.

The most obvious market risk is the same risk that is faced by an investor in shares – as the broad market moves down, the investor's shares also fall in value.

As an absolute return fund, the hedge fund often uses **leverage**, especially in arbitrage-style strategies. This form of flexibility essential for amplifying the impact of the strategy can create unique risks. In a hedge fund, leverage may be created through any of the following ways:

- Borrowing funds to create a larger position or sell short more securities than the original capital put in to the security.
- Borrowing through a margin account.

- Using derivatives (eg, futures and options) that require initial margins to gain market exposure. The margin posted will be a fraction of the full cost that is required if the underlying security was purchased in the spot market.

14.4 ABSOLUTE RETURN FUNDS (ARFs)

LEARNING OBJECTIVE

5.12.1 Analyse the key features, relative merits and limitations of investing in absolute return funds compared with other forms of direct and indirect investment: structure; income and capital growth; investment risk and return; expenses; capital protection; monitoring performance versus benchmark

An absolute return objective for an investment is a target set to achieve a positive return in a specified timeframe irrespective of market conditions. The return is not referenced to any external benchmark. Traditional mutual funds on the other hand have a relative return objective.

Hedge funds were originally promoted as a **genre** of absolute return vehicles. As noted from the previous section, given the nature of such investments, their returns cannot be evaluated using conventional benchmark portfolios. This is because the exposure, composition and investment philosophy of the fund is often radically different from conventional mutual funds. For example, hedge funds can use derivatives and even contracts for differences (CFDs) in their investment portfolios. Their strategies are often characterised by long positions in conventional and unconventional assets, combined with short selling, trading in derivatives, arbitrage, and the use of leverage.

From a historical perspective, Alfred Winslow Jones is credited with forming the first absolute return fund in New York in 1949. At that time, the first hedge fund was a long/short hedged equity vehicle. In recent years, the money management industry has embraced the use of absolute return approaches leading to the dramatic growth of hedge funds at the turn of the century. The success of these alternative investments has prompted institutional investors (even pension funds) with conservative attitudes to investment management and policies to include hedge funds as one segment in their diversified portfolios.

Absolute return funds may be confused with hedge funds in that their composition and exposures may be modelled on hedge fund products. However, absolute return funds are not exclusive products available only to a privileged group of investors, but have recently been rolled out to smaller retail investors. Essentially they are promoted as an alternative to a hedge fund. Unlike hedge funds, they do not have to be domiciled offshore and may be fully UK-regulated.

UCITS III significantly enlarged the range of investment instruments, notably allowing some use of derivatives. This makes possible for some hedge fund managers and ARF managers to launch versions of their strategies in new UCITS III-compliant wrappers, giving more investors access. The Investment Management Association (IMA) is conducting a major review (see Section 14.4.1) of its sector classifications to take into account the ramifications of the UCITS III and the Retail Distribution Review on a wide range of funds, including growth of ARFs in the industry. The implication of this reclassification and development of sector classifications that will include derivative products by the trade body is to improve approaches to benchmark construction for monitoring fund performances.

Absolute return vehicles are evaluated relative to cash deposits, the risk-free rate or LIBOR plus a specified rate to reflect the element of alpha risk taken. For example, the returns objective for such a fund may be stated as: 'achieve 20–25% regardless of the market conditions' or 'UK LIBOR plus 10%'.

The compensation structure is similar to a hedge fund. A typical charge is made up of two parts, the management fee and an incentive fee. The management fee is worked out as a percentage of the NAV per share. For most funds this can be anywhere from 1–2% of the NAV plus an incentive fee (or performance fee) that ranges from 15–30%. On the profits, the incentive fee averages out to 20%. This '2 and 20' structure is a common charge with many funds. A number also have a high water mark. This means that if the fund declined in value in one year, then the hedge fund has to recover the loss before any incentive fee is paid.

14.4.1 Measuring Performance/Benchmarking Funds

The performance of the ARFs is variable at best. A number available in the market have long/short exposures to a selected market index or its sector. Even though two funds may be classified under the same sector their returns can be quite different. This is due not only to the variations in the make-up of portfolios, but also the directional sensitivities of the funds, due to their exposures to long and short positions. ARFs with a short-selling component were primarily designed to exploit alpha opportunities during market downturns. Such a portfolio does not perform as well in an upward-trending market as a traditional long-only portfolio.

In an effort to classify sectors for use in ARF applications, to improve transparency and performance measurement, the IMA has undertaken a review. It provides the following definition of the absolute return sector (that will be subject to modification as the industry evolves in the aftermath of the UCITS 111, leading to UCITS IV):

'Funds managed with the aim of delivering absolute (ie, more than zero) returns in any market conditions. Typically funds in this sector would normally expect to deliver absolute (more than zero) returns on a 12-month basis.'

There is no asset-based monitoring for this sector, and the IMA notes that performance comparisons are likely to be inappropriate given the diverse nature of the objectives of funds in this sector.

Advisers should note that analysis of historical performances of such funds is a specialised activity and is evolving. The information for interpretation of performances is achieved by accessing information available from the sellers of the managed funds and data providers who specialise in collecting the prices obtained from the funds and fund of funds. Transparency of information and benchmarking issues present problems. In recent years there have been growing calls from investors to provide means to monitor hedge fund performances, in the same manner that traditional mutual funds are tracked. In coming years, regulation on ARF products will improve, and this will increase transparency. Issues of benchmark selection and construction and measurement are likely to persist for a lot longer, however.

As a genre of alpha generation products, advisers should note that there are several biases that they need to be aware of when interpreting the performance data of ARFs.

As this industry does not have to adhere to a regulated performance presentation standard, biases in the historical data can make it difficult to compare the relative merits and performances of candidates, leading to a distortion of data existing in the public domain. The fund performances are overstated by biases. Further the issue is complicated by the fact that disclosure of this vital investor information by fund managers is voluntary. There are no mandatory reporting standards in place, creating three main biases:

1. **Self-selection bias** – given that disclosure of information is not mandatory, managers can decide themselves whether they wish to disclose their results to a particular service that keeps historic records. Clearly, funds performing badly may not participate and will not disclose details to a public database. Poor performers will want to keep their information out of the headlines; at the same time, high-performing and large funds may not want publicity that makes them stand out from their peer grouping.

2. **Backfill bias** – some funds joining a database may not present a complete record of their past time series of performances. Fund managers may as a result decide to start reporting only when their results reach a level that makes a positive impression on their investors. This problem is being addressed by vendor services, but can still be a source of bias for analysts trying to create a true and fair assessment of each fund manager's performance.

3. **Survivorship bias** – in the industry, unsuccessful funds disappear and are dropped out of indices. Only successful funds remain and present their records over a longer time period. This history of results gives the wrong impression about fund performances into the future.

15. STRUCTURED PRODUCTS

LEARNING OBJECTIVE

5.13.1 Analyse the key features, relative merits and limitations of investing in retail structured products and investment notes compared with other forms of direct and indirect investment: structure; income and capital growth; investment risk and return; expenses; capital protection; counterparty risk.

A structured product is generally a pre-packaged investment which is based on derivatives, a single security, a basket of securities, options, indices, commodities, debt issuances and/or foreign currencies, and to a lesser extent swaps. They are primarily innovations designed to fulfil highly customised return/risk objectives. The variety of products just described is demonstrative of the fact that there is no single, uniform definition of a structured product. A feature of some structured products is a **principal guarantee** function which offers protection of the principal if held to maturity.

Structured products can be used as an alternative to a direct investment, as part of the asset allocation process to reduce risk exposure of a portfolio, or to ride the current market trend. The risks associated with many structured products, especially those products that present risks of loss of principal due to market movements, are similar to those risks involved with options.

Even in the case of a **principal-protected** product, they are only insured by the issuer, and thus they have a counterparty risk attached to them. Some firms have attempted to create a new market for structured products that are no longer trading. These securities may not be trading due to issuer bankruptcy or a lack of liquidity to insure them.

15.1   TYPES OF STRUCTURED PRODUCT

Retail structured products fall into the following categories:

Principal-Protected Investments (Investment Returns without Principal at Risk)

A principal-protected investment may be appropriate for investors unwilling to risk their principal or who have long-term financial obligations. These investments generally offer a return at maturity linked to as a broad-based equity index or a qualified basket of stocks. Investors typically give up a portion of the equity appreciation in exchange for principal protection. Maturities often range from five to seven years, and clients should intend to hold the investments to maturity.

Buffer Zone Investments (Limited Downside Protection)

A buffer zone investment may be appropriate for an investor who is comfortable taking some downside risk but would like a **buffer** to mitigate or moderate losses. In exchange for risking their principal, the investor will have greater upside potential relative to a fully principal-protected investment. In general, buffer zone investments can be structured to have a shorter maturity than principal-protected investments, often between two and four years.

Return-Enhanced Investments (Leveraged Upside in a Moderately Bullish Market)

If an investor believes that market returns are likely to be flat to slightly up over the near-term, a return-enhanced investment may be an ideal investment vehicle. In exchange for accepting full downside exposure in the underlying, a return-enhanced investment offers double or triple the equity returns up to a prespecified maximum. Return-enhanced investments tend to have maturities of one to three years.

Income-Based Investments

Other types of income-based investment offer varying degrees of principal-protection, and are primarily focused on generating one or more coupon payments during the term of the investment.

Strategic Access Investments

At times an investor may wish to have exposure to a fairly inaccessible index or to a complicated and expensive trading strategy.

Hybrid Investments

Other possible investments include equities, currencies, commodities and fixed income. These innovative investments enable investors to take investment views simultaneously across several asset classes.

The following are examples of how structured products could work in practice.

EXAMPLE – PRINCIPAL-PROTECTED INVESTMENTS

Investor **A** wants to preserve their principal but make money as equity markets rise. Investor **A** may consider the equity markets too risky for a direct investment, but is comfortable given the added protection of a principal-protected note. Investor **A** puts £1,000 in a seven-year principal-protected note linked to a broad-based equity index (such as the **S&P 500**, the **NASDAQ 100** or the **Dow Jones Industrial Average**) with an 80% participation in the index appreciation.

Scenario 1

The index is up 50% at maturity:

At maturity, the investor will receive their £1,000 principal back, plus 80% of the index appreciation, equal to 40%.

Scenario 2

The index is down 50% at maturity:

At maturity, because the index has declined, the investor will receive their £1,000 principal back.

EXAMPLE – BUFFER ZONE INVESTMENTS

Investor B is willing to accept a 20% buffer zone, meaning that they will begin to lose their principal if the index has declined more than 20% at maturity, in order to receive 85% participation in the index appreciation over three years. Investor B puts £1,000 in a three-year buffered equity note linked to a broad-based equity index (such as the S&P 500, the NASDAQ-100 or the Dow Jones Industrial Average) with an 85% participation in the index appreciation.

Scenario 1

The index is up 50% at maturity:

At maturity, the investor will receive their £1,000 principal back, plus 85% of the index appreciation, equal to 42.5%.

Scenario 2

The index is 15% down at maturity:

At maturity, the investor will receive their £1,000 principal back because the index is within the buffer zone.

Scenario 3

The index is 40% down at maturity:

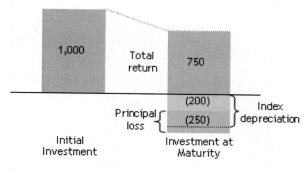

At maturity, the index is 20% below the buffer zone. The investor will lose 1.25% of their principal for each 1% the index has declined below the buffer zone, or 25% of their initial investment.

EXAMPLE – RETURN-ENHANCED INVESTMENTS

Investor C has a flat to moderately bullish market view and would like to achieve a higher return than would otherwise be possible in the current market. With a return-enhanced investment, Investor C will receive twice the appreciation in the underlying equity index as a return, subject to maximum return, or cap of 26%, at the end of two years. If the index has declined at maturity, a 1% loss in principal will occur for each 1% decline in the index. Investor C puts £1,000 in a two-year return enhanced note linked to a broad-based equity index (such as the S&P 500, the NASDAQ 100 or the DJIA).

Scenario 1

The index is up 12% at maturity:

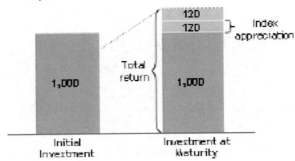

At maturity, the investor will receive their £1,000 principal back, plus double the 12% index return, equal to 24%.

Scenario 2

The index is down 12% at maturity:

At maturity, the investor will lose 1% of their investment for each 1% decline in the index.

Scenario 3

The index is up 30% at maturity:

At maturity, because the index is above the 13% upside cap, the investor will receive the maximum return of 26%.

15.2 COUNTERPARTY RISKS AND OTHER CONSIDERATIONS

The returns offered by structured products (even the principal-protected variety) are only as good as the credit quality of the issuer. Even though the cash flows and the principal in a structured product may come from a stable investment (eg, a bond), the products themselves are legally considered to be the issuer's liability. Often the products are created and sold by large global financial institutions and investment banks whose own credit rating may be less than the underlying assets held. If the issuer goes bust, then the product's principal-protected guarantee may not apply and the capital will be at risk.

Prior to the 2007/08 credit crisis, several firms that issued structured products (including Lehman Brothers) went into administration or bankruptcy during the financial crisis and could not meet their obligations. Investors in structured products had to wait along with bondholders to recover their funds invested with the banks who offered such products.

Regulatory authorities have recognised that counterparty risk was a significant issue in the post-Lehman Brothers collapse and have called for providers to describe the risks in their marketing and sales literature fully.

Structured products can be complex and may have unique characteristics that often cannot be replicated or provided by other issuers. For the investor this product differentiation creates price transparency issues. It is therefore harder to determine the intrinsic values of each competitor product in the market and to compare alternatives offered by each provider.

16. RETIREMENT PLANNING

LEARNING OBJECTIVE

5.14.1   Analyse the main types, purpose, structure and operation, tax treatment and investment characteristics of pension arrangements: defined benefit; defined contribution; personal pensions; self-invested personal pensions (SIPPs); small self-administered schemes (SSASs)

5.14.2   Analyse the key features of pension arrangements: contributions – sources, level and limits; investment selection and performance; how benefits are provided

Planning for retirement is an important element of the investment advice process – even for the youngest clients. As people live longer, and (even with rising retirement ages) face the prospect of longer periods of a possibly non-working old age, it is important that they consider the ways in which they may fund their needs as they get older. Pensions and associated products are the main retirement planning tools we will consider.

As of April 2006, a new set of pension rules were introduced, and as an adviser you will need to ensure that you are up-to-date with these, or at least in a position to refer clients to a specialist adviser in this area.

16.1   OCCUPATIONAL PENSION SCHEMES

Occupational pensions are pensions provided by an employer to its employees. They are either salary-related (also known as **defined benefit**), or money purchase (**defined contribution**).

*   **Salary-related schemes** pay a pension based on two things: the length of time the employee has been employed, and his salary. Sometimes the salary used as a reference point is his salary on retirement (a **final salary scheme**); other schemes use the employee's average salary over his time with the company. The scheme assets are looked after by trustees, who should ensure that the employer pays into the scheme regularly. Many defined benefit schemes have been phased out or closed to new members in recent years by employers, and replaced with defined contribution schemes where the risk is borne by the employee. See Chapter 6, Section 2.5.

*   **Money purchase schemes** are not directly based on the employee's salary or years of employment (though this will affect how much is paid in). Instead, an individual pension pot is built up for each employee, through contributions made by the employer and the employee – which the employee uses at retirement to convert into an income, usually by buying an annuity. The value of the employee's salary on retirement will therefore depend on:
    *   how much has been paid into the scheme over the employee's working life;
    *   how well it has performed in investment terms;
    *   what charges have been deducted; and
    *   what conditions are in the market for converting it to an income when the employee retires.

16.2   PERSONAL PENSIONS

Personal pensions are offered by commercial financial services providers, such as life companies. All personal pensions are money purchase schemes; they may be set up by a client who is arranging his pension privately – a popular option for the self-employed, or those who move between jobs regularly. Some employers also offer access to them and in this case they are not classified as occupational schemes. Personal pensions, SIPPs, group personal pensions and retirement annuity contracts are all forms of personal pension.

Again, the pension that the client will receive on retirement will depend on:

*   how much has been paid into the scheme over the individual's working life;
*   how well the scheme has performed in investment terms;
*   what charges have been deducted; and
*   what conditions are in the market for converting it to an income when the employee retires.

Stakeholder schemes are a form of personal pension which meet certain requirements, like low charges and accessible minimum contributions; they are designed to make pensions more affordable for those on lower incomes, but have also been popular with other sectors of the population on account of their apparent value for money. Like ordinary personal pensions, they are offered by commercial organisations such as life companies.

16.2.1 Annuities

People converting their pension to an annuity after 6 April 2006 now have more flexibility and choice than was previously the case – so advisers may find that some of their clients have deferred conversion, to take advantage of this. For example:

- Those in occupational money purchase schemes can **shop around** on the open market for the best annuity option for them to convert to. This may let them get considerably better value than was previously the case.
- New annuity options are available – for example, **annuity protection lump sum death benefit** is a new option which means that if the client dies before he reaches 75, his annuity does not die with him. Instead, an amount – calculated as the initial pension fund used to buy the annuity, less the income already paid from it – is paid into his estate. The payment will, however, be taxed.
- In addition to the existing alternative of **income drawdown** (also known as **unsecured pension**, an option which allows pensioners to defer converting their pension pot into an annuity for a period prior to age 75, perhaps until conditions are more favourable, by drawing on the capital of their pension fund) they can now also opt for a **short-term annuity**. This option lets them use part of their pension fund to buy a fixed-term annuity, which may be for up to five years. In the meantime the remainder of the fund stays invested in the markets. When the short-term annuity comes to an end, and depending on his view of conditions in the market at the time, the pensioner has the option to:
  - buy another short-term annuity;
  - buy a lifetime annuity;
  - move to drawdown prior to age 75;
  - switch to an **Alternative Secured Pension Fund** (ASPF) from age 75 – a way of drawing an income without converting to an annuity. The individual can draw up to 90% of the level single-life lifetime annuity he would have been able to draw from his fund, as an income. Once he is 75, he must either convert to ASPF or buy an annuity.

The Government announced in the 2010 Budget that it would scrap the requirement to purchase an annuity at age 75.

16.2.2 Small Self-Administered Schemes (SSASs)

An SSAS is a company scheme where the members are usually all company directors or key staff. A SSAS is set up by a trust deed and rules and allows members/employers greater flexibility and control over the scheme's assets.

Contributions paid to an SSAS are subject to the same rules as other registered pension schemes. Consequently there is no limit on the level of member contributions, but tax relief is restricted to the higher of £3,600 or 100% of UK earnings. Tax relief is also limited by the annual allowance.

Contributions made by the employer are also unlimited. Employer contributions are deductible against corporation tax providing that they are wholly and exclusively for the purposes of the employer's trade. If an employer's contribution is over £500,000 more than the previous year, tax relief may be spread.

Schemes with less than 12 members, and where all decisions are made unanimously or have an independent trustee, are exempt from the trustees' knowledge and understanding requirements of the Pensions Act 2004 and the member-nominated trustee requirements. If every member of the scheme is a trustee, the scheme will also be exempt from the Internal Disputes Resolution Procedure requirements.

Loans can be made to the sponsoring employer but are subject to certain conditions set by HMRC.

These include:

- The loan should not exceed 50% of the net market value of the scheme's assets.
- The loan should be secured against assets of an equal value by way of a first charge.
- The loan's terms should be no longer than five years.
- Interest of at least 1% above bank base rate should be charged on the loan.

The trustees of a SSAS can invest in a broad range of investments, including:

- commercial property and land;
- UK quoted shares, stocks, gilts and debentures;
- stocks and shares quoted on a recognised overseas stock exchange;
- futures and options quoted on a recognised stock exchange;
- OEICs, unit and investment trusts;
- hedge funds;
- insurance company funds;
- bank and building society deposits;
- gold bullion.

Shareholdings in the sponsoring employer should not exceed 5%. Shares can also be bought in more than one sponsoring employer as long the total holdings are less than 20% and shares in any one sponsoring employer are less than 5%.

There is no restriction (apart from the self-investment restrictions above) on the percentage of shares which can be held in one company.

If the scheme is deemed to be an investment-regulated pension scheme (IRPS), tax charges will apply if the scheme invests in taxable property. The definition of an IRPS includes:

- company schemes where there are less than 50 members and at least one of them (or a person related to a member) can direct, influence, or advise on investment matters relating to the scheme;
- company schemes that do not meet the above conditions but a member (or a person related to a member) can direct, influence or advise on investment matters relating to the member's arrangement.

Taxable property means investment in residential property and tangible moveable property, eg, fine wines and vintage cars.

If investments are made in taxable property, an unauthorised payment charge and a scheme sanction charge will apply. Capital gains can also apply on the sale of a taxable property.

SSASs may borrow to invest and to provide a member's benefit which has become payable. The maximum amount that can be borrowed is 50% of the net asset value of the scheme.

16.2.3 Self Invested Pension Plans (SIPPs)

SIPPS are a form of do-it-yourself pension plan that permit an investor to put their active investments into a private pension pot. They enable an investor to choose between a variety of investments, unlike other pensions, and in addition they provide the same tax advantages as other pension plans. Recent adjustments to legislation imply that SIPPs are not aimed towards those on higher incomes. Initially they were marketed to individuals with a pension fund of £200,000 or even more, but now even people with no steady income source can contribute around £3,600 into a SIPP pension.

16.3 PENSION CONTRIBUTIONS AND TAX RELIEF

There are limits on the amount of tax relief that individuals can get. The maximum amount of relief is equal to 100% of all earnings for that tax year. Although individuals can contribute to as many pension schemes as they wish, they only make contributions up to a maximum annual amount, set at £255,000 for the 2010/11 tax year. In the table below it will be noted that this maximum annual amount was reduced to £50,000 for the 2011/12 tax year. Contributions made above this limit will be subject to tax at 40%. The special annual allowance rules introduced in Finance Act 2009 were repealed in the recent budget. This new limit will not be increased by inflation until at least 2016. In addition, from April 2012 the lifetime allowance will be reduced from £1.8 million to £1.5 million.

Limits on Tax Relief – Annual Allowance Amount

Tax year	Annual allowance
2011/12	£50,000
2010/11	£255,000
2009/10	£245,000

Source: *HMRC*

Full details for transitional arrangements are given at hmrc.gov.uk/pensionschemes/annual-allowance/trans-measures.

The new lifetime allowance of £1.5 million and the £50,000 annual allowance in effect reduce the maximum annual pension that can be accumulated in final salary schemes as well as in personal pension plans and limit the rate at which they can grow. Some transitional relief is being offered as individuals can apply to retain the lifetime allowance of £1.8 million on the condition that they make no further pension saving. These rules can be complex depending upon individual circumstances and expert advice is required before making any changes to current arrangements.

KEY CHAPTER POINTS

- The net asset value of a collective is the value of its assets less its liabilities.
- OEICs pay dividends not distributions.
- Investment trusts have a closed-ended capital structure and therefore have a fixed number of shares in issue at any one time.
- The value of investment trust shares fluctuate according to supply and demand, whereas the value of the units or shares in a unit trust and OEIC are driven by the value of the underlying assets.
- Zero dividend preference shares pay no income but offer a predetermined rate of return when the investment trust is finally wound up.
- REITs pay no corporation taxes so long as they distribute 90% of their profits to shareholders as dividends.
- A fund of funds has one overall manager.
- Authorised open-ended funds can generally only borrow in certain, limited circumstances, whereas investment trusts (closed-ended vehicles) have much wider borrowing powers.
- Collective funds that invest mainly in cash deposits and interest-bearing securities pay distributions that are mostly made up of interest, and the distribution is taxed as savings income. Those investing mainly in companies make distributions that are mostly made up of dividends, and the distribution is taxed as dividend income.
- An equalisation payment is deemed to be a return of the investor's money and so is not liable to income tax.
- Capital gains made within an OEIC are exempt from tax.
- Investment trusts, provide that they comply with the relevant rules, do not pay CGT on internal gains.
- UK REITs are not subject to CGT on gains made on the disposal of property, providing that they distribute at least 90% of their profits each year to shareholders as dividends.
- Distributor funds are funds recognised by HMRC and which distribute at least 85% of their net investment income. Funds with distributor status are treated, for tax purposes, the same as UK-based funds.
- Non-distributor funds are typically those that roll up their capital gains and income. The tax treatment for UK resident investors is different and usually all gains are subject to income tax rather than capital gains tax.
- Open-ended funds may be single-priced or dual-priced.
- The dilution levy is also known as the dealing charge. It is a charge which may be imposed by the manager to cover dealing costs.
- The annual ISA investment allowance for the 2011/12 tax year is £10,680.
- Capital redemption bonds are life company products which have no life assured.
- Income tax relief is given on investments in an EIS-qualifying company subject to a minimum of £500 and a maximum of £500,000. The relief is 20% of the cost of the shares that can be set against the individual's income tax liability for the year in which the investment was made.
- VCTs are companies listed on the London Stock Exchange and are similar to investment trusts.

INVESTMENT PLANNING

This syllabus area will provide approximately 5 of the 60 examination questions

INTRODUCTION

The starting points for any investment strategy are the client's requirement for capital appreciation and/or income, the investment horizon, and the level of risk they are prepared to take in order to achieve these objectives. Once those criteria are satisfied, the adviser can then set about constructing an appropriate asset allocation to deliver the desired return.

Growth or Income

The client's requirements for capital growth or income need to be identified at the outset to ensure the correct mix of assets is used and the most appropriate funds selected. The choice of wrapper and tax consequences will also have a bearing on how the assets are invested. For example, the client's income requirements may be better met through *ad hoc* withdrawals of capital rather than recurring income payments.

Timescale

The time horizon of the client is also an important consideration. If they only require an income, then the time period may be open-ended, while clients who require capital growth may need to access some or all of their capital at a point in the future. In such circumstances, you will need to consider the liquidity and volatility of the underlying assets.

For example, if the client tells you that they need access to some of their capital in the next six months, then it is likely that an asset class that has daily liquidity and low volatility, to ensure that the capital value is preserved and accessible when needed, will be chosen. In this case, cash deposits are usually preferable.

Where the period of time is greater than six months, other fixed-interest assets may be considered.

An investment in equities may only be suitable where access is not required for five years or more. Any earlier and there is a risk that the capital value may have diminished, leaving the client with a possible shortfall.

As property can be illiquid, it should only be used for longer-term investment strategies, ie, ten years plus.

Attitude to Risk

Understanding the client's attitude to risk is a vital part of the investment decision process. A number of different methods may be used to assess how a client feels about investment risk, including questionnaires and bespoke software applications. Question-based assessments generally place clients into one of a number of risk classifications, ie, cautious, balanced, aggressive. See Chapter 7.

The combination of the client's objectives, timescale and attitude to risk is a guide to choosing a suitable asset allocation.

1.   ASSET ALLOCATION

LEARNING OBJECTIVE

6.1.1   Understand the purpose and principles of asset allocation: relationship with investment theory; achievement of performance objectives; trade-off between risk and return; stochastic modelling; active and passive management; strategic asset allocation (SAA); tactical asset allocation (TAA)

6.1.2   Understand how investment theory is applied to the process of portfolio construction

Asset allocation divides an investment portfolio among different asset classes based on an investor's financial requirements. The right mix of asset classes in a portfolio provides an investor with the highest probability of meeting their need. Each asset class selected has a long-term expected return over inflation, known as the **real** return.

Stocks and bonds are the two classic asset classes used in portfolio construction. The division between stocks and bonds is based on two factors. First, the allocation is based on the expected return that an investor requires to meet their financial objective, and second, it is based on the investor's tolerance of or capacity for risk. A successful allocation is one that achieves an investor's financial goals without so much volatility that it causes the investor to make behavioural mistakes.

Asset allocation analysis should include a correlation study between investment types. Correlation analysis shows how the price of one investment has historically moved in relation to the price of another. If two asset classes move in the same direction at the same time, they have positive correlation. If the returns have move in different directions at the same time, they have negative correlation.

Correlation is not fixed – it changes over time and in unpredictable ways. It would be ideal if two asset classes had positive real returns expectations and consistent negative return correlation with each other. Unfortunately, there are no such pairs of investments. Using historical data, it is only possible to forecast the correlation between two asset classes. See Chapter 1, Section 6.

Modern portfolio theory (MPT) is a theory of investment which tries to maximise return and minimise risk by carefully choosing different assets. Although MPT is widely used in practice in the financial industry, in recent years the basic assumptions of MPT have been widely challenged by fields such as behavioural finance. See Chapter 3, Section 3.5.

MPT is a mathematical formulation of the concept of diversification in investing, with the aim of selecting a collection of investment assets that collectively has lower risk than any individual asset. This is possible, in theory, because different types of assets often change in value in opposite ways. For example, when the prices in the stock market fall, the prices in the bond market often increase, and vice versa. A combination of both asset classes can therefore have lower overall risk than either individually.

More technically, MPT models an asset's return as a normally distributed random variable, defines risk as the standard deviation of return, and models a portfolio as a weighted combination of assets so that the return of a portfolio is the weighted combination of the assets' returns. By combining different assets whose returns are not correlated, MPT seeks to reduce the total variance of the portfolio. MPT also assumes that investors are rational and markets are efficient.

MPT was developed in the 1950s and was considered an important advance in the mathematical modelling of finance. Since then, much theoretical and practical criticism has been levelled against it. These include the fact that financial returns do not follow a Gaussian distribution and that correlation between asset classes is not fixed, but can vary depending on external events. There is also growing evidence that investors are not rational and markets are not efficient. See Chapter 3, Section 3 for a more thorough discussion of MPT.

1.1 RISK AND RETURN

MPT assumes that investors are risk-averse, meaning that, given two assets that offer the same expected return, investors will prefer the less risky one. Thus, an investor will take on increased risk only if compensated by higher expected returns. Conversely, an investor who wants higher returns must accept more risk. The exact trade-off will differ by investor based on individual risk-aversion characteristics. The implication is that a rational investor will not invest in a portfolio if a second portfolio exists with a more favourable risk/return profile – ie, if for that level of risk an alternative portfolio exists which has better expected returns.

1.2 STOCHASTIC MODELLING

Stochastic modelling is the use of historical data to model thousands of possible investment return outcomes, for almost all asset allocation combinations. Its application initially started in physics. This method allows actual or theoretical portfolios to be analysed to 'see' their risk/return profiles and determine the likely range of returns, which should be expected. These can then be matched against investors' own risk/return expectations ensuring portfolios are tailor made to individual client needs.

There are two approaches to portfolio management:

1. deterministic; and
2. stochastic.

EXAMPLE – THE DETERMINISTIC MODEL

Imagine you have to work out how many times you expect to throw heads if you flip a coin 1,000 times. The chance of throwing heads is evens, ie, 50/50. Therefore, the deterministic model of that activity is 1,000 x 50% = 500 heads.

EXAMPLE – THE STOCHASTIC MODEL

1,000 simulated coin tosses are performed, each of which has a 50/50 chance, and the number of heads is then counted and noted. You might get 487 or 505 or something else close to 500. The more simulations you run, the closer the stochastic result will get to 500, but the number simulated is also a factor that needs to be modelled and brought into account. Where the potential values are 'known' and no other variables are involved, then the outcomes (deterministic or stochastic) are virtually identical, but life and investments are not certain!

1.2.1 So Why Use Stochastic Modelling?

Where stochastic modelling comes into its own is where the outcomes are what are known as **path-dependent**.

EXAMPLE

I am building a portfolio, but also taking constant withdrawals, so the likelihood of my being able to sustain my income levels is not just affected by the impact of stock market movements, but also depends on when those falls happen. There may be on a 5% fall in one year, but there is a dramatically different impact on the sustainability of my withdrawals if that 50% fall happens in year one rather than year ten.

In this scenario, the stochastic model runs thousands of trials to chart the frequency of outcomes and thus check the robustness of this drawdown strategy.

Potential outcomes are derived from a large number of simulations (stochastic projections) which reflect the random variation in the input(s).

To achieve 20% per annum consistently for 15 years is a goal we would all aspire to. However, you would have to sell and miss the 40 worst days in the last 15 years to achieve this. By simply leaving your money invested for 15 years and not concerning yourself with buying or selling, you will achieve 1.1% per annum. By trying to get it right but actually getting the timing wrong and therefore missing some of the best days, bearing in mind that most of these best days are usually just after a fall (just after the worst days), then you rapidly reduce your annual returns.

Professionals say that trying to guess market timing never pays and these facts go some way to proving that. We should therefore spend most of our time establishing risk rating, based on the following:

- timeframe investment;
- income or growth required;
- attitude to risk;
- amount invested.

These factors will determine your risk rating, which in turn determines the asset allocation, ie, the amount required in the different asset classes to fall in line with their attitude to risk. Having established a client's asset allocation broadly in line with attitude to risk, it is still important to find the best opportunities to benefit from better-performing fund managers in each of the asset classes.

1.3   STRATEGIC ASSET ALLOCATION

In strategic asset allocation, the decisions on the portfolio mix are taken from a long-term perspective. Money managers consider both long-term client objectives as well as capital market expectations to come to this decision. This composition is called a policy portfolio and may be periodically rebalanced to adjust the portfolio to specific weights. It sets the investor's long-term exposures to systematic risk. The interpretation of **long-term** is vague as it varies with each investor. However, five years is a reasonable minimum reference point.

The policy portfolio is created by considering the long-term behaviour of a set of assets. For example, if stocks have historically returned 10% per year and bonds have returned 5% per year, a mix of 50% stocks and 50% bonds will be expected to return 7.5% per year.

1.4   TACTICAL ASSET ALLOCATION

Over the long run, a strategic asset allocation strategy may seem relatively rigid. Therefore, you may find it necessary to occasionally engage in short-term, tactical deviations from the mix in order to capitalise on unusual or exceptional investment opportunities. This flexibility adds a component of **market timing** to the portfolio, allowing you to participate in economic conditions that are more favourable for one asset class than for others.

Tactical asset allocation can be described as a moderately **active** strategy, since the overall strategic asset mix is returned to when desired short-term profits are achieved. This strategy demands some discipline, as you must first be able to recognise when short-term opportunities have run their course, and then rebalance the portfolio to the long-term asset position.

1.5   BASIC METHODS OF DIVERSIFICATION

LEARNING OBJECTIVE

6.1.3   Understand the basic ways to diversify a portfolio: asset class; geographical area; sector; currency; maturity

Diversification within the portfolio can be achieved in a number of ways including exposure to different:

*   asset classes;
*   geographical areas;
*   sectors;
*   currencies;
*   maturities.

Spreading investments across all available asset classes, eg, property, equities, cash and bonds, is the starting point for most portfolio managers. Further diversification can be achieved by spreading the exposure in a particular asset class across various geographical areas, ie, UK equities and overseas equities and emerging markets.

Sector diversification such as spreading equity exposure across manufacturing and utilities businesses can help reduce the risk of a downturn in any particular area.

Investing in various currencies can also add to the diversification of a portfolio. This may be particularly useful if the investor is based overseas.

Finally, investing in a series of fixed-interest assets with different maturities can help to limit the effects of inflation or interest rate movements on the whole portfolio. It can smooth out interest rate or investment risk.

2. INVESTMENT SELECTION

LEARNING OBJECTIVE

6.2.1   Understand the aims and characteristics of the main fund management strategies and styles: indexing or passive management; active or market timing; passive-active combinations; cash and bond fund strategies; liability driven investment (LDI); long, short and geared; sector-specific; contrarian; quantitative, trend and trading strategies

2.1   PASSIVE INVESTMENT MANAGEMENT

Passive management is seen in those collective investment funds that are described as index-tracker funds. Index-tracking, or indexation, necessitates the construction of an equity portfolio to track, or mimic the performance of a recognised equity index.

Indexation is undertaken on the assumption that securities markets are efficiently priced and cannot, therefore, be consistently outperformed. Consequently, no attempt is made to forecast future events or outperform the broader market.

Indexation techniques originated in the US in the 1970s but have since become popular worldwide.

Indexed portfolios are typically based upon a market capitalisation weighted index and employ one of three established tracking methods:

1. **Full replication** – this method requires each constituent of the index being tracked to be held in accordance with its index weighting. Although full replication is accurate, it is also the most expensive of the three methods so is only really suitable for large portfolios.
2. **Stratified sampling** – this requires a representative sample of securities from each sector of the index to be held. Although less expensive, the lack of statistical analysis renders this method subjective and potentially encourages biases towards those stocks with the best perceived prospects.
3. **Optimisation** – optimisation is a lower-cost, though statistically more complex, way of tracking an index than fully replicating it. Optimisation uses a sophisticated computer-modelling technique to find a representative sample of those securities that mimic the broad characteristics of the index tracked.

The **advantages** of employing indexation are that:

*   Relatively few active portfolio managers consistently outperform benchmark equity indices.

- Once set up, passive portfolios are generally less expensive to run than active portfolios, given a lower ratio of staff to funds managed and lower portfolio turnover.

The **disadvantages** of adopting indexation, however, include:

- Performance is affected by the need to manage cash flows, rebalance the portfolio to replicate changes in index-constituent weightings and adjust the portfolio for index promotions and demotions.
- Most indices assume that dividends from constituent equities are reinvested on the ex-dividend (xd) date, whereas a passive fund can only invest dividends when received, usually six weeks after the share has been declared ex-dividend.
- Indexed portfolios cannot meet all investor objectives.
- Indexed portfolios follow the index down in bear markets.

2.2 ACTIVE INVESTMENT MANAGEMENT

In contrast to passive equity management, active equity management seeks to outperform a predetermined benchmark over a specified time period by employing fundamental and technical analysis to assist in the forecasting of future events and the timing of purchases and sales of securities. Actively managed portfolios can be constructed on either a top-down or a bottom-up basis.

2.2.1 Top-Down Active Management

Top-down active investment management involves three stages:

- asset allocation;
- sector selection;
- stock selection.

Each of these is considered below.

Asset Allocation

Asset allocation is the result of top-down portfolio managers considering the big picture first, by assessing the prospects for each of the main asset classes within each of the world's major investment regions against the backdrop of the world economic, political and social environment.

Within larger portfolio management organisations, this is usually determined on a monthly basis by an **asset allocation committee**. The committee draws upon forecasts of risk and return for each asset class and correlations between these returns.

It is at this stage of the top-down process that **quantitative models** are often used, in conjunction with more conventional **fundamental analysis**, to assist in determining which geographical areas and asset classes are most likely to produce the most attractive risk-adjusted returns taking full account of the client's mandate.

Most asset allocation decisions, whether for institutional or retail portfolios, are made with reference to the **peer group median asset allocation**. This is known as **asset allocation by consensus** and is undertaken to minimise the risk of underperforming the peer group.

When deciding if and to what extent certain markets and asset classes should be over- or under-weighted, most portfolio managers set **tracking error**, or **standard deviation of return**, **parameters** against peer group median asset allocations, such as the **Combined Actuarial Performance Services (CAPS)** median asset allocation in the case of institutional mandates. CAPS is one of the performance measurement services that tracks the investment performance of institutional portfolios for comparison purposes.

Finally, the decision whether to **hedge** market and/or currency risks must be taken.

Recent academic studies conclude that, over the long term, asset allocation accounts for over 90% of the variation in pension fund returns.

Sector Selection

Once asset allocation has been decided upon, top-down managers then consider the prospects for sectors within their favoured equity markets. Sector selection decisions in equity markets are usually made with reference to the **weighting** each sector assumes within the **benchmark index** against which the performance in that market is to be assessed. Given the strong interrelationship between economics and investment, however, the sector selection process is also heavily influenced by economic factors, notably where in the **economic cycle** the economy is currently positioned.

Stock Selection

The final stage of the top-down process is deciding which stocks should be selected within the favoured sectors. A combination of **fundamental and technical analysis** will typically be used in arriving at the final decision.

In order to outperform a predetermined **benchmark**, usually a market index, the active portfolio manager must be prepared to assume an element of **tracking error**, more commonly known as **active risk**, relative to the benchmark index to be outperformed. Active risk arises from holding securities in the actively managed portfolio in differing proportions from that in which they are weighted within the benchmark index. The higher the level of active risk, the greater the chance of outperformance, though the probability of underperformance is also increased.

It should be noted that top-down active management, as its name suggests, is an ongoing and dynamic process. As economic, political and social factors change, so do asset allocation, sector and stock selection.

2.2.2 Bottom-Up Active Management

A bottom-up approach to active management describes one that focuses solely on the unique attractions of individual stocks. Although the health and prospects for the world economy and markets in general are taken into account, these are secondary to factors such as whether a particular company is a possible takeover target or is about to launch an innovative product, for instance.

A true bottom-up investment fund is characterised by significant **tracking error** as a result of assuming considerable active risk.

2.3   COMBINING ACTIVE AND PASSIVE MANAGEMENT

Having considered both active and passive management, it should be noted that active and passive investment strategies are not mutually exclusive. Index trackers and actively managed funds can be combined in what is known as **core-satellite management**. This is achieved by indexing, say, 70% to 80% of the portfolio's value so as to minimise the risk of underperformance, and then fine-tuning this by investing the remainder in a number of specialist actively managed funds or individual securities. These are known as the **satellites**.

The core can also be run on an **enhanced index basis**, whereby specialist investment management techniques are employed to add value. These include stock lending and anticipating the entry and exit of constituents from the index being tracked. In addition, indexation and active management can be combined within **index tilts**. Rather than hold each index constituent in strict accordance with its index weighting, each is instead marginally overweighted or underweighted relative to the index based on their perceived prospects.

2.4   BOND FUND INVESTING

The four principal strategies used to manage bond portfolios are:

- Passive, or **buy-and-hold**;
- Index-matching, or **quasi-passive**;
- Immunisation, or **quasi-active**;
- Dedicated and active.

2.4.1   Passive Bond Strategy

The passive **buy-and-hold** investor is typically looking to maximise the income-generating properties of bonds. The premise of this strategy is that bonds are assumed to be safe, predictable sources of income. Buy-and-hold involves purchasing individual bonds and holding them to maturity. Cash flow from the bonds can be used to fund external income needs or can be reinvested in the portfolio into other bonds or other asset classes.

In a passive strategy, there are no assumptions made as to the direction of future interest rates, and any changes in the current value of the bond due to shifts in the yield are not important. The bond may be originally purchased at a premium or a discount, while assuming that full par will be received upon maturity. The only variation in total return from the actual coupon yield is the reinvestment of the coupons as they occur.

On the surface, this may appear to be a lazy style of investing, but in reality passive bond portfolios provide stable anchors in rough financial storms. They minimise or eliminate transaction costs, and, if originally implemented during a period of relatively high interest rates, they have a decent chance of outperforming active strategies.

2.4.2 Indexing Bond Strategy

Indexing is considered to be quasi-passive by design. The main objective of indexing a bond portfolio is to provide a return and risk characteristic closely tied to the targeted index. While this strategy carries some of the same characteristics of the passive buy-and-hold, it has some flexibility. Just like tracking a specific stock market index, a bond portfolio can be structured to mimic any published bond index.

One also needs to consider the transaction costs associated with not only the original investment, but also the periodic rebalancing of the portfolio to reflect changes in the chosen index.

2.4.3 Immunisation Bond Strategy

This strategy has the characteristics of both active and passive strategies. By definition, **pure immunisation** implies that a portfolio is invested for a defined return for a specific period of time regardless of any outside influences, such as changes in interest rates. Similar to indexing, the opportunity cost of using the immunisation strategy is potentially giving up the upside potential of an active strategy for the assurance that the portfolio will achieve the intended desired return.

As in the buy-and-hold strategy, by design the instruments best suited for this strategy are high-grade bonds with remote possibilities of default. In fact, the purest form of immunisation is to invest in a zero-coupon bond and match the maturity of the bond to the date on which the cash flow is expected to be needed. This eliminates any variability of return, positive or negative, associated with the reinvestment of cash flows.

Duration, or the average life of a bond, is commonly referred to in immunisation, which is sometimes called duration-matching. It is a much more accurate predictive measure of a bond's volatility than maturity. This strategy is commonly used in the institutional investment environment by insurance companies, pension funds and banks to match the time horizon of their future liabilities with structured cash flows. It is one of the soundest strategies and can be used successfully by individuals. For example, just as a pension fund will use an immunisation to plan for cash flows upon an individual's retirement, that same individual could build a dedicated portfolio for their own retirement plan.

2.4.4 Active Bond Strategy

The goal of active management is maximising total return. Along with the enhanced opportunity for returns obviously comes increased risk. Some examples of active styles include interest rate anticipation, timing, valuation and spread exploitation, and multiple interest rate scenarios. The basic premise of all active strategies is that the investor is willing to make bets on the future rather than settle for what a passive strategy can offer.

2.5   LIABILITY-DRIVEN INVESTMENT (LDI)

LDI is a form of investing in which the main goal is to gain sufficient assets to meet all liabilities, both current and future.

LDIs are most prominent in the funding schemes of defined benefit pension plans, which are designed to provide a predetermined pension upon retirement. The liabilities in these funds arise as a result of the **guaranteed** pensions they are supposed to provide to members upon retirement. They can often reach into millions of pounds

In recent years, defined benefit schemes have fallen out of favour due to the significant cost involved in providing benefits to current and future members. The liabilities that the sponsoring companies and plan members must pay for has increased substantially, and this has caused some pension plans to close to new members, reduce benefits to retired members, or even shut down entirely. See Chapter 5, Section 16.

2.6   ACTIVE MARKET TIMING STRATEGY

As opposed to a passive buy-and-hold strategy, an active market timing strategy seeks to maximise returns and to minimise volatility by responding to intermediate market moves. Portfolios are positioned to take advantage of both the up-trends and the down-trends, ie, go short or long depending on conditions. Thus in theory, it is possible to make money as long as the markets are trending in one direction for a consistent period of time.

2.7   LONG/SHORT

Long/short equity is an investment strategy generally associated with hedge funds, and more recently certain progressive traditional asset managers. It involves buying long equities that are expected to increase in value and selling short equities that are expected to decrease in value. This is different from the risk reversal strategies where investors will simultaneously buy a call option and sell a put option to simulate being long in a stock.

2.8   SECTOR-SPECIFIC

A common way to diversify is through investment in various sectors of the economy. This is usually accomplished with funds that concentrate in one of the major sectors, such as natural resources or utilities.

2.8.1   What is a Sector Fund?

As the name implies, a sector fund is a collective investment fund that invests in a specific sector of the economy, such as energy or utilities. Sector funds come in many different flavours and can vary substantially in market capitalisation, investment objective (ie, growth and/or income) and class of securities within the portfolio.

- **Natural resources funds** – these funds invest in oil and gas and other energy sources, as well as timber and forestry. These funds are usually appropriate for long-term growth investors.
- **Communications funds** – these funds focus on the telecommunications sector, but can include internet-related companies as well.
- **Utility funds** – these funds invest in securities of utility companies. They are usually designed to pay steady dividends to conservative fixed-income investors, although they may have a growth element as well.
- **Financial funds** – these funds invest in the financial industry. Holdings will include securities of investment, insurance, and banking firms.
- **Healthcare funds** – these funds can cover any kind of for-profit medical institution, such as pharmaceutical companies. Many of these funds also focus on biotechnology and the companies that make pioneering advances in this industry.

- **Technology funds** – these funds seek to provide exposure in the tech sector. This sector focuses primarily on computers, electronics and other informational technology that is used in a wide range of applications.
- **Precious metals funds** – these funds provide exposure to a variety of metals, such as gold, silver, platinum, palladium and copper.

2.9   CONTRARIAN INVESTING

A contrarian investor believes that certain crowd behaviour among investors can lead to exploitable mispricings in securities markets. For example, widespread pessimism about a stock can drive a price so low that it overstates the company's risks, and understates its prospects for returning to profitability. Identifying and purchasing such distressed stocks, and selling them after the company recovers, can lead to above-average gains.

Conversely, widespread optimism can result in unjustifiably high valuations that will eventually lead to drops, when those high expectations don't pan out. Avoiding (or short-selling) investments in over-hyped investments reduces the risk of such drops.

These general principles can apply whether the investment in question is an individual stock, an industry sector, or an entire market or any other asset class.

Some contrarians have a permanent bear market view, while the majority of investors bet on the market going up. However, a contrarian does not necessarily have a negative view of the overall stock market, nor do they have to believe that it is always overvalued, or that the conventional wisdom is always wrong. Rather, a contrarian seeks opportunities to buy or sell specific investments when the majority of investors appear to be doing the opposite, to the point where that investment has become mispriced. While more **buy** candidates are likely to be identified during market declines (and vice versa), these opportunities can occur during periods when the overall market is generally rising or falling.

2.10   QUANTITATIVE INVESTMENT

Quantitative investing is a technique typically employed by the most sophisticated, technically advanced hedge funds. Computers are used to find predictable patterns within financial data. The process consists of thorough examination of vast databases searching for repeating patterns, typically positive or negative correlations among assets (**statistical arbitrage** or **pairs trading**), or price-movement patterns (**trend following** or **mean reversion**).

2.11   TREND INVESTING

Trend investing trading is a strategy that seeks to achieve gains through the analysis of an asset's price momentum either up or down. The trend investor trader enters into a long position when a stock is trending upward with successively higher highs. Vice versa, a short position is taken when the stock is in a down-trend with successively lower highs.

This investing trading strategy assumes that the present direction of the stock will continue into the future. It can be used by short-term, intermediate, or long-term investors. Regardless of their chosen time frame, investor traders will remain in their position until they believe the trend has reversed.

2.12   COSTS AND THEIR IMPACT ON INVESTMENT

LEARNING OBJECTIVE

6.2.2   Analyse and compare charges on the basis of impact, reduction in yield and total expense ratios

The impact of charges on investment funds is relatively straightforward. Higher charges reduce investment returns. In the case of initial charges, higher charges will reduce the amount of money that is actually invested in the product at the start. In the case of ongoing charges, higher charges lead to a reduction in the value of the product over time.

The higher the charges, the lower the net returns to consumers and therefore the lower the benefits to consumers from making the investment.

This is not to say that other characteristics of the product are not important; simply that, when comparing two identical funds, consumers will be better off selecting the cheaper fund, since this will ultimately lead to their having greater net returns compared with the more expensive fund.

Different types of charges also have different impacts on consumers depending on the length of time that consumers intend to invest their money. Products with high initial charges are likely to be especially costly for those customers who only hold investments for a short period of time. Products with low initial charges but high ongoing charges may end up being particularly costly for customers who hold investments for a long period of time.

Since high charges lead to consumers receiving lower net returns than they otherwise would, a failure to consider the impact of charges is likely to lead consumers to be worse off than otherwise. For these reasons, charges should, ideally, play an important role in the consumer's decision-making process.

2.12.1 Reduction in Yield (RIY)

The RIY is a measure of the impact of charges that takes into account both initial charges and ongoing charges, and is calculated over a ten-year period. Usually, the RIY is disclosed through a sentence which states something similar to the following:

'Putting it another way, this would have the same effect as bringing investment growth down from 6% a year down to 4.1% a year.'

The first growth rate that is mentioned will typically be 6% but will be 7% for an ISA and is currently prescribed by the FSA. The second figure mentioned in the sentence is calculated for the individual fund. Where fund providers have disclosure documents that cover multiple funds, instead of using the **RIY sentence** they may provide the RIY through a table listing all of the funds covered in that document.

The main advantage of the RIY is that it combines both the initial charge and any ongoing charges into one figure. In doing so, it allows consumers or advisers to compare different funds on the basis of only one figure which combines all charges. This may be especially useful for customers who struggle to compare a fund with high initial charges and low ongoing charges with a fund with low initial charges and high ongoing charges.

One limitation of the RIY is that it is presented only at one moment in time, normally after ten years. This can cause consumers and advisers to examine charging information at a point of time that does not correspond to their investment horizon.

In addition, the RIY calculation requires assumptions to be made regarding the growth of investments and this may lead some consumers to have a false expectation as to the certainty or level of any returns.

Illustrative Effect of Charges Table

At end of year	Investment to date	Effect of deductions to date	What you might get back at 6%
	£	£	£
1	3,000	158	3,020
3	3,000	290	3,280
5	3,000	447	3,560
10	3,000	981	4,390

Source: *CRA International*

As is clear from the above table, the effect of charges table shows information on charges over time – at the end of year one, three, five and ten. This should be useful for a variety of consumers, who can examine the table to see which length of time most closely matches the length of time for which they expect to invest.

The effect of charges table also shows information on charges in pounds sterling rather than in percentages. This should be useful for customers who struggle to understand percentages and find it easier to examine information in monetary terms.

2.12.2 Total Expense Ratios

Under the European Commission's UCITS Directive, a simplified prospectus must include disclosure of initial charges and exit charges as well as ongoing fund charges. The European Commission has recommended that the latter are disclosed through the total expense ratio (TER).

This is not a comprehensive measure of charges, since the TER is only a measure of ongoing charges and not initial charges. In addition, showing charges only by means of percentages may make them harder for some consumers to grasp. UK firms are therefore also required to include additional charges disclosures, which in the UK consist of a table showing the effect of charges in monetary terms (see Section 2.12.1) and a Reduction in Yield (RIY) statistic. Both of these measures were already in place in the UK investment fund market (and the life and pensions market) prior to the introduction of the simplified prospectus for UCITS-regulated funds.

2.13 RESEARCH, REPORTS AND ANALYSIS METHODS

LEARNING OBJECTIVE

6.2.3   Understand the research and reports available to financial advisers:
fundamental analysis; technical analysis; fund analysis; fund rating
agencies and screening software; broker and distributor reports;
sector-specific reports

2.13.1 Fundamental Analysis

Fundamental analysis is about using real data to evaluate a security's value. Although most analysts use
fundamental analysis to value stocks, this method of valuation can be used for just about any type of
security. Fundamental analysts attempt to study everything that can affect the security's value, including
macro-economic factors (like the overall economy and industry conditions) and company-specific
factors (like financial condition and management).

The end goal of performing fundamental analysis is to produce a value that an investor can compare
with the security's current price, with the aim of figuring out what sort of position to take with that
security (underpriced = buy, overpriced = sell or short). This method of security analysis is considered
to be the opposite of technical analysis.

An investor can perform fundamental analysis on a bond's value by looking at economic factors, such
as interest rates and the overall state of the economy, and information about the bond issuer, such as
potential changes in credit ratings.

When assessing **stocks**, this method uses revenues, earnings, future growth, return on equity, profit
margins and other data to determine a company's underlying value and potential for future growth.
In other words, in terms of stocks, fundamental analysis focuses on the financial statements of the
company being evaluated.

2.13.2 Technical Analysis

Technical analysis is a method of evaluating securities by analysing the statistics generated by market
activity, such as past prices and volume. Technical analysts do not attempt to measure a security's
intrinsic value, but instead use charts and other tools to identify patterns that can suggest future activity.

The field of technical analysis is based on three assumptions:

1. The market discounts everything.
2. Price moves in trends.
3. History tends to repeat itself.

Just as there are many investment styles on the fundamental side, there are also many different types of technical traders. Some rely on chart patterns, others use technical indicators and oscillators, and most use some combination of the two. In any case, technical analysts' exclusive use of historical price and volume data is what separates them from their fundamental counterparts. Unlike fundamental analysts, technical analysts don't worry whether a stock is undervalued. The only thing that matters is a security's past trading data and what information this data can provide about where the security might move in the future.

2.13.3 Fund Analysis

Investment fund analysis involves assessing a number of different aspects of the fund to determine whether they are appropriate to include in the portfolio. These include:

- investment objective;
- fund manager tenure;
- past performance, discrete and cumulative returns;
- volatility;
- comparison with benchmark and peers;
- initial and ongoing costs;
- independent ratings of fund and manager.

A number of independent **ratings agencies** exist including Morningstar, Lipper and OBSR, which provide analysis and pricing information on investment funds to aid both private investors and investment advisers.

2.13.4 Brokers and Distributor Reports

Research and analysis is available from a vast number of sources including brokers and distributors of funds. This is usually available as periodical updates on fund performance and market commentaries, with input from research analysts and fund managers on market direction.

2.14 FACTORS TO CONSIDER WHEN SELECTING INVESTMENT PRODUCT PROVIDERS

LEARNING OBJECTIVE

6.2.4   Analyse the factors to consider when selecting investment product providers

When choosing a suitable provider for an investment product, the following factors are worth considering:

- size and position in the market;
- administrative efficiency;
- competitive on charges;
- features and benefits of product compared to peer offerings;
- financial rating;
- assets.

2.15 WRAPS AND OTHER PLATFORMS

LEARNING OBJECTIVE

6.2.5   Understand the characteristics, uses, benefits, risks and charges
associated with wrap and other platforms

The advantages of wrap platforms are obvious. For the investor they offer an unprecedented overview and control of their investments, savings and pensions, and the possibility of a far greater choice in terms of fund managers, providers and asset classes.

For the adviser and investment adviser, they offer greater automation, much improved efficiency and the potential to offer almost instant valuations, meaning lower costs and the ability to offer a better service. In short, it should mean they can spend more time actually advising their clients and rather less on paperwork. The ability to manage client assets centrally in an administratively efficient way is proving advantageous in the post-RDR world, and enables advisers to offer a transparent fee structure and specific service levels to meet their clients' requirements.

Wraps originated in Australia but have been in use here in the UK for a number of years. Wrap platforms generally offer clients the ability to invest in a variety of different products via a single provider, eg, Transact. The wrap account provides the investor with access to:

- a cash account, used for dealing on purchases and sales, and for the payment of any associated management fees;
- a pension account with the usual tax advantages;
- an Individual Savings Account (ISA);
- an offshore/onshore investment bond.

Benefits to the investor include reduced administration and cost. In most cases, it enables the adviser to offer improved reporting to the client, allowing greater efficiency for their businesses, thereby helping to reduce costs and increase profitability.

In terms of risks, the client's assets are always held separately from those of the wrap provider and so the failure of that business will not affect them. Any assets held in the cash account are covered by the FSCS deposit protection scheme.

Wrap account providers make their money by charging a fee for using the account. Initial costs may also be levied on setting up the account and for any subsequent additional investment. Most platforms have negotiated discounts with fund managers and are able to offer reduced dealing costs on a range of investment funds.

Wraps offer complete transparency and clients can see what they are paying and to whom. Advisers are able to agree a service level and set their charges appropriately. Any trail fees from underlying investment funds are easily accounted for and may be used to subsidise the cost of the service to the client. However, trail income is expected to be phased out in the post-RDR environment.

KEY CHAPTER POINTS

- Asset allocation is an important component of financial advice, both in terms of meeting investment objectives and of reflecting the client's risk profile.
- Typically, a conservative investor will have a higher exposure to deposit-based and fixed-interest investments, and a more adventurous one will have a higher exposure to equities.
- Individual circumstances including commitments, experience, life cycle stage, age and wealth are factors to consider in designing a portfolio.
- Investment portfolios need to be affordable, taking into account changes in circumstances as far as possible, and they need to be suitable for the client. The level of accessibility must be assessed, to allow liquidity when it is needed.
- Tolerance, attitude and capacity for risk may be graded; for example, using the terms cautious, medium and adventurous. The proportion of risky asset types in a portfolio may be varied according to the desired overall level of risk.
- Risky investments should not generally be undertaken if the investment timescale is short, as short-term fluctuations can lead to losses.

INVESTMENT ADVICE

This syllabus area will provide approximately 11 of the 80 examination questions

1.   ADVISING CLIENTS

LEARNING OBJECTIVE

7.1.1   Apply a framework for providing financial advice, paying particular attention to: the nature of the client relationship, confidentiality, trust and client protection; the information required from clients and methods of obtaining it; monitoring and review of clients' circumstances; the information clients must be given under the current regulatory requirements

7.1.5   Explain to customers in a clear and non-misleading way the purpose and process of financial advice, including: gathering information and discussing objectives; planning and recommending ways to meet objectives; implementation; reporting, monitoring and review

1.1   THE NATURE OF THE CLIENT RELATIONSHIP

The relationship between a client and financial adviser is very important to the success of the planning process. We could think about this relationship from three different perspectives – the legal, the personal, and the skills which an adviser might need to foster such a relationship:

- **Legal** – in some cases, a financial adviser will be an independent financial adviser (IFA), or part of an IFA firm. The relationship with the customer is that of agent. The adviser acts as the agent of the customer in any transactions they arrange on their behalf, and is responsible for providing them with advice based on a selection of suitable options. In other cases, however, the adviser may be an employee of a single product provider (or of a provider offering its own and a small range of other providers' products) or he may be **tied** or **multi-tied** to one or more providers. In this case they act as the agent of the provider(s) and not of the client. These differing legal relationships must be disclosed to the customer, and mean different legal responsibilities to customers.

- **Personal** – in order to provide appropriate advice, financial advisers need a good deal of detailed background information about their clients. This includes not only their current financial situation, but also their plans, hopes and aspirations – and sometimes, some personal and sensitive information about their families. A client will only disclose this sort of information openly and frankly if they trust their adviser's integrity, confidentiality and capabilities.

- **Skills** – clearly, an adviser needs special skills to foster a successful relationship with his client. These include:
  - **Personal** – the adviser needs to create a trusting and open relationship with their client. They may need to be sensitive in questioning the client on personal matters, and conciliatory in persuading him to provide background details which he may not initially wish to divulge (eg, for anti-money laundering purposes).
  - **Organisational** – the busy adviser needs to be able to juggle a full diary of initial contacts and follow-up and repeat meetings. They, therefore, need to be well organised and disciplined in managing their diary and activities, and thorough in completing paperwork promptly.
  - **Technical competence** – they need to have the necessary technical knowledge and skills if they are to gain their client's confidence and provide a competent service.

- ○ **Integrity** – the client must have absolute confidence in their adviser's integrity; they trust the adviser with a great deal of sensitive financial information, which must not be improperly disclosed or otherwise abused.

1.2 INFORMATION REQUIRED OF CLIENTS, AND HOW TO OBTAIN IT

In order to be able to provide appropriate advice, the adviser needs a clear picture of the client's current and planned financial situation. To achieve this, information has to be gathered from the client – and, to ensure that this is done in an organised and structured way, this is invariably done by way of a standardised form.

The actual collection of information may be done face-to-face, or at a distance (by telephone or over the internet): this will depend on the adviser's method of delivering services. Face-to-face is still popular for many, especially those dealing with the very wealthy or those who value a high level of personal service.

The document used is often called a **fact find** or something similar. It will be a fairly lengthy document, which should collect not only the client's basic details – but also his financial background and information to build a picture of his plans and aspirations. Typically, the document will include the following:

Basic Information

- Name, residential and correspondence address of the customer and any spouse/partner, children and other dependants.
- Often, at this point, anti-money laundering information, verifying the customer's identity and address, will be sought.
- Age.
- Occupation – self-employed, employed or unemployed.
- Marital status, number of dependants and their ages.
- Possibly, some basic health information.
- Nationality and domicile (for tax purposes).

Current Financial Situation

This may take the form of a mini **balance sheet** for the individual, listing all major financial and other assets (including pensions) and liabilities such as credit card debts, mortgages and overdrafts. It will also identify their tax status – does the individual pay basic rate or higher-rate tax, or are they a non-taxpayer?

Current Income and Outgoings

Income may include such things as:

- Earned income from employment and self-employment.
- Unearned income on investments and deposits.
- Rents on investment property.
- Financial support from others – eg, a former spouse or partner.

- State benefits.

Outgoings may include:

- Rent or mortgage payments.
- Bills for food, heating and electricity.
- Rates/council tax.
- Taxes.
- TV licence.
- Maintenance paid to a former spouse or in respect of a child.
- Credit card and loan outgoings.
- Regular insurance premiums.
- Contributions to regular savings plans and pensions.
- Sums budgeted for holidays, Christmas and the like.

Expected Income and Outgoings

Here the client should list income/outgoings which are not in force at the moment but which are expected in the foreseeable future, such as school fees or a planned holiday.

Aspirations and Goals

In this section the customer should list those of his goals and aspirations which may require some financial planning (for example, early retirement). Examples may include:

- Hopes of retiring some time earlier than the state retirement age.
- A second home abroad.
- A move to a bigger house, or better area, or perhaps putting down a deposit on a first home.
- An expensive cruise to celebrate a significant anniversary.

Together, these elements give the financial adviser a snapshot of where the customer is now; an idea of his current and expected cash flows; and an idea of both his near-term objectives and where they hope to be in some years' time.

1.3   MATCHING CLIENT NEEDS WITH SOLUTIONS

This picture of where the client is – or hopes they are – headed is an important area and one where a good adviser can be of considerable help to them.

This is because, before they think about it in any structured way, many clients have a jumble of competing needs and aspirations. Some of these are more important than others, and many may not be able to be realistically achieved at all – or at least not if other aspirations are also to be prioritised. Few clients are lucky enough to have so much money that they can afford to meet all their needs, goals and aspirations immediately!

For example, in terms of importance:

- certain financial outgoings must be paid if the client is to comply with the law – TV licences (assuming the customer has a TV) and taxes, for example;

- some are very important – for example, keeping up insurance premiums to protect dependants from risks such as loss of the family breadwinner;
- others are less urgent, even if they feel more like needs than wants (an urgent desire for a new car, for example).

So clearly, certain items should be prioritised ahead of others on grounds of their importance. But even then, there may be a number of other things which the client would like to do – but which they cannot afford to do all of, or not all at once. For example, the client may want to:

- trade up to a bigger car;
- extend the house to have more space;
- take the family abroad on holiday;
- cut back on working hours by half a day a week to spend time with the children.

It may be that a financial plan can be arrived at to achieve many of these aims, if only one of them is dropped or postponed. Alternatively, the client may have some aspirations which are simply never going to be achieved in the foreseeable future.

Often, the adviser can help them organise their thoughts and prioritise which of their hopes and aspirations they are going to focus on – and which they will (for now at least) treat as merely a wishlist.

1.4   ASSESSING AFFORDABILITY AND SUITABILITY

Clients expect that their advisers are going to give them appropriate professional advice to help them achieve a sensible financial plan for their current situations, and a **roadmap** to achieving many of their objectives and aspirations.

They do not benefit from an adviser who simply tells them what they want to hear – for example, that their aims are achievable, if in fact they aren't!

Nor will they benefit from advice which benefits the adviser more than the customer (for example products paying a substantial commission, when in fact there are perhaps better solutions available which would be more cost-effective).

Financial advisers are under strict obligations to ensure that they have given their client suitable advice in light of their stated needs. The rules on this are contained in a part of the FSA's Handbook of regulatory rules, called the Conduct of Business Sourcebook.

Financial advisers should be able to demonstrate this, through the paperwork they complete. This should show how the adviser assessed the client's situation and needs, and the chosen selection of the recommended solutions.

One relatively recent development has focused advisers' and product providers' attention more closely on the issue of suitability. This is the FSA's **Treating Customers Fairly (TCF)** initiative.

1.5 TREATING CUSTOMERS FAIRLY

7.1.3 Apply the FSA's six treating customers fairly outcomes to the investment advice process and interaction with customers

In many ways, the TCF initiative should be nothing new to those in the financial services industry. Organisations already have to operate in accordance with a set of principles that include the requirement to act with integrity, consider the information needs of their customers, and other similarly **fair** approaches to doing business. TCF forces providers to demonstrate that they are behaving fairly in all areas of their activities, from the way in which they communicate with their customers, to the quality of their advice.

TCF will, therefore, be an important issue in the ongoing assessment of the suitability of advice, and advisers undertake a thorough assessment of the client's circumstances, taking into account attitude to risk and affordability. It is also more important than ever that the consequences of any recommended plan of action are clearly and properly explained to the customer, in language which they are likely to be able to understand, including the costs and risks involved.

The FSA retail regulatory agenda aims to ensure an efficient and effective market and thereby help consumers to achieve a fair deal. They hope to achieve this through the use of the TCF initiative. The TCF initiative aims to deliver six improved outcomes for retail consumers, and firms should be focused on trying to achieve these outcomes, which are listed below.

Outcome 1 – consumers can be confident that they are dealing with firms where the fair treatment of customers is central to the corporate culture.

Outcome 2 – products and services marketed and sold in the retail market are designed to meet the needs of identified consumer groups and are targeted accordingly.

Outcome 3 – consumers are provided with clear information and are kept appropriately informed before, during and after the point of sale.

Outcome 4 – where consumers receive advice, the advice is suitable and takes account of their circumstances.

Outcome 5 – consumers are provided with products that perform as firms have led them to expect, and the associated service is of an acceptable standard and as they have been led to expect.

Outcome 6 – consumers do not face unreasonable post-sale barriers imposed by firms to change product, switch provider, submit a claim or make a complaint.

1.6   PAYING FOR ADVICE

LEARNING OBJECTIVE

7.1.2   Understand how financial advice can be paid for: fees; commission; nature and frequency of service to be provided

Regulations laid down by the financial services regulator – the FSA – set out the nature, and usually the content, of information that financial advisers must provide to their clients. These obligations extend not only to the advice the adviser provides – including why they are suitable, and what the benefits, disadvantages, risks and costs are – but also to the adviser's own regulated status, how they work and on what basis changes are paid.

Financial advice can be paid for in one of the following ways:

Fees

Here the cost of the advice is fully transparent and examples of the types of fees that may be charged are usually provided to the investor at the outset. Hourly rates may be charged, or one-off fees for certain types of work, eg, the arrangement of an investment through a personal pension plan. All work and costs should be agreed in advance and no further fees charged without prior agreement with the client.

Additional fees may be levied against the value of any funds under the advice or management of the firm, and should be disclosed and agreed prior to engagement.

Commissions

In this scenario, the advice is paid through the receipt of either an upfront commission and/or commission paid from the product during its lifespan; often the latter form of commission will be built into investment products and will be a percentage of the value of the fund.

Service

The type of service provided may also differ in each scenario. If fees are charged, then it is likely that some form of service agreement will be entered into, where the person providing the advice agrees to deliver a structured service with frequent reviews. In the commission example, this is less likely to be the case, as the adviser is only remunerated when a product is sold.

1.7   KNOW YOUR CUSTOMER RULES

One of the FSA's Principles for Businesses requires a firm to take reasonable care to ensure the suitability of its advice and discretionary decisions.

To comply with this, a firm should obtain sufficient information about its private customers to enable it to meet its responsibility to give suitable advice. Similarly, a firm acting as a discretionary investment manager for a private customer should ensure that it has sufficient information to enable it to put suitable investments into the customer's portfolio.

This requirement to gather sufficient information about the private customer is generally referred to as the **know your customer** requirement. The purpose of gathering information about the client is clearly so that financial plans can be devised and appropriate recommendations made. The types of information that should be gathered include:

- **personal details** – name; address; age; health; family and dependants;
- **financial details** – income; outgoings; assets; liabilities; insurance and protection arrangements;
- **objectives** – growth; protecting real value of capital; generating income; protecting against future events;
- **tolerance and capacity for risk** – cautious; balanced; adventurous;
- **liquidity and time horizons** – immediate needs; known future liabilities; need for an emergency reserve;
- **tax status** – income; capital gains; inheritance taxes; available allowances;
- **investment preferences** – restrictions; ethical considerations.

As we will see in the Section 2, firms must ensure that any recommendations they make are both suitable and appropriate. To do so, a firm should ensure that the information they gather also includes details about:

- a client's knowledge and experience of the investment or service that will be recommended;
- the level of investment risk that the client can bear financially and whether that is consistent with their investment objectives.

1.8   SUITABILITY AND APPROPRIATENESS

Once a clear picture of the customer's requirements and needs is established, the steps expected of the firm to ensure its recommendations are suitable and appropriate will vary depending upon the needs and priorities of the customer, the types of investment or service being offered and the nature of the relationship between the firm and the private customer.

When a firm proposes to offer investment advisory services or discretionary portfolio management, it must first assess whether such services are suitable for a professional or retail client. If the firm intends to offer other investment services, then it must ensure that they are appropriate for the client.

The firm should ascertain the:

- client's knowledge and experience on the types of services and transactions;
- nature, volume, frequency and time that the client has been involved in such services and transactions;
- client's level of education, profession or relevant former profession.

The general requirement is that the firm must take reasonable steps to ensure it makes no personal recommendation to a customer unless it is suitable for that customer. Suitability will have regard to the facts disclosed by the customer and other facts of which the firm should reasonably be aware.

Having assessed what services and products are suitable and appropriate, the firm should provide the client with a **report** which should set out, among other things, why the firm has concluded that a recommended transaction is suitable for the client.

If the firm determines after assessment that the service or product is not appropriate for the client, then it should issue a **risk warning** to the client. If the client still wishes to proceed despite the warning then it is up to the firm to decide whether it will do so.

If the firm is acting as investment manager for a private customer, there is an ongoing requirement that it must ensure that the portfolio remains suitable. Equally, if a customer has agreed to the firm pooling their funds with those of others, the firm must take reasonable steps to ensure that any discretionary decisions are suitable for the stated objectives of the fund.

1.9   MONITORING AND REVIEW

LEARNING OBJECTIVE

7.1.5   Explain to customers in a clear and non-misleading way the purpose and process of financial advice, including: gathering information and discussing objectives; planning and recommending ways to meet objectives; implementation; reporting, monitoring and review

7.2.1   Analyse the main factors, resources and limitations shaping a client's current and desired financial circumstances: gather appropriate, relevant information about current and projected income, expenditure, debt and savings; consider time horizons and the relative balance of growth versus income; distinguish between what is essential and what is desirable, and prioritise accordingly; agree clear, feasible, prioritised investment objectives

7.4.7   Understand the process of periodic review to meet key criteria: regulatory requirements; appropriate frequency, taking into account client requirements and the chosen investment strategy

Financial planning is not a one-off process. In part, this is because of the possibility of change. A client's plans can change because:

- the environment changes around him – for example:
  - the tax regime changes (and remember, at the least, tax allowances are generally reviewed every year);
  - employment status alters;
  - the stock market performs better, or worse, than he had anticipated; or:
- the client's circumstances change or so do their needs, wants and aspirations. For example, when the client marries or divorces, inherits a sum of money or has a child, then not only will their needs change but their attitudes to finance may also alter and they may, for example, become more or less risk-averse.

It is important that clients review their plans and monitor progress towards objectives. Without regular updates it is impossible to know whether the financial goals are likely to be achieved. Quite small changes in financial behaviour can, together, have a big cumulative effect on a client's finances.

So a periodic review can be very helpful in ensuring that the client stays on track. By repeating the planning exercise (say) a year later, both adviser and client can see whether he is making progress towards his goal, or whether he is drifting off-target and needs to use a little financial discipline.

The adviser should agree early on whether ongoing monitoring and review is going to fall within their remit – in many cases, this will be so. If so, the adviser should have advised the customer of how frequently they can expect to see an update of the plan and any new recommendations.

Periodic reviews to clients should include the up-to-date value of the customer's investments. Investments should be valued on a basis which has already been agreed with the client (eg, where stocks and shares are involved, the valuation process should be consistent as to whether bid or mid-prices are used and what exchange rate is used for any foreign assets).

It will also generally include a statement showing any transactions undertaken over the period (including any charges that have been deducted, and any additions to or withdrawals from the customer's portfolio).

If a full periodic review is being carried out, the adviser should re-verify the customer's details and establish whether there have been any changes to his circumstances which might require an amendment to the plan. If this is the case, the adviser should check the new details, and then go through the new recommendations with the customer to ensure they understand their implications in full – just as at the outset.

1.10　INVESTMENT AND SPECULATION

As a wealth/asset manager, it is important to understand the distinction between investment and speculation. Investment can be differentiated from speculation by the timeframe adopted and the level of risk assumed by the investor. Investment is generally undertaken via a diversified portfolio of assets for the medium to long-term whereas speculation is based on profiting from the short-term price movements of individual securities or assets. Wealth/asset management can be further differentiated by its structured approach to identifying client needs and developing holistic plans that address the complete range of a client's needs.

2.   THE FINANCIAL PLANNING PROCESS

LEARNING OBJECTIVE

7.2.1   Analyse the main factors, resources and limitations shaping a client's current and desired financial circumstances: gather appropriate, relevant information about current and projected income, expenditure, debt and savings; consider time horizons and the relative balance of growth versus income; distinguish between what is essential and what is desirable, and prioritise accordingly; agree clear, feasible, prioritised investment objectives

The nature of any relationship with a client will depend upon the service being provided. This can range from providing the facilities to execute transactions without any advice to ongoing relationships that deal with selected financial areas only, investment management only or extend to in-depth wealth management or private banking.

The client relationship can, therefore, be a one-off service to satisfy a client's needs or a long-term relationship where the wealth manager is an integral part of the client achieving their investment objectives. Whatever the service, an adviser has a fiduciary duty to his client that requires them to observe the highest standards of personal conduct and fully respect the confidence and trust implicit in their relationship.

The main responsibilities of the adviser can, therefore, be seen to:

- help clients to decide on, and prioritise, objectives;
- document the client's investment objectives and risk tolerance;
- determine, and agree, an appropriate investment strategy;
- act in the client's best interest;
- where agreed, keep the products under review;
- carry out any necessary administration and accounting.

The financial planning process can be divided into five stages, each of which will be considered below.

2.1 DETERMINING CLIENT REQUIREMENTS

Individuals have varying objectives and expectations. Clearly, before advising the client the adviser must be aware of these various needs, preferences, expectations and the financial situation of the client; the adviser must **know the client** before being able to provide appropriate advice.

It is essential to establish the fullest details about the client, not only their assets and liabilities but the life assurance or protection products or arrangements that they may have in place. Their family circumstances, health and future plans and expectations are equally important. Clients often approach advisers about investment opportunities, without considering these other factors and it is important that the adviser establishes this so that they can check the suitability of existing and proposed recommendations and prioritise what needs to be dealt with first.

Below, we will consider some of the key client information that an adviser needs to establish.

2.1.1 Information to be Collected

The information that needs to be captured (known as a fact find) can be broken down into the following:

- personal and financial details;
- objectives;
- risk tolerance;
- liquidity and time horizons;

- tax status;
- investment preferences.

Personal and Financial Details

The adviser will need to establish, among other things:

- personal details;
- health status;
- details of family and dependants;
- details of occupation, earnings and other income sources;
- estimates of present and anticipated outgoings;
- assets and liabilities;
- any pension arrangements;
- potential inheritances and any estate planning arrangements, such as a will.

It is essential not to see this as a simple data collection exercise but to see beyond the headings, as to why the information is needed and what this may show about the financial position and needs of the client.

EXERCISE

Use the following table or a separate piece of paper to record why such information might be needed

Information needed	Why needed?
Personal details	
Health status	
Details of family and dependants	
Details of occupation, earnings and other income sources	
Estimates of present and anticipated outgoings	
Assets and liabilities	
Any pension arrangements	
Potential inheritances and any estate planning arrangements, such as a will	

Be aware that the scale of potential information that will be needed is significant, so there is no simple 'right' answer and it gives an indication as to why the information might be relevant. Everyone is different, so the information needed will vary from person to person.

Objectives

There are a wide range of available investment opportunities and, to understand which might be suitable for a client, an adviser needs to start with understanding what the client's investment or financial objectives are. This requires the client to consider what they are trying to achieve. The answer will determine the overall investment strategy that will drive the investment planning process.

Typical financial objectives include:

- maximising future growth;
- protecting the real value of capital;
- generating an essential level of income;
- protecting against future events.

It is also important to remember that a client may have more than one financial objective, such as funding school fees, while at the same time maximising the growth of their investments to provide the funds needed in retirement.

Having determined the client's overall financial objectives, the adviser also needs to know how this will affect the choice of investments, so investment objectives are often categorised into:

- **Income** – investors seek a higher level of current income at the expense of potential future growth of capital.
- **Income and growth** – investors need a certain amount of current income but also invest to achieve potential future growth in income and capital.
- **Growth** – investors do not seek income and their primary objective is capital appreciation.
- **Outright growth** – where the investor is seeking maximum return through a broad range of investment strategies, which generally involve a high level of risk.

Risk Tolerance

Volatility in the prices of investments or the overall value of an investment portfolio is inevitable. At a personal level this translates into the risk that prices may be depressed at the time when an investor needs funds, which will mean that they will not achieve their investment goals.

A client needs to have a very clear understanding of their tolerance to risk, as it is essential to choosing the right investment objectives. In many ways, risk tolerance is subjective and is very dependent upon the emotional make-up of a person. It is also objective, in that age will affect how much risk a client can assume because, as people get older, there is less time to recover from poor investment decisions or market falls and so appetite to take risk may change.

Although risk itself is an emotive subject, the actual establishment of a client's tolerance towards it need not be subjective. Indeed, an objective measure of a client's risk tolerance is provided by the risks that will need to be taken if the client's stated investment aims are to be met. If the client believes these risks are too great, then the client's objective will need to be revised. We will return to the subject of a client's risk profile in Section 2.6.

Liquidity and Time Horizons

It is also essential to understand a client's liquidity requirements and the time horizons over which they can invest, as these will also have a clear impact on the selection and construction of any investments.

Liquidity refers to the amount of funds a client might need both in the short and long term. When constructing an investment portfolio, it is essential that an emergency cash reserve is put to one side that the client can access without having to disturb longer-term investments.

If there are known liabilities that may arise in future years, consideration should also be given as to how funds will be realised at that time. Consideration needs to be given as to whether it is sensible to plan on realising profits from equities, as market conditions may be such as to require losses to be established unnecessarily. Instead, conservative standards suggest investing an appropriate amount in bonds that are due to mature near the time needed, so that there is certainty of the availability of funds.

Time horizon refers to the period over which a client can consider investing their funds. Definitions of time horizons vary, but short-term is usually considered to be from one to four years, while medium-term refers to a period from five to ten years and long-term is considered to be for a period of ten years or more.

Time horizon is very relevant when selecting the types of investment that may be suitable for a client. It is generally stated that an investor should only invest in equities if they can do so for a minimum period of five years. This is to make the point that growth from equities comes from long-term investment and the need to have the time perspective that can allow an investor to ride out periods of market volatility.

The lower the client's liquidity requirements and the longer their timescale, the greater will be the choice of assets available to meet their investment objective. The need for high liquidity allied to a short timescale demands that the client should invest in lower risk assets such as cash and short-dated bonds, which offer a potentially lower return than equities; if the opposite is true, the portfolio can be more proportionately weighted towards equities.

Whatever their requirements, it is important, however, that the client maintains sufficient liquidity to meet both known commitments and possible contingencies.

2.1.2   Client Information Collection Methods

LEARNING OBJECTIVE

7.1.4   Understand the purpose, merits and limitations of using questionnaires
           and interviews to elicit customer information

There is no simple way of establishing all of this information quickly. The adviser will need to undertake a detailed, and potentially lengthy, **interview** with the client in order to understand what existing assets and liabilities they have before he can turn to developing a true understanding of what their needs are.

There is also no single correct way of collecting all of the required information. Most firms use a **Know Your Customer** questionnaire that the adviser completes during their interview with the client so that the information can be collected in a logical and straightforward manner and can be available for later use.

The advantage of this approach is in its consistency, the factual record it creates and the opportunity for quality checking that it provides.

Its disadvantage is the customer's reaction to what they may perceive as a lengthy form-filling exercise, hence the need for communication skills that we will consider in Section 6. Only having completed this, can the adviser then start on the next significant exercise; that is, to identify potential solutions and then match these to the client's needs and demands.

2.2   DEVELOPING A STRATEGY

LEARNING OBJECTIVE

7.4.1   Apply a strategy and rationale that will meet the client's objectives: highlight the pertinent issues and priorities; formulate a plan to deal with them; offer proposals to achieve these objectives; explain clearly the relative merits and drawbacks of each proposal and combination thereof; agree a strategy that the client understands and accepts

Having established what the needs and objectives of the client are, a thorough assessment of their existing financial position obviously needs to be completed.

An analysis of their assets and liabilities and their income and outgoings needs to be undertaken to establish their true financial position. It is only once this has been done that an assessment can be made of both the affordability and suitability of their existing arrangements.

Once the adviser has a complete financial picture for the client, he can then move on to assess what the client is aiming to achieve and what should be the client's priorities. It needs to be remembered that financial planning is a long-term process and not a one-off exercise. Most clients will need to prioritise their needs and then deal with the most pressing first and others when the constraints of affordability allow.

The development of a strategy will involve:

* assessing where action is needed;
* prioritising what should be addressed;
* identifying where action should be left until a later date;
* developing potential solutions to address the priorities for further investigation.

2.3　ASSESSING EXISTING ASSETS AND POTENTIAL PRODUCTS

Having determined a strategy to meet the client's needs, the next stage is investigate how the potential solutions can be implemented. This will involve assessing the suitability of the client's existing assets and investigating the characteristics of products that can potentially meet their needs.

Existing assets and products will need to be checked for suitability. This will involve determining the details of each product, assessing whether they meet the client's needs and establishing any issues that may arise in moving these to alternative options. There are many factors to consider, and these will be driven by the type of asset, product or arrangement.

Some items to consider include:

- their relevance to the true needs of the client;
- whether they are affordable options;
- the degree of risk associated with the product considered against the client's risk tolerance;
- the extent of any diversification, or lack of;
- the level of charges compared to comparable products;
- income generation and tax treatment;
- performance of investments, growth achieved and any taxation treatment on encashment;
- how long any assets need to be retained to earn any bonuses;
- any encashment penalties.

This analysis will then provide the basis for continuing the financial planning process. It will identify which assets should be retained and which should be disposed of to finance meeting the client's objectives. The next steps are to identify suitable financial products that can meet the client's requirements and evaluating their features.

This part of the process essentially involves matching the investor's investment and protection objectives with the characteristics of the various financial assets and protection products. For investment-related products, the main characteristics to consider are:

- the risks associated with the investment product;
- its liquidity (that is the ease of selling it or otherwise converting it into cash);
- its tax-efficiency;
- whether it is income-producing or more suitable for capital growth.

For life assurance and protection products, the process is essentially the same in that it involves identifying the range of potentially suitable products, assessing the key product features against the client's needs and selecting the most suitable option.

2.4　PRODUCING RECOMMENDATIONS AND A FINANCIAL PLAN

So far, we have determined the needs of the client, developed a strategy to meet their needs and identified which assets should be retained and which liquidated to finance the solutions that we have identified as meeting their needs.

The final stage of the process is, therefore, to produce recommendations and a financial plan for presentation to the client. The plan should detail the following:

- Document the client's existing position.
- Identify the areas that require addressing and what the priorities are.
- Detail the recommendations made and the reasons why they are suitable and appropriate.
- Document the areas where action has been deferred until a later date.

2.5 MONITORING AND REVIEWING CLIENTS' CIRCUMSTANCES

It may be stating the obvious but, after the adviser and client have spent considerable time and effort establishing needs, objectives and plans, why wouldn't they want to make sure that these were checked from time to time to make sure they are still relevant and still meeting their planned objectives?

Whether they do so will depend upon whether the advice has been part of a one-off exercise or an ongoing service. If it is part of an ongoing proposition, such as wealth management, discretionary investment management or private banking, then ongoing management of the assets and regular reviews of the client's objectives and strategy will be integral to the service proposition. If it is a one-off transaction, then the client should be persuaded of the advantage of regular reviews.

There are often too many issues that arise from the results of the financial planning exercise than can be dealt with at one time. There are many reasons why this may be so, for example, affordability or just what the client is prepared to address at one time.

The adviser may have recommended investment in a range of collective investment schemes and, as economic or market circumstances change, a point will arise where profits need to be taken or investments switched.

Equally, a client's circumstances will change, as few things in life stay still. Further regular meetings to review the client's circumstances are clearly a sensible and practical thing to do, but one that sometimes gets lost in the busy lives that clients and advisers lead.

It is also something that is often forgotten by financial services organisations, which sometimes devote more effort to generating new business than servicing existing business. Sometimes it takes a detailed financial analysis of their performance for them to remember that looking after their existing client base is usually far more profitable than chasing new business.

It is the practice among the better financial advisers to meet regularly with their clients. This is not simple altruism. Experience has shown that a financial adviser with a client base numbering just a few hundred can earn a very acceptable income from repeat business from their clients just by ensuring they are always focused on making sure that their objectives are the same as the clients. Best practice, therefore, dictates that an adviser should agree the frequency with which they will meet to undertake a further review of the client's position.

2.6　RISK PROFILES

7.3.1　Analyse a profile of an investor's risk exposure and appetite for risk, based on the following objective and subjective factors: level of wealth; timescale; commitments; life cycle; life goals; investment objectives; attitudes; experiences; knowledge

7.3.2　Apply a client risk profile to the investment selection process

7.3.4　Assess affordability and suitability based on a range of factors including product provider quality, performance, risk, charges and client service

The risk tolerance of a client will have a considerable impact on the financial planning strategy that an adviser recommends. It will exhibit itself in the importance that is given to financial protection and in what is an acceptable selection of investment products.

Attitude to risk and its definitions are constant themes that financial services companies revisit. The reason for this is simple, namely that they want to be able to categorise a client into a risk category and then be able to say which of their products are suitable for clients with that risk profile.

However, definitions of risk profiles are imprecise and, after reviewing the suggested classification in the next section, you will understand why trying to turn this into a mathematical exercise is not straightforward. As a result, advisers need to understand even more about suitability and risk and recognise that it is only with the application of skill and knowledge that solutions can be matched with client needs.

2.6.1　Determining a Client's Risk Profile

Objective Factors

As we have seen above, determining a client's attitude to risk needs to be as accurate as possible as it will drive both priorities and solutions. There are a number of objective factors that can be established that will help define this, including:

- **Timescale** – the timescale over which a client may be able to invest will determine both what products are suitable and what risk should be adopted. For example, there would be little justification in selecting a high-risk investment for funds that are held to meet a liability that is due in 12 months' time. By contrast, someone in their 30s choosing to invest for retirement is aiming for long-term growth, and higher-risk investments will then be suitable. As a result, the acceptable level of risk is likely to vary from scenario to scenario.
- **Commitments** – family commitments are likely to have a significant impact on a client's risk profile. For example, if a client needs to support elderly relatives or children through university, this will have a determining influence on what risk they can assume. While by nature they may be adventurous investors, they will want to meet their obligations, which will make higher-risk investments less suitable.
- **Wealth** – wealth will clearly be an important influence on the risk that can be assumed. A client with few assets can ill afford to lose them, while ones whose immediate financial priorities are covered may be able to accept greater risk.

- **Life cycle** – stage of life is equally important. A client in their 30s or 40s who is investing for retirement will want to aim for long-term growth and will be prepared to accept a higher risk in order to see their funds grow. As retirement approaches, this will change as the client seeks to lock in the growth that has been made and, once they retire, they will be looking for investments that will provide a secure income on which they can live.
- **Age** – the age of the client will often be used in conjunction with the above factors to determine acceptable levels of risk, as some of the above examples have already shown.

Individual circumstances may differ widely, but some aspects of common life stages encountered in different typical age groups are described below:

- **Minors (under 18)** – someone who is under 18 may have very little in the way of direct investment needs. He is likely to be dependent on one or two parents, and have no dependants of his own.
- **Single and still young (18 to 35)** – if your client is in their early or mid-20s, they may still not yet have any dependants. They may now be financially independent of their parents, even if they are still living at home. Alternatively, they may be renting a flat or possibly even buying a house. They are unlikely to have accumulated much capital and could be spending everything that they earn. They are also more likely to be an employee than to be self-employed.
- **Married or cohabiting (20 to 30)** – they are likely to have stopped being dependent on parents at this stage and are probably either renting or buying a house.
- **Couple working but no dependants (20 to 30)** – this is the time when a couple will be building up their income at the fastest possible rate, before the expenses of looking after children begin.
- **One of a couple working, with no dependants (20 to 30)** – the client's financial life could be a little bit more fragile. Dependence upon the earnings of one person increases the possibility of difficulties if there is a fall in their earnings.
- **One of a couple working, with dependants (25 to 40)** – with all the earnings concentrated in the hands of one of the couple and with there being both a partner and at least one dependant to look after, the burden of dependency has now begun to reach its maximum.
- **Married or cohabiting, with older children (35 to 50)** – this is the point when the expenses are probably at their highest, even without school fees. Higher education costs can increase the burden – especially if it includes university. However, the couple may again have two incomes (and possibly even have a higher net income despite the higher level of expenses).
- **After children: empty-nesters (45 to 60)**. – when children have left home, their parents may have a higher net income as a result of lower expenses relating to children.
- **Retired (60 or 65 plus)** – retirement income may be significantly lower than when working, but there may be savings that have been built up. Investors may now have more free time, which they may or may not wish to devote to managing their own investments.

Subjective Factors

Establishing objective factors is clearly a preferable and more accurate way to help define a client's risk tolerance, but subjective factors also have a part to play.

A client's attitudes and experiences must also play a large part in the decision-making process. A client may well be financially able to invest in higher-risk products and these may well suit their needs but if they are by nature cautious, they may well find the uncertainties of holding volatile investments unsettling, and both the adviser and the client may have to accept that lower-risk investments and returns have to be selected.

Methods of Assessment

As will be clear from the above, establishing an investor's risk profile is not straightforward. Classifications such as cautious, moderate and adventurous, and a detailed understanding of the risks associated with different asset and product types, will clearly help.

Defining risk profiles has limitations, not least trying to help a customer to understand the difference and then agree which is applicable. As a result, many financial services companies have different methods of assessment. Some will rely on detailed client/adviser discussions, whereas others produce far more sophisticated versions of the risk classifications, which employ decision trees that require a client to answer a whole series of questions in order to determine what products might be suitable. Some companies expand this further, by applying the client's responses to sophisticated financial modelling, that aims, based on historic investment performance data, to predict the probability of certain returns, as required by the client, being achieved.

One approach is to have a written questionnaire which the individual is asked to complete. The FSA has recently alerted the industry to be more diligent in their questionnaires to improve the outcome of investment performance. The different possible answers to questions can be scored, so that someone who has a more conservative or cautious attitude to risk has a low score, while an adventurous or aggressive risk-taker will show a high score.

The questions asked to assess an individual's risk profile could include the following examples:

- How long do you expect to leave your investment in place until you sell it?
- Which outcome is most important to you from an investment portfolio: preserving asset value/ generating income/long-term growth?
- Which of the following investments have you owned before or do you now own: bank or building society deposit account/government stocks (gilts)/unit trusts or OEICs/investment trusts/individual company shares?
- Which of the following best describes your experience of investment? 'I have little investment experience beyond bank or building society savings accounts'/'I have had some experience of investment (such as unit trusts or individual shares)'/'I am an experienced investor with a portfolio managed by a financial adviser'/'I am an experienced investor and I prefer to manage my own portfolio.'
- Which of the following best describes your main objective in investing: the education of your children, your retirement, to leave money in your will?
- How large is your investment plan in proportion to your total savings? (Less than 10%; between 10% and 20%; between 20% and 30%; between 30% and 40%; 40% or more).

The key point is that the adviser needs to understand the client's attitude to risk and the risk characteristics of different assets and products, if the adviser is to match appropriate solutions with the client's needs.

2.6.2 Risk Profiles and Investment Selection

Attitude to risk will affect the investment policy that is implemented. If we look at three simple definitions of risk tolerance – cautious, moderate and adventurous – we can see how this might influence the choice of investments.

Investment Objective	Risk Tolerance	Attitude to Risk and Possible Investments
Income	Cautious	• Willing to accept a lower level of income for lower risk • Exposure to high-yield bonds and equities will be low
	Moderate	• Seeking to balance potential risk with potential for income growth • Exposure to high-yield bonds and equities will be higher
	Adventurous	• Willing to adopt more aggressive strategies that offer potential for higher income • Exposure to high-yield bonds and equities may be substantial
Income and Growth	Cautious	• Seeking maximum growth and income consistent with relatively modest degree of risk • Equities will form a relatively small percentage of the portfolio
	Moderate	• Seeking to balance potential risk with growth of both capital and income • Equities will form a significant percentage of the portfolio
	Adventurous	• Able to adopt a long-term view that permits the pursuance of a more aggressive strategy • Equities will form the principal part of the portfolio
Growth	Cautious	• Seeking maximum growth consistent with relatively modest degree of risk • Equities will form a significant percentage of the portfolio
	Moderate	• Seeking to balance potential risk with growth of capital • Equities will form the principal part of the portfolio
	Adventurous	• Able to adopt a long-term view that allows them to pursue a more aggressive strategy • Equities may form the whole of the portfolio

2.6.3 Affordability and Suitability on Investment Opportunities

Financial advisers need to assess the affordability and suitability of the range of investment opportunities available to them. Although a comprehensive and detailed formula cannot be delivered for every client, there are a series of steps that an adviser takes, based on the objectives in terms of risk and return, that have been agreed with the client, after taking into account their liquidity, constraints and other special needs.

Financial theory has established a linear relationship between risk and return. More simply, as risk taken in investment increases, return has to increase to compensate investors for the additional risk taken. The risk premium required is with the level of risk taken.

Traditionally, in a risk/return space generated by Markowitz, we can visualise the risk axis being split into zones and defined by three major asset classes that are staple products in a conventional mutual fund constructed by a traditional money manager. These zones are defined by: money market-like instruments; bond-like instruments and equity-like instruments and risk increases from money-market funds through to equity-like funds. Alternative funds are contemporary investments that have increased the risk space further and also bring with them diversification opportunities for traditional funds.

The following is a checklist to assess the suitability of an investment:

- What are you seeking from your investment – income, growth, or both?
- Risk-return trade-off – carry out an assessment for the maximum risk that can be accepted and the tolerance for maximum loss.
- What is the investment term?
- How much money is available for investment every year?
- What are your expectations of investment returns, as a percentage per annum? Is the risk assessed for the client commensurate with this level of return?
- If income is required, what is this as a percentage return from the total return: breakdown of income and capital appreciation yields.
- How likely is it that you may need access to this capital, either in part or whole, during the next five years? Impacts on liquidity.
- Is the income or growth guaranteed?
- When your investment term is complete, what do you intend to do with the money? Is this matched to a liability falling due at that time?
- What is your view of charges, ie, would the lowest charging company be the best for you, or do you seek a company that has been obtaining better consistent returns?
- Do you want the flexibility to move in a charge-efficient manner from fund to fund?
- Are there any market sectors you would (not) like to invest in? Consider ethical investments if required.
- Is simplified administration important to you?
- Is tax efficiency important?
- How much of the ISA allowance is available for this tax year?
- Is your tax position likely to change for any reason in the foreseeable future, or when you retire?
- What are your immediate and future liquidity requirements?
- Do you have any other requirements and investment constraints?
- Carry out due diligence on product providers.
- Which product provider meets all of these client requirements?
- Will client service meet expectations? Are the charges levied by the provider acceptable?
- Performance attribution of product providers and their selection.

The checklist will provide information on the following and will be used to build up an investment policy:

- Objectives – return requirements and risk tolerance.
- Constraints – liquidity, horizon, regulations, taxes and unique needs.

After an assessment of the client needs, the policies will focus mainly on:

- Active or passive management.
- Asset allocation – proportions of the mix in terms of asset classes and their composition.
- Risk positioning.
- Tax positioning.
- Income generation.

An example of a matrix of objectives for a variety of investors is as follows.

Type of Investor	Return Requirement	Risk Tolerance
Individual and personal trusts	Life cycle (education needs, children, retirement)	Life cycle dependent (old more risk averse)
Mutual funds	Variable	Variable
Pension funds	Assumed actuarial rate	Depends on proximity of payouts
Endowment funds	Determined by current income needs and need for asset growth to maintain real value	Generally conservative
Life insurance company	Should exceed new money rate by sufficient margin to meet expenses and profit objectives; also actuarial rates are important	Conservative
Non-life insurance companies	No minimum	Conservative
Banks	Interest rate spread	Variable

Source: Investments 9th Edition

EXAMPLE 1

A neighbour who has learnt that you have successfully passed your examination in Investment, Risk and Taxation with the CISI has come to you for advice. He and his wife are both in their early 50s and have just finished mortgage payments on their house in which they have lived for the last fifteen years. Their two children have both completed their university education, have gained employment and have moved out of the family home. Your neighbour and his wife are planning for retirement.

What advice on investing their retirement savings would you give? If they are very risk-averse what would you advise?

This is an open-ended question and you need to be careful in providing advice until you have thoroughly understood the client's needs and current position. Follow the steps outlined in the checklist before drafting an investment policy statement. At a general level, check that they have both used up their tax allowances and invested in tax-efficient schemes. A high level of risk aversion suggests that asset allocation decisions will most likely be tilting in favour of bond-like investments where income and capital protection is necessary over a long term. A risk-tolerant investor on the other hand will prefer investment growth and will not be averse to losing some capital in return for higher returns. The asset allocation decision in this case will tilt towards equity-like investments to achieve growth.

3. ETHICAL AND SOCIALLY RESPONSIBLE INVESTMENT STRATEGIES

LEARNING OBJECTIVE

7.3.5   Understand the purpose of different ethical and socially responsible investment strategies and the circumstances in which it may be appropriate to discuss them

An individual investor or an organisation may wish to make investment decisions that take into account their **ethical beliefs** or **social values**. Churches and charities that have funds to invest on stock markets may want to avoid buying shares or bonds issued by companies involved in certain activities – eg, the manufacture or sale of alcohol products, the provision of gambling facilities, arms-dealing.

Indeed, in some cases the investor must avoid certain areas, perhaps because it is written into its constitution that it must do so. Tthis might be the case for a charitable trust set up by a wealthy benefactor, for example, who wanted his values and wishes reflected in the charity's trust deed.

3.1 GENERAL PERSONAL ETHICAL CONSIDERATIONS

Some people want to avoid having investments in their portfolios that fund businesses of which they do not approve; this is generally referred to as **ethical investment**.

Ethical investment strategies will vary according to the views of the investor (ie, with regard to his own particular ethics) – but may involve **screening out** investments in companies involved in specific areas. For example, an investor might specify that he wishes to avoid any companies which are involved in:

- animal testing;
- genetic modification or engineering;
- intensive farming;
- arms dealing or dealings with the military;
- nuclear power;
- pornography or other similar industries; and/or
- those with a poor record on human rights.

The firm managing his portfolio will need to screen investments for the above **negative criteria**.

Still others want to ensure that their investments are in areas of which they positively approve; for example, enterprises that exhibit a degree of social responsibility or are proactive in certain desirable activities. This is generally referred to as '**socially responsible investment (SRI)**'.

Examples of strategies which are SRI-friendly would be screening for **positive criteria** – eg, an investor might require that his portfolio is invested in companies involved in any of the following fields:

- good corporate governance;
- a good record of contribution to the community;
- equal opportunities;

- positive products and services, such as ecologically friendly cleaning products;
- sound supply-chain practices, such as ensuring that a fair price is paid to the producers from whom they source raw materials or supplies.

Such investments are possible, whether within a portfolio of individual stocks or collective funds. Indeed, they are common enough that there is now a relatively wide range of product providers, and products, offering bank accounts and packaged investments such as unit trusts which meet certain stated ethical standards. The Ecology Building Society, for example, grants mortgages on properties that help the environment (eg, energy-efficient houses). Its savers know that the money they place on deposit with it is used to make funding available to, for example, projects aimed at **low-impact lifestyles**.

In addition, for direct investments, there are a small number of **indices** which measure the performance of companies meeting certain ethical standards. For example, in the FTSE series of indices, the FTSE4Good index covers the performance of stocks meeting certain criteria; it recently began to include factors relating to how much a company contributes to climate change among the matters it considers.

The Ethical Investment Research Service (EIRIS) provides research and guidance to organisations and investors interested in such an investment approach.

3.1.1 Restrictions on Portfolio Construction and Implications for Performance

Depending on the investor's values and expectations, different restrictions may need to be applied to a portfolio constructed to meet ethical or SRI standards. For example, as already explained:

- one investor might just want to avoid areas they saw as harmful;
- another might want to be more proactive, and invest in a way that supports activities that are positively helpful to the environment.

Further, investors have different areas of interest. One person might be more interested in helping people in poorer countries, for example, while another might be more interested in projects closer to home, or supportive of animal welfare instead of that of people.

It is therefore important that, when an investor is interested in ethical investment or SRI, they ensure that their wishes are reflected in the portfolio's restrictions and limits so that the manager knows what is expected. If they are investing in a packaged product such as a unit trust, OEIC or life product, then this will not be tailored to their needs. They should read the product literature carefully to ensure that they understand the limits within which the product will be invested, and that these reflect their concerns.

Ethical or SRI-orientated funds generally state explicitly the criteria they use in selecting investments, so that investors can decide if a particular fund meets their needs. Such funds may use either negative criteria or positive criteria in the process of screening the companies they invest in. Once it has been established whether a company meets the criteria of the fund, investment managers can decide whether the company is worth investing in at the current price based on other, more common, investment criteria such as fundamental analysis (see Chapter 6, Section 2.13).

Portfolios may be constructed to avoid investments that are involved in or have a poor record in some or all of the following areas:

- Alcohol production or sale.
- Animal exploitation.
- Animal testing in cosmetics.
- Animal testing for pharmaceutical products.
- Environmental degradation and damage.
- Gambling.
- Genetic engineering and modern biotechnology.
- Genetically modified organisms (GMO).
- Health and safety breaches.
- Human rights breaches.
- Intensive farming.
- Military-related enterprises.
- Nuclear power.
- Offensive or misleading advertising.
- Oppressive regimes.
- Pesticides.
- Pollution breaches.
- Pornography.
- Third World exploitation.
- Tobacco production or sale.
- Tropical hardwoods.
- Water pollution.

Examples of positive criteria might include:

- Community involvement.
- Training and education policies.
- Full disclosure and openness about activities.
- Good relations with customers and suppliers.
- Equal opportunities.
- Good employment practices.
- Environmental improvement.
- Environmental management; energy and resource conservation.
- Positive goods and services produced.

Ethical or socially aware investors should remember that the more restrictions they place on a portfolio, the more they are likely to limit its potential for good performance; there are just fewer options for its manager to select from.

In addition, by placing restrictive criteria on it, they may inadvertently be increasing the risk within the portfolio – because its investments may be less diversified than would otherwise be the case, and/or because there is a concentration of investment in areas with a strong correlation to one another. Due to their activities, larger companies may be screened out of ethical funds, thereby limiting the overall selection pool to mainly smaller, potentially more risky companies.

Those in favour of ethical and SRI policies sometimes argue that the performance of individual companies selected on ethical grounds tends – over the long term – to be better than that of some other companies, in part because they tend to have strong internal governance criteria, which feeds through into better overall management controls. Others argue that the additional restrictions placed on a company complying with SRI or ethical criteria can only limit its abilities to make decisions in the (financial) best interests of its shareholders – so performance must be lower.

In 1999, EIRIS produced some research comparing the performance of ethical/SRI investments against those managed without such limitations. Its conclusion, at the time, was that ethical/SRI criteria can have both a positive and negative influence on a portfolio but that, overall, performance seemed to be broadly similar.

You might want to look at the performance of the FTSE4Good indices yourself to see how performance compares with that of the wider market indices; consider whether current trends – the publicity given to climate change, for example – may be benefiting companies investing in SRI and ethical ways, and, as a consequence, such indices.

3.1.2 Corporate Social Responsibilty (CSR)

Corporate social responsibility (CSR), also known as corporate responsibility, corporate citizenship, responsible business and corporate social opportunity, is a form of corporate self-regulation integrated into a business model.

Ideally, CSR policy functions as a built-in, self-regulating mechanism whereby, businesses monitor and ensure their adherence to law, ethical standards, and international norms. Businesses embrace responsibility for the impact of their activities on the environment, consumers, employees, communities, stakeholders and all other members of the public sphere.

Furthermore, such businesses proactively promote the public interest by encouraging community growth and development, and voluntarily eliminating practices that harm the public sphere, regardless of legality. Essentially, CSR is the deliberate inclusion of public interest into corporate decision-making, and the honouring of a triple bottom line: **people, planet, profit**.

The practice of CSR is subject to much debate and criticism. Proponents argue that there is a strong business case for CSR, in that corporations benefit in multiple ways by operating with a perspective broader and longer than their own immediate, short-term profits. Critics argue that CSR distracts from the fundamental economic role of businesses; others argue that it is nothing more than superficial window-dressing; others argue that it is an attempt to pre-empt the role of governments as a watchdog over powerful multinational corporations.

Along with CSR, there has been increasing debate in recent years about including environmental, ecological, social and governance issues in investment and corporate decisions. The recent climatic change and CO_2 concerns, financial, economic, and debt crisis, the nuclear catastrophe in Japan, and the crisis in the Arab region have all highlighted the fact that CSR policies need to be widened in scope to take into account the global environmental, social and governance (ESG) responsibility. Pressure groups have responded to the recent crises outlined above and state that the global economy has to be aligned with ESG criteria. They argue that measures and ideas need to be geared towards avoiding financial, economic, confidence, social, and ecological crises in the future.

The European Federation of Financial Analysts Societies (EFFAS) Commission on Environmental, Social and Governance (CESG) was founded in October 2007 in Vienna. Its main objective is to facilitate the integration aspects of ESG in relation to corporate performance into investment processes. Within EFFAS a committee on ESG has been set up and the body comprises investment professionals from leading European and global sell-side and buy-side firms. Members are predominantly fund managers, financial analysts and equity sector specialists and the committee has been considering processes that need to become more and more a part of traditional investment analysis (mainstreaming).

CESG philosophy is aimed at integrating ESG into classic investment research and decisions from the perspective of traditional investors and financial analysts. Hence, CESG fills the gap between political and high-level industry initiatives supported by many global investment houses on the one hand, and the need of corporates to enhance corporate reporting on the other.

Encouraging other stakeholder groups to enter into dialogue, CESG does not confine itself to discussions but rather strives to: define positions on extra-financials; produce outcome such as papers; recommendations; and seeks to play an active role in the dialogue with both investment professionals and corporates.

3.1.3   Social, Environmental and Other Ethical Issues

The following covers some of the issues that are commonly of concern to investors seeking to apply social, environmental and ethical principles to their investments.

The first thing you should remember when assessing the social, environmental and overall ethical performance of a company or an ethical fund is there is no such thing as a perfect company. All are involved in activities that someone somewhere will object to; none goes far enough in terms of positive social and environmental contribution to satisfy all of the people all the time. With that in mind, ethical/socially responsible investment is about **compromising** and **prioritising**.

Before constructing an ethical portfolio or choosing an ethical fund, the investor should think through their concerns. They should decide what types of corporate activities they are concerned about and how strongly they feel about them. Some of the common issues that are of concern to many ethical investors are described below. Of course they may have other concerns not covered here that they may want to discuss with their financial adviser or broker.

Traditional Ethical Issues

For many, the first introduction to ethical investment came as a response to the human rights abuses in South Africa under apartheid. Since then, investors have extended the boycotting approach to other oppressive regimes. Such negative coverage has given companies an impetus to adopt human rights policies or codes of business conduct.

Policies of this kind are particularly relevant to operations in countries with poor human rights records. While some investors seek to avoid involvement in oppressive regimes altogether, for others it is what the company does in a country that is of interest. Is it an influence for good, or does the business either benefit from or somehow support a climate of repression?

Other, often connected issues are armaments (production and sales) in the Third World and corporate activities such as commodity extraction, breast milk substitution, pharmaceutical marketing and holding debt.

Alcohol, gambling and tobacco were the traditional concerns of the temperance movement back in the 1900s, where the origins of ethical investment can be found. For some these are still of significant concern today, particularly with the adverse effects on health; and likewise pornography, animal testing, intensive farming and fur have been longstanding issues for the UK ethical investor in particular. Attitudes vary between different countries and cultures.

Environmental Issues

Public concerns about the degradation of the environment are becoming increasingly widespread. Protests, shareholder actions, boycotts and other campaigns have brought these concerns to the attention of business. Some companies have also started to engage with stakeholders, including employees, communities, shareholders and campaign groups such as Friends of the Earth and Greenpeace. Calls for increased transparency in company activities have led to an increase in reporting on environmental performance. A number of organisations, notably the Global Reporting Initiative (GRI), have published guidance documents in an attempt to standardise the format used. However, many companies have been criticised for publishing **greenwash** to improve public relations without including meaningful performance data.

In addition, there are specific environmental issues that continue to be of concern to responsible investors. Examples include: climate change exacerbated by companies' greenhouse gas emissions and use of ozone-depleting chemicals (ODCs); the use of pesticides and genetic engineering; the use of tropical hardwood; (air and water) pollution; and industries associated with nuclear power, mining and quarrying and fossil fuels.

Social Issues

These encompass a wide range of issues related to how a company behaves towards its stakeholders, ie, customers, employees, suppliers, shareholders and the community within which it operates and what standards it might set. For example, when assessing a company's attitude towards its employees EIRIS looks at several areas, including equal opportunities, training and development, and job creation and security.

When looking at a company's standards with regard to suppliers, one might wish to investigate how companies ensure that core labour rights apply throughout their supply chain, particularly where their suppliers are based in countries where child labour is common. Community involvement and charitable giving have also become areas where companies have come under scrutiny, to see if they make a positive effort to contribute to the communities they work in and to society at large, whether via donations or other means.

Positive Products and Services

Knowing whether the product or service provided by a company contributes positively to society is something that has been of interest to many ethical investors for a number of years. Ethical investment is not only about avoiding companies but also about actively supporting companies that are contributing positively to society and/or the environment.

Of course, there will be different views about what products or services should be regarded as positive; and perhaps one can supply a basically 'good' product or service in a way that does not benefit the world.

Products and services that are often identified as positive include basic necessities, environmental products/services and other services which help make the world a safer and better place. Examples might be wind power generators, pollution abatement technology, public transport and bicycles, safety and protection systems such as fire alarms, healthcare including medicines, housing, utilities and educational services.

Governance and Ethics

Concern about the governance of public companies has increased immensely over the last few years, particularly following corporate scandals such as Enron. Corporate governance has been on the SRI agenda for some time and includes issues such as board structure and practices. This encompasses factors such as women on the board and directors' remuneration, the latter having received massive media and public interest in the so-called **fat-cat** scandals about large pay rises for directors, when shareholders felt they had not done enough to justify these substantial pay increases. Questions such as does the company have a code of ethics and does it make any political donations also come under this umbrella.

3.2 ISLAMIC FINANCE

LEARNING OBJECTIVE

7.3.6   Understand the main considerations for investing in accordance with Sharia'a law

Islamic banking refers to a system of banking or banking activity that is consistent with the principles of Islamic law (Sharia'a) and its practical application through the development of Islamic economics.

Sharia'a prohibits the payment of fees for the renting of money (*Riba*, usury) for specific terms, as well as investing in businesses that provide goods or services considered contrary to its principles (*Haraam*, forbidden).

The overarching principle of Islamic finance is that all forms of interest are forbidden. The Islamic financial model works on the basis of risk-sharing. The customer and the bank share the risk of any investment on agreed terms, and divide any profits between them. The main categories within Islamic finance are: Ijara, Ijara-wa-iqtina, Mudaraba, Murabaha and Musharaka.

- **Ijara** is a leasing agreement whereby the bank buys an item for a customer and then leases it back over a specific period.
- **Ijara-wa-Iqtina** is a similar arrangement, except that the customer is able to buy the item at the end of the contract.
- **Mudaraba** offers specialist investment by a financial expert in which the bank and the customer share any profits. Customers risk losing their money if the investment is unsuccessful, although the bank will not charge a handling fee unless it turns a profit.

- **Murabaha** is a form of credit which enables customers to make a purchase without having to take out an interest-bearing loan. The bank buys an item and then sells it on to the customer on a deferred basis.
- **Musharaka** is a investment partnership in which profit-sharing terms are agreed in advance, and losses are pegged to the amount invested.

3.3 OTHER FAITH-BASED INVESTMENT PRODUCTS

LEARNING OBJECTIVE

7.3.7 Understand the main considerations for investing in accordance with other faith values

A branch of SRI, faith-based investing, has been around for a long time. In the 1800s, the Quakers, who were anti-slavery and anti-war, avoided investing in weapons production. Today, faith-based investing is often a combination of SRI plus the screening out of several other things germane to a particular religion. Each group decides both what their financial goals are and their strategies to achieve those goals. They also look at their social and religious teachings and that leads them to be willing to hold certain things in their portfolios.

3.4 INVESTMENT FOR CHARITIES

LEARNING OBJECTIVE

7.3.8 Understand the main considerations that should be taken into account when investing for charities

3.4.1 Introduction

Many charities have surplus funds not needed to fund their immediate charitable activities; often the trustees invest some or all of this surplus in order to generate extra income to fund future activities. The basic principle governing trustees' decisions about investing their charity's funds is that they must take a prudent approach. When investing charitable funds (especially which those represent permanent endowment), trustees must seek to strike the right balance for their particular charity between the two objectives of:

- providing an income to help the charity carry out its purposes effectively in the short term; and
- maintaining and, if possible, enhancing the value of the invested funds, so as to enable the charity effectively to carry out its purposes in the longer term.

In order to discharge the duty to adopt a prudent approach to the investment of the charity's funds, trustees must:

- know their investment powers;
- discharge their duties properly when they take decisions about investments;
- have proper arrangements in place for holding investments on behalf of the charity;

- follow certain legal requirements if they are going to use an institution to manage the charity's investments on their behalf;
- know what they can and cannot do if they are going to apply an ethical approach to the charity's investments.

If the size of the funds to be invested justifies it, trustees should decide on a formal investment policy for the charity. This will, of course, vary in the level of detail and complexity depending on the size of the charity, and on whether the function of investment has been delegated.

3.4.2 Definition of an Investment

Conceptions of what constitutes investment vary – in this context it needs to be distinguished from other forms of income-generation, such as trading and gambling. For most trustees, particularly of smaller charities, the examples of what are and are not investments in the following paragraphs should be sufficient as a guide.

Examples of Investments

The term investment is not defined in statute. Instead the courts have interpreted the phrase. While not exhaustive, some common examples of investments include:

- shares in companies;
- land rented or leased out by the charity to tenants;
- interest-bearing loans by the charity, for example, government bonds, company loan stock, deposits at banks and building societies; and
- units in collective investment schemes, such as unit trusts, open-ended investment companies or common investment funds.

Examples of What Are Not Investments

Some examples of what do not constitute investments are:

- Land purchased and developed with a view to sale. This will usually be regarded as trading rather than investment, and hence may attract only limited tax relief.
- Commodities such as gold or vintage wine, acquired with a view to resale in the future at a profit. This is the only prospect of a financial benefit from the transaction. The purchase and sale of such items will also usually be viewed as trading.

3.4.3 Trustees' Powers of Investment

Under the Trustee Act, most trustees will have a very wide power of investment. In practice this means that most trustees are able to invest in almost anything regarded under trust law as an investment. See Section 3.4.2 for examples of what falls within the trust law definition.

There are certain circumstances in which trustees do not have the power of investment which the Trustee Act confers, or where certain conditions apply when using powers of investment. These general powers of investment are not available if:

- The charity is a charitable company (except when the company is itself acting as a charity trustee);

- The charity's governing document excludes or restricts the Trustee Act power (although in certain circumstances this statutory power overrides restrictions or exclusions in the governing document); for instance, the governing document may restrict the trustees to investing in certain types of investment (eg, shares traded on the London Stock Exchange) or prohibit investment in certain industries (eg, armaments or tobacco).

If the Trustee Act powers are not available, trustees must rely on any powers within their governing document when making investments.

3.4.4 Trustees' Duties

When managing a charity's investments, trustees must act according to certain standards as defined in the Trustee Act, whether they are using the investment powers in that Act or not.

Firstly, there is the **general duty of care**, which is the duty to exercise such care and skill as is reasonable in the circumstances. This applies both to the use of any power of investment and to the discharge of the specific duties which the Act attaches to the use of investment powers. A higher level of care and skill is expected of a trustee who is or claims to be knowledgeable about or experienced in investments, or who is paid.

Secondly, trustees must comply with the following **specific duties**:

- Trustees must consider the **suitability** for their charity of any investment. This duty exists at two levels. The trustees must be satisfied that the type of any proposed investment (eg, a common investment fund or a deposit account) is right for their charity (including whether it is consistent with an ethical investment policy if the charity has one). They also have a duty to consider whether a particular investment of that type is a suitable one for the charity to make. Trustees should, at both levels, try to consider the whole range of investment options which are open to them; how far they should go here will, of course, depend on the amount of funds available for investment.
- Trustees must consider the need for **diversification**, ie, having different types of investment, and different investments within each type. This will reduce the risk of losses resulting from concentrating on a particular investment or type of investment. Again, how far the trustees can go here will depend on the amount of funds available for investment.
- Trustees must periodically **review** the investments of the charity. The nature and frequency of these reviews is up to the trustees to decide, but the reviews should be proportionate to the nature and size of the charity's investment portfolio. To review too infrequently may result in losses or missed opportunities; changing investments too frequently may incur unnecessarily high levels of transaction charges.
- Before exercising any power of investment, and when reviewing the charity's investments, trustees must obtain and consider proper **advice** from a suitably qualified adviser (who may be one of the trustees), unless the size of the funds available for investment is so small that seeking investment advice would not be cost-effective.

The Trustee Act requires the objective consideration of the points mentioned above. The trustees of charitable companies have similar obligations, even though the act does not apply to them expressly. All trustees must also take into account any relevant provisions in their charity's governing document.

Trustees of all charities with permanent endowment have a duty to be **even-handed** between the interests of **present and future beneficiaries** of the charity. In practice this means that they must consider whether an investment provides a suitable balance between providing income for current needs and preserving or increasing the value of the investments so that the charity can operate effectively in future.

Some other duties of trustees with respect to investments are to:

- manage the risks their charity faces, balance those risks against the potential returns from particular investments, and be careful to avoid undue risk to their charity's funds;
- invest in markets where financial services are closely regulated, and where compensation schemes are in place;
- have a suitably diversified investment portfolio;
- be particularly wary of making speculative forms of investment.

A charity's **annual report** must include a description of the policies used by the trustees to select the charity's investments. Larger charities must, as part of their compliance with accounting requirements, also report on the performance of their investments.

Trustees are not liable to make good any loss to the charity incurred simply because an investment made by them is unsuccessful. However, trustees may be liable if, in making or retaining the unsuccessful investment, they have acted outside the scope of their powers, or failed to discharge the duties.

3.4.5   Delegation of Investment Management

Many charity trustees will consider it best to place the management of the charity's investments in the hands of a specialist.

There are two main ways of doing this:

- investing in one or more collective investment schemes, such as unit trusts, open-ended investment companies or common investment funds for charities; or
- delegating their investment decisions by appointing an investment manager.

For smaller charities the first option may well be a cost-effective way of achieving a professionally managed and balanced portfolio. But trustees must still fulfil the investment duties described in the paragraphs above and satisfy themselves of the suitability of any collective scheme as an investment vehicle for their charity.

Larger charities with significant funds may consider appointing an investment manager, which is unlikely to be cost-effective for smaller charities. This involves the trustees in a number of extra duties in appointing an investment manager, providing them with direction as to the charity's investment policies, and reviewing their performance.

The advantage of using an investment manager is, of course, that the manager can pursue an investment strategy which is tailor-made to the needs of the particular charity. But this advantage comes at a cost, both in terms of fees charged for the service, and in terms of the trustees having to discharge the extra responsibilities referred to above in their relationship with the investment manager.

3.4.6 Investment Policy

The charity trustees will decide on an investment policy for their charity, record it clearly in writing, and keep it under regular review. If they have delegated their investment function to an investment manager these are legal requirements. Without an investment policy, trustees are likely to find it difficult to demonstrate that they are making good use of the charity's funds.

Any investment policy should, for example, address the following considerations:

- the need for enough resources for the charity to carry out its present and future activities effectively;
- the level of acceptable risk and how to manage it;
- the charity's stance on ethical investment.

Ethical Investment

The question of basing an investment policy on ethical considerations can be an important one for charities. The essentials are dealt with briefly here.

If trustees are to adopt an ethical investment policy, or follow one laid down in the charity's governing document, they need to keep in mind their duty to invest in a way that furthers the purpose of the charity. This will normally be achieved by seeking the maximum return from a set of investments which have been selected prudently. An ethical investment policy can be entirely consistent with this duty, but there can also be a risk that the exclusion from consideration, or preference, of certain investment classes or particular investments may detract from the objective of obtaining the best direct financial returns from investment.

Trustees may well consider that the adoption of a particular ethical investment policy does not detract from the objective of obtaining the best direct financial return from investment. They must, of course, then be able to justify their position, through being able to show that they have, in following the policy, fully discharged the investment duties referred to above.

Some trustees may, however, wish to adopt an ethical investment policy even though it does, or may, detract from the objective of obtaining the best direct financial return. The circumstances in which they may wish to do this are outlined in the following paragraph.

Trustees are able to adopt an ethical investment policy which will involve avoiding investments:

- in a particular business that would for practical reasons conflict with the aims of the charity; for example, a charity with objectives for the protection of the environment and wildlife may decide not to invest in businesses which pollute what the charity is trying to protect;
- that might hamper a charity's work, either by making potential beneficiaries unwilling to be helped because of the source of the charity's money, or by alienating supporters.

This requires trustees to strike a balance between the likely cost of lost support, if the charity were to hold the investments, and any risk of financial underperformance if those investments are excluded from its portfolio.

There may be some cases where the two previous statements do not apply, but the trustees will still wish to make investment decisions on moral grounds. This may include using positive or negative criteria, or a combination of both. In all these cases, however, the trustees must be particularly clear that their decisions will not place the charity at risk of significant financial detriment, due to underperformance by the preferred investments or by the exclusion from consideration of forms of investment to which the trustees are opposed.

Trustees are unlikely to be criticised for adopting a particular policy if they have considered the correct issues, taken appropriate advice and reached a rational result.

Note that **ethical** investment is not the same as **social investment**. Also known as **programme-related investment (PRI)**, this is an entirely separate concept, and is not investment in the financial sense, as its primary aim is to carry out the objectives of a charity.

3.4.7 Tax Implications

Most investments are treated as **qualifying investments** by HM Revenue & Customs. However, the making of certain types of investment may be treated as **non-qualifying investments**. This can lead to a restriction of the charity's tax reliefs. Trustees making such investments will need to be able to satisfy HM Revenue & Customs that the investments are made for the financial benefit of the charity and not for the avoidance of tax, whether by the charity or by any other person.

Guidance on the tax implications of investment by charities can be found on the HM Revenue & Customs website.

3.5   INVESTMENT FOR TRUSTS

LEARNING OBJECTIVE

7.3.9   Understand the main considerations that should be taken into account when investing for trusts

A personal trust is created for a person or persons. Personal trusts can be used by beneficiaries to accomplish a variety of financial objectives. Personal trusts are separate legal entities that have the authority to buy, sell, hold and manage property for the benefit of their beneficiaries.

There are typically three main parties to a trust:

1. The **trust creator**, sometimes (in Scotland) called the grantor but usually (in England and Wales) the **settlor**, is the person who began as owner of the property that is to be transferred to and held by the trust.
2. The **trustee** is the person or institution (such as a bank or trust company) that holds the legal title to the trust estate. There may be one or more trustees. If a trustee is unwilling or unable to serve, then a successor trustee steps in to hold and manage the trust estate. The trustee is obliged to act in accordance with the terms of the trust for the benefit of the trust beneficiaries.
3. The **beneficiaries** are the persons who the trust creator intended to benefit from the trust estate.

The law in the area of personal trusts is complex. In the sections that follow we present the key guiding principles of the legislation that advisers need to be aware of when investing for trusts. In England and Wales, the legislation covering trusts and trustees is contained in the Trustees Act 2000. It has given professional trustees far greater investment freedom whilst making them more accountable. In addition, trustees are now required to seek professional guidance and investment advice. Trustees should take legal advice if uncertain. The Act covers five areas of trust law: the duty of care imposed upon trustees, trustees' power of investment, the power to appoint nominees and agents, the power to acquire land, and the power to receive remuneration for work done as a trustee. It sets a new duty of care, both objective and standard, massively extends the trustees' power of investment and limits the trustees' liability for the actions of agents, also providing for their remuneration for work done in the course of the trust. The legislation now requires that trustees should ensure that any adviser they are proposing to use is competent to give advice.

There are three main areas of responsibility that a trustee managing investment trusts should be aware of:

1. A statutory duty of care.
2. General powers of investment.
3. Rules on the appointment of nominees, custodians and investment managers.

3.5.1 Duty of Care

This duty for trustees is enshrined in statue law. Trustees have a duty of care under the Trustee Act 2000.

The new uniform statutory duty of care for trustees makes sure that individuals show such skill and care as is reasonable in the circumstances of the case, making allowance for their specialised knowledge, experience or professional status. The act requires the delivery of a certain standard of consistency and competence expected of trustees. This makes it more difficult to ignore or overlook their overall responsibilities.

The standard of care takes account of the trustees' experience and professional training. For example, in relation to the purchase of stocks and shares, a higher standard may be expected of a trustee who has specialist knowledge in the area of finance (ie, is an investment banker, specialising in equities), other than of a trustee who is a beekeeper, particularly if the investment banker is acting as a trustee in the course of their investment banking business.

According to Section I of the Act, the duty of care must be exercised when:

*   investing trust capital or reviewing investments;
*   acquiring or managing land;
*   appointing someone to give proper advice or reviewing/selecting agents to carry out delegated responsibilities;
*   insuring trust properties;
*   exercising powers to compound liabilities;
*   dealing with audits and valuations of trust property.

The trustee may be liable under law for any act or default by their appointed agents if they fail to deliver the duty of care responsibilities when drawing up investment policy statements or entering into or reviewing compliance matters. For professional trustees the duty of care is taken further in the sense that they must select investments with the **prudent man rule**, looking after the interests of others. In addition, when investing trust monies, trustees must treat the beneficiaries impartially and seek to balance the interests of providing income and preserving capital value.

The following steps have to be taken by the trustees:

- Review the trusts aims and objectives.
- Decide which responsibilities should be delegated to agents.
- Review and reconcile the investment management, nominee and custodian arrangements with trust rules.
- Trustees of charitable trusts must act in accordance with Charity Commission rules on the selection and appointment of custodians and nominees.
- Check that investment advice and management is provided by qualified professionals.
- Prepare, review and revise the trust's investment policy statement.

3.5.2 Investment Powers

In the Trustee Act 2000, trustees have been given the flexibility to make investments in any asset classes that are expected to produce an income or capital return. The Act refrains from defining the nature of the investment narrowly: it should be in an asset class that is suitable or appropriate for the needs of the trust. The responsibility requires that the trustee employs appropriate skills in stock selection within each asset class. Finally, the investment portfolio should be diversified.

From a practical point of view, this implies that the trustees must engage in the following process:

- Create and review investment objectives and define the requirements precisely. Trustees must continually refer back to the standard investment criteria to check that they are being fulfilled.
- Work with the appointed investment manager to set and review the investment policy statement of the fund. This ensures that the money manager is fully conversant with the plan requirements.
- Agree the terms of the investment engagement with the investment manager and secure a written agreement. The policy must be written so that all the functions are carried out in the best interests of the trust.

Examples of the contents of the **investment policy** are as follows:

- Frequency of review and performance reporting.
- Overall return expected, minimum yield required and risks.
- Income or capital requirements.
- The ability to distribute capital in the place of income, ie, total return.
- The nature and timing of any liabilities.
- The liquidity requirement, including dates of planned expenditure.
- The marketability of the investments – important if capital needs to be raised quickly.
- The time horizon of the trust - less than five years or long-term.
- Asset allocation considerations.
- Selection of the benchmark.
- The time horizon over which performance will be assessed.
- The base currency of the trust.

- The residence and tax status of the trust and the beneficiaries.
- Any socially responsible investment constraints.
- Other tax and legal constraints.

3.5.3 Appointment of Nominees, Custodians and Investment Managers

Trustees have been given the power under the Act to appoint a nominee to hold the title to the trust's investments and/or a custodian to look after the documents of the title.

These agreements have to be made in writing and trustees have to check that the nominee:

- is separately incorporated from the investment manager;
- is a non-trading company;
- provides an insurance cover/indemnity over and above the statutory limits.

4. THE ADVANTAGES OF REPAYING MORTGAGE AND OTHER BORROWINGS

LEARNING OBJECTIVE

7.2.2   Analyse the merits and disadvantages of paying off mortgage or debt compared with investing surplus funds

4.1 THE RELATIONSHIP BETWEEN INVESTMENT AND BORROWINGS

At different points in the investor's financial life cycle, the typical individual will tend to:

- have surplus funds (for example, someone in middle age and middle management, with solid earnings, having paid off the mortgage and seen any children reach adulthood); or
- be cash-poor and tending to have a certain amount of indebtedness (perhaps someone in young adulthood, while in the early stages of a career, with young children to raise and a mortgage).

Of course, these are only stereotypes and not everyone follows such a pattern. In addition, there are times when people have both debt and investable cash.

It may seem irrational to invest money while also paying interest on a loan. After all, loan interest is typically higher than the interest paid on savings accounts of similar size and term. Sometimes, however, it will be appropriate to allow the investor to remain in some debt, and invest any liquid capital he has in the markets. At other times, this may not make financial sense. It may be more prudent to pay off existing debts before risking committing capital to the markets.

In weighing up the merits of repaying debt, against those of investing surplus cash instead, the factors to be considered will include:

- whether the debt is fixed-rate or variable (will the client be able to keep up the repayments if interest rates go up, if their money is tied up in the markets?);
- any penalties on early repayment of the loan;
- the likely direction of interest rates;
- the nature of the debt (for example, it may be appropriate to allow a fixed-rate, fixed-term mortgage to run rather than paying it off, if the investor has a good deal on it and wishes to begin investing for the future);
- the investor's tax status: if an investment is particularly tax-favourable, then this may be an additional factor to weigh against the disadvantages of carrying a debt burden.

Many people with capital available to invest will also be owner-occupiers (homeowners) with a mortgage. Should such a person use free capital to pay off all or part of their mortgage rather than invest the money? The cost of maintaining the mortgage can be quantified in terms of the interest cost.

Suppose that an individual has a repayment mortgage for £50,000 and also has £50,000 in cash. If the interest rate on the mortgage is 5% and the after-tax rate of interest paid on deposits is 3%, then the net cost of keeping the mortgage, rather than using the money to pay it off, is 2% (£50,000 x 2% = £1,000 per annum).

What if the individual is considering investing the available sum of £50,000 in equities? This obviously involves taking a risk with the money, and the sum could either grow or fall in value.

Generally, it is well worth someone considering paying off part of their mortgage if they can. This will reduce their interest repayments in the future, and may bring forward the day when they are free of mortgage debt. The alternative of investing the money will also be considered by some, and is a valid strategy for someone who is not risk-averse.

It is also worth bearing in mind that a homebuyer who has an interest-only mortgage backed by a repayment vehicle (such as an equity ISA) is effectively choosing to take the risk of investing in equities (through the ISA) rather than withdrawing and using those funds to partially repay the mortgage.

There are various ways that an individual can consider balancing the relationship between borrowings and capital for investing. The availability of **offset mortgages** which allow the net outstanding borrowing to be set against cash balances has increased the flexibility that can be employed in reaching a balance that suits the individual.

5. INVESTMENT SOLUTIONS

LEARNING OBJECTIVE

7.4.2   Apply an appropriate investment allocation strategy that best meets the following criteria: client's financial objectives and priorities; client's risk tolerance; appropriate fees and charges; total expense ratio (TER) and portfolio turnover ratio (PTR); client suitability requirements; adequate diversification and correlation benefits; additional risk, timing and liquidity factors where asset accumulation and decumulation are relevant features

5.1   INVESTOR CIRCUMSTANCES

It is possible to identify a typical financial life cycle (and the financial needs that accompany this) – but bear in mind that every case is different, and there may be many variations in individual circumstances that cannot easily be fitted into standard categories. In any event, we can identify certain factors that affect an investor's circumstances.

When considering an investor's objectives and risk profile, his **wealth** is an important consideration. If there is free capital to invest, then clearly it is sensible for the individual to take steps to make the best use of that capital.

It is possible, although not generally advisable, for someone with little wealth to gain exposure to investment markets, for example, by borrowing money to invest, or by using investments such as derivatives or spread betting to gain a greater exposure than the individual's free resources. When investing in risky assets such as equities, a good principle is the often-stated one that someone should only invest what they can afford to lose. Someone who borrows to invest without having other capital to back it up if things go wrong has the problem that they may end up with liabilities in excess of assets.

An investor who uses instruments such as derivatives to increase his exposure to the markets should maintain other accessible resources (for example, cash on deposit) that can be used to meet losses that may arise. Clearly, it is also important that he understands and accepts the risks involved.

The age of an investor, their stage in the life cycle, and their commitments, all affect their **risk profile**. Adventurous risk-taking may be unwise for someone with heavy financial commitments, for example, to children and other dependants. Further, time can be a factor: someone who works full-time and has a family may have little time left to manage their investments (even if they had the inclination and skills to do so). Their time commitments may mean that they are more likely to use professional financial advice and management.

5.2   AFFORDABILITY AND SUITABILITY

In considering what recommendations to make to an investor, a planner or adviser needs to take into account not just the factors external to that investor – the investment and economic environment – but also those internal to them. These factors include their own financial situation, and psychological factors such as their appetite for risk. They affect what investments will be suitable for them, in their current situation – and what investments they may be able to afford on an ongoing basis.

There is little point in recommending a regular savings product if the investor is unlikely to be able to keep up the payments. Indeed, to do so may end up being very costly for them, as some packaged products carry heavy penalties if they are discontinued in the early years and the investor may end up losing as much as 100% of what they have paid in.

Whether an investor is making their own financial planning decisions, or is being advised by a financial adviser, it may seem obvious to state that investments chosen should meet a test of suitability. An adviser clearly needs to follow the regulatory principle of know your client in order to be able to assess the suitability requirements of a client.

In order to ensure that recommendations meet the test of suitability, client needs should be quantified and the shortfall (if any) between needs and the client's existing arrangements should be assessed.

For each quantified need, the adviser should draw up a list of suitable products and strategies from those available. From the list of suitable products and strategies, the most suitable combination should be identified. This can generally be achieved by a process of elimination, bearing in mind such factors as risk, flexibility, access, cost, complexity, match with the investor's investment objectives, and charges.

5.3 INVESTMENT ALLOCATION STRATEGY

Asset allocation strategy is the construction stage of the portfolio management process. Bearing in mind the mandate from the investment policy statement, an investment manager gets to work on the selection of assets, processing capital market expectations and developing the model inputs that are required to build a suitable portfolio that meets the client's objectives.

The traditional asset classes from which a portfolio is constructed include the following:

- **Domestic ordinary shares** – market capitalisation is used as a criterion to distinguish amongst large-cap, intermediate and small-cap issues as distinct sub-asset classes. Moreover, the decision-making may include an element of style that is captured by following value or growth opportunities.
- **Domestic fixed income** – here the focus may be on short, intermediate or long-term maturities. In particular, recently, inflation-protected securities have been used to distinguish between nominal bonds and inflation-protected bonds.
- **Money market securities** – these securities are of a maturity of less than one year and offer the advantages of easy conversion to meet short- or near-term liquidity needs in a portfolio.
- **International equities** – investment in this area may further be sub-divided into developed, emerging and frontier markets, as permitted within the policy statement.
- **International bonds** – as with international equities, the asset class is sub-divided mainly into permitted developed and emerging markets.
- **Real estate and commodities** – the major asset classes above are the primary asset classes used in the construction of financial portfolios. In the recent decade, however, interest in non-financial asset classes has increased as money managers have sought better diversification opportunities and yield enhancement. Real estate, commodities and private equity all belong to this unique asset class, often called **alternative investments**.

It is important to note that when investing in international assets, investors will need to consider the following special issues:

*   **Currency risk** – exchange rate movements will affect both the total return and the volatility of an asset. The currency risk is often of the same order as the **equity risk**, but it is considerably greater for bond and money market investments. As a result money managers will want to develop capital market expectations about currency movements and then to decide whether the new position will need to be hedged or left unhedged.
*   **Stress-induced correlation increase** – investors should be aware that, during episodes of market stress, correlations across international markets will increase, limiting opportunities for diversification.
*   **Emerging markets concerns** – a number of issues may be present that fund managers will be wary about. These include: political instability; limitations on ownership of securities by international investors; the quality and content of information available on foreign securities; and non-normality of security returns.

5.3.1   Weighting of Asset Classes

In strategic asset allocation, the money manager has to determine the asset allocation or the proportions of weights given to each asset class that is invested in a portfolio. Asset allocation reviews are carried out on a regularly basis during the management of a funded portfolio. For each asset class that is considered as a viable class for the portfolio, there will be a comprehensive view of capital market expectations formed over the investment period.

With capital market expectations and the portfolio objectives in hand, the asset allocation decision is then taken. The inputs to this decision are often fed into an **optimiser**. A large number of fund managers nowadays use established procedures that have a **quantitative** flavour. The optimisation methodologies are beyond the scope of this syllabus and use variants of the Markowitz mean-variance approach. Some investment advisers on the other hand, particularly those serving individual investor clientele, may use a **qualitative** approach to allocation based on their experiences. In actual fact most professional advisers utilise both quantitative and qualitative judgements in making recommendations.

Experience-Based Approaches

Although qualitative approaches offer a disciplined basis to the asset allocation process, there are advisers who prefer an experience-based qualitative method that is also grounded in financial theory. The lengthy training and experience of an adviser adopting a qualitative approach has worked well for some clients in the past.

Some popular experience-based approaches are:

*   **A 60/40 stock/bond allocation** – this may be a good starting point for an average investor. This allocation pre-dates modern portfolio theory and has been suggested to be neutral for an average investor under **normal** market conditions. The 60% equity allocation provides the long-term growth to the fund, while the 40% bond weight in the bond portfolio provides the risk-reduction and income contribution.
*   **Increase bond weighting as risk aversion increases** – conservative investors value low volatility. Hence, increasing the allocation to bonds should lead to lower portfolio risks.

- **Increase allocation to stocks as the investment time period gets longer** – this is based on an idea called time diversification, which has shown that, over a longer time period stocks are less risky. The rule-of-thumb suggested by some practitioners in the US market is that the allocation to equities could use the following simple formula: **% equity allocation = 100 – age of the investor**. This view is based on the works of Malkiel (2004), who put forward a life-cycle investment guide to asset allocation. For example, as a starting point for the investment allocation decision for a 30-year-old investor, the adviser may start with a 70/30 equity/bond mix. A 60-year-old investor on the other hand will be given a 40/60 equity/bond mix.

5.3.2 Rebalancing

After a portfolio allocation decision has been taken and the fund is fully invested, the portfolio will have to be rebalanced over the investment time period. Rebalancing may be done on a calendar basis (ie, quarterly or semi-annually). In a strategic asset allocation setting, since the timeframes are long, the rebalancing is only necessary if underlying asset prices have changed appreciably and have moved the portfolio weights away from target weights past the tolerance limit agreed within the investment policy statement (IPS) frameworks.

Rebalancing may also be done on percentage-of-portfolio basis. This form of rebalancing occurs when an asset-class weight passes a threshold or a trigger point. When this occurs, the asset weight must be rebalanced all the way back to original target weight.

5.4   IDENTIFYING SUITABLE PRODUCT SOLUTIONS

7.3.3   Assess the following factors when selecting suitable product solutions: impact of new solutions on existing arrangements; range of solutions available to suit different circumstances; range of criteria for matching solutions to client needs and demands

An adviser needs to be able to analyse a wide range of potentially suitable investment products, taking account of the investor's existing arrangements. Depending on the terms of their engagement, they are likely to need to take a comprehensive approach in arriving at the proposed solutions.

The client's needs and demands should be considered in order to match possible appropriate solutions to these needs and demands, in the light of the features of the various investment alternatives. It is not necessarily the case that only one possible solution should be recommended. There may be a number of feasible solutions that can be discussed with the client.

5.4.1   The Impact of New Solutions

It is not always realistic or beneficial to chop and change between different products as they are launched; some products carry penalties for people encashing them early, and others simply need time to deliver their benefits. But in a rapidly evolving and dynamic market such as that which exists in the UK, it is possible for better-value options to be developed into which the investor can switch, in some cases.

Various considerations may be involved when taking over an existing portfolio and reconstructing it, though there will be the usual need to consider the individual's requirement for accessibility and liquidity, income needs, attitude to risk, timescale and tax position. If clients have investments that no longer meet current requirements and circumstances, they should clearly be changed. However, an adviser may face a dilemma if there are existing life assurance policies or products, which could carry heavy surrender penalties on early encashment.

There may also be tax penalties if investments are disposed of, making it hard to carry out a wholesale realignment. For property, shares and collective investments not sheltered within an ISA, there may be a capital gains tax charge. Encashment of a life assurance investment bond may create a chargeable event, resulting in a possible higher-rate tax liability.

5.4.2 Matching Investment Solutions to Client Circumstances

Depending on an adviser's status – independent, tied or multi-tied – they may be required to advise their client on solutions from the whole of the market, from just one provider, or from a limited number of providers. It is important that this is made clear to the investor, so that they can consider the effects of this on the advice received.

Advisers need to be able to apply a range of criteria when matching investment solutions to client needs.

The financial adviser must recognise that each client has their own views, goals and attitudes. Attitudes to risk vary widely and, accordingly, investment choices vary widely too. Some individuals will be reluctant to take on any significant risk of loss of their capital, while others are prepared, in effect, to **gamble** with their savings.

People are likely to take notice of the growth potential of an investment, while some could be less willing to appreciate the risk involved. The adviser needs to take especial care to make such a client aware of risks.

Attitudes to risk vary according to the different objectives of the investor. An investor may have a core holding of deposits that they wish to keep as an emergency fund, while they may be prepared to take greater risks with other funds they hold.

If a client has a specific target for a particular investment – for example, to pay for children's education, or to pay for a vacation – then the adviser may choose lower-risk investment solutions for the funds intended to reach that target than they will for the client's other investments. If an individual is prepared to take on risks for a proportion of their savings and does not require those funds for a specific purpose, then equities may be an appropriate choice for that individual.

6.   PRESENTING RECOMMENDATIONS

LEARNING OBJECTIVE

7.4.3   Understand the factors which influence the way in which
           recommendations are presented

Providing a **written report** to clients is an important part of the process of giving financial advice.

A written report provides a way of putting across recommendations that have already been made orally in meetings with clients. The written format makes some aspects of observations and recommendations easier for the client to understand.

Furthermore, providing a written report is clearly an important way of providing a record of what is being recommended, and on what key information it is based. A report in writing should avoid the potential for misunderstandings about the advice that has been given, thus acting as a safeguard for the adviser in justifying his work, as well as a document of record for the client.

The parts of a financial planning report to a client are normally as follows:

- A statement of the client's objectives.
- A summary of the client's income and assets and other relevant circumstances or problems.
- Recommendations, including any proposals for immediate action as well as longer-term suggestions for the client to consider in the future. These should be backed up by the reasoning behind them – why they are felt to be suitable – and any risks or inflexibilities inherent in the proposed solutions. These recommendations should include timescales for implementation.
- Appendices, including any data that is best presented separately, if appropriate.

Product quotations, illustrations and brochures should be presented in an orderly way, possibly with an index listing the various items being sent to the client. The language in the report should be written as concisely and clearly as possible. The language used should not include jargon except where necessary to explain points being made.

Following the preparation of a written report, it is often sensible to have a face-to-face meeting with the client, to give him an opportunity to clear up any misunderstandings that may have arisen with regard to his objectives, and to allow him to ask questions where needs be.

6.1   CLIENTS' UNDERSTANDING

7.4.4   Understand how to check clients' understanding of recommendations

Firms are required by the FSA to have regard for the information needs of their clients, taking into account the client's level of sophistication and experience. An adviser should not recommend a transaction or act as an investment manager for a customer unless they have taken reasonable steps to help the customer understand the nature of the risks involved.

In particular, where highly risky investments are involved, specific **risk warnings** are required; the same applies to investments that are not readily realisable. The adviser should also explain any likely difficulties in establishing a market price.

Following the recording of recommendations in a report, the adviser may be well advised to check whether the client has read and understood the contents of the report, and should ascertain whether they have any questions to ask about it.

7.   CONSUMER RIGHTS AND REGULATORY REQUIREMENTS

7.4.5   Apply consumer rights and the regulatory requirements to the provision of investment advice

7.1   REGULATORY PRINCIPLES AND AUTHORISATION

The Financial Services Authority (FSA) was established under the Financial Services and Markets Act 2000 (FSMA), as the **single regulator** for the UK's financial services industry. This is a slight misnomer, as there are still some other bodies exercising powers over financial services operators. For example, the Office of Fair Trading still oversees the Consumer Credit legislation and issues licences to lenders under it.

The FSA's objectives are to:

*   support market confidence;
*   support financial stability
*   provide an appropriate measure of protection to financial services consumers;
*   reduce financial crime.

It has established 11 **Principles for Businesses**. These encapsulate the basic obligations of any authorised business, including – of course – financial advisers. The FSA has described these Principles as '...*a general statement of the fundamental obligations of firms under the regulatory system*'.

The Principles are as follows:

1. **Integrity.** A firm must conduct its business with integrity.
2. **Skill, care and diligence.** A firm must conduct its business with due skill, care and diligence.
3. **Management and control.** A firm must take reasonable care to organise and control its affairs responsibly and effectively, with adequate risk-management systems.
4. **Financial prudence.** A firm must maintain adequate financial resources.
5. **Market conduct.** A firm must observe proper standards of market conduct.
6. **Customers' interests.** A firm must pay due regard to the interests of its customers and treat them fairly.
7. **Communications with clients.** A firm must pay due regard to the information needs of its clients, and communicate information to them in a way which is clear, fair and not misleading.
8. **Conflicts of interest.** A firm must manage conflicts of interest fairly, both between itself and its customer and between a customer and another client.
9. **Customer's relationship of trust.** A firm must take reasonable care to ensure the suitability of its advice and discretionary decisions for any customer who is entitled to rely on its judgment.
10. **Clients' assets.** A firm must arrange adequate protection for clients' assets when it is responsible for them.
11. **Relationship with regulators.** A firm must deal with its regulators in an open and co-operative way, and must disclose to the FSA appropriately anything relating to the firm of which the FSA would reasonably expect notice.

These are all clearly very general – hence the term principles – and therefore, to help firms understand how they should be complying in the context of the specific activities they carry on, the Principles are underpinned by a series of rules and sets of guidance, contained in the FSA's Handbook.

The Handbook itself is divided into smaller sourcebooks, covering specific areas – for example, Systems and Controls (SYSC); Conduct of Business (COBS); and the Approved Persons Regime (APR). They are very detailed, and fairly voluminous, but provide detailed rules and guidance on a wide area of activities, many of which are directly relevant to how advisers deal with their clients:

*   exercising a significant influence on the conduct of an authorised person's affairs; or
*   dealing with customers in connection with regulated activities (eg, advising on investments); or
*   dealing with the property of customers in connection with regulated activities.

So a person is likely to need to be approved if they are to take on any of the following roles:

*   discretionary investment manager;
*   customer adviser or trader;
*   director or chief executive of an authorised firm;
*   appointed actuary of an insurance company;
*   money laundering reporting officer;
*   senior manager;
*   head of compliance;
*   internal auditor.

Authorised businesses must maintain clear and appropriate apportionment of significant responsibilities for senior managers, and keep a record of them. There must also, as we saw under the Principles for Businesses, be appropriate systems and controls, and there should be an effective compliance system in place, overseen by a director or senior manager.

The FSA has also laid down a series of seven **Principles for Approved Persons**, which the relevant individuals must follow themselves. Some of them are very similar to those that apply to the firms as a whole – but they apply at the personal level. These Principles are applicable to all those who are subject to individual registration as discussed above. They are:

1. An approved person must act with integrity in carrying out his controlled function.
2. An approved person must act with due skill, care and diligence in carrying out his controlled functions.
3. An approved person must observe proper standards of market conduct in carrying out his controlled functions.
4. An approved person must deal with the FSA and with other regulators in an open and co-operative way and must disclose appropriately any information of which the FSA would reasonably expect notice.
5. An approved person performing a significant influence function must take reasonable steps to ensure that the business of the firm for which he is responsible in his controlled function is organised so that it can be controlled effectively.
6. An approved person performing a significant influence function must exercise due skill, care and diligence in managing the business for which he is responsible in his controlled function.
7. An approved person performing a significant influence function must take reasonable steps to ensure that the business of the firm, for which he is responsible in his controlled function, complies with the regulatory requirements on that business.

7.2　COMPLAINTS AND COMPENSATION

The FSA states that a **complaint** is *'any expression of dissatisfaction, whether oral or written and whether justified or not'*. This can cover a wide range of communications, from a minor grumble to a claim for a serious amount of compensation.

The rules on complaints procedures only apply to **eligible complainants**. This means someone who is any of the following:

*   a private individual;
*   a business with annual turnover of less than £1 million;
*   a charity with annual income of less than £1 million;
*   a trust with a net asset value of less than £1 million.

This means that certain clients are not eligible complainants. This does not mean, of course, that their complaints should not be properly and fairly dealt with – simply that the detailed FSA regime in connection with complaints procedures doesn't apply to them.

When a customer has a complaint against his financial product provider or adviser, he should – in the first instance – take it to the provider/adviser to give them an opportunity to investigate and if possible (and providing that the complaint is justified) put matters right.

The FSA requires that firms have **written complaints procedures**. They must refer – in writing – to the availability of a copy of their complaints procedures, at or immediately after the point of sale. Copies of complaints procedures must also be published and copies provided on request. Firms which have branches to which clients have access must display a notice stating that they are subject to the Financial Ombudsman Service's regime (see Section 7.2.1).

In addition, they must be given to any complainant on receipt of a complaint – except where the complaint can be resolved by the close of business on the business day after it is received.

All complaints must be investigated by a competent and independent employee who has the authority to settle them. In a firm which is big enough to merit it, this may mean having a separate complaints officer, or having complaints investigated by the compliance department. All relevant employees must be aware of the firm's complaints procedure, so that they know to whom complaints should be referred.

Complaints must be handled fairly and consistently. In addition, they should be handled promptly, and the FSA lays down rules as to what this means in practice:

- Complaints must be acknowledged within five days of receipt.
- A final response must be sent after eight weeks – or, if the complaint cannot yet be resolved, because it is still being investigated, a further holding response must be sent at that point.

When a complaint has been investigated and the facts considered, a decision must be made as to whether to uphold it (that is, acknowledge that the complainant is correct and that the situation should be rectified), or to reject it. The decision is sent to the complainant as a final response, and in the same letter the firm must remind the complainant that if he is not satisfied with its response he can refer the matter on to the **Financial Ombudsman Service (FOS)**. A firm must also advise a complainant of his right to refer to the FOS if it cannot reach a final response within eight weeks from receipt of the complaint – for example, if it needs longer to investigate the circumstances.

If a complaint is upheld, the firm must make an offer of appropriate compensation, or other remedial action. This might, for example, involve undoing a transaction which should not have been carried out in the first place, so as to put the customer back in his original position.

If the client accepts the firm's offer of redress, the matter can be closed. However, if he is not satisfied (or if the firm rejected his complaint and he is unhappy), he can refer to the FOS.

7.2.1   The Financial Ombudsman Service (FOS)

The FOS is established under FSMA and is responsible for receiving and investigating complaints against authorised persons, where they cannot be satisfactorily resolved between the two parties directly. All authorised persons come under the FOS's compulsory jurisdiction – that is, they have to co-operate with it when it investigates complaints and they are bound by its decisions. Some other, non-authorised firms are also voluntarily under its jurisdiction.

The FOS's objective is to resolve disputes quickly and effectively. It has a number of advantages over taking a dispute to court:

- It is free to the complainant.

- It is less intimidating than going to court – many individuals will be nervous of approaching a lawyer, quite apart from the time and cost of the legal process.
- It can take into account factors other than the strict letter of the law (eg, what current common market practice was at the time).
- It is private, whereas court actions are often made public.

Authorised firms are required to co-operate fully with the FOS. In reviewing a case, the FOS can require either party to produce information or documents it deems necessary; failure to do so may be treated as contempt of court. It will investigate cases fully and can allow each side the chance to put its side.

The FOS determines complaints on the basis of what is **fair and reasonable** meaning it can consider matters other than the strict letter of the law (although of course this is also important). This means that the FOS can sometimes come to a conclusion which is fairer to all sides than the outcome of legal action might have been. The FOS will consider:

- the facts of the case;
- the law;
- FSA rules and guidance;
- commonly accepted good market practice.

Once it has made a decision, it will write to both parties to tell them the outcome, with its reasoning. The complainant then has a certain time, set by the FOS at that point, to accept or reject the decision:

- If they accept it, the decision will be binding on the firm being complained about.
- If they reject it, they can take the matter to court.
- If they fail to reply to the FOS, the FOS will treat this as a rejection and the firm will not be bound by its decision.

Where it finds in favour of a complainant, the FOS can award compensation for any loss they have suffered, and/or require the firm to take remedial action; assuming the complainant has accepted the FOS's decision, the firm must comply.

The maximum the FOS can award, in monetary terms, is:

- £100,000;
- plus the complainant's costs;
- plus an award for suffering, damage to reputation, distress or inconvenience, if appropriate.

It can recommend an award higher than £100,000, but this will not be binding on the firm; therefore a complainant who believes they may deserve more than this may be best advised to take legal action immediately, instead.

7.3   OTHER REGULATIONS

As set out in the Principles for Businesses, financial advisers – and the providers of the products recommended – are required to communicate information to a customer in a way which is clear, fair and not misleading. They must also communicate in a way which has regard for the customer's knowledge of the business. This implies that firms should be considering their customers' level of financial sophistication, tailoring the language they use accordingly, and ensuring that any matters that may need explanation are made clear.

There are specific and detailed rules in connection with:

- **Financial promotions** – these refer to communications that are or may be **inducements** to clients, in connection with regulated activities, through any medium. The intention is to ensure that promotions are **fair and not misleading**, and that their target audience receives clear and adequate information which is appropriate to its level of understanding.
- **Status disclosure** – firms must tell clients and potential clients about their status (independent, or tied) and the way in which they are remunerated, in a prescribed format.
- **Terms of business and client agreements** – the FSA has rules on when firms must provide their clients with their **terms of business**, and what these must contain.
- **Know your customer and suitability** – the FSA requires that financial advisers ensure that they have found out enough about their customer to ensure that their advice is appropriate to his circumstances.
- **Execution-only transactions** – the term execution-only refers to a transaction or account where no advice is given, and the provider exercises no discretion. The client makes their own decisions as to what transactions are to be undertaken, and instructs the provider to put them into effect. There are various differences between the regulatory regime for this type of business and for business where the provider gives advice or exercises discretion.
- **Charges, commissions and product disclosure** – advisers have to disclose a considerable amount of information about the way in which they are paid.
- **Cancellation and cooling-off** – cancellation provisions apply to a number of packaged products and allow clients, who have bought on the basis of advice, the opportunity to consider what they have done for a short period after the transaction has been effected – and, if they believe it is appropriate, to change their minds. This period for reflection is known as the **cooling-off** period. Cancellation notices must be issued in respect of a range of packaged investment and insurance products. They are not applicable to non-packaged investments such as the purchase of direct shareholdings.

8.   PERFORMANCE BENCHMARKS

LEARNING OBJECTIVE

7.4.6   Assess the factors influencing the choice of benchmark and the basis for review: portfolio's asset allocation; risk/return profile; alternative investments; taxation; peer groups; maintenance of capital value

Once the portfolio has been constructed, the portfolio manager and client need to agree on a realistic benchmark against which the performance of the portfolio can be judged. The choice of benchmark will depend on the precise asset split adopted and should be compatible with the risk and expected return profile of the portfolio. Where an index is used, this should represent a feasible investment alternative to the portfolio constructed.

Portfolio performance is rarely measured in absolute terms but in relative terms against the predetermined benchmark and against the peer group. In addition, indexed portfolios are also evaluated against the size of their tracking error, or how closely the portfolio has tracked the chosen index. Tracking error arises from both underperformance and outperformance of the index being tracked.

It is essential that the portfolio manager and client agree on the frequency with which the portfolio is reviewed, not only to monitor the portfolio's performance but also to ensure that it still meets with the client's objectives and is correctly positioned given prevailing market conditions.

KEY CHAPTER POINTS

- Financial advice extends well beyond investment matters, to areas such as budgeting, borrowing and protection.
- The process of giving financial advice requires that the adviser establishes a sound relationship with his client.
- Financial advice is not usually a one-off process; periodic monitoring and review of a client's arrangements can be important.
- The review will lead to the creation of a set of portfolio objectives that will summarise the client's risk and return requirements.
- The process of understanding a client's precise requirements along with the objectives will lead to the development of a comprehensive investment policy statement.
- Investment decisions will take into account investors' unique requirements that will include ethical and social considerations.
- Non-financial factors need to be taken into account along with investment decisions that include corporate, social, environmental and governance issues.
- The role of trustees is to have a duty of care over the powers they have been given to look after the financial needs of their beneficiaries. They must act in accordance with the principles of the Trustee Act.
- Investment managers have a duty not only to meet the requirements as set out in an investment policy statement, but to also prepare regular written reports for clients to explain and justify the investment decisions taken as a matter of record-keeping and also to protect the adviser against unwarranted criticism.
- The FSA is the regulatory body that has powers to hear complaints and to find remedies for eligible entities. The Financial Ombudsman Service (FOS) is available to those consumers who are unhappy and still have concerns about their complaints. Authorised firms are required to co-operate fully with the FOS in reviewing a case.
- Performance measurement is a specialised area of portfolio monitoring. Suitable benchmarks need to be identified at early stages of the portfolio management process for both actively and passively managed portfolios. Passive managers seek to minimise tracking error against benchmarks. In their search for alpha, active managers seek to beat benchmark returns.

CHAPTER EIGHT

PORTFOLIO PERFORMANCE AND REVIEW

This syllabus area will provide approximately 5 of the 80 examination questions

1.   PURPOSE AND CONCEPT OF BENCHMARKING

LEARNING OBJECTIVE

8.1.1   Understand the purpose and limitations of portfolio evaluation

8.1.2   Understand the concept and purpose of benchmarking

If the performance of an investment fund or investment manager is to be assessed, then the first issue to address is how to measure that performance. Investment performance is usually monitored by comparing it to a relevant benchmark.

There are three main ways in which portfolio performance is assessed:

- Comparison with a relevant bond or stockmarket index.
  - An index comparison provides a clear indication of whether the portfolio's returns exceed that of the bond or stock market index that is being used as the benchmark return.
  - As well as the main stock market indices that are generally seen, many sub-indices have been created over the years which allow a precise comparison to be made.
- Comparison with similar funds or a relevant universe comparison.
  - Investment returns can also be measured against the performance of other fund managers or portfolios which have similar investment objectives and constraints.
  - A group of similar portfolios is referred to as an 'investment universe'.
- Comparison with a custom benchmark.
  - Customised benchmarks are often developed for funds with unique investment objectives or constraints.
  - If a portfolio spans several asset classes, then a composite index may need to be constructed by selecting several relevant indices and then multiplying each asset class weighting to arrive at a composite return.

1.1   STOCKMARKET INDICES

LEARNING OBJECTIVE

8.1.3   Know the construction and weighting methods of the following indices: FTSE 100; FTSE All Share Index; FTSE Actuaries Government Securities Indices; MSCI World Index; Dow Jones Industrial Average Index; S&P 500 Index; Nikkei 225

Stockmarket indices have the following uses:

- To act as a market barometer. Most equity indices provide a comprehensive record of historic price movements, thereby facilitating the assessment of trends. Plotted graphically, these price movements may be of particular interest to technical analysts, or chartists, and to momentum investors, by assisting the timing of security purchases and sales, or market timing.
- To assist in performance measurement. Most equity indices can be used as performance benchmarks against which portfolio performance can be judged.

- To act as the basis for index tracker funds, exchange-traded funds (ETFs), index derivatives and other index-related products.
- To support portfolio management research and asset allocation decisions.

There are three main types of market index:

- **Price-weighted index** – these are constructed on the assumption that an equal number of shares are held in each of the underlying index constituents. However, as these equal holdings are weighted according to each constituent's share price, those constituents with a high share price relative to that of other constituents have a greater influence on the index value. The index is calculated by summing the total of each constituent's share price and comparing this total to that of the base period. Although such indices are difficult to justify and interpret, the most famous of these is the Dow Jones Industrial Average (DJIA).
- **Market value-weighted index** – in these indices, larger companies account for proportionately more of the index as they are weighted according to each company's market capitalisation. The FTSE 100 is constructed on a market capitalisation-weighted basis.
- **Equal-weighted index** – in certain markets, the largest companies can comprise a disproportionately large weighting in the index, and therefore an index constructed on a market capitalisation basis can give a misleading impression. An equal-weighted index assumes that equal amounts are invested in each share in the index. The Nikkei 225 is an example of an equal-weighted index.

Most of the major indices used in performance measurement are market value-weighted indices such as: the S&P 500 and other S&P indices; the Morgan Stanley Capital International index; and the FTSE 100 and FTSE All Share indices.

1.1.1 FTSE 100

The FTSE 100 is a market capitalisation-weighted index representing the performance of the 100 largest UK-listed blue chip companies. It is free-float-weighted to ensure that a true investable opportunity is represented within the index, and screened for liquidity to ensure that the index is tradeable. Capital and total return versions are available. It is reviewed and its components rebalanced every quarter in March, June, September and December. The index represents approximately 80% of the UK's market capitalisation and is used as the basis for investment products, such as funds, derivatives and exchange-traded funds.

1.1.2 FTSE All Share Index

The FTSE All Share measures the performance of companies listed on the London Stock Exchange's main market. It covers close to 700 companies representing, approximately 98% of the UK's market capitalisation. It is a market capitalisation-weighted index and screened for size and liquidity. It is considered to be the best performance measure for the overall London equity market and is the basis for a wide range of investment-tracking products.

1.1.3 FTSE Actuaries Government Securities Indices

FTSE also produces indices based on British government securities. The indices are divided into conventional gilts and index-linked gilts and are also available in maturity bands. There is also a yield index that provides the term structure of the gilt market from one year up to 50 years.

1.1.4 MSCI World Index

The MSCI World index is a free-float-adjusted market capitalisation-weighted index that is designed to measure the equity market performance of developed markets.

The index includes securities from 23 countries and is calculated on a capital or total return basis and in both dollars and other currencies. It is the common benchmark index used for global funds.

1.1.5 Dow Jones Industrial Average

The Dow Jones Industrial Average was introduced over 100 years ago in 1896 and was the first convenient benchmark for comparing individual stocks to the performance of the market or for comparing the market with other indicators of economic conditions.

It is the best-known index in the world and its 30 stocks account for close to 25% of the total US equity market. It was designed in the pre-computer era and is based on a simple price-weighted arithmetic calculation, making it less suitable for index products.

1.1.6 S&P 500 Index

The S&P 500 is regarded as the best indicator of the US equity markets. It focuses on the large cap segment of the US market and provides coverage of approximately 75% of US equities that trade on NYSE and NASDAQ. It is a market capitalisation-weighted index that requires a free float of at least 50% and a minimum market capitalisation of US$4 billion. It is widely used as the basis for index products.

1.1.7 Nikkei 225

The Nikkei 225 or Nikkei Stock Average is Japan's most widely watched index of stockmarket activity and is the oldest and most-watched Asian index. As mentioned above, it is an equal-weighting index which is based on each constituent having an equal weighting based on a par value of 50 yen per share. Because it is an equal-weighting index, it needs to be rebalanced periodically.

The Nikkei 225 is designed to reflect the overall market, so there is no specific weighting of industries. The 225 components of the Nikkei Stock Average are among the most actively traded issues on the first section of the Tokyo Stock Exchange (TSE).

1.2   COMPOSITE BENCHMARKS

LEARNING OBJECTIVE

8.1.4   Understand the differences between a single and a composite
(synthetic) benchmark

As mentioned in Section 1, customised benchmarks are often developed for funds with unique investment objectives or constraints. If a portfolio spans several asset classes then a composite index may need to be constructed by selecting several relevant indices and then multiplying each asset class by a weighting to arrive at a composite return.

An example is the private investor indices produced by FTSE and the Association of Private Client Investment Managers and Stockbrokers (APCIMS). The indices are based on three portfolios which each have different asset allocations and are composed of related indices.

The current allocations and respective indices within the APCIMS indices are as follows:

Asset class	APCIMS income	APCIMS growth	APCIMS balanced	Underlying index
UK shares	45	47.5	42.5	FTSE All Share
International shares	10.0	30	22.5	FTSE World Ex-UK index calculated in sterling
Bonds	35	5	17.5	FTSE Gilts All Stocks index
Cash	5	5	5	7-Day LIBOR –1% (London Interbank Offer Rate)
Commercial property	5	5	5	FTSE UK Commercial Property index
Hedge funds	–	7.5	7.5	FTSE Hedge
Total	100	100	100	

1.3   ALTERNATIVE BENCHMARKING METHODS

LEARNING OBJECTIVE

8.1.5   Understand the alternative ways of benchmarking: GIPS (Global
Investment Performance Standards); peer group average (WM and
CAPS)

Rather than use an established index to benchmark portfolio performance, a peer group average is often employed. **WM** or **WM (World Markets)** company is a worldwide independent investment information services company which provides, among other services, performance measurement services to pension funds and other investing institutions.

Combined Actuarial Performance Services (CAPS) is an independent investment performance measurement service for the UK, covering over 1,800 pension funds. CAPS was set up as a joint venture of firms of consulting actuaries.

Most pension funds adopt cautious investment policies, and the guidance and benchmarks they set for fund managers means that most schemes keep their asset allocation close to the CAPS or WM averages.

Both create universes which are an aggregation of funds or portfolios with similar investment briefs or types of owner and are used for peer group comparisons. There are many specialist sub-groups of universe groupings to cater for a wide range of fund structures and investment management styles to provide a relevant and accurate relative comparison.

Global investment performance standards (GIPS) are not a way of benchmarking performance, but are global standards for calculating and presenting performance figures. As such, they represent a great leap forward for the performance measurement industry. Originally established in 1999 by the CFA Institute, GIPS were significantly enhanced in 2005 and have been voluntarily adopted by industry representative organisations in over 20 countries in order to help promote best standards.

1.4   PERFORMANCE ATTRIBUTION

LEARNING OBJECTIVE

8.1.6   Apply suitable benchmarks when measuring and evaluating investment performance

Investors, trustees and plan sponsors will want to assess the returns achieved by a fund manager to determine which elements of the strategy were responsible for results and why.

The process is known as performance attribution and attributes the performance to:

* asset allocation;
* sector choice;
* security selection.

To determine the returns produced by **asset allocation** you need to apply the following formula for each asset class:

(fund value at start of period x portfolio manager asset class weightings x benchmark asset class returns)

minus

(fund value at start of period x benchmark asset class weightings x benchmark asset class returns)

This isolates that part of the return attributable to diligent asset allocation by comparing the portfolio manager's exposure to asset classes and geographical areas to that of the benchmark and then multiplying this difference by the benchmark returns. To determine a portfolio manager's stock selection skill, you need to subtract the fund value resulting from asset allocation from the actual fund value at the end of the period. We will look at how performance is attributed by way of an example.

EXAMPLE

We will assume that the investment fund we are analysing had a fund value of £20 million at the start of the period we are considering and was valued at £18.75 million at the end, producing a negative return of 6.25%. The asset allocation of the fund was 75% in equities and 25% in gilts.

The benchmark used for the fund assumed an asset allocation of 50% in equities and 50% in gilts. Over the period equities produced a negative return of 10% and gilts a negative return of 5%.

1. Fund performance relative to benchmark performance

Using the figures given above, we can determine the performance of the benchmark as follows:

Benchmark	Asset Allocation	Value at Start of Period	Return	Value at End of Period
Equities	50%	£10m	–10%	£9.0m
Bonds	50%	£10m	–5%	£9.5m
Total		£20m		£18.5m

The fund has therefore outperformed the benchmark by £0.25 million.

The next step is to calculate the absolute outperformance or underperformance of the fund relative to the benchmark attributable to asset allocation.

2. Fund performance attributable to asset allocation

The contribution of asset allocation to fund returns is established by applying the formula referred to above to both the fund's equity and gilt weightings and to the benchmark returns. The benchmark returns are as shown above and the fund's returns are:

Benchmark	Asset Allocation	Value at Start of the Period	Return	Value at End of Period
Equities	75%	£15m	–10%	£13.5m
Bonds	25%	£5m	–5%	£4.75m
Total		£20m		£18.25m

Poor asset allocation has caused the fund to underperform the benchmark by £0.25 million.

The final stage is to consider the impact that stock selection has had.

3. Effect of stock selection

The fund value at the end of the period is £18.75 million, whilst the fund value attributable to asset allocation is £18.25 million. Therefore, good stock selection has added £0.5 million to performance.

The outcome of this performance attribution is summarised in the diagram below.

2. PORTFOLIO MEASUREMENT

LEARNING OBJECTIVE

8.2.1　　Apply the theory of investment risk and return to the measurement of portfolio performance: holding period return; relative return; standard deviation; risk-adjusted returns

2.1　RISK AND RETURN

There are three different methods used to measure portfolio performance:

- holding period yield – sometimes referred to as total return;
- money-weighted rate of return;
- time-weighted rate of return.

The holding period yield simply measures how much the portfolio has increased in value over a period of time and expresses it as a percentage. It suffers from the limitation of not taking into account the timing of cash flows into and out of the fund and so is not a particularly useful measure for most investment funds. Instead, the money-weighted and time-weighted rate of returns are used.

2.1.1　Money-Weighted Rate of Return

The money-weighted rate of return is used to measure the performance of a fund that has had deposits and withdrawals during the period being measured. It is also referred to as the internal rate of return of the fund. The standard money-weighted return measurement used in the UK is the Modified BAI Method as discussed in Chapter 3, Section 2.3.2.

One of the main drawbacks of this method is that to calculate the return is an iterative process and so is a more time-consuming calculation than other methods.

2.1.2 Time-Weighted Rate of Return

The time-weighted rate of return (TWRR) removes the impact of cash flows on the rate of return calculation. The TWRR is established by breaking the investment period into a series of sub-periods. A sub-period is created whenever there is a movement of capital into or out of the fund. Immediately prior to this point, a portfolio valuation must be obtained to ensure that the rate of return is not distorted by the size and timing of the cash flow. The TWRR is calculated by compounding the rate of return for each of these individual sub-periods, applying an equal weight to each sub-period in the process. This is known as unitised fund performance as discussed in Chapter 3, Section 2.3.2.

This can be seen in the following example:

EXAMPLE

A portfolio is valued at £1,000 at the beginning of October and grows in value to £1,100 by 15 October. It receives a cash inflow of £215 on 16 October and at 31 October is valued at £1,500.

Using TWRR, a percentage return is calculated for each separate period as follows:

Period 1 : r = $\dfrac{1,100}{1,000}$ − 1 = 0.10

Period 2 : r = $\dfrac{1,500}{1,315}$ − 1 = 0.141

TWRR = [(1 + 0.10) (1 + 0.141)] − 1 = 1.2551 − 1 = 25.51%

In many cases, the differences between money-weighted rate of return and time-weighted rate of return will be relatively small, but in certain circumstances wide variations can occur. As a result, the time-weighted rate of return is more widely used.

2.2 STANDARD DEVIATION

The standard deviation of a set of data is simply the square root of the variance and is the most commonly used measure of dispersion. Although the variances and standard deviations of both ordered raw and frequency distribution data can be calculated quickly and easily by using a scientific calculator, it is useful to understand how to work through their calculation manually. In summary, the steps you should take in making these calculations manually are as follows:

*   Obtain the arithmetic mean.
*   Obtain the set of deviations from the mean.
*   Square each deviation.

- Divide the sum of the squared deviations by the number of observations to obtain the population variance.
- Take the square root of the variance in each case to obtain the standard deviation.

To ensure precision in the calculation of the variance and standard deviation, statistical rules require a slight change to the formula if measuring a sample. The limitations of small data sets include the fact that they may not provide a representative picture of the population as a whole and so sampling error may arise. As a result, a slight adjustment to the standard deviation formula is made by reducing the number of observations by one.

The formulas for both calculations are expressed as follows:

Population standard deviation =

$$\sqrt{\frac{\sum (x - \bar{x})^2}{n}}$$

Sample standard deviation =

$$\sqrt{\frac{\sum (x - \bar{x})^2}{n - 1}}$$

In effect, by taking the square root of the variance, the standard deviation represents the average amount by which the values in the distribution deviate from the mean. With sufficiently large data, the pattern of deviations from the mean will be spread symmetrically on either side and if the class intervals are small enough, the resultant frequency distribution curve may look like a cross-section of a bell, ie, a bell-shaped curve.

Statistical analysis shows that in a normal frequency distribution curve:

- Approximately two thirds or 68.26% of observations will be within one standard deviation either side of the mean.
- Approximately 95.5% of all observations will be within two standard deviations either side of the mean.
- Approximately 99.75% of all observations will be within three standard deviations of the mean.

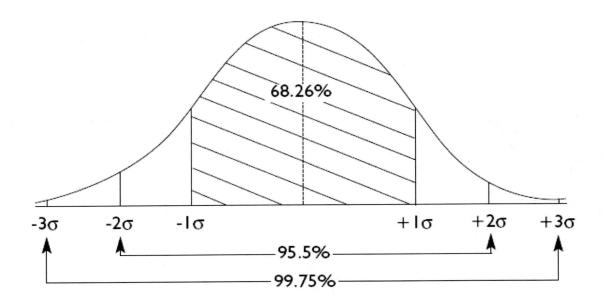

Figure 1: Normal Frequency Distribution Curve

Data does not always conform to a normal pattern and is then referred to as **skewed**. If the peak of the curve is to the left of centre it is said to be positively skewed and, if to the right, negatively skewed. Most long-run distributions of equity returns are positively skewed. That is, equity markets produce more extreme positive and negative returns than should statistically be the case – a phenomenon known as **kurtosis** – but these extreme positive values far outweigh the negative ones.

2.3   RISK-ADJUSTED RETURNS

Having calculated how a portfolio has performed the next stage is to compare its performance against the market as a whole or against other portfolios. This is the function of risk-adjusted performance measurements of which there are four main methods in use, as covered in Chapter 3, Section 2.4.

- Sharpe ratio;
- Treynor ratio;
- Jensen measure;
- Information ratio.

2.4 ABSOLUTE AND RELATIVE RETURN

8.2.2 Analyse portfolio performance in terms of: absolute and relative return; absolute and relative risk; risk-reward ratios; contributions to return arising from asset allocation, currency movements, stock selection and timing; impact of new money and timing factors

There are a number of methods that advisers can use to analyse the performance of an investment portfolio. This next section aims to offer some practical examples to assist you in carrying out this task for your clients.

The effort involved in considering the performance of a large, diverse portfolio may be considerable, and a number of tools are available, which have been specially developed to assist with this task.

Both Lipper and Morningstar provide performance statistics and risk measures for individual funds. Trustnet also provide this information in the form of individual factsheets available via their website www.trustnet.com.

Whichever tool you decide to use, it is important to establish a process for reviewing each component within the portfolio against its sector (or benchmark), and then relating the performance of the portfolio as a whole against its chosen benchmark, whilst also taking account of the movement of capital into and out of the portfolio.

Let us consider the various performance and volatility measures that we discussed earlier in the book.

- **Alpha** – a positive alpha is a measure of how much a fund has outperformed its benchmark, and a negative alpha is a measure of how much a fund has underperformed its benchmark. It is often seen as a key measure of the added value of an active fund manager.

- **Beta** – a measure of a fund's sensitivity to market movements. The beta of the market is 1.00 by definition. A beta of 1.10 shows that the fund has performed 10% better than its benchmark index in up markets and 10% worse in down markets, assuming all other factors remain constant. Conversely, a beta of 0.85 indicates that the fund is expected to perform 15% worse than the market's excess return during up markets and 15% better during down markets.

- **Information ratio** – the information ratio assesses the degree to which a fund manager uses skill and knowledge to enhance returns. This is a versatile and useful risk-adjusted measure of actively managed fund performance, calculated by deducting the returns of the fund benchmark from the returns of the fund and dividing the result by its tracking error. It is generally considered that the higher the number the better, with 0.75 reflecting a very good performance and 1.00 outstanding performance, with the caveat that the R-squared correlation between the fund and its benchmark must be strong if any reliance is to be placed upon the information ratio.

- **R-Squared/R^2** – a measure of the percentage of a fund's movements that can be accounted for by changes in its benchmark index. An R-squared of 100 indicates that a fund's movements are perfectly correlated with its benchmark. Thus, index funds that invest only in S&P 500 stocks typically could have an R-squared close to 100. Conversely, a low R-squared indicates that little of the fund's movements can be explained by movements in its benchmark index. An R-squared measure of 35, for example, means that only 35% of the fund's movements can be explained by movements in the benchmark index. R-squared can be used to ascertain the significance of a particular beta. Generally, a higher R-squared will indicate a more reliable beta. If the R-squared is lower, then the beta is less relevant to the fund's performance.

- **Sharpe ratio** – a risk-adjusted measure developed by Nobel laureate William Sharpe. It is calculated by using standard deviation and excess return to determine reward per unit of risk. The higher the Sharpe Ratio, the better the fund's historical risk-adjusted performance. The Sharpe ratio is calculated for the previous 36-month period by dividing a fund's excess returns by the standard deviation of a fund's excess returns. Since this ratio uses standard deviation as its risk measure, it is most appropriately applied when analysing a fund that is an investor's sole holding. The Sharpe ratio can be used to compare two funds directly on how much risk they had to bear to earn excess return over the risk-free rate. There is no definition of a good or bad Sharpe beyond the thought that a fund with a negative Sharpe ratio would have been better off investing in risk-free products.

- **Volatility/3-year volatility** – three-year standard deviation is used to represent volatility, and demonstrates a fund's propensity to rise/fall in value over a specified period of time. Standard deviation measures how far actual fund returns have deviated from the sector average. The more a fund's returns have varied from the sector average, the higher the volatility. The volatility of a fund is partly attributable to the assets in which it invests. For example, a fund that invests totally in equities is likely to have a higher volatility than a fund solely invested in cash.

EXAMPLE

Armed with this understanding, we can now analyse the performance of this fund using the information supplied by Trustnet below.

a Financial Express website

Factsheet as at : August 01, 2010

Jupiter Financial Opportunities

Fund objective

To achieve long-term capital growth principally through investment in equities of financial sector companies on an international basis.

Detailed fund information

Unit name	Jupiter Financial Opportunities
Crown rating	n/a
OBSR rating	AAA
S&P rating	AAA
Sector	Specialist
Launch date	01-Jun-1997
Fund size (as at 31-May-2010)	£ 1,125.5m
Primary asset class	Equity

Price and charges

Bid price	(as at 30-Jul-2010)	GBX 372.71
Offer price	(as at 30-Jul-2010)	GBX 395.48
Initial charge		5.25%
Annual charge		1.50%

Investment

Minimum initial	£500
Minimum additional	£250

Dividend policy
Income distributed 31 December and 30 June.

Codes

Citicode	JU02
SEDOL	0479019

Management information

Address	1 Grosvenor Place, London
Tel	020 7314 7699 (Broker Line)
	020 7314 4933 (Fax Number)
	011 7971 1177 (IFA Support)
	005 0005 0096 (Literature)
	020 7314 7600 (Main Number)

Website
http://www.jupiteronline.co.uk/

Email
brokerdesk@jupiter-group.co.uk

Past performance overview fund vs. sector

■ Jupiter Financial Opportunities (59.11%)
■ Specialist (39.07%)

29/07/2005 - 01/08/2010 © Financial Express Holdings 2010

Cumulative performance (%)

	1m	3m	6m	1y	3ys	5ys
Jupiter Financial Opportunities	+3.1	-6.7	-0.9	+6.5	+15.8	+59.1
Specialist	+2.5	-4.0	+5.1	+19.4	+3.7	+39.1

Performance figures are calculated on a bid price to bid price basis. All prices in Pence Sterling (GBX) unless otherwise specified.

Discrete calendar year performance

■ Jupiter Financial Opportunities
■ Specialist

© Financial Express Holdings 2010

Discrete performance (%)

	YTD	2009	2008	2007	2006	2005
Jupiter Financial Opportunities	-4.5	+11.9	+7.3	+1.9	+15.7	+34.0
Specialist	+2.9	+30.4	-23.8	+3.9	+15.4	+29.4

Performance figures are calculated on a bid price to bid price basis. All prices in Pence Sterling (GBX) unless otherwise specified.

Key ratios & analysis

powered by

■analytics

Ratios

	1y	3y
Volatility	19.29	15.88
Alpha	-17.31	4.44
Beta	1.44	0.54
Sharpe	0.08	0.06
Info Ratio	-1.00	0.21
R^2	0.70	0.29

Quartiles: 1 2 3 4

Volatility

If we begin by considering the volatility measure, you can see that the returns achieved by the fund manager deviated from the sector average by some 19.29% over one year and 15.88% over three years.

Alpha

In terms of alpha it is clear that the fund underperformed its benchmark by 17.31% over one year and exceeded it by 4.44% over three years.

Beta

The beta measure shows that the return achieved by the fund fluctuated by 44% over one year and 46% over three years, In a climbing market over one year, the fund would have produced a return greater than the index by 44%. In a declining market over the same period the fund would have exceeded the loss on the index by 44%. Over three years the fund would have underperformed the benchmark in a rising market by 46% and similarly it would have lost 46% less than the index when the market declined.

Sharpe

The Sharpe ratio is positive, which demonstrates that the investor has benefited from taking the additional risk over investment in risk-free assets such as cash.

Information Ratio

The negative information ratio over one year implies that the fund manager's contribution in terms of skills and knowledge is low. If +1 suggests outstanding performance, then –1 is the opposite end of the spectrum. A positive 0.21 over three years is more encouraging.

R^2

R-squared shows that 70% of the fund's performance over one year was down to market movement and followed the benchmark. Over three years this figure reduced to 29%.

Overall View

It is clear from these figures that the fund manager takes an active approach. However, the measures over one year illustrate that the investor would have benefited from holding an index tracker rather than the fund.

Given the nature of the underlying assets (financial sector/equities) and the fund's objective (long-term capital growth) this fund can only be viewed as a medium- to long-term investment. As such, the measures discussed above suggest that the investor would benefit from holding the fund rather than the index tracker over a three-year period.

This view is supported by the cumulative performance figures shown on the factsheet, which show that the return achieved by the fund exceeded the benchmark over three and five years.

The following is an example of an investment summary from Morningstar, which again shows performance and volatility data, but with some more additional detail to consider.

EXAMPLE

Advisor Workstation Office Edition℠ | Print Date: 10/11/2009   Page 1 of 1

IP Income Acc GB0033031260

Investment Summary

	Data as of 31/10/2009	Currency GBP	Benchmark 1 FTSE AllSh TR GBP	Benchmark 2 MSCI World LCL

Trailing Return

	Total Return %	+/- BM1	+/- BM2	Cat % Rank
1 Mo	-0.08	1.74	2.23	10
3 Mo	8.69	-2.05	4.64	93
6 Mo	13.14	-8.03	-4.06	97
YTD	6.10	-15.02	-9.15	98
1 Yr	13.03	-10.44	4.13	95
3 Yr	-1.00	1.71	8.76	24
5 Yr	9.93	3.87	10.41	2
10 Yr	9.78	7.71	12.24	2
15 Yr	—	—	—	—

Ratings as of 31/10/2009

	Overall	3 Year	5 Year	10 Year
Rating	5★	4★	5★	5★
Risk		2.30	1.88	2.36
Return		-6.80	4.04	4.32
# Investments Rated	376	376	286	167

Risk/Reward

Versus Benchmark 1	3 Year	5 Year	10 Year
Alpha	-0.69	3.58	7.21
Beta	0.79	0.80	0.82
R-Squared	89.64	87.67	74.57
Tracking Error	8.20	7.11	9.08
Information Ratio	0.21	0.54	0.89
Excess Return	1.71	3.87	7.71

Miscellaneous	3 Year	5 Year	10 Year
Standard Deviation	15.53	13.17	14.72
Sharpe Ratio	-0.55	0.36	0.47
Sortino Ratio	-0.53	0.38	0.59
Max Drawdown (Mo)	17	17	17
Max Drawdown (%)	-31.21	-31.21	-31.21
Peak Date	01/11/2007	01/11/2007	01/11/2007
Valley Date	31/03/2009	31/03/2009	31/03/2009

Manager Information

Neil Woodford. Since 10/1990.

Investment Strategy

The Invesco Perpetual Income Fund aims to achieve a reasonable level of income, together with capital growth. The fund intends to invest primarily in companies listed in the UK, with the balance invested internationally. In pursuing this objective, the fund managers may include investments that they consider appropriate which include transferable securities, money market instruments, warrants, collective investment schemes, deposits and other permitted investments and transactions.

Operations

Minimum Initial Investment	500
Inception Date	06/04/1999
Management Fees	Actual: 1.50% Max: 1.50%
Sales Fees	5F
Management Group	INVESCO Fund Managers Ltd
Telephone	353 1 439 8100
Web Address	http://broker.invescooffshore...

Performance

	1999	2000	2001	2002	2003	2004	2005	2006	2007	2008	10/2009	History
	—	20.54	2.65	-11.92	23.53	22.42	26.50	27.47	7.29	-19.58	6.10	Total Return %
	—	26.45	15.94	10.76	2.67	9.59	4.45	10.72	1.97	10.35	-15.02	+/- Benchmark 1
	—	31.32	17.90	13.27	0.77	12.94	12.76	13.95	4.46	20.53	-9.15	+/- Benchmark 2
	—	—	—	—	—	—	—	—	4.90	31.03	31.09	Turnover Ratio %
	—	—	—	—	—	—	—	—	—	3.482	4.036	Share Class Assets (mil)
	—	—	—	—	—	—	—	—	—	—	1.68	Expense Ratio
	—	—	99.72	97.77	89.30	88.45	90.09	87.49	92.64	75.95	Stock %
	—	—	0.00	0.00	0.00	0.00	1.50	0.56	0.16	1.69	Bond %

Holding Analysis as of 30/09/2009

	Net %	#
Cash	6.1	—
Equities	95.5	74
Bond	-5.2	2
Other	1.6	—
Total	**100.0**	**99**

Equity Style %

18	44	17
10	2	5
3	2	1

Val Core Grth

Market Cap	%
Giant	45.2
Large	32.9
Mid	14.5
Small	5.2
Micro	2.2
Avg Market Cap (mil)	13,191.5

Value Factors	%	Growth Factors	%
Price/Earnings	10.68	LT Earn Gr	6.04
Price/Book	2.07	Hist Earn Gr	-0.76
Price/Sales	0.95	Book Val Gr	0.73
Price/Cash Flow	5.63	Sales Gr	12.02
Dividend Yield	5.11	Cash Flow Gr	6.12

Fixed Income Style

Short Interm Long

Avg Eff Duration	—
Avg Eff Maturity	—
Avg Credit Quality	—
Avg Wtd Coupon	—
Avg Wtd Price	1,045.93

% as of —

Credit Rating Breakdown	%	Maturity Breakdown	%
AAA	—	1-3	2.9
AA	—	3-5	3.3
A	—	5-7	9.8
BBB	—	7-10	76.8
BB	—	10-15	0.4
B or below B	—	15-20	0.7
Not Rated	—	20-30	1.6
		30+	4.6

Top Holdings as of 28/02/2009

	Style Box	Sector	Mkt Cap GBP (mil)	% Mkt Val
BG Group PLC			46.097	6.57
BP PLC			119.697	6.16
GlaxoSmithKline PLC			79.053	5.97
British American Tobacco PLC			51.132	5.19
AstraZeneca PLC			46.282	5.04
Vodafone Group PLC			93.885	5.02
Reynolds American, Inc.			9.787	4.84
National Grid PLC			21.687	4.77
Tesco PLC			37.349	4.61
Imperial Tobacco Group PLC			24.334	4.28
BT Group PLC			16.010	3.10
Drax Grp			2.511	2.86
Altria Group Inc.			31.813	2.61
Capita Grp			5.882	2.39
Centrica PLC			18.884	2.36
Reckitt Benckiser Grp			27.249	2.24
Scottish and Southern Energ...			16.074	2.07
Rolls-Royce Group PLC			7.628	2.06
Reed Elsevier			8.244	1.66
International Power plc			—	1.33
Top 20 Holdings				75.1

Top 3 Equity Sectors	%	Rel BM1%	Rel BM2%
Consumer Goods	22.97	179.22	168.48
Health Care	18.37	223.41	189.29
Utilities	18.08	513.49	412.22

Top 3 Fixed Income Sectors	%	Rel BM1%	Rel BM2%
Asset-backed	—	—	—
Cash	—	—	—
Convertible	—	—	—

CISI CHARTERED INSTITUTE FOR SECURITIES & INVESTMENT

2.5 THE IMPACT OF ASSET ALLOCATION ON THE RETURNS ACHIEVED BY THE PORTFOLIO

EXAMPLE

Using the table below, calculate the returns achieved by the following asset allocation models over three years.

AA1	AA2
Cash 10%	Cash 5%
Fixed Interest 20%	Fixed Interest 15%
Commercial Property 30%	Property 50%
Equity 40%	Equity 30%

Asset Class	1-Year Return	3-Year Return
Cash	2%	7%
Fixed Interest	3%	10%
Commercial Property	4%	12%
Equities	5%	15%

AA1	
Cash	10% x 7% = 0.70%
Fixed Interest	20% x 10% = 2.00%
Commercial Property	30% x 12% = 3.60%
Equity	40% x 15% = 6.00%
Total Return	12.30%

AA2	
Cash	5% x 7% = 0.70%
Fixed Interest	15% x 10% = 2.00%
Commercial Property	50% x 12% = 3.60%
Equity	30% x 15% = 6.00%
Total Return	12.35%

As you can see in this example, increasing the portfolio exposure to equities and commercial property by a further 10% has only improved the return by 0.05%.

2.6   THE IMPACT OF CURRENCY MOVEMENTS

Currency fluctuations can have a dramatic impact on investment returns.

EXAMPLE

Exchange rate at date of investment:		**£1.00 – $1.50**
Amount invested:		**£20,000**
Price per unit:		**$2.00**
Number of units purchased:		**15,000**
Exchange rate of date of valuation:		**£1.00 – $1.90**
Price per unit:		**$2.50**
$ Proceeds:	**15,000 x $2.50**	**$37,500**
£ Proceeds:	**$37,500/$1.90**	**£19,736**

Although the underlying unit price has increased 25%, the decline of the dollar against sterling has meant that the client is left with a loss of £264 (£20,000–£19,736).

2.7   WHAT DOES RISK/REWARD RATIO MEAN?

This is a ratio used by many investors to compare the expected returns of an investment to the risk taken. Essentially, an inverse of this ratio is more common as a rule of thumb and is used by many traders to pick profitable trades. A 2:1 or a 3:1 reward ratio is considered an attractive proposition by some traders and may be justification to enter into a deal.

Every deal involves an element of risk and the trade may result in a loss. Hence, the maximum downside loss possible is calculated first and then the trader determines the expected profit. This ratio may also be calculated mathematically as:

$$\text{Reward to Risk Ratio} = \text{Expected Profit/Possible Loss}$$

EXAMPLE

A trader wishes to buy 100 shares of Topbuy plc at £2.50 each. He will put a stop loss order at £1.50 if the price drops unexpectedly over his holding period. Hence, his maximum loss will be £1.00 per share.

On the upside, his view is that prices will rise to £5.00 but he will actually take profits if prices were to move up to £4.50: an expected profit of £2.00.

Risk/reward ratio= £1.00/£2.00 = 0.5.

Alternatively his reward/risk ratio is: £2.00/£1.00 = 2:1.

Many traders may decide to screen off trading opportunities offering a minimum of 2:1 reward ratio over their holding period.

3.   PORTFOLIO REVIEW

LEARNING OBJECTIVE

8.3.1   Understand the importance of regularly reviewing the client's portfolio

8.3.2   Apply measures to address the factors that require attention as part of the portfolio review and administration process: changes in client circumstances; changes in the financial environment; new products and services available; administrative changes or difficulties; investment-related changes (eg, credit rating, corporate actions); portfolio rebalancing; benchmark review

3.1   THE IMPORTANCE OF PORTFOLIO REVIEWS

It is important to ensure that the management of a client's portfolio is reviewed regularly. The frequency of review should be agreed with the client and should take into account any changes in the client's circumstances or requirements. For example, the portfolio may have been initially created to generate a capital return, while the client may now require a regular income.

Changes in the performance of the underlying assets may also require a rebalancing of the asset allocation. For example, the outperformance of the equity holding compared to the other assets such as bonds and property may alter the risk profile of the overall portfolio.

Various portfolio-balancing techniques could be employed to ensure that the asset allocation is adjusted to remain in line with what was originally agreed.

Regular reviews are also necessary for the purposes of calculating performance and reporting to the client, including the calculation of any performance related fees.

3.2   FACTORS REQUIRING REVIEW

3.2.1   Changes in Client Circumstances

Changes in the client's personal circumstances can have a bearing on the structure of the portfolio and will require a review, eg, a requirement for regular income instead of growth or access to a lump sum to assist with an unplanned expense.

When creating a portfolio it is important to consider the client's requirements and ensure that some tolerance is built in to cope with unforeseen events, ie, ensuring that some capital remains accessible for emergencies.

3.2.2 Changes in the Financial Environment

Economic changes can impact the portfolio and will require a review to assess their impact and determine a strategy for minimising their impact.

Examples include a change to tax laws and rates of taxation of gains or income generated from within an investment portfolio, including amendments to legislation surrounding certain investment vehicles such as pensions, Enterprise Investment Schemes and ISAs.

3.2.3 New Products and Services

The introduction of new products onto the market can also require a review due to improved charging structures or additional features and benefits that were not offered by the original contract.

3.2.4 Administrative Changes or Difficulties

If the ongoing management of the portfolio is proving difficult due to issues dealing with a particular platform, technology or provider which is proving detrimental to the efficient and timely dealing, then a review may be appropriate.

3.2.5 Investment-Related Changes

Changes to the underlying holdings within a portfolio due to a corporate action should trigger a review of the portfolio to ensure that the level of overall exposure to that particular stock has not been altered significantly.

3.3 PORTFOLIO REBALANCING

Portfolio rebalancing relates to adjustments in the levels of exposure to the various asset classes and should be reviewed as part of the scheduled portfolio review or earlier if changes in the economic cycle mean that a greater or less exposure is required in other areas.

Various methods are employed in the industry including automatic rebalancing, where assets are sold or purchased continually to ensure that the right balance is maintained.

3.4 BENCHMARK REVIEW

A review of the benchmark may be required if it is no longer representative of the portfolio objective or contains assets which the portfolio no longer has exposure to.

3.5 THE PORTFOLIO REVIEW PROCESS

In practice the adviser should ensure that they have a strict administrative process in place to ensure that the portfolio is reviewed, both at the agreed anniversary dates and during the interim period when any changes occur.

Ensuring reviews are carried out at the agreed points during the year is relatively straightforward, and requires nothing more than a simple diary system that is made available to the adviser and his support team. This should be checked frequently and a list of forthcoming reviews for the next time period shared with the team.

Capturing changes to the client's circumstances is a different matter. Some individuals like to keep their adviser informed and will contact them as and when changes occur, or are anticipated. Indeed, part of the adviser's job should be to encourage this form of regular communication or information-sharing. For those clients who are less forthcoming, the adviser should take steps to incorporate a regular email or phone call into their diary, to ensure that any changes or developments in the client's personal circumstances are known.

The adviser may also consider preparing a cut-down version of a fact-find as a 'review questionnaire' to send to the client in advance of the next review, which can incorporate changes to income/expenditure, employment, personal status, assets/liabilities and revised/new financial objectives. The completion of such a questionnaire can then be used to set the agenda for the next review meeting and mean the adviser is prepared to discuss in outline what changes they feel may need to be made.

In terms of reviewing the investment portfolio, the adviser will need to consider how to ensure that changes to the following areas are captured, then communicated to the investor and acted upon:

- Asset allocation changes.
- Corporate actions (rights issues).
- Recommended fund switches (if advisory).

Changes to the client's personal circumstances may also require the input of other professionals such as solicitors or accountants. Most firms these days have links with firms to whom they are happy to refer their clients for advice on matters relating to divorce, starting a new business or selling an existing business. If these links are not already in place, then it makes good business sense to arrange them and ensure that your clients are aware of these additional services.

KEY CHAPTER POINTS

- There are three main ways in which portfolio performance is assessed: comparison with a relevant bond or stockmarket index, comparison to similar funds or a relevant universe comparison, and comparison to a custom benchmark.
- There are three main types of market index: price-weighted index, market value-weighted index, and equal-weighted index.
- The FTSE All Share index measures the performance of companies listed on the London Stock Exchange's main market. It covers close to 700 companies representing approximately 98% of the UK's market capitalisation.
- The FTSE 100 is a market capitalisation-weighted index representing the performance of the 100 largest UK-domiciled blue chip companies.
- The Dow Jones Industrial Average is the best known index in the world and its 30 stocks account for close to 25% of the total US equity market.
- Performance attribution is a process that seeks to attribute investment performance to asset allocation, sector choice and security selection.
- There are three different methods used to measure portfolio performance: holding period yield – sometimes referred to as total return; money-weighted rate of return; and time-weighted rate of return.
- There are four main methods of risk-adjusted performance measurement in use: Sharpe ratio; Treynor ratio; Jensen measure; and information ratio.
- The absolute return is simply a measure of the gain or loss on an investment portfolio expressed as a percentage of invested capital.
- Relative return is a measure of the return of an investment portfolio relative to a theoretical passive reference portfolio or benchmark.
- Regular portfolio reviews are necessary for the purposes of calculating performance and reporting to the client, including the calculation of any performance-related fees.

Tax Return 2011
Tax year 6 April 2010 to 5 April 2011

Your tax return

This notice requires you, by law, to make a return of your taxable income and capital gains, and any documents requested, for the year from 6 April 2010 to 5 April 2011.

Deadlines
We must receive your tax return by these dates:
- if you are using a **paper** return – by **31 October 2011**, (or 3 months after the date of this notice if that's later), or
- if you are filing a return **online** – by **31 January 2012**, (or 3 months after the date of this notice if that's later).

If your return is late you will be charged a **£100 penalty**. If your return is more than 3 months late, you will be charged daily penalties of £10 a day.

If you pay late you will be charged interest and a late payment penalty.

How to file your return
To file online, go to **www.hmrc.gov.uk/online**

To file on paper, please fill in this form using the rules below.

Use black ink and capital letters

Cross out any mistakes and write the correct information below

4	Name of bank or building society
	ANY BANK

8	State Pension lump sum
	2 4 9 5 0 ·
	4 9

| 9 | Tax taken off box 8 |
| £ | 4 7 0 1 · |

Please round up tax paid: £4,700.21 would be £4701

| 10 | Pensions (other than State Pension), retirem |

- Enter your figures in whole pounds – ignore the pence. Round down income and round up expenses and tax paid – it is to your benefit.
- If a box does not apply, please leave it blank – do not strike through empty boxes or write anything else.

Starting your tax return

Before you start to fill it in, look through your tax return to make sure there is a section for all your income and claims – you may need some separate supplementary pages (see page TR 2 and pages TRG 2 to 6 of the tax return guide). If you need help please use the tax return guide, phone the number shown above or **0845 9000 444**, or go to **www.hmrc.gov.uk/sa**

Your personal details

| 1 | Your date of birth – *it helps get your tax right* DD MM YYYY |

| 3 | Your phone number |

| 2 | Your name and address – *if it is different from what is on the front of this form. Please write the correct details underneath the wrong ones, and put 'X' in the box* |

| 4 | Your National Insurance number – *leave blank if the correct number is shown above* |

What makes up your tax return

To make a **complete** return of your taxable income and gains for the year to 5 April 2011 you may need to complete some **separate supplementary pages**. Answer the following questions by putting 'X' in the 'Yes' or 'No' box.

1 Employment

If you were an employee, director, office holder or agency worker in the year to 5 April 2011, do you need to complete *Employment* pages? Please read page TRG 3 of the tax return guide before answering.

Fill in a separate *Employment* page for each employment, directorship etc., for which you need to complete an *Employment* page and say how many sets of pages you are completing.

Yes ☐   No ☐   Number ☐

2 Self-employment

Did you work for yourself (on your 'own account' or in self-employment) in the year to 5 April 2011? (Answer 'Yes' if you were a 'Name' at Lloyd's.) Fill in a separate *Self-employment* page for each business and say how many sets of pages you are completing.

Yes ☐   No ☐   Number ☐

3 Partnership

Were you in partnership? Fill in a separate *Partnership* page for each partnership you were a partner in and say how many sets of pages you are completing.

Yes ☐   No ☐   Number ☐

4 UK property

Did you receive any income from UK property (including rents and other income from land you own or lease out)?

Yes ☐   No ☐

5 Foreign

If you:

• were entitled to any foreign income, or income gains
• have, or could have, received (directly or indirectly) income, or a capital payment or benefit from a person abroad as a result of any transfer of assets
• want to claim relief for foreign tax paid

please read the notes on page TRG 4 to decide if you have to fill in the *Foreign* pages.

Do you need to fill in the *Foreign* pages?

Yes ☐   No ☐

6 Trusts etc.

Did you receive, or are you treated as having received, income from a trust, settlement or the residue of a deceased person's estate?

Yes ☐   No ☐

7 Capital gains summary

If you disposed of any chargeable assets (including, for example, stocks, shares, units in a unit trust, land and property, goodwill in a business), or had any chargeable gains, or you wish to claim an allowable loss or make any other claim or election, read page TRG 5 of the guide to decide if you have to fill in the *Capital gains summary* page.

Do you need to fill in the *Capital gains summary* page?

Yes ☐   No ☐

8 Residence, remittance basis etc.

Were you, for all or part of the year to 5 April 2011, one or more of the following – not resident, not ordinarily resident or not domiciled in the UK and claiming the remittance basis; or dual resident in the UK and another country?

Yes ☐   No ☐

9 Supplementary pages

If you answered 'Yes' to any of questions 1 to 8, please check to see if, **within this return**, there is a page dealing with that kind of income etc. If there is not, you will need separate supplementary pages. Do you need to get and fill in extra loose supplementary pages?

Yes ☐   No ☐

If 'Yes', you can go to **www.hmrc.gov.uk** to download them, or phone **0845 9000 404** and ask us for the relevant page.

*Some less common kinds of income and tax reliefs (not covered by questions 1 to 8), and details of disclosed tax avoidance schemes, should be returned on the **Additional information** pages enclosed in the tax return pack. Do you need to fill in the **Additional information** pages?*

Yes ☐   No ☐

Student Loan repayments

Please read page TRG 6 of the tax return guide before filling in boxes 1 and 2.

1 If you have received notification from the Student Loans Company that repayment of an Income Contingent Student Loan began before 6 April 2011, put 'X' in the box

☐

2 If your employer has deducted Student Loan repayments enter the amount deducted

£ ☐☐☐☐☐☐☐ . ☐ ☐

Tax return: Page TR 2

HMRC 12/10

Income

Interest and dividends from UK banks, building societies etc.

1 Taxed UK interest etc. – *the net amount after tax has been taken off (see notes)*

£ _____ . 0 0

2 Untaxed UK interest etc. – *amounts which have not been taxed (see notes)*

£ _____ . 0 0

3 Dividends from UK companies – *do not include the tax credit (see notes)*

£ _____ . 0 0

4 Other dividends – *do not include the tax credit (see notes)*

£ _____ . 0 0

5 Foreign dividends (up to £300) – *the amount in sterling after foreign tax was taken off. Do not include this amount in the Foreign pages*

£ _____ . 0 0

6 Tax taken off foreign dividends – *the sterling equivalent*

£ _____ . 0 0

UK pensions, annuities and other state benefits received

7 State Pension – *the amount due for the year (see notes)*

£ _____ . 0 0

8 State Pension lump sum

£ _____ . 0 0

9 Tax taken off box 8

£ _____ . 0 0

10 Pensions (other than State Pension), retirement annuities and taxable triviality payments – *give details of the payers, amounts paid and tax deducted in the 'Any other information' box, box 19, on page TR 6*

£ _____ . 0 0

11 Tax taken off box 10

£ _____ . 0 0

12 Taxable Incapacity Benefit and contribution-based Employment and Support Allowance – *see notes*

£ _____ . 0 0

13 Tax taken off Incapacity Benefit in box 12

£ _____ . 0 0

14 Jobseeker's Allowance

£ _____ . 0 0

15 Total of any other taxable State Pensions and benefits

£ _____ . 0 0

Other UK income not included on supplementary pages

Do not use this section for income that should be returned on supplementary pages. Share schemes, gilts, stock dividends, life insurance gains and certain other kinds of income go on the *Additional information* pages in the tax return pack.

16 Other taxable income – *before expenses and tax taken off*

£ _____ . 0 0

17 Total amount of allowable expenses – *read page TRG 14 of the tax return guide*

£ _____ . 0 0

18 Any tax taken off box 16

£ _____ . 0 0

19 Benefit from pre-owned assets – *read page TRG 15 of the guide*

£ _____ . 0 0

20 Description of income in boxes 16 and 19 – *if there is not enough space here please give details in the 'Any other information' box, box 19, on page TR 6*

_____

_____

_____

Tax reliefs

Paying into registered pension schemes and overseas pension schemes

Do not include payments you make to your employer's pension scheme which are deducted from your pay before tax or payments made by your employer.

1 Payments to registered pension schemes where basic rate tax relief will be claimed by your pension provider (called 'relief at source'). Enter the payments and basic rate tax

£ _____ • 0 0

2 Payments to a retirement annuity contract where basic rate tax relief will not be claimed by your provider

£ _____ • 0 0

3 Payments to your employer's scheme which were not deducted from your pay before tax

£ _____ • 0 0

4 Payments to an overseas pension scheme which is not UK-registered which are eligible for tax relief and were not deducted from your pay before tax

£ _____ • 0 0

Charitable giving

5 Gift Aid payments made in the year to 5 April 2011

£ _____ • 0 0

6 Total of any 'one-off' payments in box 5

£ _____ • 0 0

7 Gift Aid payments made in the year to 5 April 2011 but treated as if made in the year to 5 April 2010

£ _____ • 0 0

8 Gift Aid payments made after 5 April 2011 but to be treated as if made in the year to 5 April 2011

£ _____ • 0 0

9 Value of qualifying shares or securities gifted to charity

£ _____ • 0 0

10 Value of qualifying land and buildings gifted to charity

£ _____ • 0 0

11 Value of qualifying investments gifted to non-UK charities in boxes 9 and 10

£ _____ • 0 0

12 Gift Aid payments to non-UK charities in box 5

£ _____ • 0 0

Blind Person's Allowance

13 If you are registered blind on a local authority or other register, put 'X' in the box

☐

14 Enter the name of the local authority or other register

☐

15 If you want your spouse's, or civil partner's, surplus allowance, put 'X' in the box

☐

16 If you want your spouse, or civil partner, to have your surplus allowance, put 'X' in the box

☐

Other less common reliefs are on the *Additional information* pages enclosed in the tax return pack.

Service companies

1 If you provided your services through a service company (a company which provides your personal services to third parties), enter the total of the dividends (including the tax credit) and salary (before tax was taken off) you withdrew from the company in the tax year – *read page TRG 21 of the guide*

£ _____ • 0 0

Tax return: Page TR 4

HMRC 12/10

CISI
CHARTERED INSTITUTE FOR
SECURITIES & INVESTMENT

Finishing your tax return

ⓘ **Calculating your tax** – if we receive your tax return by 31 October 2011, or if you file online, we will do the calculation for you **and** tell you how much you have to pay (or what your repayment will be) before 31 January 2012.

But if you want to calculate your tax ask us for the *Tax calculation summary* pages and *notes*. The *notes* will help you work out any tax due or repayable, and if payments on account are necessary.

Tax refunded or set off

1	If you have had any 2010-11 Income Tax refunded or set off by us or Jobcentre Plus, enter the amount

£ ⬜⬜⬜⬜⬜⬜⬜⬜ . 0 0

If you have not paid enough tax

Use the payslip at the foot of your next statement (or reminder) from us to pay any tax due.

2	If you owe tax for 2010-11 and have a PAYE tax code, we will try to collect the tax due (if less than £2,000) through your tax code for 2012-13, unless you put 'X' in the box – *read page TRG 22 of the guide*

3	If you are likely to owe tax for **2011–12** on income other than employed earnings or pensions, and you do **not** want us to use your 2011-12 PAYE tax code to collect that tax during the year, put 'X' in the box – *read page TRG 22 of the guide*

If you have paid too much tax

We will repay direct to your bank or building society account – this is the safest and quickest method. Tell us where you would like us to make any repayment by filling in boxes 4 to 14.

If you would like us to send some, or all, of your repayment to charity please use the *Giving your tax repayment to charity* form in your tax return pack.

4	Name of bank or building society

5	Name of account holder (or nominee)

6	Branch sort code

⬜⬜ – ⬜⬜ – ⬜⬜

7	Account number

8	Building society reference number

9	If you do not have a bank or building society account, or if you want us to send a cheque to you or to your nominee, put 'X' in the box

10	If you have entered a nominee's name in box 5, put 'X' in the box

11	If your nominee is your tax adviser, put 'X' in the box

12	Nominee's address

13	and postcode

14	To authorise your nominee to receive any repayment, you must sign in the box. A photocopy of your signature will not do

Tax return: Page TR 5   HMRC 12/10

Your tax adviser, if you have one

This section is optional. Please see the note on page TRG 24 about authorising your tax adviser.

15 Your tax adviser's name

17 The first line of their address and the postcode

16 Their phone number

18 The reference your adviser uses for you

Any other information

19 Please give any other information in this space

Signing your form and sending it back

20 If this tax return contains provisional or estimated figures, put 'X' in the box

21 If you are enclosing separate supplementary pages, put 'X' in the box

22 If you give false information, you may have to pay financial penalties and face prosecution. Please sign and date this form.

The information I have given on this tax return and any supplementary pages is correct and complete to the best of my knowledge and belief

Date *DD MM YYYY*

Signature

23 If you have signed on behalf of someone else, enter the capacity. For example, executor, receiver

25 If you filled in boxes 23 and 24 enter your name

24 Enter the name of the person you have signed for

26 and your address

Finally, please send us your completed form in the envelope provided.

Syllabus Unit/ Element		Chapter/ Section
ELEMENT 1	**ASSET CLASSES**	**CHAPTER 1**
1.1	**Cash and Equivalents**	
	On completion, the candidate should be able to:	
1.1.1	understand the main types of deposit account:	1.7
	• current	
	• instant access	
	• National Savings & Investment products	
	• notice	
	• fixed rate	
	• term	
	• money market	
1.1.2	analyse the main characteristics, risk and returns of cash deposits:	1
	• liquidity	
	• rates of interest	
	• past returns	
	• real returns	
	• deposit takers	
	• statutory protection	
	• risks, interest rate risk and institutional risk	
	• credit risk assessment of deposit taking institutions	
	• foreign currency deposits	
	• costs, charges and penalties	
1.1.3	analyse the main characteristics, risks and returns of money market funds	1.8
	• cash assets only	
	• near-cash assets	
	• pricing, liquidity and fair value	
	• costs, charges and penalties	
1.1.4	analyse the factors to take into account when selecting between different types of cash deposits, accounts and money market funds	1
1.2	**Fixed Income Securities**	
	On completion, the candidate should be able to:	
1.2.1	know the main issuing institutions and purposes for issuing fixed income securities:	2
	• sovereign states and governments	
	• public authority	
	• corporate	
	• credit institutions	
	• supranational	

Syllabus Unit/ Element		Chapter/ Section
1.2.2	analyse the main sources of investment risk and return associated with fixed income securities:	2.4, 2.5
	• capital return	
	• interest or yield	
	• liquidity	
	• rates of interest	
	• real returns	
	• credit ratings	
	• credit enhancements	
1.2.3	analyse the characteristics and differences between the main types of fixed income securities:	2
	• fixed rate bonds	
	• floating rate notes	
	• zero coupon bonds	
	• inflation-linked bonds	
	• other index-and asset-linked bonds	
	• asset-backed securities	
	• convertible bonds	
	• subordinated bonds	
	• perpetual bonds	
	• eurobonds and foreign issuer bonds	
1.2.4	understand how fixed-income securities are traded and settled:	2.6
	• primary and secondary markets	
	• decentralised market	
	• clearing, settlement and safe custody	
	• pricing, liquidity and fair value	
	• coupon	
	• nominal value	
	• market price	
	• clean and dirty prices	
	• redemption date	
	• transaction costs and charges	
1.2.5	understand the purpose and construction of the main bond indices, and the considerations needed for less liquid markets	2.7
1.2.6	analyse the factors to take into account when selecting bonds and bond funds:	2.8
	• bond characteristics	
	• direct bond strategies	
	• indirect investment	
	• investing in bonds through funds	
	• advantages and disadvantages of investing in bonds and bond funds	

Syllabus Unit/ Element		Chapter/ Section
1.3	**Equities**	
	On completion, the candidate should be able to:	
1.3.1	understand the characteristics and differences between the main types of shareholder equity:	3.2
	• ordinary	
	• redeemable	
	• non-voting	
	• preference	
	• convertible preference	
1.3.2	understand the characteristics and differences between the main types of private equity share capital	3.3
1.3.3	analyse the main sources of investment risk and return associated with equities:	3.4, 3.5
	• capital return	
	• dividends	
	• liquidity	
	• credit ratings	
	• corporate actions	
	• company liquidation	
	• market conditions	
1.3.4	understand the issues involved in dealing for clients in equity markets:	3.6
	• regulated and designated investment exchanges	
	• over-the-counter (OTC) and alternative trading platforms	
	• access to markets	
	• principal and agency trading	
	• listed and unlisted securities	
	• quoted and unquoted securities	
	• admission to trading	
1.3.5	understand how equity securities are traded and settled:	3.7
	• liquidity, pricing and fair value	
	• cost of purchase and sale	
	• nominal value	
	• market price	
	• cum- and ex-dividend	
	• transaction costs and charges	
1.3.6	understand the purpose and construction of the main equity indices, and the considerations needed for less liquid markets	3.8
1.3.7	analyse equity securities and equity funds using the following valuation measures:	3.9
	• price earnings (PE) ratio	
	• earnings per share	
	• dividend yield	

Syllabus Unit/ Element		Chapter/ Section
	• dividend cover	
	• borrowings	
	• net asset value	
	• past performance	
1.3.8	analyse the factors to take into account when selecting equities and equity funds:	3.10, 3.11
	• equity fund strategies – growth, income, market capitalisation, sector, region, customised	
	• growth/dividend prospects	
	• direct versus indirect investment	
	• advantages and disadvantages of investing in equities	
	• cost, turnover, liquidity and ease of trading	
1.4	**Property**	
	On completion, the candidate should be able to:	
1.4.1	understand the differences, characteristics, risks and returns of the main property markets and sectors:	4
	• residential and buy-to-let	
	• commercial – retail space, hotel, office, industrial/warehouse	
1.4.2	analyse the main sources of investment risk and return associated with property investment, both direct and indirect	4
	• capital growth	
	• yield	
	• location and quality	
	• occupancy rate	
	• tenant creditworthiness, tenancy and rental agreement	
	• term and structure of lease	
	• asset liquidity	
	• market volatility and risk	
	• sector risk	
1.4.3	understand how the direct residential and commercial property markets operate:	4
	• ownership and lease structures	
	• conveyancing, buying and selling	
	• costs – transactional, management	
	• property valuation	
	• finance and gearing	
	• investment performance measurement and the role of the Investment Property Databank	
1.4.4	analyse property and property funds using the following valuation measures:	4.10
	• cash flow and average yield	

Investment, Risk & Taxation

Syllabus Unit/ Element		Chapter/ Section
	• capitalisation rate	
	• rental value, review	
	• reversionary value	
	• average repair costs	
	• comparative analysis	
	• market indices and trends	
1.4.5	analyse the factors to take into account when selecting property and property funds:	4.11
	• property shares, OEICs, REITs, bonds, trusts, funds, funds of funds, limited partnerships	
	• property fund strategies	
	• growth/ dividend prospects	
	• direct versus indirect investment	
	• pricing, liquidity and fair value	
	• advantages and disadvantages of investing in property	
	• costs and ease of trading	
1.5	**Alternative Investments**	
	On completion, the candidate should be able to:	
1.5.1	understand the purpose, characteristics, risks and returns of the main types of alternative investments:	5
	• gold and other metals	
	• commodities	
	• art	
	• antiques	
	• forestry	
1.5.2	analyse the factors to take into account when investing in alternative investments:	5
	• direct versus indirect investment	
	• investment time horizon	
	• features – quality, durability, provenance	
	• transaction, delivery and ongoing costs	
	• pricing, liquidity and fair value	
	• advantages and disadvantages of investing in alternatives	
1.6	**Correlation of Asset Classes**	
	On completion, the candidate should be able to:	
1.6.1	analyse combinations of asset classes based on:	6
	• historical returns	
	• index and benchmark comparisons	
	• correlation of performance between asset classes	
	• advantages and limitations of relying on historical data	

Syllabus Unit/ Element		Chapter/ Section
ELEMENT 2	**THE MACRO-ECONOMIC ENVIRONMENT**	**CHAPTER 2**
2.1	**Macro-Economic Trends and Indicators**	
	On completion, the candidate should be able to:	
2.1.1	understand the main long-term global trends and the effects of technological changes/advancements:	1
	• ageing population	
	• rising living standards	
	• access to education	
	• growth of the service sector	
	• changing patterns of the economy	
	• productivity of capital and labour	
	• wealth and income distribution	
	• growth of developing economies	
2.1.2	understand the impact of the following on global trades and asset classes:	2
	• international markets	
	• globalisation of business and finance	
	• market failures	
2.1.3	understand the main stages of economic, financial and stock market cycles, including:	4
	• trade cycles	
	• business cycles	
	• asset price bubbles	
	• economic shocks	
	• difficulty in forecasting national and international trends	
2.1.4	interpret key economic and business indicators:	5
	• gross domestic product	
	• interest rates	
	• consumer price and inflation indices	
	• retail sales	
	• unemployment rate	
	• industrial production	
	• stock market indices	
	• money supply changes	
	• foreign exchange indices	
	• leading, lagging and coincident indicators	
	• pro-cyclic, counter-cyclic and acyclic indicators	
2.2	**Financial Investment in the Economy**	
	On completion the candidate should be able to:	
2.2.1	understand the role of government and central banks in fiscal and monetary policy	6
	• interest rate setting process	

Syllabus Unit/ Element		Chapter/ Section
	• money market operations	
	• fiscal easing	
	• other interventions	
2.2.2	understand how the money supply affects:	6.4
	• inflation	
	• deflation	
	• disinflation	
	• interest rates	
	• exchange rates	
	• relationship between money supply, inflation and employment	
2.2.3	understand the impact of surpluses and deficits on business and the economy	6.5
2.2.4	understand the composition of the balance of payments, and the factors behind and benefits of international trade and capital flows:	6.5
	• current account	
	• imports	
	• exports	
	• effect of low opportunity cost producers	
2.2.5	understand the role of financial investment in the economy:	7.1
	• primary markets as introducers of new funds to business and government	
	• secondary markets enabling investors to adjust investments to meet individual needs	
2.3	**Influences on Asset Classes**	
	On completion the candidate should be able to:	
2.3.1	analyse the impact of macro-economic influences on each of the main asset classes	7.2
	• fixed income	
	• alternative investments	
	• cash	
	• property	
	• equities	
ELEMENT 3	**PRINCIPLES OF INVESTMENT RISK AND RETURN**	**CHAPTER 3**
3.1	**Time Value of Money**	
	On completion, the candidate should be able to:	
3.1.1	understand the effects of compound interest and the time value of money	1.1, 1.4
3.1.2	calculate the present value of:	1.2
	• lump sums	
	• regular payments	
	• annuities	
	• perpetuities	

Syllabus Unit/ Element		Chapter/ Section
3.1.3	calculate the future value of:	1.3
	• lump sums	
	• regular payments	
3.1.4	calculate real and inflation-adjusted returns:	1.5
	• nominal returns	
	• real or inflation-adjusted returns	
	• total returns	
3.2	**Investment Risk and Return**	
	On completion, the candidate should:	
3.2.1	analyse and explain the main types of risk and the implications for investors:	2.2
	• systemic risk	
	• market risk – asset price volatility, currency, interest rates, foreign exchange rates, commodity price volatility	
	• concentration and diversification	
	• long-term investment risk	
	• liquidity, credit risk and default	
	• gearing	
	• fraud and financial crime	
	• counterparty and institutional risk	
	• market timing	
3.2.2	understand the main risk and return measures, and how they are used within asset and portfolio evaluation, and their purposes:	2.3
	• holding period return	
	• total return and its components	
	• standard deviation	
	• volatility	
	• covariance and correlation	
	• risk-adjusted returns	
	• benchmarking	
3.3	**Models of Investment Theory**	
	On completion, the candidate should be able to:	
3.3.1	understand the main propositions and limitations of the efficient markets hypothesis (EMH)	3.1
	• strong form	
	• semi-strong form	
	• weak form	
3.3.2	understand the main principles of modern portfolio theory (MPT), the capital asset pricing model (CAPM), its application and limitations:	3.2, 3.3
	• risk-free rate of return	
	• risk premium	

Syllabus Unit/ Element		Chapter/ Section
	• cost of capital and return on capital	
	• excess returns	
	• correlation measures	
	• systematic and unsystematic risk	
	• risk and diversification	
	• efficient frontier, portfolio optimisation and leverage	
	• assumptions and shortcomings	
3.3.3	understand the main principles behind arbitrage pricing theory (APT), its application and limitations:	3.4
	• factor structure and analysis	
	• macro-economic and market factors	
	• arbitrage theory and mechanics	
	• relationship with CAPM	
	• assumptions and shortcomings	
3.3.4	understand the principles of behavioural finance:	3.5
	• loss aversion	
	• price reaction and price trends	
	• barriers and biases – practical and psychological	
	• relationship with EMH	
	• assumptions and shortcomings	
3.3.5	understand the types and uses of multi-factor models, their assumptions and limitations	3.6
3.3.6	understand how to reduce portfolio risk through diversification and hedging:	3.7
	• significance of alpha and beta	
	• correlation and relative risk	
	• principles of asset allocation	
	• hedging and immunisation	
	• active and passive strategies	
ELEMENT 4	**TAXATION OF INVESTORS AND INVESTMENTS**	**CHAPTER 4**
4.1	**Income Tax**	
	On completion, the candidate should be able to:	
4.1.1	understand how a private individual's income tax liability is determined using:	1
	• tax rates	
	• tax rate bands	
	• personal allowances	
4.1.2	understand how the income tax liability for a trust is determined based on:	2
	• trust type	
	• tax rates	
	• tax rate bands	

Syllabus Unit/ Element		Chapter/ Section
4.1.3	understand the application of income tax in respect of:	2
	• individuals	
	• trusts	
	• charities	
4.2	**Taxation of Investment Income**	
	On completion the candidate should be able to:	
4.2.1	understand the tax treatment of investment income:	3.1
	• savings income	
	• dividend income	
4.2.2	understand the tax treatment of rental income from property and property investment funds for both the fund and UK investors	3.2.3
4.3	**National Insurance Contributions**	
	On completion the candidate should be able to:	
4.3.1	understand the basis on which national insurance contributions (NICs) are levied:	4
	• employers	
	• employees	
	• self-employed	
	• voluntary	
4.4	**Capital Gains Tax**	
	On completion the candidate should be able to:	
4.4.1	understand the application of capital gains tax in respect of:	5
	• individuals	
	• trusts	
	• charities	
4.4.2	understand the application of capital gains tax to the sale of assets, such as:	5
	• shares	
	• government bonds	
	• corporate bonds	
	• real estate	
	• chattels	
4.5	**Inheritance Tax**	
	On completion the candidate should be able to:	
4.5.1	understand the application of inheritance tax (IHT):	6
	• chargeable transfers	
	• potential exempt transfers	
	• transfers on death	
	• nil rate band	
	• exemptions and reliefs	
	• gifts with reservation	
	• valuation of assets	

Syllabus Unit/ Element		Chapter/ Section
	• deed of variation	
4.5.2	understand how intestacy rules may apply in England and Wales, and the implications of these rules for estate planning	6.3
4.5.3	understand the application of IHT to:	6
	• transfers into trusts	
	• assets held in trusts	
	• transfers out of trusts	
4.6	**Residence and Domicile**	
	On completion the candidate should be able to:	
4.6.1	understand the impact of the rules on residency and domicile and the implications for income tax and CGT	7.1
4.6.2	understand the use of double taxation treaties	7.2
4.6.3	understand how withholding tax is applied based on:	7.3
	• residency	
	• product	
	• tax regime (at source or reclaimable)	
	• beneficiary	
	• European Savings Directive	
	• qualified intermediaries scheme	
4.6.4	know the impact of residency and domicile on the liability to IHT	7.4
4.7	**Stamp Duty**	
	On completion the candidate should be able to:	
4.7.1	understand the application of stamp duty and stamp duty reserve tax (SDRT) to the purchase of securities, including:	8.1
	• company shares	
	• share options	
	• unit trusts and open ended investment companies (OEICs)	
	• government bonds	
	• corporate bonds	
	• exchange-traded funds (ETFs)	
4.7.2	understand the application of stamp duty land tax (SDLT), including the main reliefs and exemptions, to the purchase of property	8.2
4.8	**Value Added Tax**	
	On completion the candidate should be able to:	
4.8.1	understand how liability to value added tax (VAT) arises and is charged	9
4.9	**Corporation Tax**	
	On completion the candidate should be able to:	
4.9.1	understand how liability to corporation tax (CT) arises and is charged:	10
	• companies and organisations: trading, non- trading	
	• taxable profits and accounting periods	
	• rates, allowances and reliefs	

Syllabus Unit/ Element		Chapter/ Section
	• taxation of franked income	
4.10	**Tax Compliance**	
	On completion the candidate should be able to:	
4.10.1	understand how tax is accounted for and an adviser's duties regarding tax compliance, avoidance and evasion	10
4.11	**Tax Planning**	
	On completion the candidate should be able to:	
4.11.1	apply the key principles of investment tax planning:	11.1
	• use of personal allowances	
	• spouses' personal allowances	
	• children's tax position	
	• pension contributions	
	• use of tax wrappers	
	• use of capital gains tax exemptions	
	• tax deferral	
	• use of life assurance bonds	
4.11.2	analyse the criteria for selecting a tax-planning strategy	11.2
4.11.3	apply the key principles of IHT planning	11.3
	• lifetime gifts	
	• trusts	
	• transferability of nil rate band	
4.11.4	apply common tax computations for:	11.4
	• an individual's liability to income tax	
	• age allowance	
	• CGT liability on share disposals	
	• IHT liability on lifetime transfers and at death	
4.11.5	apply the above principles to basic recommendations relating to the taxation of investments and pensions	11.4
ELEMENT 5	**INVESTMENT PRODUCTS**	**CHAPTER 5**
5.1	**Open-Ended Funds**	
	On completion the candidate should be able to:	
5.1.1	understand the main types, purposes, common investment characteristics and behaviours of funds, collectives and other products	1, 2 & 3
5.1.2	understand the structure of multi manager and multi asset funds	1.2
5.1.3	understand when and why borrowing/gearing is used by funds, and the benefits and risks associated with it	3.3
5.1.4	understand the tax treatment within the fund and for UK investors of income arising from collective investments:	4
	• open-ended investment companies (OEICs)	
	• investment companies with variable capital (ICVCs)	
	• unit trusts	

Syllabus Unit/ Element		Chapter/ Section
	• investment trusts	
	• exchange-traded funds (ETFs)	
	• real estate investment trusts (REITs)	
5.1.5	analyse the common differences, merits and limitations of direct investment in securities and assets compared with indirect investment through collectives and other products, in terms of:	5
	• risk	
	• return	
	• tax treatment	
	• turnover, liquidity and access	
	• expenses – transaction and ongoing	
	• management and administration	
5.1.6	understand the main types, purposes, common investment characteristics and behaviours of:	5
	• onshore collective investment funds	
	• offshore collective investment funds	
5.1.7	understand the tax treatment of UK investors investing in offshore funds, including:	5.1
	• differences between distributor and non-distributor offshore funds and reporting funds	
	• taxation of offshore funds	
5.1.8	analyse the charges and pricing of collective investments:	6
	• initial, annual, exit and performance fee charging structures	
	• single pricing	
	• bid/offer pricing	
	• dilution levies	
	• forward pricing	
	• premiums	
	• discounts	
5.1.9	analyse the relative merits and limitations of investing in a collective investment fund compared with other forms of direct and indirect investment, in terms of:	6
	• risk	
	• return	
	• tax treatment	
	• turnover, liquidity and access	
	• expenses – transaction and ongoing	
	• management and administration	
5.2	**Exchange-Traded Funds and Exchange-Traded Commodities**	
	On completion the candidate should be able to:	
5.2.1	understand the main types, purposes, common investment characteristics and behaviours of :	7
	• exchange-traded funds (ETFs)	

Syllabus Unit/ Element		Chapter/ Section
	• exchange-traded commodities (ETCs)	
5.2.2	analyse the relative merits and limitations of investing in exchange-traded funds (ETFs) or exchange-traded commodities (ETCs) compared with other forms of direct and indirect investment, in terms of:	7
	• risk	
	• return	
	• tax treatment	
	• turnover, liquidity and access	
	• expenses – transaction and ongoing	
	• management and administration	
5.3	**Closed Ended Funds and Investment Companies**	
	On completion the candidate should be able to:	
5.3.1	understand the main types, purposes, common investment characteristics and behaviours of:	3
	• onshore closed-ended funds and investment companies	
	• offshore closed-ended funds and investment companies	
5.3.2	analyse the relative merits and limitations of investing in closed ended funds and investment companies compared with other forms of direct and indirect investment, in terms of:	3
	• risk	
	• return	
	• tax treatment	
	• turnover, liquidity and access	
	• expenses – transaction and administration	
	• management and administration	
5.4	**Individual Savings Accounts and Child Trust Funds**	
	On completion the candidate should be able to:	
5.4.1	analyse the key features, restrictions and tax treatment of ISAs and child trust funds (CTFs):	8.1, 8.2
	• eligibility	
	• eligible investments	
	• subscriptions	
	• transfers	
	• withdrawals	
	• use in investment and tax planning	
5.5	**National Savings & Investments**	
	On completion the candidate should be able to:	
5.5.1	analyse the key features, restrictions and tax treatment of National Savings & Investments:	8.4
	• eligibility	
	• eligible investments	
	• subscriptions	

Syllabus Unit/ Element		Chapter/ Section
	• transfers	
	• withdrawals	
	• premium bonds	
	• use in investment and tax planning	
5.6	**Life Assurance Based Investments**	
	On completion the candidate should be able to:	
5.6.1	analyse the key features, relative merits and limitations of investing in onshore and offshore life assurance-based investments compared with other forms of direct and indirect investment:	9
	• risk	
	• return	
	• tax treatment	
	• turnover, liquidity and access	
	• expenses – transaction and ongoing	
	• management and administration	
5.6.2	understand the impact of the Policy Holder Protection Act 1997	9.3
5.7	**Private Equity Funds**	
	On completion the candidate should be able to:	
5.7.1	understand the main types, purposes, structures, tax treatment and investment characteristics of private equity funds	10
5.8	**Venture Capital Trusts and Enterprise Investment Schemes**	
	On completion the candidate should be able to:	
5.8.1	analyse the key features, relative merits and limitations of investing in venture capital trusts (VCTs) and enterprise investment schemes (EISs) compared with other forms of direct and indirect investment:	11
	• partners/ investors	
	• investment management	
	• tax characteristics	
	• past performance in terms of risk and returns	
	• discounts	
	• premiums	
	• secondary market liquidity	
5.9	**Broker Funds and Distributor Influenced Funds (DIFs)**	
	On completion the candidate should be able to:	
5.9.1	understand the main types, purposes, structure and arrangement, tax treatment and investment characteristics of:	12
	• broker funds	
	• distributor influenced funds	
5.9.2	analyse the key features, relative merits and limitations of investing in a broker- or distributor-influenced fund compared with other forms of direct and indirect investment:	12
	• roles and responsibilities of underlying parties	

Syllabus Unit/ Element		Chapter/ Section
	• fee structure	
	• expenses and commissions	
	• tax characteristics	
	• investment performance and risk	
	• other risks – distributor power and expertise, conflicts of interest, suitability	
	• secondary market liquidity	
5.10	**Derivatives**	
	On completion the candidate should be able to:	
5.10.1	understand the purposes, structure and risk/reward characteristics of the main types of financial derivatives pertaining to each main asset class:	13
	• futures	
	• forward contracts	
	• options	
	• warrants	
	• contracts for differences	
5.10.2	understand the effects of implementing simple derivatives strategies for the purposes of hedging or speculation in terms of:	13
	• risk transfer and risk/reward payoff	
	• transaction costs and margin	
	• ease of implementation and unwinding	
5.11	**Hedge Funds**	
	On completion the candidate should be able to:	
5.11.1	analyse the key features, relative merits and limitations of investing in hedge funds compared with other forms of direct and indirect investment:	14
	• main types of hedge fund	
	• regulatory environment	
	• investment risk	
	• use of short and long positions	
	• custody and safe keeping practices	
	• limitations in respect of voting capital	
	• funds of hedge funds (FoHFs)	
5.12	**Absolute Return Funds (ARFs)**	
	On completion the candidate should be able	
5.12.1	analyse the key features, relative merits and limitations of investing in Absolute Return Funds (ARFs) compared with other forms of direct and indirect investment:	14.4
	• structure	
	• income and capital growth	
	• investment risk and return	
	• expenses	

Syllabus Unit/ Element		Chapter/ Section
	• capital protection	
	• monitoring performance versus benchmark	
5.13	**Structured Products**	
	On completion the candidate should be able:	
5.13.1	analyse the key features, relative merits and limitations of investing in retail structured products and investment notes compared with other forms of direct and indirect investment:	15
	• structure	
	• income and capital growth	
	• investment risk and return	
	• expenses	
	• capital protection	
	• counterparty risk	
5.14	**Pension Arrangements**	
	On completion the candidate should be able:	
5.14.1	analyse the main types, purpose, structure and operation, tax treatment and investment characteristics of pension arrangements:	16
	• defined benefit	
	• defined contribution	
	• personal pensions	
	• self invested personal pensions (SIPPs)	
	• small self-administered schemes (SSASs)	
5.14.2	analyse the key features of pension arrangements:	16
	• contributions – sources, level and limits	
	• investment selection and performance	
	• how benefits are provided	
ELEMENT 6	**INVESTMENT PLANNING**	**CHAPTER 6**
6.1	**Asset Allocation**	
	On completion the candidate should be able to:	
6.1.1	understand the purpose and principles of asset allocation:	1
	• relationship with investment theory	
	• achievement of performance objectives	
	• trade-off between risk and return	
	• stochastic modelling	
	• active and passive management	
	• strategic asset allocation (SAA)	
	• tactical asset allocation (TAA)	
6.1.2	understand how investment theory is applied to the process of portfolio construction	1
6.1.3	understand the basic ways to diversify a portfolio:	1.5
	• asset class	
	• geographical area	

Syllabus Unit/ Element		Chapter/ Section
	• sector	
	• currency	
	• maturity	
6.2	**Investment Selection**	
	On completion the candidate should be able to:	
6.2.1	understand the aims and characteristics of the main fund management strategies and styles:	2
	• indexing or passive management	
	• active or market timing	
	• passive-active combinations	
	• cash and bond fund strategies	
	• liability driven investment (LDI)	
	• long, short and geared	
	• sector-specific	
	• contrarian	
	• quantitative, trend and trading strategies	
6.2.2	analyse and compare charges on the basis of impact, reduction in yield and total expense ratios	2.12
6.2.3	understand the research and reports available to financial advisers:	2.13
	• fundamental analysis	
	• technical analysis	
	• fund analysis	
	• fund rating agencies and screening software	
	• broker and distributor reports	
	• sector-specific reports	
6.2.4	analyse the factors to consider when selecting investment product providers	2.14
6.2.5	understand the characteristics, uses, benefits, risks and charges associated with wrap and other platforms	2.15
ELEMENT 7	**INVESTMENT ADVICE**	**CHAPTER 7**
7.1	**Advising Clients**	
	On completion the candidate should be able to:	
7.1.1	apply a framework for providing financial advice, paying particular attention to:	1
	• the nature of the client relationship, confidentiality, trust and client protection	
	• the information required from clients and methods of obtaining it	
	• monitoring and review of clients' circumstances	
	• the information clients must be given under the current regulatory requirements	
7.1.2	understand how financial advice can be paid for:	1.6
	• fees	

Syllabus Unit/ Element		Chapter/ Section
	• commission	
	• nature and frequency of service to be provided	
7.1.3	apply the FSA's six treating customers fairly outcomes to the investment advice process and interaction with customers	1.5
7.1.4	understand the purpose, merits and limitations of using questionnaires and interviews to elicit customer information	2.1.2
7.1.5	explain to customers in a clear and non-misleading way the purpose and process of financial advice, including:	1
	• gathering information and discussing objectives	
	• planning and recommending ways to meet objectives	
	• implementation	
	• reporting, monitoring and review	
7.2	**Client Fact Finding**	
	On completion candidates should be able to:	
7.2.1	analyse the main factors, resources and limitations shaping a client's current and desired financial circumstances:	2
	• gather appropriate, relevant information about current and projected income, expenditure, debt and savings	
	• consider time horizons and the relative balance of growth versus income	
	• distinguish between what is essential and what is desirable, and prioritise accordingly	
	• agree clear, feasible, prioritised investment objectives	
7.2.2	analyse the merits and disadvantages of paying off mortgage or debt compared with investing surplus funds	4
7.3	**Risk and Suitability**	
	On completion candidates should be able to:	
7.3.1	analyse a profile of an investor's risk exposure and appetite for risk, based on the following objective and subjective factors:	2.6
	• level of wealth	
	• timescale	
	• commitments	
	• life cycle	
	• life goals	
	• investment objectives	
	• attitudes	
	• experiences	
	• knowledge	
7.3.2	apply a client risk profile to the investment selection process	2.6
7.3.3	assess the following factors when selecting suitable product solutions:	5.4
	• impact of new solutions on existing arrangements	
	• range of solutions available to suit different circumstances	

Syllabus Unit/ Element		Chapter/ Section
	• range of criteria for matching solutions to client needs and demands	
7.3.4	assess affordability and suitability based on a range of factors including product provider quality, performance, risk, charges and client service	2.6
7.3.5	understand the purpose of different ethical and socially responsible investment strategies and the circumstances in which it may be appropriate to discuss them	3, 3.1
7.3.6	understand the main considerations for investing in accordance with Sharia'a law	3.2
7.3.7	understand the main considerations for investing in accordance with other faith values	3.3
7.3.8	understand the main considerations that should be taken into account when investing for charities	3.4
7.3.9	understand the main considerations that should be taken into account when investing for trusts	3.5
7.4	**Planning and Recommendations**	
	On completion the candidate should be able:	
7.4.1	apply a strategy and rationale that will meet the client's objectives:	2.2
	• highlight the pertinent issues and priorities	
	• formulate a plan to deal with them	
	• offer proposals to achieve these objectives	
	• explain clearly the relative merits and drawbacks of each proposal and combination thereof	
	• agree a strategy that the client understands and accepts	
7.4.2	apply an appropriate investment allocation strategy that best meets the following criteria:	5
	• client's financial objectives and priorities	
	• client's risk tolerance	
	• appropriate fees and charges	
	• total expense ratio (TER) and portfolio turnover ration (PTR)	
	• client suitability requirements	
	• adequate diversification and correlation benefits	
	• additional risk, timing and liquidity factors where asset accumulation and decumulation are relevant features	
7.4.3	understand the factors which influence the way in which recommendations are presented	6
7.4.4	understand how to check clients' understanding of recommendations	6.1
7.4.5	apply consumer rights and the regulatory requirements to the provision of investment advice	7
7.4.6	assess the factors influencing the choice of benchmark and the basis for review	8
	• portfolio's asset allocation	

Syllabus Unit/ Element		Chapter/ Section
	• risk/return profile	
	• alternative investments	
	• taxation	
	• peer groups	
	• maintenance of capital value	
7.4.7	understand the process of periodic review to meet key criteria:	1.9
	• regulatory requirements	
	• appropriate frequency, taking into account client requirements and the chosen investment strategy	
ELEMENT 8	**PORTFOLIO PERFORMANCE AND REVIEW**	**CHAPTER 8**
8.1	**Selection and Use of Benchmarks**	
	On completion the candidate should be able:	
8.1.1	understand the purpose and limitations of portfolio evaluation	1
8.1.2	understand the concept and purpose of benchmarking	1
8.1.3	know the construction and weighting methods of the following indices:	1.1
	• FTSE 100	
	• FTSE All Share Index	
	• FTSE Actuaries Government Securities Indices	
	• MSCI World Index	
	• Dow Jones Industrial Average Index	
	• S&P 500 Index	
	• Nikkei 225	
8.1.4	understand the differences between a single and a composite (synthetic) benchmark	1.2
8.1.5	understand the alternative ways of benchmarking:	1.3
	• Global Investment Performance Standards (GIPS)	
	• peer group average (WM and CAPS)	
8.1.6	apply suitable benchmarks when measuring and evaluating investment performance	1.4
8.2	**Portfolio Measurement**	
	On completion the candidate should be able:	
8.2.1	apply the theory of investment risk and return to the measurement of portfolio performance:	2
	• holding period return	
	• relative return	
	• standard deviation	
	• risk-adjusted returns	
8.2.2	analyse portfolio performance in terms of:	2.4
	• absolute and relative return	
	• absolute and relative risk	
	• risk-reward ratios	

Syllabus Unit/ Element		Chapter/ Section
	• contributions to return arising from asset allocation, currency movements, stock selection and timing	
	• impact of new money and timing factors	
8.3	**Portfolio Review**	
	On completion the candidate should be able:	
8.3.1	understand the importance of regularly reviewing the client's portfolio	3
8.3.2	apply measures to address the factors that require attention as part of the portfolio review and administration process:	3
	• changes in client circumstances	
	• changes in the financial environment	
	• new products and services available	
	• administrative changes or difficulties	
	• investment-related changes (eg, credit rating, corporate actions)	
	• portfolio rebalancing	
	• benchmark review	

EXAMINATION SPECIFICATION

Each examination paper is constructed from a specification that determines the weightings that will be given to each element. The specification is given below.

It is important to note that the numbers quoted may vary slightly from examination to examination as there is some flexibility to ensure that each examination has a consistent level of difficulty. However, the number of questions tested in each element should not change by more than plus or minus 2.

		Questions
ELEMENT 1	ASSET CLASSES	14
ELEMENT 2	THE MACRO-ECONOMIC ENVIRONMENT	6
ELEMENT 3	PRINCIPLES OF INVESTMENT RISK AND RETURN	6
ELEMENT 4	TAXATION OF INVESTORS AND INVESTMENTS	16
ELEMENT 5	INVESTMENT PRODUCTS	17
ELEMENT 6	INVESTMENT PLANNING	5
ELEMENT 7	INVESTMENT ADVICE	11
ELEMENT 8	PORTFOLIO PERFORMANCE AND REVIEW	5
	TOTAL	80

CISI Membership

Studying for a CISI qualification is hard work and we're sure you're putting in plenty of hours, but don't lose sight of your goal! This is just the first step in your career, there is much more to achieve!

The securities and investments industry attracts ambitious and driven individuals. You're probably one yourself and that's great, but on the other hand you're almost certainly surrounded by lots of other people with similar ambitions. So how can you stay one step ahead during these uncertain times?

Entry Criteria:	Pass in either:
	• Investment Operations Certificate (IOC, formerly known as IAQ), IFQ, ICFA, CISI Certificates in, eg, Securities, Derivatives or Investment Management, Advanced Certificates
	• one or two CISI Diploma/Masters papers
Joining Fee:	£25 or free if applying via prefilled application form
Annual Subscription (pro rata):	£115
International Annual Subscription:	£86.25

Using your new CISI qualification* to become an Associate (ACSI) member of the Chartered Institute for Securities & Investment could well be the next important career move you make this year, and help you maintain your competence.

Join our global network of over 40,000 financial services professionals and start enjoying both the professional and personal benefits that CISI membership offers. Once you become a member you can use the prestigious ACSI designation after your name and even work towards becoming personally chartered.

* ie, Investment Operations Certificate (IOC, formerly known as IAQ), IFQ, CISI Certificate Programme

Turn over to find out more about CISI membership

> **" ... competence is not just about examinations. It is about skills, knowledge, expertise, ethical behaviour and the application and maintenance of all these "**
>
> April 2008
> FSA, Retail Distribution Review Interim Report

Becoming an Associate member of CISI offers you...

- ✓ Use of the CISI CPD Scheme
- ✓ Unlimited free CPD seminars
- ✓ Highly recognised designatory letters
- ✓ Free access to online training tools including Professional Refresher and Infolink
- ✓ Free webcasts and podcasts
- ✓ Unlimited free attendance at CISI Professional Interest Forums
- ✓ CISI publications including S&I Review and Regulatory Update
- ✓ 20% discount on all CISI conferences and training courses
- ✓ Invitation to CISI Annual Lecture
- ✓ Select Benefits — our exclusive personal benefits portfolio

Plus many other networking opportunities which could be invaluable for your career.

To upgrade your student membership to Associate,

get in touch...

+44 (0)20 7645 0650
memberservices@cisi.org
cisi.org/membership

CISI

CHARTERED INSTITUTE FOR
SECURITIES & INVESTMENT

CISI Elearning Products

You've bought the workbook.....
...now test your knowledge before your examination

CISI elearning products are high quality, interactive and engaging learning tools and revision aids which can be used in conjunction with CISI workbooks, or to help you remain up to date with regulatory developments in order to meet compliance requirements.

Features of CISI elearning products include:

• Questions throughout to reaffirm understanding of the subject

• All modules now contain questions that reflect as closely as possible the standard you will experience in your examination*

• Interactive exercises and tutorials

* (please note, however, they are not the CISI examination questions themselves)

Price per elearning module: £35

Price when purchased with the CISI workbook: £100 (normal price: £110)

For more information on our elearning products call:
+44 20 7645 0756

Or visit our web site at:
cisi.org/elearning

To order call CISI elearning products call Client Services on:
+44 20 7645 0680

Feedback to CISI

Have you found this workbook to be a valuable aid to your studies? We would like your views, so please email us (learningresources@cisi.org) with any thoughts, ideas or comments.

Accredited Training Providers

Support for examination students studying for the Chartered Institute for Securities & Investment (CISI) Qualifications is provided by several Accredited Training Providers (ATPs), including 7City Learning and BPP. The CISI's ATPs offer a range of face-to-face training courses, distance learning programmes, their own learning resources and study packs which have been accredited by the CISI. The CISI works in close collaboration with its accredited training providers to ensure they are kept informed of changes to CISI examinations so they can build them into their own courses and study packs.

CISI Workbook Specialists Wanted

Workbook Authors

Experienced freelance authors with finance experience, and who have published work in their area of specialism, are sought. Responsibilities include:

* Updating workbooks in line with new syllabuses and any industry developments
* Ensuring that the syllabus is fully covered

Workbook Reviewers

Individuals with a high-level knowledge of the subject area are sought. Responsibilities include:

* Highlighting any inconsistencies against the syllabus
* Assessing the author's interpretation of the workbook

Workbook Technical Reviewers

Technical reviewers provide a detailed review of the workbook and bring the review comments to the panel. Responsibilities include:

* Cross-checking the workbook against the syllabus
* Ensuring sufficient coverage of each learning objective

Workbook Proofreaders

Proofreaders are needed to proof workbooks both grammatically and also in terms of the format and layout. Responsibilities include:

* Checking for spelling and grammar mistakes
* Checking for formatting inconsistencies